A GIFT FROM

Richard Morgan

Education and the Creation of Capital in the Early American Republic

This book argues that schools were a driving force in the formation of social, political, and financial capital during the market revolution and capitalist transition of the early republican era. Grounded in an intensive study of schooling in the Genesee Valley region of upstate New York, it traces early sources of funding and support for education (including common schools and various forms of higher schooling) to their roots in different social and economic networks and trade and credit relations. It then interprets that story in the context of other major developments in early American social, political, and economic history, such as the shift from agricultural to nonagricultural production, the integration of rural economies into translocal capitalist markets, the organization of the Second Great Awakening, the transformation of patriarchy, the expansion of white male suffrage, the emergence of the Second American Party system, and the formation of the modern liberal state.

Nancy Beadie is a professor and historian of education in the area of educational leadership and policy studies at the University of Washington, Seattle. She is a co-editor of *Chartered Schools: Two Hundred Years of Independent Academies, 1727–1925* (2002). She has twice received the History of Education Society's prize for best article published in a refereed journal, and her articles have appeared in numerous journals, including *Social Science History*, *History of Education Quarterly*, *History of Education*, and *Paedagogica Historica*.

Education and the Creation of Capital in the Early American Republic

NANCY BEADIE
University of Washington, Seattle

CAMBRIDGE
UNIVERSITY PRESS

CAMBRIDGE UNIVERSITY PRESS
Cambridge, New York, Melbourne, Madrid, Cape Town, Singapore,
São Paulo, Delhi, Dubai, Tokyo, Mexico City

Cambridge University Press
32 Avenue of the Americas, New York, NY 10013-2473, USA

www.cambridge.org
Information on this title: www.cambridge.org/9780521196284

© Nancy Beadie 2010

This publication is in copyright. Subject to statutory exception
and to the provisions of relevant collective licensing agreements,
no reproduction of any part may take place without the written
permission of Cambridge University Press.

First published 2010

Printed in the United States of America

A catalog record for this publication is available from the British Library.

Library of Congress Cataloging in Publication data

ISBN 978-0-521-19628-4 Hardback

Cambridge University Press has no responsibility for the persistence or
accuracy of URLs for external or third-party Internet Web sites referred to in
this publication and does not guarantee that any content on such Web sites is,
or will remain, accurate or appropriate.

For Don

Contents

List of Tables	page ix
List of Maps and Illustrations	x
List of Abbreviations	xi
Acknowledgments	xiii

PART I: EDUCATION AND SOCIAL CAPITAL FORMATION

1	Introduction – The Place of Schooling in a Transforming Political Economy	3
2	Creating Social Capital – Norms of School and Community Building	18
3	A Matter of Trust – Neighbors and Strangers	36
4	Discipline – Evangelicalism as an Educational Movement	55
5	Bonding and Bridging – The Methodist Economy	72
6	Development – Evangelicalism and Capital Formation	89

PART II: SCHOOLS AS AGENCIES OF POLITICIZATION

7	Between Markets and the State – Venture Schools and Academies	107
8	Political Economies of Schooling – Academies and Common Schools	123
9	Education and Civic Engagement – Schools and Politics	139
10	Diffusing Intelligence – Education and the Formation of the Liberal State	158
11	Education and Coalition Building	176
12	Denominational Politics and Institution Building	193

PART III: EDUCATION AND ECONOMIC TRANSFORMATION

13	Education as an Object of Capital Investment	215
14	Varieties of Trust – Education and Economic Competition	233
15	Controlling Capital – Education and the Politics of Economic Change	248
16	Success – Education and the Culture of the Market	267
17	Panic – Education and the Discipline of the Market	282
18	Friends – An Education in Trust	301
	Conclusion – Education and the Creation of Capital	317
	Appendix	329
	Index	333

List of Tables

1	Sources of Funding for Teacher Wages, Lima School District No. 4, 1825	*page* 148
2	Length of School Year and Rates of Attendance by School District, Town of Lima, 1825	149
3	Length of School Year, Lima School District No. 4, 1815–1835	149
4	Number and Proportion of Male and Female Students Studying Various Higher Level Subjects at Genesee Wesleyan Seminary, 1834	275

Appendix Tables

1	Per Capita Land Values and Improved Acreage, 1820, Lima and Neighboring Towns	329
2	Percentage of Land Improved, Lima, 1820, as Compared with Clark's 4 Massachusetts' Towns and Median % for Pritchard's 152 Counties	329
3	Population Density, 1830, Lima and Surrounding Towns	330
4	Population Density and Per Capita Land Values for Lima, 1820/1830/1850, as Compared with Pritchard's Categories of Economic Development, 1850–1860	331

List of Maps and Illustrations

1	Town of Lima, New York, in Relation to Major Cities and Transportation Routes, circa 1840	*page* 2
2	Lima School Districts, circa 1813	40
3	Hamlets, Towns, and Churches in and around Lima, circa 1820	46
4	Territory of the Genesee Conference of the Methodist Episcopal Church, 1810–1824	78
5	Territory of the Genesee Conference of the Methodist Episcopal Church, 1829	194
6	Genesee Wesleyan Seminary, Lima, New York, circa 1848	214

List of Abbreviations

BFP	Bronson Family Papers, New York Public Library, New York, New York
CUDRMC	Cornell University Division of Rare and Manuscript Collections, Cornell University, Ithaca, New York
GVHC	Genesee Valley Historical Collection, State University of New York (SUNY), Geneseo, New York
GWSC	Genesee Wesleyan Seminary Collection, Syracuse University Archives, Syracuse, New York
LCCO	Livingston County Clerk's Office, Geneseo, New York
LCHO	Livingston County Historian's Office, Geneseo, New York
LHS	Lima Historical Society, Lima, New York
LTH	Lima Town Historian, Lima, New York
LPC	Lima Presbyterian Church, Lima, New York
MAC	Middlebury Academy Collection, Wyoming, New York
MAHC	Methodist Archives and History Center, Drew University, Madison, New Jersey
MMC	Methodist Manuscript Collection, Special Collections Research Center, Syracuse University Library, Syracuse, New York
NYSHA	New York State Historical Association, Cooperstown, New York
OCHS	Ontario County Historical Society
OCRAIMS	Ontario County Records, Archives, and Information Management Service, Canandaigua, New York
OMTH	Office of the Mendon Town Historian, Mendon, New York

SDL	Swasey Divinity Library, Colgate Crozer Seminary, Rochester, New York
URSC	University of Rochester Special Collections, Rochester, New York
WNYCA	Western New York Conference Archives, United Methodist Conference Center, West Amherst, New York

Acknowledgments

This project has a long history to which many people have contributed both direct assistance and general support. My greatest debt is to those who kept faith in me and in the project through its many iterations – or at least suspended disbelief long enough to allow me to write the next page.

Chief among those people is my husband, Don Argus, whose own knowledge of the historical places I describe in many ways exceeds my own, whose encouragement and practical assistance have been unerring at every point along the way, and whose love of learning and discovery is a joy to share. My experience of such faith, support, and love of knowledge begins with my parents, Tom and Norma Beadie.

My colleagues at the University of Washington and at many institutions around the country have honored me with their questions, stimulated me with their comments, and offered many practical words of advice and encouragement. In particular I thank Kim Tolley, David Labaree, Linda Eisenmann, Chris Ogren, Barbara Beatty, Jon Zimmerman, Kate Rousmaniere, Debby Kerdeman, Walter Parker, Diane Jones, and Lee Nelson, but there are many others as well. In the town of Lima I am grateful to a number of people but especially Fran Gotcsik and Martha Sempowski of the Lima Historical Society, who rewarded me with their interest, supplied me with information, and welcomed me into their homes over repeated visits. At Syracuse University, where I did my graduate work and started down this path with great intellectual stimulation and support, I thank John Briggs, D. W. Meinig, the late Thomas F. Green, John Scott Strickland, James Roger Sharp, Joan Burstyn, Sari Biklen, and Emily Robertson. At Cambridge University Press I thank Lewis Bateman, who saw the first version of this work years ago and managed not to forget.

The people who have directly assisted me in practical ways include many at archives and historical societies, in particular Mary O'Brien, Syracuse University Archives; Diane C. Ham, Mendon Town Historian; Jo Ann Lanphear, Ontario County Records, Archives, and Information Management Service; and Anne Bullock, Village Historian for Honeoye Falls. I also am grateful for excellent assistance with data entry and analysis over the years from Taylor Kokjohn, Erin Peinado, Angela Gonzalez, and Aurora Graf. Grants from the Spencer Foundation, the Royalty Research Fund, and the Zesbaugh Scholarship Fund at the University of Washington paid for that assistance at important points in the project and supported my own time and travel. In addition, the University of Washington supported me with two sabbaticals, one at the beginning and one at the end of this project. Thanks go to Arthur Whiteley, Kathy Cowell, and the Helen Riaboff Whiteley Center for creating and sustaining the fabulous faculty retreat facility at Friday Harbor Laboratories, where I wrote major sections of the manuscript.

I am grateful to the anonymous reviewers for Cambridge University Press and for the various journals where I have published my work over the years for their knowledgeable insights and suggestions: *History of Education Quarterly*, *Social Science History*, *Paedagogica Historica*, and the *American Journal of Education*. In particular, portions of the introduction and conclusion of this book first appeared as part of the text of my 2007 presidential address to the History of Education Society, subsequently published in *History of Education Quarterly* 48:1 (February 2008).

Special thanks to Don Argus for preparing the maps and index for this book. You really came through.

PART I

EDUCATION AND SOCIAL CAPITAL FORMATION

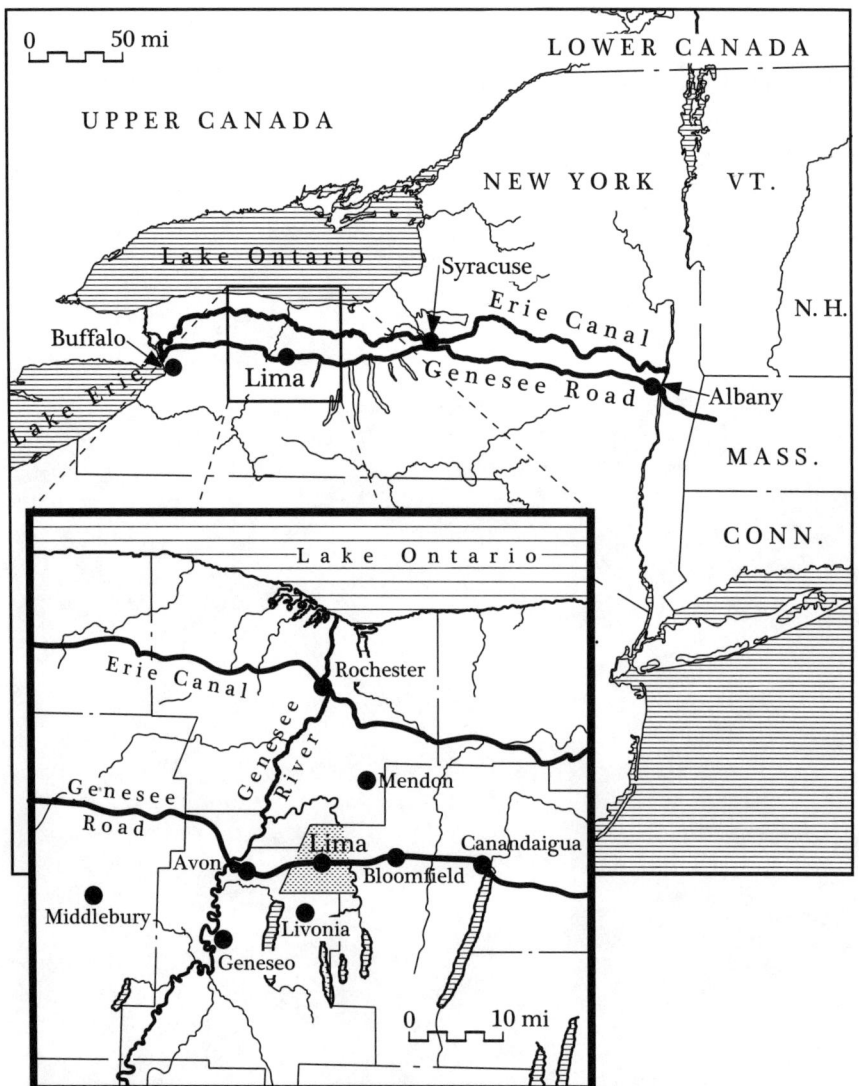

FIGURE 1. Town of Lima, New York, in Relation to Major Cities and Transportation Routes, circa 1840. The economy and society of the northern United States underwent a significant shift around 1840, marked by increased rates of capital accumulation and mobility, a shift of capital resources from agricultural to nonagricultural production, and the growth of interior cities like Rochester and Syracuse. This "capitalist transition" was preceded by, and predicated on, a process of commercial expansion and market integration before 1840 that some scholars refer to as "the market revolution," facilitated by the development of interior transportation routes like the Genesee Road and the Erie Canal. Coincident with this earlier development, schooling also expanded and became a centerpiece of community and social life.

I

Introduction – The Place of Schooling in a Transforming Political Economy

> I have left home and friend and for the present must learn to depend upon myself.
>
> Livingston and Onondaga County woman's diary
> [diary of Clarissa Pengra], 1838–1842, November 2, 1840[1]

In the fall of 1840, twenty-four-year-old Clarissa Pengra journeyed from a small town in western New York to the growing city of Syracuse to take up a new teaching position. She began by heading north by carriage on a plank road to Rochester, where she would catch a canal boat east. Arriving in Rochester in the evening, after what she described as "an unpleasant ride," she decided to spend the night at a boarding establishment rather than at the home of a family friend, "in order to be convenient for the boat in the morning." While in the city, she finished her "shopping," a term she had never used in the context of her rural hometown. Already, Clarissa had traveled a social and psychological distance. In the hours, weeks, and months that followed, her sense of dislocation would continue. At 6 A.M. on the morning after she arrived in Rochester, she boarded the canal boat for a trip that would take twenty-four hours, ending in Syracuse the following day "before daylight." On the boat, Clarissa encountered whist players, whiskey drinkers, and a follower of the Calvinist evangelist Charles Finney, each in his own way somewhat at odds with her own principles and ideas. With respect to the trip as a whole, she expressed a sense of adventure, tempered by a hint of anxiety. "I have left home and friend," she wrote in her journal, "and for the present must learn to depend upon myself."[2]

The dual note of possibility and foreboding Clarissa expressed on the eve of her journey makes sense from a historical perspective. On the one hand,

---

[1] Livingston and Onondaga County woman's diary [diary of Clarissa Pengra], 1838–1842, November 2, 1840, Microfilm, Collection #6230, CUDRMC. Holder of original material, Chris Densmore, University of Buffalo Archives. I have identified the woman as Clarissa Pengra.
[2] Ibid.

3

Clarissa's move was part of an expansion of opportunity for young women in a growing labor market for teachers. It also represented something of a career move for her. As a student at a thriving academy in the small town of Lima, New York, Clarissa had acquired cultural knowledge and some practical experience as an assistant teacher of young children. She had then parlayed that knowledge and experience into employment as an independent teacher in a rural pay school. Now she was going to a growing city with a more competitive school market, larger potential school enrollments, and correspondingly greater potential remuneration. Socially, Clarissa's journey represented a move toward something like individual independence, as she left the structure of a patriarchal household and entered a world that allowed her a degree of autonomy. In all these ways, Clarissa's move was one of opportunity. On the other hand, as a wage earner and something of a migratory worker, Clarissa joined an increasing number of people – from day laborers, to clerks, to factory operatives and itinerant preachers – who effectively and repeatedly had to sell themselves in order to live, and who regularly experienced the unsettling reality of unemployment or underemployment. The closing of a school, a decline in enrollment, the disappearance of trustee or parental support, and increased competition from other schools were all common experiences in the lives of teachers.[3] In such an eventuality, Clarissa might well prefer the support of a patriarchal family or the help of a friend to depending on herself. Clarissa had reason, in other words, to feel trepidation as well as excitement on the eve of her journey.

Clarissa's personal journey was emblematic of a broader shift in economy and society around 1840. At the same time that Clarissa moved from a rural farming community to the growing trade center of Syracuse, the economy of the northern United States underwent a significant shift from agricultural to nonagricultural production. That shift was associated with other changes, such as increases in rates of capital accumulation and fundamental alterations in the social organization of labor. These changes are sometimes referred to as the "capitalist transition." The capitalist transition was preceded by, and predicated on, a process of commercial expansion and market integration before 1840 that some scholars refer to as "the market revolution." Together the market revolution and the capitalist transition led to a condition of accelerated economic growth that economists associate with modern industrial society.[4]

---

[3] For discussions of the market realities of teachers' lives in the early national and antebellum periods, see Kim Tolley and Nancy Beadie, "Socio-Economic Incentives to Teach in New York and North Carolina: Toward a More Complex Model of Teacher Labor Markets, 1800–1850," *History of Education Quarterly*, 46:1 (Spring 2006): 36–72; Tolley, "How Mrs. Sambourne Earned a 'Comfortable Living for Herself and Her Children': Music Teachers in the North Carolina Education Market, 1800–1840, *Social Science History* 32:1 (April 2008), 75–106; Tolley and Margaret Nash, "Leaving Home to Teach: The Diary of Susan Nye Hutchison, 1815–1841," in Beadie and Tolley, eds. *Chartered Schools: Two Hundred Years of Independent Academies in the United States, 1727–1925* (New York: Routledge Press, 2002): 161–185; and Teri L. Castelow, "'Creating an Educational Interest': Sophia Sawyer, Teacher of the Cherokee," ibid., 186–210.

[4] Vast scholarly literatures lie behind this brief description of nineteenth-century economic change. These literatures will be referenced further in the notes that follow and discussed

Historians who study and interpret this process of transformation often echo the ambiguity that Clarissa expressed as she embarked on her journey. In his major synthetic work on the market revolution, historian Charles Sellers portrayed the period from 1815 to 1846 as marked by conflict between two different social orders and ways of looking at the world. One pattern was rooted in rural society, communitarian social values, and a politics of democratic localism. The other pattern was shaped by commercial competition, individualism, and a politics of cosmopolitan nationalism. Sellers' project was to identify and describe these two competing orders in all their social, political, and cultural dimensions, and then to chronicle and explain how the cosmopolitan, commercial culture came to prevail over that of democratic localism.[5] In Sellers' account, this historical shift is tinged with a sense of loss.

Since the publication of Sellers's 1991 book, scholars from a wide range of historical subfields have used his formulation to frame the significance of their work on religion, society, culture, and politics in the early American republic. Critics of Sellers's account have taken issue with some of his specific claims and often with his interpretive emphasis – for example, with what some scholars regard as an unwarranted sense of nostalgia for a "democratic localism" that was essentially patriarchal.[6] Other scholars have argued that Sellers's categorical distinctions are too neatly drawn and that his account of historical change is too strongly dominated by impersonal forces.[7] Highlighting some of the ambiguities and contingencies of market transformation, they have used Sellers's work as a starting point for investigating the dynamics of social communalism and market integration within particular regional, racial, and ethnic communities – from Native Americans in the Southeast, to French-Canadians in rural Vermont, and African Americans in the urban North.[8] In

---

fully elsewhere in the book. For the brief summary provided here I rely primarily on Christopher Clark, *The Roots of Rural Capitalism: Western Massachusetts, 1780–1860* (Ithaca, NY: Cornell University Press, 1990) and Howard Bodenhorn, *A History of Banking in Antebellum America: Financial Markets and Economic Development in an Era of Nation-Building* (Cambridge: Cambridge University Press, 2000).

[5] Charles Sellers, *The Market Revolution: Jacksonian America, 1815–1846* (Oxford: Oxford University Press, 1991).

[6] The concept of "market revolution" generally, and the specific argument of Sellers's book, were the subject of a 1994 conference the University College of London and of a resulting edited book comprised of papers written from multiple perspectives by leading scholars of U.S. history for the period. Among the participants who criticized Sellers's account as essentially nostalgic were Richard Ellis and Daniel Walker Howe. See Ellis, "The Market Revolution and the Transformation of American Politics, 1801–1837," in Melvyn Stokes and Stephen Conway, eds. *The Market Revolution in America: Social, Political and Religious Expressions, 1800–1880* (Charlottesville: University Press of Virginia, 1996): 149–176; and Howe, "The Market Revolution and the Shaping of Identity in Whig-Jacksonian America," ibid., 259–281.

[7] Among those who criticized Sellers's account as too neatly drawn and dominated by impersonal forces – though from very different perspectives – were Christopher Clark and Richard Cawardine. See Clark, "The Consequences of the Market Revolution in the American North," and Cawardine, "'Antinomians' and 'Arminians:' Methodists and the Market Revolution," in Stokes and Conway, eds. *The Market Revolution in America*, 23–42 and 282–310, respectively.

[8] See, for example, essays collected by Scott C. Martin, ed. *Cultural Change and the Market Revolution in America, 1789–1860* (Lanham, MD: Rowman and Littlefield, 2006), including

so doing they have highlighted the agency of individuals and social groups in shaping their relationships to the market and the meaning of market participation within their communities. They have shown, for example, how certain market commodities and ideas could be used simultaneously to pursue competitive economic and political advantage, and to revitalize symbolic systems and social ties within communities. In these accounts, the market revolution is often illuminated by possibility as well as marked by loss.

This book aims to recapture a similar sense of complexity and contingency in the relationship between education and economic change in the early republic. Nearly a century and a half after Clarissa journeyed to Syracuse, I began a reverse journey in time and space to recover the world from which Clarissa came. At the time, I had not yet discovered Clarissa or her diary, but I had been looking closely at many of the social, economic, and political circumstances – and even at some of the individual people – that shaped her way of thinking, her social and career possibilities, and her eventual disappointments and misfortunes. To be specific, I had been tracing sources of support for what was one of the largest educational institutions in New York State during the first half of the nineteenth century: the Methodist-affiliated academy known as Genesee Wesleyan Seminary that Clarissa attended in Lima, New York, and where she worked for a brief time as an assistant teacher in the mid-1830s. The records of this institution, including a complete set of financial records, had, like Clarissa, ended up in Syracuse.[9] In discovering and analyzing those records and putting them in historical context, I had, without quite knowing it, embarked on an effort to understand the place of schooling in a transforming political economy.

In the beginning I focused on the role of church and state in education. In particular, I concentrated on understanding the vast and elaborate structure of the academy's denominational sponsor, the Methodist Episcopal Church, and on the distinctive system of Regents academies chartered and subsidized by New York State. The further I went in my research, however, and the

---

James Taylor Carson, "Native Americans, the Market Revolution, and Cultural Change: The Choctaw Cattle Economy, 1690–1830," ibid., 71–88; Kevin Thornton, " A Cultural Frontier: Ethnicity and the Marketplace in Charlotte, Vermont, 1845–1860," ibid., 47–69; and Patrick Rael, "The Market Revolution and Market Values in Antebellum Black Protest Thought," ibid., 13–46.

[9] GWSC. In 1850 the seminary spawned the organization of an affiliated college, Genesee College, and in 1871 the Central New York Conference of the Methodist Episcopal Church essentially removed the college to become the nucleus of Syracuse University. Local residents actively protested the move and won a civil court case on the matter, but the ruling was effectively circumvented as most faculty and students formally withdrew from the institution to resume at the new university founded with a considerable outlay of funds from Syracuse. The Methodists apparently took most of the seminary's records as well as the college's with them. Thus the seminary's records have become part of the Syracuse University archives. For an account of this progress of events, see Nancy Beadie, "From Academy to University in New York State: The Genesee Institutions and the Importance of Capital to the Success of an Idea, 1848–1871," *History of Higher Education Annual* 14 (1994), 13–38.

Introduction

further back in time I went, the more I also found myself delving into local history to recreate the social and economic networks that mobilized the institution's initial sources of capital – the further, in other words, to borrow a phrase from a particular body of scholarship, I found myself delving into the "roots of rural capitalism."[10]

Increasingly, historians agree that the roots of antebellum capitalist transformation were largely rural, that the dynamic that propelled antebellum economic growth came from the countryside, that the increasing capacity of farmers and rural merchants to realize the value of surplus goods and labor on domestic commodities markets fostered the creation of new sources of capital, and that the investment of increasing amounts of this rural capital in nonagricultural enterprises fueled the "takeoff" of the U.S. economy – a point variously located sometime after 1840, when growth in per capita output and income accelerated and became a "normal condition" of society.[11]

In his intensive study of the roots of capitalism in rural western Massachusetts, the social historian Christopher Clark identified two phases in this transformation. The first he called a period of "involution," characterized by the intensification of rural production and trade practices from the 1780s to the 1820s. During this phase, rural households increased their productive capacity and their capacity to realize the value of surplus labor and goods while retaining control of production itself and of the terms of trade. The second phase Clark referred to as a period of concentration, from the 1830s to the 1860s. During this period, certain households accumulated capital and increased their influence over the distribution of labor and the trade of goods while other households lost control of production and the terms of trade. Clark devoted considerable attention to describing the processes that led to the shift from one phase to the next. In particular, he explored how merchants and entrepreneurs increased their influence in local economies through the development of outwork manufacturing.[12]

By focusing on a single place and following closely local patterns of household organization, production, and exchange, Clark brought a degree of specificity and precision to both the chronology and the theory of capitalist transition in the North. The results of his analysis also dovetailed with the findings of economic historians who described and analyzed change at more macro-economic levels, including the work of some historians with whom Clark differed over issues of interpretation. Winifred Rothenberg,

---

[10] This phrase is borrowed from the title of Christopher Clark's 1990 book, *The Roots of Rural Capitalism*. The titles of other books belonging to the same body of literature convey a similar idea. For example, Stephen Hahn and Jonathan Prude, eds. *The Countryside in the Age of Capitalist Transformation* (Chapel Hill: University of North Carolina Press, 1985) and Alan Kulikoff, *The Agrarian Origins of American Capitalism* (Charlottesville: University Press of Virginia, 1992).

[11] An excellent survey of the literature on antebellum economic development is provided in Bodenhorn, *A History of Banking*, 1–27.

[12] Clark, *The Roots of Rural Capitalism*.

for example, found a convergence in agricultural commodities prices across localities in the northeast from 1780 to 1820. She concluded from this that the process of market integration was largely complete by the end of that period.[13] Although Rothenberg and Clark differed in their interpretations of this development, with Clark highlighting the persistence of alternatives to the market, their basic findings and chronologies are not necessarily incompatible. As Alan Kulikoff pointed out in his 1989 review of the literature on the capitalist transition, it is entirely possible that noncommercial patterns of production and exchange intensified at the same time as commodities markets became more integrated.[14] Both could be evidence of the increased productive capacity of rural households.

Meanwhile, some historians have tried to combine micro-economic and macro-economic perspectives on early economic development. In his study of antebellum banking, Howard Bodenhorn combined the study of specific lending practices by banks in different places with a broadly comparative analysis of capital mobility and interest rates across localities. He also synthesized the literature on economic change and development from multiple perspectives. His results suggest a chronology of capitalist economic development that adds to the findings of Clark and Rothenberg. In Bodenhorn's synthesis, banking contributed to a significant increase in capital mobility and accumulation in the period from 1820 to 1840, a process that in turn facilitated a shift of capital from agricultural to nonagricultural production and thus eventually to the acceleration of economic growth.[15]

To summarize, the literature provides an account of the transition to capitalism in the North that distinguishes among three main phases before the Civil War. Although the phases certainly overlapped, they can be roughly periodized as follows: 1) 1780–1820, a period of intensified agricultural production and increased trade of surplus labor and goods both within local exchange networks and on increasingly integrated commodities markets; 2) 1820–1840, a period of increased capital accumulation and mobility and of increased power of local capitalists, merchants, and entrepreneurs; and 3) 1840–1860, a period of increased concentration of capital resources in nonagricultural production.

Where is the place of schooling in this history? In the 1970s and 1980s, a number of scholars debated the relationship between education and economic and social changes in the nineteenth century. Initially, however, they focused their studies almost entirely on urban and industrial settings and issues. In his influential 1968 study, *The Irony of School Reform,* Michael Katz surveyed a wide range of educational institutions, ideas, and policies in Massachusetts

---

[13] Winifred Barr Rothenberg, *From Market Places to a Market Economy: The Transformation of Rural Massachusetts, 1750–1850* (Chicago: University of Chicago Press, 1992).
[14] Alan Kulikoff, "The Transition to Capitalism in Rural America," *William and Mary Quarterly,* 3rd Ser. 46 (1989):120–144.
[15] Bodenhorn, *A History of Banking.*

that were not limited to urban settings. From the start, however, he made "industrialization and urbanization" organizing concepts of his analysis, and he explored ways to connect the campaign for state intervention in schooling to the new class relations presented by large-scale manufacturing and the growth of cities.[16] Similarly, in their 1975 study of education and social change in the Canadian Province of Ontario, Katz and his associates focused most of their analysis on the leading cities and industrial centers of Toronto and Hamilton.[17] Meanwhile, in 1973, Carl Kaestle provided a complex study of urban schooling in New York City from 1750 to 1850.[18]

In the context of 1970s policy concerns with urban education and issues of educational equity, the Katz and Kaestle studies generated secondary analyses by scholars in other social science fields who were interested in the extent to which schools were agencies of social mobility or social control. The most influential of these analyses was *Schooling in Capitalist America*, published by the economists Samuel Bowles and Herbert Gintis in 1976. Leaning heavily on Katz but referring broadly to the work of Kaestle and others, Bowles and Gintis reinforced the conclusion that "the expansion of mass education and the evolution of its structural forms" were "sparked by demographic changes associated with the industrialization and urbanization of economic and social activity."[19]

Not until the 1980s was this preoccupation with urban and industrial contexts corrected. In their 1980 study of education and social change in Massachusetts, Carl Kaestle and Maris Vinovskis documented substantial rural/urban differences in school attendance patterns. Enrollment rates were substantially higher in rural areas than in large commercial towns. In fact, enrollment rates were inversely related to town size, with the smallest towns enrolling the highest proportion of their children in school and the largest towns enrolling the lowest proportion of all children in school. These urban/rural differences already existed by the 1820s in both New York and Massachusetts, and they developed as a result of a considerable increase in rural school enrollments over the previous thirty to forty years. The differences were substantial. In 1826, the lowest and highest enrollment rates differed by as much as 37 percentage points when all forms of schooling were considered (including venture schools and academies) and by as much as 55 percentage points when only town-supported common schools were considered.[20] Similarly, in 1985 Maris Vinovskis established that in 1860 high

---

[16] Michael B. Katz, *The Irony of School Reform: Educational Innovation in Mid-Nineteenth Century Massachusetts* (Cambridge, MA: Harvard University Press, 1968).
[17] Michael B. Katz and Paul H. Mattingly, eds. *Education and Social Change: Themes from Ontario's Past* (New York: New York University Press, 1975).
[18] Carl F. Kaestle, *The Evolution of an Urban School System: New York City, 1750–1850* (Cambridge, MA: Harvard University Press, 1973).
[19] Samuel Bowles and Herbert Gintis, *Schooling in Capitalist America: Educational Reform and the Contradictions of Economic Life* (New York: Basic Books, 1976).
[20] Carl F. Kaestle and Maris A. Vinovskis, *Education and Social Change in Massachusetts* (Cambridge: Cambridge University Press, 1980).

school attendance varied with town size, with much higher proportions of relevant age cohorts attending in small towns than in larger towns and cities.[21] These findings gave substance and specificity to the substantially higher rural than urban attendance patterns that the economists Lee Soltow and Edward Stevens were finding in their systematic study of literacy and school attendance in national census data.[22] Clearly, the expansion of common schooling was rooted in the countryside.

With these well-documented discoveries regarding the chronology and social geography of school expansion, prevailing ideas about the nature of the relationship between education and economic change were fundamentally challenged. Those ideas included both the more positivist ideas of some economists regarding the significance of schooling in the formation of human capital and the critical ideas of other economists about the significance of schooling as a means of imposing certain kinds of work discipline and ideologies on wage workers. These arguments simply did not make sense for rural areas in the early national period, where school expansion had actually occurred. Kaestle and Vinovskis, in particular, mounted a substantial critique of the focus on urbanization and industrialization that had dominated the previous decade of scholarship.[23] Far from being explained by urbanization, the expansion of schooling seemed to be a primarily rural phenomenon. Rather than being driven by industrialization, this growth occurred largely before 1820, and thus before any significant shift toward factory production and wage-labor.

It was possible that schooling had different relationships to economic development at different times, Kaestle and Vinovskis pointed out. Schooling may have become more significant for inculcating work discipline after 1840 than it had been previously, for example. Similarly, after 1880, the already well-established system of both primary and secondary schooling may have been more important as a means of human capital formation and selection than schools had been earlier in the century. Neither of these ideas about the relationship between schooling and economic change seemed to apply to

---

[21] Maris A. Vinovskis, *The Origins of Public High Schools: A Reexamination of the Beverly High School Controversy* (Madison: University of Wisconsin, 1985).

[22] Portions of this analysis and of the supporting data were first reported in Lee Soltow and Edward Stevens, "Economic Aspects of School Participation in Mid-Nineteenth Century United States," *Journal of Interdisciplinary History* 8 (Autumn, 1977): 221–243. The analysis was then incorporated into a larger work: idem, *The Rise of Literacy and the Common School in the United States: A Socioeconomic Analysis to 1870* (Chicago: University of Chicago, 1981). The norm of higher attendance in small towns and rural areas than in cities of the North continued, by the way, well into the twentieth century. Economists Claudia Goldin and Lawrence Katz discovered similar rural/urban variations in high school attendance data through 1940. See Claudia Goldin and Lawrence Katz, "Human Capital and Social Capital: The Rise of Secondary Schooling in America, 1910–1940," *The Journal of Interdisciplinary History* 29:4 (Spring 1999): 683–723.

[23] Kaestle and Vinvoskis, *Education and Social Change.*

the period from 1780 to 1840, however, when the most dramatic expansion of schooling occurred and was concentrated in small towns and rural areas. Overall, Kaestle and Vinovskis cautioned, connections between education and economic change were difficult to establish, and the tightness of the links should not be overestimated.[24]

Since then, scholars in the history of education have for the most part taken Kaestle and Vinovskis's advice, especially with regard to periods before the Civil War. Although substantial bodies of scholarship exist on the significance of schooling for human capital formation and economic development, that scholarship is largely written by economists and concentrates almost exclusively on the role of secondary institutions after 1880 and especially after the turn of the twentieth century.[25] Similarly, while a critical tradition remains salient in interpreting schooling and school reform during the progressive era, the tradition is now largely silent with regard to the early national and antebellum eras, and the single greatest critical work in the history of education continues to be James Anderson's study of education for blacks in the South after the Civil War.[26]

One way in which relationships between education and economic and social changes have continued to be investigated for the early nineteenth century is as a family or household strategy for social reproduction. Much of this scholarship is rooted in women's history and is aimed at explaining the phenomenal expansion of women's participation in schooling as both students and teachers that occurred in the early national and antebellum eras. That expansion occurred both at the common school level, in the period from 1780 to 1820, and at the level of higher schooling, where women were the majority of all students in the North by the mid-1840s. Clearly families were finding the education of girls an increasingly worthy object of household investment. Historians have explored a range of social and economic factors to explain this development, beginning with the declining significance of female labor in household production identified by Nancy Cott in 1977 and the "marriage gap" and decline in land availability cited by David Allmendinger in 1979.[27]

---

[24] Ibid.
[25] Theodore Schultz, "Capital Formation by Education," *Journal of Political Economy* 68:6 (Dec. 1960): 571–583; idem., "Investment in Human Capital," *The American Economic Review* 51:1 (1961): 1–17; Goldin and Katz, "Human Capital and Social Capital"; Claudia Goldin, "America's Graduation from High School: The Evolution and Spread of Secondary Schooling in the Twentieth Century," *The Journal of Economic History* 58:2 (June, 1998): 345–374; John L. Rury, "Social Capital and Secondary Schooling: Interurban Differences in American Teenage Enrollment Rates in 1950," *American Journal of Education* 110 (August 2004): 1–22.
[26] James Anderson, *The Education of Blacks in the South, 1860–1935* (Chapel Hill: University of North Carolina, 1988).
[27] Nancy Cott, *The Bonds of Womanhood: "Women's Sphere" in New England, 1780–1835* (New Haven, CT: Yale University Press, 1977); David F. Allmendinger, "Mount Holyoke Students Encounter the Need for Life Planning, 1837–1850," *History of Education Quarterly* 19 (Spring 1979): 27–46.

Some explanations emphasize the significance of schooling for women as an alternative to productive labor and as a marker of upperclass status, especially in commercial towns and cities.[28] At the other end of the spectrum, some scholars associate increased female participation in schooling in rural communities with certain forms of production, such as dairy-making, where women had some influence over economic decision making, and with towns where the distribution of wealth and political power was relatively equitable across households.[29] A growing body of work also emphasizes the significance of schooling as a source of social and financial security for women from middling and often rural backgrounds. Historians of women's education have together established a more or less continuous account from the 1780s to the 1920s of women who sought and pursued education as a means of securing self-improvement, middle class status, and self and family support, chiefly as teachers.[30]

Still, the literature on schooling during the early republican era remains largely disconnected from broader historical literatures on social, economic, and political changes. In all the vast scholarship on Jacksonian politics, evangelical religion, the market revolution, and the capitalist transition, schools

---

[28] This is the interpretation developed in Cott, *Bonds of Womanhood* and in Barbara Solomon's survey of the history of women's education, *In the Company of Educated Women: A History of Women and Higher Education in America* (New Haven, CT: Yale University Press, 1985). More recently, Jane Hunter developed this interpretation with reference to the development of urban high school culture among the set of fairly affluent women she studied in *How Young Ladies Became Girls: The Victorian Origins of American Girlhood* (New Haven, CT: Yale University Press, 2002). For a recent essay review that distinguishes the interpretation presented in these works from those developed in some works discussed in the following notes, see Christine A. Ogren, "'Precocious Knowledge of Everything': New Interpretations of Women's Higher Schooling in the US in the late-18th and early-19th centuries," *Journal of Curriculum Studies* 39:4 (2007): 391–402.

[29] Joan Jensen, *Loosening the Bonds: Mid-Atlantic Farm Women, 1750–1850* (New Haven, CT: Yale University Press, 1986); Kathryn Kish Sklar, "The Schooling of Girls and Changing Community Values in Massachusetts Towns, 1750–1820," *History of Education Quarterly* 33:4 (Winter, 1993): 511–42; Kathryn Kerns, "Ante-bellum Higher Education for Women in Western New York State" (unpublished Ph.D. dissertation, University of Pennsylvania, 1993); Doris Jeanne Malkmus, "Capable Women and Refined Ladies: Two Visions of American Women's Higher Education, 1760–1861" (unpublished Ph.D. dissertation, University of Iowa, 2001). Malkmus explicitly distinguishes between a "genteel" tradition of women's education rooted in large towns and cities of the east coast in the early republican period and a "productionist" tradition of evangelical coeducation rooted in the countryside of the eastern interior and the Midwest in the antebellum period.

[30] Margaret Nash, *Women's Education in the United States, 1780–1840* (New York: Palgrave/MacMillan, 2005); Kerns, "Ante-bellum Higher Education"; Malkmus, "Capable Women and Refined Ladies"; Kim Tolley, "How Mrs. Sambourne Earned a "Comfortable Living for Herself and Her Children"; Tolley and Beadie, "Socio-Economic Incentives to Teach"; Tolley, *The Science Education of American Girls: A Historical Perspective* (New York: Routledge/Falmer Press, 2003); Polly Welts Kaufman, *Women Teachers on the Frontier* (New Haven, CT: Yale University Press, 1984); and Christine Ogren, *The American State Normal School: "An Instrument of Great Good"* (New York: Palgrave/MacMillan, 2005).

Introduction

are barely mentioned, despite the fact that schools were more universal agencies of association than churches, reform societies, or political parties. When they do mention schooling, social and political historians often seem unaware that in the North schooling was much more universal in rural areas than in cities, and that it achieved near universality long before it was publicly funded or state-administered.[31] As a result, the place of education in the social and economic transformations of the countryside remains largely unexplored.

This book is a case study of rural education during the capitalist transition. It tells the story of one town and its schools and connects that story with broader literatures and events in social, economic, and political history. The case of Lima, New York, is a fruitful place for making such connections. Throughout the period, Lima remained a rural and predominantly agricultural town. Officially organized in 1796, it had a population of just under 2000 in 1820 and just under 2500 in 1850.[32] And yet, in 1820, the town of Lima was poised for economic development. Located in the fertile Genesee Valley region of western New York, it had already achieved the level of agricultural improvement, population density, and per capita land values that economic historians identify as characterizing a commercial farming economy. During the period from 1820 to 1840, the town of Lima experienced many of the same aspects of economic change that scholars have identified as characterizing the transition to capitalism. Among these were the development of outwork manufactures, the accumulation of capital by local merchants and entrepreneurs, and the establishment of factory production. Also, beginning around 1818 and continuing for more than a decade until 1830, the town of Lima experienced the intense evangelical activity that scholars have associated most strongly with upstate New York, and to which they have attributed the social and cultural deconstruction of the patriarchal household as the primary

---

[31] I have in mind here the large literature surveyed by Charles Sellers in *The Market Revolution* (cited earlier) and more specifically the influential work of Mary P. Ryan, who did so much to illuminate the significance of antebellum revivalism and voluntary associations for enabling women and youth to conceive of themselves as independent social and economic agents, and who later went on to analyze the significance of such associations in shaping politics and the public sphere: Ryan, *Cradle of the Middle Class: The Family in Oneida County, New York, 1790–1865* (Cambridge: Cambridge University Press, 1981); idem., *Women in Public: Between Banners and Ballots, 1825–1880* (Baltimore, MD: Johns Hopkins University Press, 1990); idem., *Civic Wars: Democracy and Public Life in American Cities during the Nineteenth Century* (Berkeley: University of California Press, 1997). Although Ryan argues for the paramount importance of intermediate levels of association for mediating between the individual and the polity, she ignores schools as sites of association, socialization, and identity formation among youth and/or women, seems to assume that schooling was not present or significant unless state-directed, and believes mistakenly that public support for common schools did not develop in New York State until 1840.

[32] Population figures taken from the federal censuses for 1820 and 1850: *Census for 1820* (Washington, DC: Gales and Seaton, 1821) and U.S. Bureau of the Census, *Seventh Census of the United States* (1850) (Washington, DC: Department of the Interior, U.S. Bureau of the Census, 1854).

locus of production and authority. Coincident with these developments, the town of Lima made schooling a centerpiece of local community life. Beginning with the construction of the first brick school house in 1803 and continuing under the first state laws providing for systematic public support of schools in the period from 1812 to 1815, people in Lima devoted substantial local resources to common school building and operations. By 1820 the town had already achieved the virtually universal common school attendance that historians of education associate with the expansion of rural common schooling in the early national period. It had also achieved a level of school funding and operations far beyond anything required or supported by common school law. In 1830, local credit-brokers built on this history of school and community building and forged a coalition that successfully won the site of a Methodist-sponsored academy. By 1840, this academy would be the largest and one of the most heavily capitalized educational institutions in the state.[33]

The exceptional size and success of this institution in a small, otherwise unexceptional, rural town provided the initial impetus for this study. Juxtaposed against the rise and demise of a local textile mill in the mid-1830s, the case of the academy at Lima highlights the peculiar significance of certain kinds of social institutions and social practices in the process of capitalist transformation. The founding and substantial capitalization of the academy at Lima did not occur *de novo* through direct endowment by the state or a grant of church lands, as might have occurred during the colonial era. Nor did it occur through the intervention of an industrialist philanthropist or by federal land grant as might have occurred after the Civil War.[34] Rather, the founding and initial capitalization of the academy at Lima drew on a pattern of community building and trade and barter among neighbors that dated back at least to the founding and construction of the first brick school house in town three decades earlier.

Starting with the story of that first brick school house, this study traces patterns of school and community building in one town in the Genesee Valley region of western New York. The study builds on what scholars have done before but takes a somewhat different approach. In the 1970s and 1980s, scholars studied the relationship between education and economy as a matter of social demography. They asked who promoted, resisted, and participated in schooling, and then analyzed the social and economic backgrounds of those people. Issues of interpretation focused on the extent to which schools expressed the interests of any particular class, and on the ideological significance of schooling in the shift toward capitalist production and wage-labor.

---

[33] In 1850 the academy would spawn the organization of Genesee College. Although the latter institution would eventually move to Syracuse and become the nucleus of Syracuse University in 1871, the academy survived in Lima until 1940. Beadie, "From Academy to University."

[34] For a comparative discussion of these antebellum and postbellum methods of capitalizing "higher" education, with reference specifically to the Genesee case, see Beadie, "From Academy to University."

Introduction

The approach taken here, by contrast, has a somewhat different starting point. Instead of dividing people into classes, I trace the roots of school support to different social networks and then connect those networks to broader patterns of social, political, and economic changes.

The proposition here, then, is that schools, together with other social institutions, played a significant role in the market revolution and capitalist transition, and in the political and economic integration of the modern liberal state. It is the aim of this book to describe and analyze what this role was and to do so with considerable attention to the specificity of place and the contingency of history. The book is about the place of schooling in a transforming political economy. But it is also about a specific place. The aim of the book, in other words, is both narrative and theoretical. One purpose is to make claims about the significance of education in the process of economic development and state formation. Another purpose is to highlight the human dimensions of that history.

The book operates at multiple levels. At one level, it is the story of one town and its schools. It is an account of people such as the self-described "young Men of the town" who organized the first congregational society and built the town's first "brick school house" in 1803. It is the story of the teachers of a local "woman school," "select" school, and common schools, such as Harriet Partridge, Anson Tuthill, and Thomas Caulkins. It is the story of the rebellious taxpayer and parent William Gray; the Methodist circuit preacher Benajah Williams; local credit-brokers and opportunists such as Asahel Warner and Augustus Bennett; the New York capitalist Isaac Bronson; and the luckless mill-owners Amon Lamphere and Othaniel Gilbert. And it is the story of students such as Clarissa Pengra, Frances Smith, and A. J. Warner, who sought and sometimes found career opportunities and true friends at school, but who also learned the hazards of bankruptcy, migration, and betrayal in the transforming economy of the 1830s and 1840s.

At another level the book is a study of the norms of everyday life and educational practice in the early republican era. While grounded in specific stories, each chapter explicates certain norms of the time, such as the practice of local barter and exchange in the building of schools and the hiring of teachers; the technique and culture of revivalism as practiced by itinerant preachers; the rhythm of home study, work, schooling, visiting, and teaching common to many youth; and the role of local "credit-brokers" in mediating exchanges for both commercial and noncommercial enterprises.

At a third level the book is a study of the meanings of these norms and practices as represented by certain ideas. Each section aims at illuminating how particular ideas were understood at the time, such as "the Methodist economy," "the diffusion of intelligence," "liberty of conscience," "communities of interest," and "the importance of friends."

At a fourth level the book is a study of historical change, particularly transformations of society, politics, and economy. By situating education in this town in relation to studies of social and economic changes in other towns in western New York and other areas of the United States, the book connects the history of education in this period to the larger movements and developments of which the events were a part, such as the transformation of patriarchy, the transition to capitalism, the emergence of the Second American Party System, and the expansion of market culture.

Finally, at a theoretical level, the book develops an argument about the significance of education and social capital in the process of economic development and state formation in the early American republic. That argument is framed in the language of social capital and is previewed in the following paragraphs.

The book is organized in three parts. Part I focuses on the social dimensions of education in the early republican era, particularly relationships between church and school. It establishes how early schools, like churches, served as loci for the formation of local social capital – that is, networks of association and trust. It then goes on to examine the expansion and transformation of these networks of association through the Second Great Awakening. Specifically, it examines the Second Great Awakening as an *educational movement* and as an *organizing process* that transformed individual identities through a common discipline and organized social and financial capital across localities. In the language of social capital theory, the evangelical educational movement facilitated the formation of two types of social capital: *bonding* and *bridging*.

Part II focuses on schools as agencies of politicization in the early republican era. It establishes that early academies and common schools emerged in the context of existing education markets in which institutions competed for students and funds. It goes on to examine from a local perspective the significance of laws allocating shares of state funds to schools that already commanded substantial household resources and nearly universal school attendance on a tuition basis. It then considers the political significance of bringing educational decisions into the public realm during a period of expanded suffrage, party formation, and state investment in economic development. In this context, I argue, state support for education helped to integrate ordinary households and social networks into translocal party politics and a state political economy. In effect, state policy converted the already considerable social capital commanded by schools into political capital for the modern liberal state. At the same time, it also made schools sites of political coalition and conflict, at both local and state levels.

Part III focuses on the economic dimensions of education in the antebellum era, particularly on relationships between schools and the capitalist transition. Specifically, it considers the founding of one denominationally sponsored educational institution as a case of corporate capitalization and a site of economic competition and conflict in a time of economic change. In 1834, a significant conflict developed in the New York State Legislature over Genesee Wesleyan's corporate charter. Understanding what was at stake in this battle from various perspectives, how and why it occurred as it did, and with what consequences provides something of a narrative arc and focus for this section of the book. That such a political battle occurred over the incorporation of an educational institution in New York in 1834 makes social, economic, political, and cultural sense. Acts of incorporation were first and foremost about the consolidation and control of capital. A battle over incorporation was thus a battle over the control of capital – social, financial, political, and cultural capital. That local petitioners from Lima essentially lost the battle over control of an educational institution in their town is indicative of a larger shift in politics and political principle at the time, and in the organization of social, political, and financial capital in the state.

Finally, the book considers the meaning of education in this transforming economy. For years, scholars who considered the place of education in the early republic focused on class formation and social control. More recently, scholars have moved beyond the framework of class analysis as a way of understanding historical relationships between economy and society, focusing more broadly on the market revolution and market culture. This book concludes by arguing that systematic organization and support of schools promoted the formation of translocal friendship networks and the currency of social "credentials" sought by youth trying to negotiate the hazards and opportunities of a capitalist market economy. Among the youth negotiating such hazardous opportunities was the hopeful yet anxious Clarissa Pengra.

2

Creating Social Capital – Norms of School and Community Building

> Social capital ... refers to the features of social organization, such as trust, norms and networks, that improve the efficiency of society by facilitating coordinated actions.
>
> Robert Putnam, *Making Democracy Work*, 1993[1]

> Americans of all ages, all stations in life, and all types of dispositions are forever forming associations. ... Americans combine to give fetes, found seminaries, build churches, distribute books and send missionaries to the antipodes. Hospitals, prisons and schools take shape in that way. ... In every case, at the head of any new undertaking, where in France you would find the government or in England some territorial magnate, in the United States you are sure to find an association.
>
> Alexis de Tocqueville, *Democracy in America*, 1848[2]

> The young Men of the Town ... taking into consideration the many advantages arising to society in the improvement of knowledge, the promotion of virtue and good Morrals and the cultivation of manners, all of which we believe may be promoted by the preaching of the Gospel; and seeing with concern, the failure of several attempts for its support by the elder Class of Citizens: we do therefore with these considerations, hereby form ourselves into a Society for the encouragement of the preaching of the Gospel.
>
> Minutes of the Charleston [Lima] Congregational Society, 1801[3]

---

[1] Robert Putnam, *Making Democracy Work: Civic Traditions in Modern Italy* (Princeton, NJ: Princeton University Press, 1993): 167.

[2] Alexis de Tocqueville, *Democracy in America*, J. P. Mayer ed., Vol. II, Part I, Chap. 5 (New York: Anchor Books, 1969 [orig., 1840, 1848]): 513.

[3] "Subscription" [c. December 1801] copied into "Minutes, first Congregational Society in Charleston, Beginning Jan. 6, 1802," LPC. While the original subscription circular was not itself dated, the date can be roughly determined as sometime during the month or so before the "original warning" of the first meeting of the subscribers, which was issued on December 30, 1801. Originally named Charleston in 1796, the town changed its name to Lima in 1808, but the congregational society retained its original corporate name until 1852. "Ontario County General Session Records," November 1796, OCRAIMS; n.a., *Official Index to the Unconsolidated Laws Being the Social, Private and Local Statutes of the State of New York from Feb. 1778 to Dec. 31, 1919* (Albany: J.B. Lyon printer, 1920): 252.

Creating Social Capital

> The Society met according to adjournment. 1st voted to let a subscription paper Circulate to get siners [sic.] for Building a Schoolhouse; 2ndly voted Matthew Warner, Willard Humphrey and Asahel Birchard as a Committee to forward [said] Paper; 3rd voted to Build the house Thirty-two feet by twenty six to be Built of Brick.
>
> Minutes of the Charleston [Lima] Congregational Society, January 17, 1803[4]

In the aftermath of the American Revolution, when established church authority had been eliminated in all but the New England states, and when property ownership still defined and limited participation in civil government, schools were important agencies of social capital formation. To achieve social aims at the turn of the nineteenth century, ordinary rural households could not rely on the intervention of the state, the endowments of an established church, or the sponsorship of proprietors. Instead they depended on their own initiative. Drawing on networks of kinship, trade, and trust; employing the practice of raising subscriptions; and using the tool of general incorporation law, they chose to contribute shares of their own surplus goods and labor toward the goals of securing basic education for their children and continued discipline and enlightenment for themselves and their society. In the process, they created social capital.

This chapter introduces the idea of social capital through the example of early school and community building in the town of Lima, New York. By the time local leaders and residents in Lima launched their bid for the site of the Methodist academy in 1830, they already had thirty years of experience with school and community building in their town. This experience dated back to the turn of the nineteenth century, when residents first raised subscriptions to establish a local congregational society and build the town's "brick school house." Soon after settling in the area in the mid-1790s, a group of residents who identified themselves as "the young men of the Town" organized a society for "the improvement of knowledge, the promotion of virtue and good morrals [sic] and the cultivation of manners."[5] In December 1801, the founders of the society circulated a "subscription" and collected pledges of support from forty-three subscribers. They then called a meeting, drew up a constitution, and applied for incorporation as a church society. Having achieved that object in 1802, the members went on to raise a second subscription to construct the town's first community building, known thereafter as "the brick school house." Completed in 1803 and located at the center of town on the main east-west highway through New York State at the time, Genesee Road, the brick school house sufficed for a decade as the town's main meeting place. It housed town and church meetings as well as a school.

As the example of the brick school house illuminates, the practice of school and community building occurred according to certain norms and principles.

---

[4] "Minutes, the Charleston Congregational Society," January 17, 1803.
[5] "Subscription," 1801.

Subscriptions followed a common format and assumed norms of long-term debt accounting. The process of incorporation, meanwhile, embodied principles of joint ownership, shared governance, and voluntary consent. This chapter describes the norms of school and community building at the turn of the nineteenth century. In the process it illuminates the significance of schools as social institutions and education as a social purpose in early American society.

Raising Subscriptions

Raising a subscription was the normal way of launching a group endeavor in the late eighteenth and early nineteenth centuries. The practice was common not only to church and school organization, but also to the formation of clubs, libraries, and debating societies and to the provision of many shared services and facilities, such as fire companies, bridges, and bell towers. In the eighteenth century, the quintessential subscriber and subscription organizer was Benjamin Franklin, who in his autobiography recorded his involvement in a number of subscription enterprises, including everything from commissioning a system of street cleaning to founding the Philadelphia Academy. The practice of raising subscriptions became common in rural as well as urban locations, including both social reform causes, such as temperance and antislavery, and transportation and business enterprises, such as turnpikes, canals, and factories. When Alexis de Tocqueville made his famous comments in 1840 about the propensity of Americans to form associations, he had the practice of raising subscriptions in mind.[6]

As a document, a subscription typically consisted of two parts, a text and a list of signatures. The text often began with a preamble that stated the larger social and moral purposes of the enterprise. In the case of the first religious society in Lima, the self-described young men of the town claimed to have considered "the many advantages arising to society" from the preaching of the gospel, including the improvement of knowledge, virtue, morals, and manners. Given these advantages of religious instruction and seeing "with concern" the "failure of several attempts for its support by the elder class of citizens," the signers determined to form themselves into a "Society for the encouragement of the Gospel" in late 1801. They then circulated their statement of purpose among local residents to enlist members and collect pledges of support.[7]

With its declaration of principles and list of signatures, a subscription resembled a petition. Unlike a petition, however, a subscription did not stop at declaring an opinion or making demands of an authority. A subscription was not simply a form of speech; it was a form of action. In the case of the congregational society in Lima, the "young men of the town" did not just complain

---

[6] Benjamin Franklin, *The Autobiography* (New York: Vintage Books, 1990): 114–121; Tocqueville, *Democracy in America*, Vol. II, Part I, 513.
[7] "Subscription," 1801.

Creating Social Capital 21

about the absence of a church and meeting house. They took matters into their own hands. They formed an association and raised money to accomplish the task themselves. In so doing, they acted out a certain understanding of the meaning of self-government.

This understanding emphasized voluntary initiative and group accountability. In signing a subscription, a person volunteered the resources of his household in support of a goal he claimed as his own. He even determined the amount of his contribution according to his own assessment of his duty and his means. In the case of the first congregational society in Lima, the text of the subscription expressed this idea of voluntary commitment in an actual pledge statement. "We the subscribers," the document stated, "agree to pay to a commity [sic] which we shall hereafter choose for the purpose, the sums annexed to our respective names." Turning then to the matter of accountability, the document went on to detail the terms under which the funds should be collected and expended. Once the total amount pledged had reached the sum of $100, the organizers would notify the subscribers and schedule a meeting to elect a committee charged with collecting and disbursing the funds. Immediately thereafter, the money subscribed would be paid into the hands of the committee "and an account of the same by them kept in a book by them provided for that purpose." In the book the committee would also register an account of exactly how the funds had been spent. Should any money be left after the end of a year, it would be the option of each individual member of the society either to receive his proportionate share of the remainder and thereby dissolve the association, or to continue in society.[8]

Even as they allowed for subscribers to dissolve their membership in the association, however, the founders of the first religious society in Lima looked ahead to making the organization more permanent through incorporation. Acting in the New England congregational tradition of completely independent local churches, residents of Lima had organized their first "church," or church society, on a wholly voluntary basis, without any superintending religious authority. And yet, without the state legal structure that provided tax support for local churches in New England, residents of Lima and other towns in New York had to secure support for such societies or churches by other means. They did so under corporate law.

Corporate Ownership

Organizing a religious society was the normal way of forging neighborhood and community identity at the turn of the nineteenth century. Until the revised school law of 1815, it was also the only means for ordinary people in New York to own property in common as a corporate entity without making special application to the legislature.[9] When the founders of the congregational society

---

[8] Ibid.
[9] Ronald Seavoy, *The Origins of the American Business Corporation, 1784–1855* (Westport, CT: Greenwood Press, 1982).

filed for incorporation in 1802, they acquired a legal basis for joint ownership of property. They also laid the groundwork for future community building.

From the perspective of the twenty-first century, it can be difficult to appreciate the significance of incorporation in early American society. Then, as now, incorporation enabled a group of people to establish a legal identity as a corporate body, to perpetuate that identity beyond the lives and interests of the founding members, to pool resources for a common purpose, and to protect such resources from appropriation by others. In the context of early republican society, however, corporate organization could have a somewhat different meaning than it does now. Without incorporation, property used for common purposes often remained in the hands of individual proprietors, and thus in their control. The town of Geneseo, for example, about twenty miles southwest of Lima, belonged almost entirely to William Wadsworth, the major proprietor and speculator in western New York lands who made his headquarters there. As town supervisor, an office he held for twenty-one consecutive years, Wadsworth directed that a tax be raised to construct a meeting house "for the use of the town" in 1797. Residents complied by contributing a portion of their farm production for the purpose, and also by performing the labor of construction. Title to the land on which the building was sited remained in Wadsworth's hands, however, until 1805, when townspeople physically removed the building to "meeting house hill," a site owned by the local congregational society.[10] In this context, corporate ownership represented an alternative to aristocratic proprietorship.

The men who organized the congregational society in Lima actively sought this alternative. They could have built a town house the way Geneseo did, but chose not to. In the proprietary tradition, landowners in Lima initially decided to "raise $400 to build a town house" in 1799. Meeting in the home of the man who owned the single largest amount of land at the time, Reuben Thayer, the town specified that $200 be collected in the present year and $200 in the next year, "to be paid in wheat." Because the state at this time did not recognize towns as corporate entities, the land on which the town house was sited would have remained in private hands. At the annual meeting the following year, however, local landowners voted to revoke the earlier decision to build a town house on proprietary terms.[11] Instead, "the young men of the town" proceeded to organize a religious society and build a meeting house under corporate ownership.

Who were these "young men?" The federal census at this time did not record the ages of male heads of household or the names of men who were not heads of the households in which they lived, let alone their wealth or occupations.

---

[10] "Geneseo Town Book, 1797," microfilm, LCHO, Geneseo, New York. On Wadsworth see Neil Adams McNall, *An Agricultural History of the Genesee Valley, 1790–1860* (Philadelphia: University of Pennsylvania Press, 1952) and Donald W. Meinig, "The Geography of Western Expansion, 1785–1855," in John H. Thompson, ed. *The Geography of New York State* (Syracuse, NY: Syracuse University Press, 1966): 141–171.

[11] "Town Book, 1797–1818," LHS.

Details about the lives and identities of the organizers and subscribers of the first religious society in Lima are thus only available incidentally. Nonetheless, from later tax, census, and cemetery records, and from miscellaneous surviving papers of those who stayed in town long enough to be noted, we can surmise that the leaders of the society were landowners of some means, and that several were in the early years of starting their own families.

Of the forty-three men who signed the original subscription paper in 1801, just over half (23) had been listed as heads of household in the 1800 census. Some had migrated to the area as sets of siblings with older parents or as local caretakers of lands owned by absentee parents. For these men the act of founding a religious society seems to have been less about rejecting the authority of their own fathers and more about making a claim to town leadership and declaring joint independence from certain proprietors, such as Reuben Thayer. The census of 1800 itself provided the opportunity for this shift in the balance of power, as county officials at that time redistricted the town to include territory north of its original boundaries, extending to the site of Norton's Mills on Honeoye Creek. As a result of this annexation of territory, Reuben Thayer lost his position as owner of the largest amount of land in town to two other major landholders, Zebulon Norton, of Norton's Mills, and Asahel Warner.[12]

Asahel Warner took the lead in organizing the town's first religious society and building its first meeting house, as he would in virtually every other community project for decades to come. Warner did not assume that role alone, however. Rather, he forged a leadership coalition, including some men with whom he enjoyed family connections and others who had actually preceded his family in buying and settling land in the area. A number of these founding members of the church society would appear near the top of the town's first highway tax assessment in 1803. Ranked according to the number of days' labor each was assessed for local road work, they numbered among the town's top dozen landowners in 1803 and were also among the original subscribers to the church society in 1801. Altogether, twenty-four (56%) of the forty-three original subscribers to the society were known landowners.[13] In cooperating to organize a society independent of town government and aristocratic proprietorship, these men clearly did not object to the principle of property

---

[12] Although the change in boundaries is not generally recognized in local town histories, it is indicated by indirect statements in the Charleston town record book and by a comparison of the boundaries recorded in 1796 when the town was established with those recorded for the town in 1801 as part of state law. See "Ontario County General Session Records," November 1796; "An Act for dividing the counties of this state into towns," *Session Laws of New York, 24th Session, 1801* (Albany: State of New York, 1801): 435; and "Town Book, 1797–1818."

[13] Names of subscribers were matched against those listed in the 1803 highway tax list, in which the amount of labor assessed against each household was proportional to the amount of land (if any) each pole owned or leased, as well as against various land deeds. "Minutes, first Congregational Society"; "A list of the Poles supposed to be Taxable on Highways in the Town of Charleston for 1803," June 10, 1803, Town Record Book, 1797–1812, LHS; "Ontario County Deeds," Libers 1–10, OCRAIMS.

ownership as a basis for leadership. Rather, they regarded land ownership as conferring certain social responsibilities that had not been properly assumed. In assuming these responsibilities themselves, Warner and his associates also demonstrated a keen and current knowledge of the law and the opportunities it afforded. Specifically, leaders of the society took advantage of the provisions of general incorporation law.

General Incorporation Law and Religious Liberty

A general incorporation law specified the terms on which any of a whole category of similar institutions could acquire corporate status. By thus making explicit the rules and procedures of incorporation, such laws eliminated much of the political maneuvering and patronage otherwise necessary for obtaining corporate charters. In the absence of a general incorporation statute, a group or institution seeking corporate legal status had to apply for an individual charter in the state legislature and put together the political coalition necessary to achieve the bill's passage. Under a general incorporation law, by contrast, an organization had only to file a document meeting certain criteria with a county clerk. Eventually, general incorporation statutes would be written for business corporations such as banks, insurance companies, and manufactories. Until the 1840s and 1850s, however, profit-seeking enterprises were exceptions rather than the rule among corporations. The general incorporation of banks and other businesses was an innovation of the 1830s that built on an earlier tradition of general incorporation for social institutions such as churches, schools, and charities.[14]

The first category of institution to be named in general incorporation law in the United States was that of religious organizations. In New York State, the legislature passed a general incorporation statute for religious congregations in January 1784, at its first peacetime session following the end of the Revolutionary War. The significance of this law was that it provided an alternative to an established church. Under its provisions, a group of people seeking to organize a church or build a meeting house could do so on a voluntary basis, rather than by tax. They thus could raise the money on their own, without convincing the town's electors of the purpose or levying a tax on unwilling taxpayers. Also under this law, a group of people seeking an alternative to an existing church, whether for reasons of theology or geography, could acquire the means to do so without seeking permission from existing institutions. In this way, the general incorporation of religious societies embodied the principle of religious liberty.[15]

---

[14] Seavoy, *Origins*.

[15] Ibid. "An Act to enable all the religious denominations in this State to appoint trustees who shall be a body corporate, for the purpose of taking care of the temporalities of their respective congregations, and for other purposes therein mentioned," April 6, 1784, *Laws of New York* (Albany: State of New York, 1784), 8th Session, Chap. 18.

The legislators who drafted the law specifically conceived it in these terms. As stated in the original 1784 legislation, the New York Constitution had declared that the free exercise of religions "without discrimination or preference" should forever be allowed within the state. By making it possible for congregations of any denomination to acquire legal status on the same terms and without direct recourse to political authority, the legislature effectively institutionalized this understanding of "liberty of conscience."[16] Founders of the congregational society in Lima echoed this idea of religious liberty in their own constitution. The preamble of the document began by declaring it the duty of all men to worship "the Supreme Being" according to "their own minds and will." In pursuit of this idea, the preamble continued, the people of the town had formed a congregational society to worship God "in the Manner and Season most agreeable to the Dictates of our own Consciences."[17]

The principle of religious liberty lay not only in the alternative to established religion it made possible, however, but also in the model of governance it represented. To be recognized by the state as a corporate body, an organization had to establish an elected board of trustees to serve as representatives of the organization in legal documents and proceedings. Trustees had the power to buy or sell property, to represent the organization in court, and to assume or collect debts in the organization's name. One of the main points of incorporation was to register the name of the organization with the state and provide an account of how its representatives could be recognized as legitimate. Corporate charters thus spelled out the rules by which trustees were to be elected, the qualifications of voters allowed to participate, the length of trustees' terms, the nature and extent of their authority, and the procedures for their replacement. To acquire status as a corporation, then, was to adopt an elective model of governance.

Elective Governance

Founders of the congregational society in Lima established a particularly high standard of elective governance for their organization. Citing a revised version of the 1784 general incorporation law, the society's 1802 constitution specified that trustees of the society would be chosen in a manner "agreeable to an act passed by the legislature of the State of New York the 27 of March 1801 for the incorporation of religious societ[ies]." Specifically, they would be chosen by a majority of the society at its annual meeting. When it came to specifying the powers of trustees, however, founders of the congregational society in Lima reserved more decisions for the membership and required a higher standard of group accountability than that specified by law. The law empowered trustees to make all decisions regarding "the temporalities" of

---

[16] Ibid.
[17] "The Form of the Constitution of the Charleston Congregational Society," November 1, 1802, in "Minutes, first Congregational Society."

the church except that of fixing the salary of the minister, which was left to a majority vote of the membership as a whole.[18] Trustees of the society in Lima, by comparison, would exercise authority in all matters except "settling ministers, building [houses] and raising money for that purpose."[19] The congregational society in Lima, in other words, reserved *all* major financial decisions to the membership as a whole. For these matters, moreover, the society required a two-thirds rather than a simple majority vote.

By adopting this high standard of group consensus, founders of the congregational society effectively safeguarded the liberty of its members. Should they find a potential minister objectionable or a proposed financial burden excessive, members could readily gather the votes necessary to prevent that decision. The power to influence group decision making was not the same as the freedom to do as one pleased, however. When they joined the society, members gained a voice in its proceedings, but they also accepted a long-term commitment to submit to the will of the majority. This commitment had financial implications that could not be accepted or rejected at will. Decisions about how to raise or spend money would be made "in the way that two thirds of the society shall think best," but, once made, they would "be binding upon the whole."[20] In other words, if two-thirds of the society voted to hire a minister, all members would be expected to contribute a share of his support.

In these and other respects, membership in the congregational society resembled a Lockean social compact. As the most widely accepted statement of republican theory in the eighteenth century, John Locke's *Second Treatise on Government* captures the logic of much that had become ordinary thought and practice in Anglo-American society by 1800.[21] Writing in the wake of the Glorious Revolution of 1689, Locke was primarily concerned with explicating the grounds of legitimacy for civil government. The applicability of his theory to a religious society thus at first may not seem obvious. In the case of the congregational society at Lima, however, it was precisely this sense of legitimacy that the founders were after. As theorized by Locke, the legitimacy of any government rested on voluntary consent. "The only way whereby anyone devests himself of his Natural Liberty [a condition of the State of Nature], and puts on the bonds of Civil Society, is by agreeing with other men to joyn and unite into a Community," Locke explained.[22] For members of the congregational society at Lima, this expression of consent was literal. To join the society,

---

[18] "An Act to provide for the Incorporation of Religious Societies," March 27, 1801, *Laws of New York*, 24th Session, Chap. 74 (Albany: State of New York, 1801).
[19] "Form of the Constitution."
[20] Ibid.
[21] On the currency of Locke's theoretical statements, and, generally, on the way in which such statements reflected ordinary political practice in the republican era, see Pauline Maier, *American Scripture: Making the Declaration of Independence* (New York: Random House, 1997): esp. 87 and 47–96.
[22] John Locke, *Two Treatises of Government* (New York: Cambridge University Press, 1960), Second Treatise, Chap. VIII, pp. 374–375.

one simply indicated acceptance of its principles by signing the articles of the constitution. In signing the constitution, members acted out Locke's theory of self-rule in a way they would never have the opportunity to do in civil government. At the same time, however, they also assumed a certain obligation. As Locke explained, "... every Man, by consenting with others to make one Body Politick under one Government, puts himself under an Obligation to every one of that society, to submit to the determination of the majority, and to be concluded by it."[23]

Locke regarded this obligation as essentially permanent, except in rare cases where a government failed to honor the fundamental ends and principles of its organization, a situation that justified revolution. Similarly, in the case of the congregational society at Lima, the obligations assumed by members were regarded as conclusive and enduring, with limited exceptions. Only two conditions could excuse a member from continuing to honor his commitments to the society. First, anyone belonging to the society who moved out of town would no longer be "holden." Second, anyone who dissolved his relationship with the society by joining another church could be excused from further obligation. In this respect, joining the society was more like entering into a marriage (or what Locke referred to as the *original* social compact) than it was like joining the average membership organization in the twenty-first century. The relationship and its attending moral and financial obligations were considered permanent unless formally terminated. "If any one of the members of this Society should be convinced in his own Confession that some other Religious Denomination is higher," the twelfth and final article of the society's constitution read, "and he actually joins himself to some other church," then "he shall be excepted."[24]

Residents of Lima would invoke this understanding of religious liberty a number of times in subsequent decades. As conceived by the authors of the constitution in 1802, however, the point of these provisions was not to counter existing threats of religious oppression, but to establish the broadest possible basis for congregational membership. At the same time as founders of the society imitated the logic of a Lockean social compact, they also extended the membership of the society beyond that typically encompassed by civil government. In Locke's account, the primary motive for joining civil society was property-based. Having created wealth through labor, men sought society as a means "to secure enjoyment of their properties" in comfort, peace, and safety. They thus formed a government with the power to make and enforce law and to provide for mutual defense. In the case of the congregational society in Lima, by contrast, membership was not property-based. No specific pledge of financial support was required of members at the time of joining. Nor, though the law allowed for it, did the society make voting rights dependent on previous financial support. The constitution did require that at least fifty

---

[23] Ibid., 375.
[24] "Form of the Constitution."

signatures, forty from freeholders, be collected in order for the document to be binding. As contrasted with suffrage qualifications for political office at the time, however, property ownership was not a condition of voting.[25]

This relative inclusiveness with respect to property ownership extended to religious affiliation as well. Somewhat surprisingly, perhaps, neither the constitution nor the original subscription made any mention of baptism, creed, or any other religious criteria for membership, although the law allowed for such conditions. Rather, in the most liberal possible interpretation of its preamble, the constitution formally opened membership to all according to their own wills and consciences. In this way, founders of the congregational society established a group identity with the broadest possible base of community support. By making membership open to all adult males without regard to property or creed, by adopting a high standard of group consent over funding decisions, and by allowing for the dissolution of obligation on grounds of both religion and geography, the organizers of the society aimed at attracting the broadest possible constituency and laying the strongest possible foundation for future community building.

In this objective they were fairly successful. As indicated by a comparison of the signatures on the original subscription with those appended to the 1802 constitution, the congregational society doubled its membership between the end of 1801 and the end of 1802. The new membership list included a very high proportion of all known landowning families (more than 75%), as well as a number of families (19, or 23% of the 82 signatories) who apparently owned no land.[26] It also included both old and new settlers. New members included some close relatives of the original subscribers. Even as organizers of the society enlisted the support of relatives, however, they also succeeded in soliciting members from families who had not supported the original subscription. Beyond the known landowners and householders, the list of signateurs included a number of men about whom nothing else is known. Some may have been laborers or tenants of other subscribing households. Others simply migrated into town after 1800 but left before 1810, leaving no record in either census. Given these gaps and uncertainties, it is not possible to make a precise count of the proportion of total households represented by the society's founding members. Nonetheless, a reasonable estimate is that the signateurs to the 1802 constitution represented about 50 percent of all households in town.[27]

With a strong base of support among landowners and additional support from unpropertied residents, leaders of the congregational society succeeded

---

[25] Ibid.
[26] Names of subscribers were matched against those listed in the 1803 highway tax list, as well as against land deeds recorded with Ontario County. See note 13. "Minutes, first Congregational Society"; "A list of the Poles supposed to be Taxable on Highways 1803"; and "Ontario County Deeds."
[27] Subscribers were matched against names of householders in the 1790, 1800, and 1810 federal censuses.

in achieving on a voluntary basis what townsmen had failed to achieve on proprietary terms. They established a group identity with both the political authority and the social legitimacy necessary to undertake a community building project. Having obtained the requisite signatures to the constitution, leaders of the society acted quickly to establish corporate legal status. They then proceeded with a plan to erect a physical symbol of that corporate identity in the form of a community building. Again, the leaders followed closely the provisions of the law in pursuing this object. The 1801 incorporation law had specified that electors "shall have belonged to a church or congregation the last twelve months" before voting on funding decisions. Accordingly, leaders of the society prepared to launch the town's first community building project almost precisely a year after the society had formed under the original subscription. On January 17, 1803, at its first meeting following the adoption of a constitution and the election of a corporate board of trustees, the society took up the question of a meeting house as its first item of business. Even before deciding to hire a preacher for the ensuing year, members voted "to let a subscription paper circulate to get signers for building a school house."[28]

Educational Purpose

The decision to build a school house proved significant in the history of Lima in a number of ways. Materially, the "brick school house," as it came to be known, would be the first local community building. It thus established a physical identity for the town that had not existed before. Socially, the school house provided a space for future community organization and activity, including not only school instruction but town meetings and church meetings led by ministers of diverse denominations. Politically, the school building helped solidify the town's leadership. The men who succeeded in forging the coalition and raising the funds for the school house went on to assume formal political offices and spearhead community efforts for decades to come. Symbolically, the brick school house also proved important. It established education, or more specifically schooling, as a central end of community support and investment. It also established a precedent for future relationships between church and school in community building.

In one way, the fact that the congregational society voted to construct a school house comes as no surprise. The decision drew on a long tradition of church sponsorship of education. In cities, churches were the presumed source of charity schooling for the poor, and they often also sponsored grammar instruction for aspiring youth. Similarly, in small towns and rural areas, ministers often combined their work as preachers with teaching the young, whether in formal schools or informally as tutors. More specifically, the building of school houses was a well-established practice of the church. The original 1784 legislation for the general incorporation of religious societies explicitly

---

[28] "Minutes, first Congregational Society," January 17, 1803.

enumerated the power to "erect and build ... school houses" among the prerogatives of churches and congregations, and this power was reiterated in the 1801 revision of the law.[29]

The fact that the congregational society *could* build a school house under corporate authority is not enough to explain why it actually did so, however. The general incorporation law not only empowered trustees to build school houses, but also to build "churches," "meeting houses," "dwelling houses for the use of their ministers," and "other buildings for the use of such church, congregation or society."[30] Working within the parameters of the law, the leaders and members of the congregational society nonetheless made a very specific choice when they decided to build a "school house" rather than a church or meeting house.

Considered as a choice, the decision to build a school house says a number of things about the strategy and intentions of the town's aspiring leadership. It suggests, first of all, that the intentions of the leaders who founded the congregational society were not exclusively religious. From the perspective of the twenty-first century, present observers are apt to regard any evidence of church activity as an expression of religious fervor or sectarianism. In fact, in Lima in the 1810s and 1820s, some townspeople would participate in evangelical revivals characteristic of the Second Great Awakening and organize rival churches. Responding in part to that context, the congregational society would construct the town's first separate church building in 1815, to be followed by churches of other denominations. At the very beginning of the century, however, when the existence of the town as a unit of government was less than a decade old, and when a symbol of town identity had yet to emerge in the landscape, church organization was a practical means of getting a number of things done. It was a way to hire preaching, for sure, but also a way to forge a community with a shared identity, and to give that identity some solidity in the form of a community building.

By choosing to identify that building as a school house, rather than as a church or meeting house, the aspiring leadership of the town continued in the direction of forging a community identity that was more inclusive than exclusive in character. More ecumenical than either the property-based coalition that defined town government or the broad religious coalition associated with the congregational society, a school house potentially served whole families and the town at large. The building itself would of course be used for multiple purposes. That was exactly the point. A building with an identity expansive enough to hold the possibility of multiple common purposes promised a broad foundation for the future.

Building a school house also expressed a commitment to education as an idea. From the beginning, community builders in Lima had framed their purpose in educational terms. In making the original case for religious organization, they

---

[29] "An Act to incorporate," 1801.
[30] Ibid.

wrote of the advantages that would result for the "improvement of knowledge" and the "promotion of virtue." These two phrases were quintessential expressions of enlightened educational ideals in the late eighteenth and early nineteenth centuries. They were common to virtually every statement of republican mission and purpose in education, from Benjamin Franklin's *Proposals Relating to the Education of Youth in Pensilvania* in 1749 to Emma Willard's *Plan for Improving Female Education* in 1818.[31] Similarly, when it came to constitutional principle, the founders of the congregational society expressed their idea of religious duty in the language of enlightenment thought. Under the rubric of their constitution, religious practice would be directed by members' "own minds and will" rather than by any ecclesiastical, or even divine, authority. From the perspective of these rhetorical precedents, the decision to build a school house reflected a broad faith in education and human improvement on the part of the town's leadership.

Educational ideals continued to motivate community building in Lima for decades to come. Some school building efforts responded to state directives. When the state legislature passed the first common school law in 1812, it directed the organization of school districts and allowed for the construction of school houses in those districts. In compliance with the law, the town levied a school tax and laid out the boundaries of its first school districts in 1813. At this time, the state had not yet made any provisions for the corporate status of school districts. Once the state amended the school law to allow for the general incorporation of school districts in 1815, however, townspeople in Lima organized additional neighborhood schools.[32] Even as schooling became an object of state policy in the 1810s and 1820s, however, it also continued to be a focus of voluntary initiative. The men who organized the First Universalist Society of Lima in 1825, for example, proceeded in much the same way as had the founders of the original congregational society more than twenty years earlier. They raised a subscription, drafted a constitution, and acquired corporate status as a religious society. They also looked to school building

---

[31] Benjamin Franklin, *Proposals Relating to the Education of Youth in Pensilvania* (Philadelphia: Franklin and Hall, 1749), reprinted in Thomas Woody, ed. *Educational Views of Benjamin Franklin* (New York: McGraw-Hill, 1931); Emma Willard, *An Address to the Public, Particularly to the Members of the Legislature of New-York, Proposing a Plan for Improving Female Education*, 2nd edition (Middlebury, VT: J. W. Copeland, 1819 [reprinted by Middlebury College, 1918]). On the significance of Willard's plan, see Nancy Beadie, "Emma Willard's Idea Put to the Test: The Consequences of State Support for Female Education in New York, 1819–1867," *History of Education Quarterly* 33:4 (1992): 543–562.

[32] "An Act for the establishment of Common Schools," June 19, 1812, *Laws of New York*, 35th Session, Chap. 242; "An Act for the better establishment of Common Schools," April 15, 1814, *Laws of New York*, 37th Session, Chap. 192; "An Act to amend the act, entitled 'An act for the better establishment of Common Schools," April 18, 1815, *Laws of New York*, 38th Session, Chap. 252; "Record of School districts in the Town of Lima as determined by the School Commissioners of said Town according to the Act for the Establishment of Common Schools passed the Nineteenth Day of April, 1812" in "Town Book, 1797–1818"; and "School Minutes, 1814–1854," School District 4, LHS.

to solidify their identity and create a permanent meeting place. Initially, the society proposed adding a second floor to an existing school building in the hamlet of Norton's Mills. After the school's trustees rejected this proposal, however, the society commissioned a separate building to be located in the hamlet of Smith's Mills. Like the original brick school house, this building served educational as well as religious purposes, becoming known as "the North Bloomfield School."[33]

In each of these cases, school building mobilized support through local social networks and solidified that support in the form of a corporate institution. Schools in this way were important social bonding institutions. They both commanded and forged substantial social capital. Over time, this capital accumulated, becoming a renewable resource with potential for expansion in new school and community building projects.

The Idea of Social Capital

In the largely rural society of western New York, as in much of the rest of the country in the early nineteenth century, the household was both the primary social unit and the primary locus of production and trade. To sustain themselves and to create surplus wealth, ordinary people employed the labor of their own households and traded with the households of relatives and neighbors. Trade among households included not only goods (the product of labor) but labor itself, including that of children, servants, wards, and apprentices as well as of heads of household and other adults. In some cases, the households involved were those of merchants, mill owners, or proprietors of large estates who collected goods from a number of local households and sold the combined stores on distant markets, or who pooled the labors of a number of local men, women, and children to produce a quantity of particular marketable goods. For the most part, however, trade occurred among neighbors, relatives, or acquaintances who knew or were known to each other and who negotiated the distribution and value of labor and goods directly. Social relationships, in other words, were essential to the creation of wealth. They both motivated production and mediated exchange. They shaped the capacity to command the goods and services of others and the likelihood of receiving fair value for one's own household goods and services in return.[34]

More to the point, social relationships endured beyond a single transaction. This durability was itself an economic resource. Like land and cash, it allowed people to store the value of goods or labor for the future. In other words, it enabled them to turn surplus goods and labor into capital. In the ordinary give and take of a rural social economy, the exchange of (often perishable) goods and (temporarily available) labor among neighbors seldom constituted

---

[33] "Minutes of the Universalist Society of Lima, 1825–1885," LHS.
[34] This description of local trade is derived from a wide range of sources. See Chapters 13, 14, and 17.

immediate trades of precisely equal value. Instead, people exchanged the resources of their households on credit and over time. Maintaining what are referred to as long-term debt accounts, they offered goods or services when available in exchange for the promise of future goods and labor when needed. Sometimes several debts accumulated for months or even years on one side of a ledger before a credit on the other side canceled some or all of the value of the debts with goods or services provided in return. Other times a credit exceeded the value of existing debts, temporarily converting the debtor into a creditor with respect to that relationship. Now and then a pair of households purposefully balanced their accounts, perhaps with a payment of cash to even things out. Occasionally, relationships ruptured through death, migration, betrayal, or a simple change in needs or business. Almost never would a household seek to settle all its accounts at once, however, for that would mean a major break with the past and a disruption of the future. In a very real sense, the social and economic well-being of a household depended on the continual renewal of indebtedness or, to put the same point another way, the continual renewal of trust. Through trust, people projected the social and economic resources of the past into the future.

This renewal of trust was social capital in the making. Robert Putnam defines social capital as "the features of social organization, such as trust, norms and networks, that improve the efficiency of society by facilitating coordinated actions."[35] Social scientists like Putnam often use examples from rural society to illustrate the concept of social capital. Putnam borrows one such example from James Coleman: "In a farming community ... where one farmer got his hay baled by another and where farm tools are extensively borrowed and lent, social capital allows each farmer to get his work done with less physical capital in the form of tools and equipment."[36] In this example, the meaning of social capital is represented by the norms of rural exchange relations, that is, by the direct barter or trade of labor, goods, and services. To further illustrate the loss of value that occurs in the absence of social capital, Putnam borrows a second farming example from the philosopher David Hume: "Your corn is ripe today; mine will be ripe tomorrow. 'Tis profitable for us both that I shou'd labor with you today, and that you shou'd aid me tomorrow." But, Hume goes on to explain, "[If] I have no kindness for you and know that you have as little for me ... I will not ... take any pains on your account; ... I leave you to labor alone; and you treat me in the same manner. The seasons change; and both of us lose our harvests for want of mutual confidence and security."[37]

[35] Putnam, *Making Democracy Work*, 167.
[36] James S. Coleman, *Foundations of Social Theory* (Cambridge, MA: Harvard University Press, 1990): 307, as quoted in Robert Putnam, *Democracy at Work*, 167.
[37] David Hume (*A Treatise of Human Nature*, Book 3, Part2, Section 5, [1740]) as quoted by Robert D. Putnam in *Bowling Alone: The Collapse and Revival of American Community* (New York: Simon and Schuster, 2000): 134. Putnam in turn borrowed the citation from Robert Sugden, *The Economics of Rights, Cooperation and Welfare* (Oxford: Basil and Blackwell, 1986): 106.

The point of these examples is that without relationships of trust and reciprocity, farmers would not be able to realize the full value of their labor or "capital." In both examples, the value of social capital is realized (or not) by the individual farmer. But as Putnam is otherwise at pains to point out, the value of social capital does not only accrue to individuals, but also to the community at large. The case of rural school funding makes this notion concrete. In the town of Lima, the norms and networks of rural social economy made possible not only the increased accumulation of wealth by individual households but also the creation of common wealth or community assets, including schools. Moreover, without such norms and networks it is unlikely that such corporate assets would have been created, because other sources of capital or long-term credit such as bank loans or commercial bonds were not available for such projects at the time.[38] Schools in this way did not simply divert capital from some existing source. Rather, in the old agrarian sense, they created capital where none existed before.[39]

In the case of the academy founded in Lima in 1830, more than 150 heads of household from Lima and the vicinity would pledge the value of future goods and labor in amounts ranging from 50 cents to $600, for a total of nearly $11,000.[40] To raise that capital, Lima residents drew on a network of social relationships and a tradition of community building that dated back at least thirty years to the founding of the first congregational society in 1801 and the building of the first brick school house in 1803.

By the time people in Lima launched their bid for the site of the Methodist academy in 1830, they had organized and reorganized eleven different school districts and erected at least as many school houses. They had also organized three new church societies and contributed to the construction of three new church buildings. In many respects, the bid for the Methodist academy in 1830

---

[38] On banking practices see Howard Bodenhorn, *A History of Banking in Antebellum America: Financial Markets and Economic Development in an Era of Nation-Building* (Cambridge: Cambridge University Press, 2000); also Bray Hammond, *Banks and Politics in America from the Revolution to the Civil War* (Princeton, NJ: Princeton University Press, 1957); James Roger Sharp, *The Jacksonians versus the Banks: Politics in the States after the Panic of 1837* (New York: Columbia University Press, 1970); and John Denis Haeger, *The Investment Frontier: New York Businessmen and the Economic Development of the Old Northwest* (Albany: State University of New York Press, 1981). See also Chapter 13.

[39] I refer to the idea of French physiocrats and Scottish enlightenment thinkers that agriculture was the source of all real increase in wealth. See Drew R. McCoy, *The Elusive Republic: Political Economy in Jeffersonian America* (Chapel Hill: University of North Carolina Press for the Institute of Early American History and Culture, 1980), esp. Chap. 1, 13–47; Michael Merrill, "Self-Sufficiency and Exchange in Early America: Theory, Structure, Ideology," (unpublished Ph.D. dissertation, Columbia University, 1985), esp. Chap. 5, "The Principles of Agrarian Realism," pp. 292–317; David Hume, "On Commerce," and "Of Refinement in the Arts," in David Hume, *Political Essays,* Knud Haakonssen, ed. (Cambridge: Cambridge University Press, 1994): 93–104 and 105–114; and Adam Smith, *An Inquiry into the Nature and Causes of the Wealth of Nations,* Edwin Cannan, ed. (New York: Random House, 1994): 718–746.

[40] These contributions are detailed in Chapters 12 and 13. Lima Subscription, Account Book #102, GWSC.

would be just the next in a long line of community building projects, albeit on a much larger scale. As before, local residents invoked traditions of voluntary organization, corporate legal status, and subscription funding to win the bid for the academy. They also drew directly on the experience of past practice.

Even as Lima's bid for the academy built on a long tradition of school and community building, however, it also engaged the force of a powerful evangelical movement that gained considerable momentum in upstate New York in the 1810s and 1820s. This movement animated participation and involvement in many Protestant denominations in the United States. No denomination advanced and capitalized on the evangelical movement more, however, than the Methodist Episcopal Church. By the 1830s the Methodist Church was the largest denomination in the country. In making a bid for the site of a Methodist academy, Lima residents successfully enlisted the considerable power of this organization for local community building, education, and growth. At the same time, they linked the town's future to an outside corporate power with its own structure of governance, its own network of leadership and political influence, and its own principles and priorities. Operating at a different scale and in a changing social, economic, and political context, this outside corporate power challenged local expectations regarding the norms of community building. Eventually this conflict came to a head in the state legislature in a battle over the academy's corporate charter. The roots of this conflict, however, lay in the fundamental reorganization of social life effected by the evangelical movement of the 1810s and 1820s. Illuminating the educational significance of this movement is the project of the next four chapters.

3

A Matter of Trust – Neighbors and Strangers

> ... on this Said plan I do obligate myself to live and to settle among the people as their Minister trusting to their sense of Duty liberality and honor to fulfill their Engagements....
>
> The Rev. Ezekiel Chapman, 1808[1]

> Voted that the school house shall be opened for the Christian societies to hold meetings in.
>
> Minutes of Lima School District No. 4, May 4, 1818[2]

> Though a resident of one place, it was not in his nature to be a local man.
>
> Memoir of Rev. Joseph Badger, 1854[3]

During the first decades of the early republican era, the normative ideal of a central community church and associated school still dominated in Lima and many places in the Northeast, despite the fact of religious disestablishment everywhere outside of a few New England states.[4] Increasingly, however, the

---

[1] "Minutes, first Congregational Society in Charleston," November 22, 1808, LPC.
[2] "Minutes of Lima School District no. 4," May 4, 1818, LHS, Lima, New York.
[3] E. G. Holland, *Memoir of Rev. Joseph Badger* (New York: C. S. Francis & Co.; Boston: Benjamin H. Greene, 1854): 214. I am grateful to Diane Ham, Mendon Town Historian, for bringing this memoir to my attention and providing me with a copy of the text.
[4] Massachusetts was the last state to abolish tax support for established churches, in 1833. For an in-depth discussion of the norms and ideals of the central community church and of the long process by which disestablishment occurred in Massachusetts, see Johann N. Neem, "The Elusive Common Good: Religion and Civil Society in Massachusetts, 1780–1833," *Journal of the Early Republic* 24 (Fall 2004): 381–417. Connecticut ended tax aid for established churches in 1818. New Hampshire continued the practice but allowed the possibility of exemption to any Christian in 1819. For a precise enumeration of various establishment and disestablishment provisions in each colony and state, see John K. Wilson, "Religion under the State Constitutions, 1776–1800," *Journal of Church and State* 32:4 (Autumn 1990): 753–764. For a deeper philosophical and historical discussion of the meaning of religious liberty and how it emerged in different colonial and U.S. contexts, see Chris Benneke, *Beyond Toleration: The Religious Origins of American Pluralism* (Oxford: Oxford University Press, 2006); and William Lee Miller, *The*

fact of religious diversity and the dynamic of educational expansion challenged this ideal. That early school laws should have had a decisive effect on the organization of church life in a town like Lima is a fact that historians have so far not recognized. And yet a close look at the everyday practice of church and school organization makes plain that early school laws challenged existing social and religious authority in a number of ways. In Lima, implementation of New York's first common schools laws undermined the educational authority of the established minister, the Reverend Ezekiel Chapman, and unsettled his contractual arrangement with the local congregational society. It also fractured support for the central brick school by providing a corporate organizational framework for the support of other schools in town. In a context of increased religious pluralism fostered by the Second Great Awakening, these schools in turn became sites of itinerant preaching and religious association, further challenging the authority and support of a central community church and the terms of trust between ministers and communities.

This chapter describes how the structure of organized religion changed in the 1810s and 1820s, and how schools as institutions and education as a social process promoted and facilitated that change. Evangelicalism and schooling followed similar patterns of diffusion and expansion during the early nineteenth century, both spatially and structurally. Spatially, schools and evangelical churches moved into hamlets on the fringes of settled towns, becoming nodes of social organization in outlying districts, often sharing facilities. Structurally, evangelical religion and the expansion of schooling both promoted a loss of authority for central community churches and their ministers. After 1812, ministers in New York lost educational authority to elected school commissioners, trustees, and inspectors for schools that acquired the status of independent corporations. At the same time, central churches and their ministers lost religious and civic authority as they competed for congregants and financial support with itinerant preachers of other denominations. This change in norms and ideals is captured by the distinction between the "settled minister" and the "itinerant preacher" – differences illuminated in Lima by the contrasting stories of the Reverend Ezekiel Chapman and the Reverend Joseph Badger.

The Concept of "Settlement"

When Ezekiel Chapman became Lima's first "settled" minister in 1808, he had already been serving the congregation for several years. Since November 1804, the congregational society had repeatedly employed Chapman as a preacher and teacher for periods of six months to a year at a time, with salaries to be paid partly in cash and partly in produce. Disputes over compensation plagued

First Liberty: Religion and the American Republic (New York: Alfred A. Knopf Press, 1985). I am grateful to Chris Benneke for recommending the work of Neem and Wilson.

the relationship, with the terms renegotiated more than once and the congregation at one point voting to sever the relationship altogether. Eventually both parties accepted terms that fixed the total salary amount and specified that the half to be paid in produce would consist of wheat, rye, or pork. Even after this compromise had been achieved, however, it took another two and a half years for Chapman and the congregation to reach a permanent "settlement."[5]

Struggles over compensation between ministers and congregations were not at all unusual.[6] The life of an ordinary minister often bordered on penurious. As Benjamin Franklin reported about conditions in the early eighteenth century, the drawbacks of the ministry lay not only in the expensive college education it required, but also in "the mean living many so educated were afterwards able to obtain."[7] In the early nineteenth century, moreover, the livelihoods of preachers became even more insecure. A number of factors contributed to this financial difficulty. Among these were the long-term effects of religious disestablishment. In New England, the cultural home of congregationalism, some vestige of tax support for local churches survived as late as 1833.[8] In New York and other middle states, however, ethnic and religious diversity undermined the legal basis for such provisions in the early Revolutionary era. Without the universality of taxation or the compulsion of the law, ministers depended on voluntary pledges and an enduring sense of religious duty for support. Subject to the vicissitudes of individual fortune and the volatility of human relations, this support often proved insufficient.[9]

Given these conditions, Chapman, like other ministers, regarded an invitation to "settle" with a congregation cautiously. In November of 1807, Lima's congregational society voted to raise a subscription and appoint a committee "to treat with Mr. Chapman" over a settlement agreement.[10] To accept a call to a congregation was a major life decision. In the congregational tradition it meant committing oneself to a specific group of people through all life's eventualities. Not unlike a marriage, this commitment was presumed to be permanent. The vast majority (85%) of congregational ministers at the turn of the nineteenth century assumed a single pastorate for the duration

---

[5] "Minutes, first Congregational Society," November 4, 1804–November 22, 1808.
[6] Donald M. Scott, *From Office to Profession: New England Ministry, 1750–1850* (Philadelphia: University of Pennsylvania, 1978): 4. Scott summarizes New England congregationalist norms of preacher hiring and tenure for the period before the Second Great Awakening using statistical data on pages 3–9. See also Daniel H. Calhoun, *Professional Lives in America: Structure and Aspiration, 1750–1850* (Cambridge, MA: Harvard University Press, 1965): 88–177.
[7] Benjamin Franklin, *The Autobiography* (New York: Vintage Books, 1990): 9.
[8] William Lee Miller, *The First Liberty*, 45–46 and 204–205; Calhoun, *Professional Lives in America*, 115.
[9] Scott, *From Office to Profession*, 70–73 and 113–114; Calhoun, *Professional Lives in America*, 164–165.
[10] "Minutes, first Congregational Society," November 10, 1807.

of their careers. Another 14 percent held only two pastorates over their lifetimes.[11] The decision to settle with a congregation thus was not a decision to enter into lightly. In effect, the years that Chapman preached in Lima on temporary contracts served as an engagement period through which both Chapman and the congregational society tested their desire for a long-term commitment. Having learned by trial and error the extent and limits of what they could expect from each other, they then negotiated an official "plan of settlement."

To consider what "a plan of settlement" meant in this context is to conjoin several senses of the word that have since diverged. On the one hand, a "settlement" is a place, but a place identified by signs of human habitation rather than by topographical features of the land. Correspondingly, "to settle" was to take up more or less permanent residency in such a place, or, as Chapman put it, "to live and settle among the people." At the same time, a settlement is also an agreement. It is an agreement reached by negotiation. Such agreements are often financial in character. To settle in this sense is to come to terms over matters of money or property. In this case, accepting a "plan of settlement" meant reaching an agreement with the congregation over the financial terms on which Chapman would take up residence among the people "as their minister."[12]

By his own account, Ezekiel Chapman accepted the plan of settlement offered by Lima only after "mature deliberation." No doubt he hesitated in part because of his past experience with the Lima congregation. This in turn may have given him cause to worry about the future. In a rural community, people made financial commitments for the long term, negotiating payment over time in the give and take of local barter exchange. As Chapman knew, and as he and his successors repeatedly confirmed by experience, the promise of compensation was not the same as its actual provision. Securing a living as a preacher depended on yet another meaning of the term "settlement": the payment of debts, or the settlement of accounts. To accept a plan of settlement meant not only agreeing to the stated terms of a congregation's offer, but trusting the congregation to meet its obligations. As for a woman weighing a marriage proposal, this leap of faith carried certain risks.

Chapman weighed these risks carefully. His formal statement of acceptance indicated both his hopes and his concerns:

This certifies that after mature Deliberation I have accepted the plan of settlement which has been lately circulated in Lima and that on this Said plan I do obligate myself to live and to settle among the people as their Minister *trusting to their sense of Duty liberality and honor to fulfill their Engagements* and that through Divine aid I shall be enabled to serve them faithfully in the Gospel of the Savior.[13]

---

[11] Scott, *From Office to Profession*, 3.
[12] "Minutes, first Congregational Society," November 22, 1808. Scott describes the norms of settlement in *From Office to Profession*, 3–11.
[13] Ibid., emphasis added.

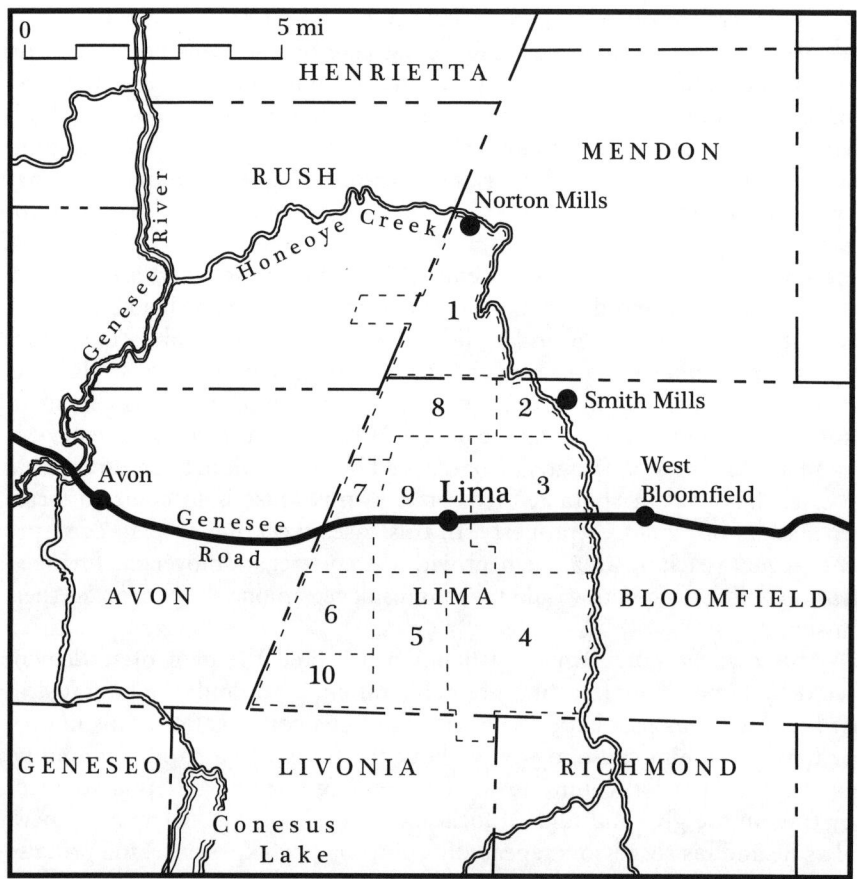

FIGURE 2. Lima School Districts, circa 1813. Early school laws had a significant effect on the organization of church and town life after 1812. They undermined the educational authority of the established minister and fractured support for a central church and school by providing a corporate organizational structure for the support of other schools and meeting houses in town. School district lines shown here are approximate, reconstructed from the original survey recorded by Lima's first school commissioners in "Town Book, 1797–1818, LHS." Base map from David H. Burr, *An Atlas of the State of New York* (New York: by the author, 1829).

With his reference to living "among the people" Chapman expressed a normative idea of "settlement" as rooted in face-to-face relationships among neighbors. He also signaled that, after settlement, his relationship with the congregation would no longer be merely contractual, but dependent on deeper and broader ties of community, long-term trust, and obligation. At the same time, Chapman's insistence on spelling out the qualities that settlement required of congregants suggested the possibility that such trust might prove misplaced. The willingness of Chapman to "settle" in Lima despite past disputes over compensation implied some faith in the formative power of the pastoral relationship and of the collective itself. Over time, Chapman had to hope, the body of the church would knit together and the social ties among community members would strengthen, rather than fray. Through this binding together, the affective power of the group's collective identity would increase and the capacity of the community to mobilize internal resources for a common purpose would grow, making the future "liberality" of the church potentially larger than its present. In theoretical terms, this model of social capital formation depended on the intensification of existing networks of trust, or bonding.[14]

In response, the congregation imitated Chapman's guarded expression of faith in a collective future. After recording his statement in the official record book, members of the congregation voted "that the Above answer be considered sufficient."[15] The Reverend Ezekiel J. Chapman thus became Lima's first settled minister. Perhaps the congregation recognized a note of ambivalence in Chapman's commitment, as the clipped language of the record of its vote seems to suggest. Even by the standards of the time, the period of trial and negotiation in this case was long, a condition that could have been read as a warning in this, as in other kinds of relationships. What eventually unraveled the relationship between Chapman and the congregation, however, was not a particular breach of trust, but a fundamental change in the structure that supported it.

Consequences of New York's First Common School Laws

New York's first permanent common school laws consisted of a series of laws passed over several years, from 1812 through 1815. The first of these laws established the terms on which local schools would be eligible to receive shares of income on endowed state funds dedicated to the support of common schools. The state apportioned funds on a matching basis, based on population. For a town to be eligible, local school commissioners had to raise an equal amount through local taxes. The combined local and state funds would then be distributed to individual schools according to the number of school-aged children resident in the district. To provide for the administration of such funding, the laws detailed procedures for dividing towns into districts, electing school officials, assessing local taxes, and distributing state and local funds.[16]

---

[14] Robert Putnam distinguishes between "bonding" and "bridging" social capital in *Bowling Alone: The Collapse and Revival of American Community* (New York: Simon and Schuster, 2000): 22–23. He attributes the terms to Ross Gittell and Avid Vidal, *Community Organizing: Building Social Capital as a Development Strategy* (Thousand Oaks, CA: Sage, 1998). The distinction is discussed in detail in Chapter 5.

[15] "Minutes, first Congregational Society," November 22, 1808.

[16] Although New York's Common School Fund was established in 1812, the law directed that the first income on the fund be distributed in 1815. In the intervening years the legislature

When Lima's town officials received official notice of the first permanent common school law in 1812, they acted quickly to comply with its provisions. At the next annual town meeting, held in April 1813, the town clerk read aloud the letter from the county outlining the terms on which state school funds would be distributed in the future. In accordance with those specifications, attendees at the meeting voted to assess themselves the "sum of money necessary" to match the state allotment and thus entitle the town to its share of state funding.[17] Also at this meeting, townspeople elected two sets of school officials: three school commissioners to organize the town into school districts, and six school inspectors who would oversee the actual operation of the schools. For commissioners, who were charged with negotiating school district boundaries, the town appointed major landholders. For school inspectors, whose jurisdiction included the examination of teachers, the electors chose four established householders who had often assumed town offices in the past and two men who had never been elected for town office in Lima before and never would be again. The first of these two men was a man named Smith Weeks. The second was the Reverend Ezekiel Chapman.[18]

Whether Smith Weeks won his office more as a representative of his neighborhood or as a representative of Methodism cannot be determined. According to various records, Weeks was an early Methodist preacher who at some point resided in the hamlet of Norton's Mills, though the timing of this association is unclear.[19] By 1818 Norton's Mills was a developing mill site and a center of Methodist organization in the area, but the origins of this development

---

passed a series of laws specifying structures for administering those funds: "An Act for the establishment of Common Schools, Passed January 19, 1812," *Laws of New York*, 35th Session, Chap. 242 (Albany: State of New York, 1813): 258–266; "An Act Supplementary to the act, entitled 'An act for the establishment of Common Schools,' Passed March 12, 1813," *Laws of New York*, 36th Session, Chap. 52 (Albany: State of New York, 1814): 266–268; "An Act for the better establishment of Common Schools, Passed April 15, 1814," *Laws of New York*, 37th Session, Chap. 192 (Albany: State of New York, 1815): 228–243; and "An Act to amend the act, entitled 'An act for the better establishment of Common Schools,' Passed April 15, 1815," *Laws of New York*, 38th Session, Chap. 252 (Albany: State of New York, 1816): 260–264.

[17] "Town Book, 1797–1818," April 6, 1813, LHS.
[18] Ibid.
[19] Some sources refer to Weeks as working as an itinerant preacher in the Norton's Mills area as early as 1797. The origin of this reference appears to be a listing of the "Pastors of the Methodist Church, Honeoye Falls, New York, 1797–1997," held by the village historian of Honeoye Falls and presumably compiled from records of the existing Methodist church in Honeoye Falls. However, since formal organization of that church did not occur until the period 1818–1820, the earliest Genesee Conference records to make reference to the Bloomfield circuit date from 1813, and the earliest reference to Norton's Mills as a location of Methodist activity dates to 1818, this 1797 reference seems somewhat suspect. Nor is Weeks listed anywhere in the conference records from this period as a professional preacher with the Genesee Conference (even though the official minutes ostensibly list all the preachers "in connection" with the church every year). *Minutes of the Annual Conference of the Methodist Episcopal Church for the Years 1773–1828*, Vol. I (New York: T. Mason and G. Lane, 1840): 229 (1813) and *passim*. Smith Weeks does appear as early as 1802 as a Methodist circuit preacher in the

cannot be precisely dated. It is worth noting, however, that Weeks' successor as school inspector in 1815, John Dixson, would also be associated both with Methodism and with the hamlet of Norton's Mills.[20]

For his part, Ezekiel Chapman certainly owed his election as school inspector to his position as Lima's only settled minister. At the time, ministers commonly assumed authority over local educational matters. School teaching and ministerial duties were regarded as mutually reinforcing, especially in a minister's early career. The former undergirded the latter in the manner of an apprenticeship. Students of the ministry often combined school teaching with formal study as a way of subsidizing their educations, perhaps assisting a minister with whom they were also reading or training. In small congregations like Lima's, ministers might continue to combine school teaching with preaching well into their careers, as a means of supplementing their incomes.[21]

Given these norms of practice, Chapman may well have chafed at sharing the role of school inspector with five other men. Such an arrangement insulted his traditional authority as an ordained minister. At the same time, the new school law also directly threatened his livelihood. It not only provided for the levying of taxes and the election of school officials at the town level, it also directed the division of the town into multiple school districts.[22] In Lima, the newly elected school commissioners divided the town into ten school districts in 1813.[23] Each of these districts then became eligible for a share of the funds apportioned by the state and raised through town tax assessments. Each also

---

Seneca District in New York's southern tier. It seems then that Weeks may have later settled in Honeoye Falls and become associated with the church there, which then back-dated its origins to his early ministry. Michael George Nickerson, *Sermons, Systems and Strategies: The Geographic Strategies of the Methodist Episcopal Church in its Expansion into New York State, 1788-1810* (Ph.D. dissertation, Syracuse University, 1988), 352. It would not be the only time I have run into some creative back-dating by a local Methodist church of its origins in a particular place. Multiple references to Weeks do indicate that he was active in the Norton's Mills area from sometime before 1813 through at least 1820. A reference to "Elder Weeks" for 1820 appears in the Journals of Benajah Williams (himself a Methodist preacher), 1817-1862, Vol. I, p. 173, SDL. Smith Weeks is also a signatory to the deed for the land purchased as the site of the Methodist church at Honeoye Falls in 1820. I am grateful to Anne Bullock, Village Historian for Honeoye Falls, for investigating Weeks on my behalf and for passing a copy of the deed with Weeks' signature to me.

[20] A James Dixson was the second signatory to the deed mentioned above. However, it is not clear whether he was related to John Dixson. According to Ham, *Migration to Mendon*, p. 61, John Dixson (or Dixon) opened the first store in Norton's Mills in 1810 and "bought a cloth dressing establishment from Smith Wicks" with his brother Amos Dixon. In 1822, John Dixson signed a petition to the Genesee Conference requesting that the next annual meeting at the conference be held at the chapel at Mendon. "A petition from the towns of Lima and Mendon on Bloomfield Circuit," June 24, 1822, Conference Records, Box 1: Genesee Conference, Folder 2: Genesee Conference Papers, 1820-29, MAHC.

[21] Scott, *From Office to Profession*, 54-75.

[22] "An Act for the establishment of Common Schools, Passed January 19, 1812," *Laws of New York*, 35th Session, Chap. 242 (Albany: State of New York, 1813): 258-266.

[23] "Record of School Districts in the Town of Lima as determined by the School Commissioners of Said Town according to the Act for the Establishment of Common Schools Passed the

acquired the authority to raise its own additional funds to meet the costs of building a neighborhood school house and pay teacher salaries.[24] This multiplication of new funding authorities undermined Chapman's base of financial support by fracturing its integrity. Once required to pay taxes to support schools in their own neighborhoods, householders were less likely to support a central church and school under Chapman's authority.

Chapman and the congregational society certainly recognized the ways in which the new school law challenged their normal way of doing things. After all, the commissioners charged with carrying out the new school law and the trustees of the town's congregational society were essentially the same persons. In the spring and summer of 1814, as the newly organized school districts were preparing to hold their first school meetings, the Reverend Ezekiel Chapman and the members of the congregational society formally recognized the changing circumstances. At the next meeting of the congregational society, held March 28, 1814, the Reverend Ezekiel J. Chapman requested a "dismission" from his position as minister of Lima's congregational church. For their part, members of the congregational society accepted Chapman's request without comment and appointed a committee to negotiate the terms of the final separation.[25] Lima's first settled preacher had been unsettled.

Education and the Expression of Religious Liberty

The new school law did not only unsettle the minister from his position; it also unsettled the church from its meeting place. Having accepted Chapman's resignation in March, the congregational society went on in August to construct a new church. Although the building of a new church might at first seem unrelated, in fact it was a logical outcome of implementing the new school law.

As encouraged by the law, one of the first acts undertaken by the newly organized school districts was the siting of a district school. Meeting in September 1814, at the home of Francis Stevens, inhabitants of school district no. 4 voted to build a school house "on Thomas Gorton's land a little north of where the said Gorton family dwelt." Plans for the school house did not proceed right away, however; instead, the district repaired Thomas Gorton's old house for interim use as a school. Construction of a new school building waited until the inhabitants negotiated some changes in the existing social arrangements with the town's congregational society.

Nineteenth Day of April, 1812," inserted in "Town Book, 1797–1818," after the Minutes of the 1815 Town Meeting. However, the document itself was dated December 1, 1813.

[24] "An Act for the establishment of Common Schools, Passed January 19, 1812," *Laws of New York*, 35th Session, Chap. 242 (Albany: State of New York, 1813): 258–266; also "An Act Supplementary to the act, entitled 'An act for the establishment of Common Schools,' Passed March 12, 1813," *Laws of New York*, 36th Session, Chap. 52 (Albany: State of New York, 1814): 266–268; and "An Act for the better establishment of Common Schools, Passed April 15, 1814," *Laws of New York*, 37th Session, Chap. 192 (Albany: State of New York, 1815): 228–243.

[25] "Minutes, first Congregational Society," March 28, 1814.

A Matter of Trust

When the inhabitants of the district met again the following January 1815, they reiterated their plan of locating a new school house "a little north of the house [where] Elder Gorton formerly dwelt."[26] To effect the plan, however, they first appointed a committee of two "to consult the church and society on the question."[27] The "society" to which they referred was the congregational society, to which some of them belonged. John Phillips, for example, who actually owned the land on which Thomas Gorton had apparently dwelled as a tenant, was among the original members of the town's congregational society in 1801. So was Francis Stevens, in whose home the first meeting of the district took place. As members of the town's central church, these district residents already shared the cost of maintaining the existing brick school house. By "consulting" with the society, they sought release from that obligation so that they could transfer their support to school building in a different part of town.

One result of the school law, then, was to redirect resources away from a central school into schools in outlying neighborhoods. At the same time, the school district in which the original brick school house was now located – district no. 9 – required its own dedicated facility. To resolve this situation, the congregational society took two actions. It undertook the construction of a new church meeting house and it sold the existing brick school house to a group of subscribers who bought it on behalf of the district.

This decision to construct the first dedicated church building in Lima was symbolic of the larger change in social structure being effected by the new school laws. The new school laws effectively selected out the business of common schooling, once embedded in the law regulating religious societies, and set it apart as the business of new corporations – *school* corporations – with their own independent authority and resources. An 1815 revision of the common school law made this corporate dimension of the change explicit when it specified that any property granted to a school district for the use and benefit of that school "shall be to them and their successors in office, in the same manner as if they were a body corporate in law."[28] In effect, the revised law constituted a general incorporation law for common schools. In Lima in 1815, these new school corporations were the *only* other organizations besides the congregational society to hold corporate powers. Not even the town government itself had the power to hold common property.[29]

To assert this corporate independence, men like John Phillips effectively invoked the principle of religious liberty embedded in the constitution of the

---

[26] "Minutes of Lima School District #4," September 8, 1814.

[27] Ibid., January 9, 1815.

[28] "An Act to amend the act, entitled 'An act for the better establishment of Common Schools,' Passed April 15, 1815," *Laws of New York*, 38th Session, Chap. 252 (Albany: State of New York, 1816): 260–264.

[29] On the early history of general incorporation laws in New York, including church, school, and town laws, see Ronald Seavoy, *The Origins of the American Business Corporation, 1784–1855* (Westport, CT: Greenwood Press, 1982).

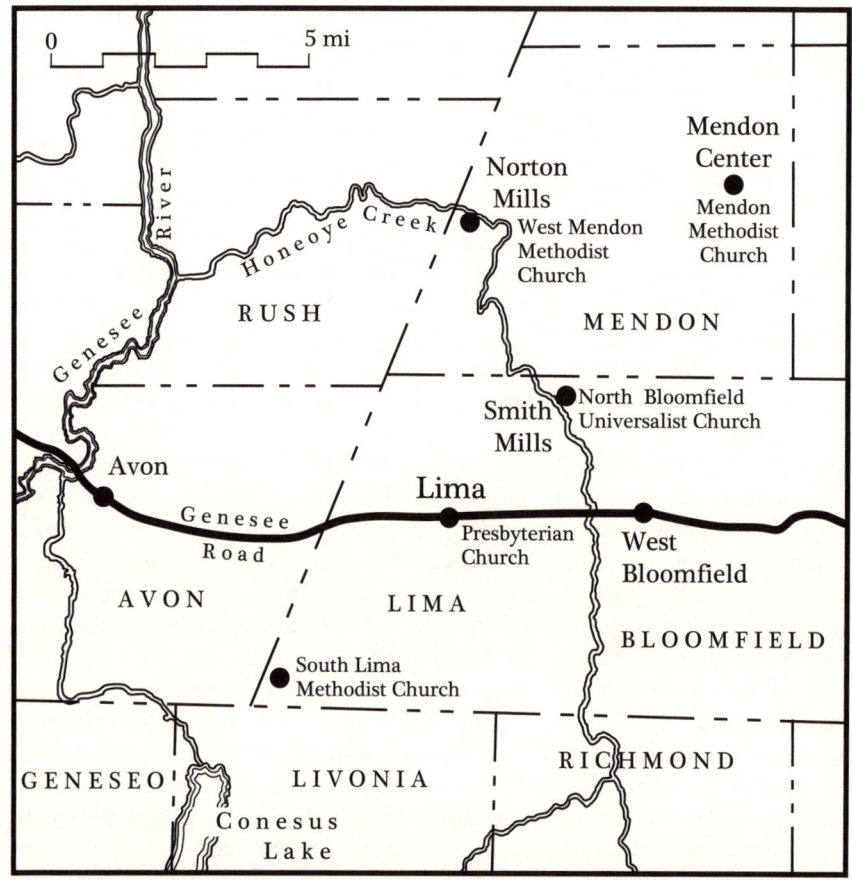

FIGURE 3. Hamlets, Towns, and Churches in and around Lima, circa 1820. Evangelicalism and schooling followed similar patterns of diffusion and expansion during the 1810s and 1820s. Geographically, schools and evangelical churches moved into hamlets on the fringes of settled towns, becoming nodes of social organization in outlying districts, often sharing facilities. Base map from David H. Burr, *An Atlas of the State of New York* (New York: by the author, 1829).

congregational society. As codified there, "anyone belonging to this society" who either moved out of town or became "convinced in his own Confession that some other Religious Denomination is higher" could be excepted from the financial obligations conferred on him as a member of the society.[30] Although the drafters of the constitution did not anticipate the organization of independent schools as an occasion requiring implementation of this provision, the significance of members' withdrawal to a separate church or a separate school

[30] "The Form of the Constitution of the Charleston Congregational Society," November 1st, 1802, in "Minutes, first Congregational Society."

was essentially the same. Moreover, as the election of Methodist Smith Weeks as school inspector suggests, the issue of religious conscience was not necessarily irrelevant to the matter of district school organization. Different neighborhood schools were in fact associated with different religious denominations. Indeed, John Phillips' own family would be among the founders of the first Baptist church in Lima, which began by holding meetings at the school house in district no. 4.[31]

Another consequence of the new school laws, in other words, was the promotion of social and religious pluralism. The creation of independent school districts undercut the authority of the existing congregational society as the central agent of community identity and initiative. School, church, and town no longer cohered into a single structure with a common membership and leadership corps. To establish a system of multiple school districts was to recognize first of all that different hamlets and neighborhoods already existed within towns, and that some of these neighborhoods already supported their own schools on a voluntary basis. Thus, not everyone shared the same level of interest in maintaining a central school. Beyond the matter of funding equity, however, was also an issue of social and religious pluralism. To establish a system of multiple school inspectors was to entertain the notion that different neighborhoods might represent not simply different geographies, but different interests, and even different ideas about education – or, to use the religiously weighted but educationally significant term – different *disciplines*.

Finally, the new school laws promoted pluralism through school facilities themselves. Once established, school houses became sites of neighborhood activity and social organization in their own right. In 1818, school district no. 4 voted that their school "shall be opened for the Christian societies to hold meetings in."[32] Schools in this way were incubators of social and religious pluralism. In the late 1810s and 1820s, hamlets in and around Lima became sites of increasing evangelical activity characteristic of the Second Great Awakening. The hamlets of South Lima, Norton's Mills (West Mendon), and North Bloomfield (Smith's Mills) in particular were nodes of this development.

The Second Great Awakening

Throughout Anglo-America, church activity quickened in the 1810s and 1820s. People of all ages, both sexes, and diverse social backgrounds participated in religious revivals, declared themselves converted Christians, joined

---

[31] "Minutes of Lima School District no. 4," passim; also, many references to the Phillips family and the Baptist congregation in town appear in the diaries from 1856 and 1860 held at the Lima Historical Society and identified as the "Chapin diaries," but which are most certainly the diaries of a woman named Innocent Briggs, whose family was closely inter-related with the Phillips family (as indicated by evidence internal to diaries and corresponding census information).

[32] "Minutes of Lima School District no. 4," May 4, 1818.

existing churches, and organized new ones. Within this broad trend, historians have long identified upstate New York, including the area between the Finger Lakes and the Genesee Valley, where Lima is located, as a region especially rife with religious fervor. In part, this reputation rests on the success of the most famous evangelical preacher of the era, Charles Grandison Finney, who made central and western New York his special project in a series of well-documented revivals in the 1820s and 1830s. Also, in part, the reputation derives from the number of new religions and quasi-religious experiments that emerged and took root in upstate New York in the decades that followed the Finney revivals, including, most famously, Mormonism and Alfred Noyes's Oneida Community. As the historian Whitney Cross noted in 1950, however, and as subsequent historians have since detailed further, the success of Finney and his utopian successors built on previous episodes of religious fervor. Based on contemporaneous accounts, Cross concluded that "western New York was more intensively engaged in revivalism than were other portions of the Northeast" as early as the 1810s.[33] Using early church records, other historians have filled in this picture for certain localities. Interpreting spikes in church membership as evidence of revivalism, they have identified waves of religious enthusiasm for every year from 1813 through 1821, for the years of the Finney revivals in 1825–1826 and 1830–1834, and again for 1837–1838 and 1843.[34] Although the precise pattern varies somewhat from account to account and locale to locale, Cross's summary still holds up well: "Strenuous evangelism mounted irregularly from the 1790s to reach a grand climax between 1825 and 1837."[35]

One indicator of this activity in Lima, as elsewhere, was increased religious pluralism. For the period from 1801 to 1813, the congregational society was the only church or religious organization in Lima for which any reference survives. After 1813, references to other church societies begin appearing in surviving records. This new pluralism had geographic as well as religious roots. Each of the new church societies developed first in a hamlet outside Lima's town center. The hamlets of Norton's Mills (West Mendon), South Lima, Smith's Mills, and West Bloomfield in particular became sites of alternative religious activity in the 1810s. Once again, schools were at the center of this community building. Encouraged by the first permanent common

---

[33] Whitney Cross, *The Burned-over District: The Social and Intellectual History of Enthusiastic Religion in Western New York, 1800–1850* (New York: Harper & Row, 1965 [Cornell University Press, 1950]): 11.

[34] Curtis D. Johnson, *Islands of Holiness: Rural Religion in Upstate New York, 1790–1860* (Ithaca, NY: Cornell University Press, 1989): 72 and Table B3, p. 183; Mary Ryan, *Cradle of the Middle Class: The Family in Oneida County, New York, 1790–1865* (Cambridge: Cambridge University, 1981): 75–104 and Tables C1–C9, pp. 257–262; Paul E. Johnson, *A Shopkeeper's Millennium: Society and Revivals in Rochester, New York, 1815–1837* (New York: Hill and Wang, 1978): 4–8; Appendix B, Rochester Church Records, pp. 152–161; and note 28, p. 189.

[35] Cross, *The Burned-over District*, 13.

A Matter of Trust 49

school law in New York in 1812, residents of Lima focused new energy on the construction and support of district schools in outlying neighborhoods. Once established, these neighborhood schools became meeting places for itinerant preachers and diverse religious societies as well as for school instruction. As might be expected, this increased pluralism did not occur without disturbing existing social arrangements.

The Itinerant Preacher

When Joseph Badger first began preaching in school houses around Lima, the town may have been particularly attractive to itinerants, because its central church lacked a settled minister. After Chapman resigned in March 1814, the congregational society focused its attention on constructing a new building. To provide the congregation with preaching, they hired two different interim ministers, a Mr. Brown in 1814 and Gordon W. Cook in 1815 and again in mid-1817. These engagements do not appear to have been continuous, however, and a concerted effort to find a new permanent preacher waited until after the society completed the new church and implemented a plan for satisfying the society's construction debts. The congregation finally settled a new minister in December 1818 – more than four and a half years after Chapman's resignation.[36] In the meantime, Badger and other itinerants actively worked the territory in and around Lima. When available, neighborhood schools housed these itinerant church meetings.

Joseph Badger took credit for organizing two religious societies in Lima in the years 1817–1818, one in the hamlet of Norton's Mills, later known as West Mendon, and one in the hamlet of South Lima. Sorting out the denominational affiliations of these societies is difficult for several reasons, one of which is Badger's own changing denominational identity. A more important source of uncertainty, however, is probably the lack of clear distinctions among preachers and societies at the time. Itinerants of multiple and sometimes unspecified church affiliations worked the same territory concurrently, and groups of neighbors who assembled for such events did not necessarily identify themselves in denominational terms. While he later ascribed the formal organization of the South Lima church to his own "instrumentality," Badger nonetheless acknowledged that "other Gospel Ministers" had also "favoured" that area with "occasional visits" over the previous year.[37]

Itinerant preaching was not new in Lima in the 1810s. The first ministers to preach in the area in the 1790s did so on an itinerant basis. Even after the organization of the congregational society in 1801, local residents continued to hire itinerants off and on before "settling" Ezekiel Chapman in 1808. Most of these early itinerants, however, probably sought a permanent pastorate.

---

[36] "Minutes, first Congregational Society," 1814–1818, LPC.
[37] "A Record of the Church of God at South Lima, Livingston County, State of New York, Organized June 17 AD 1818 Through the instrumentality of Joseph Badger," LCHO.

What was new in Lima, as elsewhere, in the 1810s, was the idea of itinerancy as a lifelong career and a principle of religious leadership. This idea challenged the livelihoods of settled ministers and the legitimacy of central churches. It also transformed the structure and culture of church life.

Badger's first few months of travel in western New York were fairly typical of itinerant practice. Beginning in November 1816, he worked a wide territory around the lower Genesee River. Making the town of Pittsford, just south of the river's mouth (and of the future city of Rochester) his home base, Badger alternated periods of preaching in Pittsford with periods of preaching in other towns in the region. During the second week of January 1817, for example, he conducted meetings for four days in a row in the town of Avon, the next town south on the Genesee River from Pittsford and the first town west of Lima on the Genesee Road. After a week back in Pittsford, he returned to the area again on January 19, this time spending a week in Lima, where "he administered baptism and attended to holy communion." At the close of the week, he went back to Pittsford. Then, in early February, he again traveled to the Lima vicinity, this time holding meetings in West Bloomfield, a hamlet on Lima's eastern border, and in the town of Bristol, to the south and east. Touching base again in Pittsford, he circled back through Lima for three days, February 12–14, preaching first in Avon, then in Lima, and finally in Norton's Mills. Passing a few weeks back in Pittsford, Badger then set out for new territory to the west of the Genesee River on Lake Ontario, going as far as Lewiston and and into Canada. At the end of March, he returned to the Avon-Lima circuit, preaching in each of those towns, respectively, before again cultivating new territory to the west.[38]

One way to look at Badger's travels in this period is as an exploratory survey not unlike that made by many other young men in search of good land and farming opportunities. Like many other migrants to western New York, Badger came from northern New England, having grown up in New Hampshire and the eastern territories of Canada. As a younger son in a large family, Badger's decision to take on the work of itinerant preaching coincided closely with his coming of age and effectively granted him independence from the authority of his family. Also like many of his peers, however, he found northern New England lacking in opportunities for him to establish himself. Seeking better prospects elsewhere, he, like many other young men at the time, saw the possibilities as more promising in western New York. In the spring of 1817, he went home to collect his young family and relocated to the Genesee region.[39]

It is impossible to know exactly how Badger imagined his future when he returned to western New York in the summer of that year. At first, he established his family in Pittsford, where he had concentrated most of his efforts so far and had succeeded in organizing a church society. Whether he ever

[38] Holland, *Memoir of Joseph Badger*, 156–173.
[39] Holland, *Memoir of Joseph Badger*, 176.

envisioned a more settled relationship with this or another church is unknown. In any case, he did not maintain one. As his biographer would say of him with reference to his later home in Norton's Mills, "Though a resident of one place, it was not in his nature to be a local man."[40] In this respect, then, Badger, like other itinerant preachers of the era, bore an entirely different relationship to his home community than a settled preacher, and took an entirely different approach to his future than his peers who took up farming. Though he established a home and family in a locale, he did not make his living primarily in or from that place. Like other itinerant preachers, he took up collections where he preached and depended on the families with whom he visited, prayed, and remonstrated to provide him food and lodging. Perhaps, if his labors proved successful, they would offer him something else besides. By collecting a little bit from a lot of places, and doing so on an occasional rather than a steady basis, an itinerant preacher like Badger did not require the same concentration of resources as did a settled preacher. Nor did he depend on the same long-term social relationships.

In this way, the practice of itinerancy effectively inverted the traditional relationship between the minister and congregation[41]: Where once the congregation had called the preacher, now the preacher effectively called the congregation. Preparing the way by going door-to-door, making home visits, and advertising a future "appointment" to preach, an itinerant minister endeavored to collect new congregations that had not necessarily gathered before. In assessing prospects for the future, then, an itinerant like Badger did not need to weigh the same kinds of risks. His situation required no less trust than that of a settled minister, but it was not a long-term trust in individual people. Nor, however, was it simply a trust in providence. Rather, the unknown and open-ended quality of day-to-day life for an unsettled preacher seemed to require that the preacher trust in himself. Unable to fall back on long-term personal relationships, he had to depend for his livelihood and identity on his enduring capacity to kindle the interest of strangers. This element of self-reliance in an itinerant's work was conveyed by Badger's biographer, E. A. Holland, in a passage that referred to the period of Badger's initial sojourn in western New York:

In these six months, he, an entire stranger in the land of his labors, creates the material and organizes it, on which he is willing to rely for his future support and cooperation.[42]

Of course, from the perspective of the settled ministry, this entrepreneurial aspect of itinerancy was precisely the problem. Wherever an itinerant succeeded in taking up regular collections or organizing an alternative church

---

[40] Ibid., 214.
[41] On the change in the structure and culture of the ministry as a profession, which occurred in the Northeast beginning in the late 1810s, see Scott, *From Office to Profession,* passim, and Calhoun, *Professional Lives in America,* 88–177.
[42] Holland, *Memoir of Joseph Badger,* 176.

society, he directed potential resources away from an existing church and its regular minister. In addition to threatening ministers' livelihoods in this way, itinerants often also challenged the authority of ministers and their churches. According to his memoir, Badger, like many evangelical preachers, came into conflict with a number of local churchmen. In Pittsford, he dared leaders of the local Presbyterian church to try to prevent him from organizing a competing religious society.[43] In Avon, he debated two Baptist ministers, including the Reverend Thomas Gorton, formerly of school district no. 4 in Lima, over the issue of who should be admitted to communion.[44] In Lima, he went head-to-head with an interim minister of the congregational church, Gordon W. Cook, over a passage of scripture. According to Badger, Cook's opposition to Badger's interpretation "was evidently to his own hurt."[45]

When challenging churchmen on their own turf, Badger, like many itinerant evangelicals, assumed a stance that must have come across to many as both aggravating and contradictory. On the one hand, he claimed the cause of the universal church, in which all eventually shared a common Christianity. On the other hand, he insisted on the prerogative of pluralism, in which independent preachers like himself freely founded multiple, competing churches. In a letter addressed to a deacon of the Presbyterian church in Pittsford, Badger first decried the many divisions among Christians in the world. Then, turning to the local situation, he announced his intention to organize an independent church, explaining that before proceeding, he had a "few propositions" he would like to lay before the deacon. Because he truly hated the thought of a divided church, he would like to propose that he and the Presbyterians together hold an open meeting for the purpose of forming a united church. In the new church, presumably, leadership and financial support would be shared. Religious truth, however, would be better served. In the context of a united church, any differences of scriptural interpretation could be entertained in the spirit of friendship and mutual improvement. "Each shall offer his light in friendship on the subject, which is the only way for truth to shine in its various luster," Badger wrote, adding, "the truth will make us free."[46]

With this letter, Badger apparently accepted the premises of a central community church even as he challenged them. At the beginning of the nineteenth century, community churches often tolerated a fairly wide range of positions on doctrinal matters, on the theory that such differences could be negotiated within the framework of a common church. From this perspective, it was Badger himself who had introduced dissension into Pittsford's Christian community, by preaching and organizing communicants outside the existing church establishment. But Badger effectively took this argument and turned it back on his would-be critics. According to the terms of his argument, the

---

[43] Holland, *Memoir of Joseph Badger*, 166–169.
[44] Holland, *Memoir of Joseph Badger*, 159–161.
[45] Holland, *Memoir of Joseph Badger*, 181.
[46] Holland, *Memoir of Joseph Badger*, 166–169.

organization of a competing church would be a sign of the Presbyterians' intolerance, rather than an act of divisiveness on his part.[47]

Apparently the Presbyterians did not take this bait, for Badger proceeded to organize an independent church in a western hamlet of Pittsford in February 1817. "Some little opposition appeared," he noted, but that did not deter him or his congregants. "Weapons formed against Zion are never destined to prosper," he commented.[48] Neither, however, did Badger long maintain his association with the Pittsford congregation. In the summer of 1817, when he returned to Pittsford, he brought with him not only his family, but an assistant or "coadjutor" named John Blodgett. This "minister of the same evangelical faith" was "prepared to supply the increasing demand made on Badger's labors."[49] In August, Blodgett took over pastoral responsibilities for the church and Badger went back to full-time itinerancy, eventually organizing two church societies in Lima. This pattern would repeat itself in subsequent situations. Occasionally Badger would arrange an affiliation with a particular congregation, presumably receiving some initial financial support. No sooner would he negotiate such an arrangement, however, than he would leave the congregation and set out to evangelize a new territory.[50]

Although Badger was perhaps somewhat extreme in his avoidance of ordinary pastoral duties, he was not alone in doing so. Methodism, which systematized the logic and logistics of itinerant preaching, was organized precisely to free the ordained minister from the day-to-day intricacies of congregational relations that typically came with dependence on a local congregation. In the process, Methodism inverted traditional assumptions regarding the relative status of the settled minister and the itinerant preacher. Once, the aspiring minister sought success in the form of an enduring tenure with a respectful congregation, while the failed minister moved from place to place. Now, many new ministers sought success precisely through mobility – by evangelizing new territories, moving from location to location, and building a reputation among fellow preachers as effective revivalists. In Methodism, the relationship between a "local" preacher and a "traveling preacher" was hierarchical, a career step that marked the transition from local lay leader to fully ordained minister. By contrast, the position of "located" or "stationed" preacher was often relegated to the ill, or the "superannuated."

It is hard to imagine a version of the ministry more directly opposed to the tradition of "settlement." Instead of depending on long-term relations of trust among neighbors, the itinerant preacher relied on new and temporary relations with strangers. Rather than develop the concentrated collective power of a particular group of people over time, the itinerant diffused power by continually stimulating the formation of new networks of association. Structurally

---

[47] Ibid.
[48] Holland, *Memoir of Joseph Badger*, 169.
[49] Holland, *Memoir of Joseph Badger*, 177.
[50] Holland, *Memoir of Joseph Badger*, 177 and passim.

and spatially, schools facilitated this process by undermining the concentrated power and authority of central community churches and providing alternative nodes of association on the borders of established towns and communities. From the perspective of the settled minister, these changes may well have looked like the unraveling of the core social relationships that constituted society – a violation of bonds of trust. From the perspective of the itinerant minister, however, evangelicalism was itself a powerful social and educational movement that fundamentally redefined the basis of membership in society on new terms.

4

Discipline – Evangelicalism as an Educational Movement

> In December 1818, trials arose with Roxey Moon, as she professed to have trials with certain members of the church and refused to labour with them or to tell the church the cause of her dissatisfaction, thus she left our meetings and returned to folly [whited out] as all exertions to reclaim her proved abortive agree it was duty to withdraw ourselves from her.
>
> A Record of the Church of God at South Lima, [December 1818], 1825.[1]

> Whereas on 25th of May 1820, by a vote in which there was but one dissenting voice, this church resolved to adopt the Presbyterian Form of Government and Discipline – And whereas James Sterling at that time a member of this church, did then avail himself of the opportunity to withdraw himself from our communion and fellowship: We therefore after affording him the space of more than two years & a half for reflection & after having used with him such means as Christian prudence seemed to dictate to bring him to a sense of his duty, do now feel it our duty publickly to declare that we consider him as having no connexion whatever with this church. & that we do not consider ourselves as responsible for any of his conduct since the date before mentioned. Concluded with prayer. Adjourned.
>
> John Barnard Pastor. Presbyterian Session Records, January 2, 1823.[2]

As a forty-nine-year-old male in 1820, James Sterling probably did not recognize his fellow town resident, Roxey Moon, as a kindred soul in church matters. If he knew her at all, he may have regarded her as part of the problem rather than as a victim of circumstances similar to his own. Yet, whether they knew it or not, James Sterling and Roxey Moon had a lot in common. Both were founding members of a church society. Both managed to get themselves

---

[1] "A Record of the Church of God at South Lima, Livingston County, State of New York, Organized June 17 AD 1818 Through the instrumentality of Joseph Badger," LCHO. As explained below, although the events described occurred in December 1818, the account of events was (re-)written in 1825.

[2] Lima Presbyterian Session Records, Book #1, 1820–1831, January 2, 1823, microfilm, LCHO.

on the wrong side of a church examining committee. And both ended up being expelled from the churches they'd helped organize. Sterling's fall from grace occurred at a church established as the cornerstone of town identity. Roxey Moon, by contrast, was expelled from an upstart congregation established on the town's southwestern border. Nonetheless, both Sterling and Moon experienced the simultaneous impulses toward pluralism and conformity that characterized the Second Great Awakening.

This chapter shows how the evangelicalism of the Second Great Awakening reconstructed society on new terms. Instead of assuming that individuals belonged to a more or less permanent set of social relationships rooted in locality, kinship, and patriarchal households, the new evangelicalism imagined a society constituted by indeterminate social relationships that transcended place, sex, age, household structure, and social or family status. Membership in this society would be the result of evangelical education and moral certification rather than birth and connection, and would bridge the experience of social and geographic mobility. Evangelicalism, in other words, offered a pedagogical model for forging social identity. Through initiation into a common discipline, an individual acquired access to social capital and membership in a network of moral peers. In Lima the significance of this new social discipline is illuminated by the case of James Sterling and the fate of Roxey Moon.

Membership and Identity in the Evangelical Church

The alternative model of society represented by the evangelicalism of the Second Great Awakening is apparent in the church that Joseph Badger helped to organize in the hamlet of South Lima in the summer of 1818. Founding members of the South Lima society differed significantly from those who formed the town's first congregational society in 1801. Instead of the leading landholders and male heads of families who described themselves as "the young men of the town" in 1801, the list of founding members for the South Lima church consisted entirely of young people who had not yet reached the age of majority, most of them women.[3]

According to Joseph Badger's retrospective account, the origins of the church society at South Lima lay with his own and other ministers' visits "to the vicinity of South Lima" in 1817. "Several persons in the course of the year" were converted, or "brought to rejoice in Christ the Lamb of God." Early the following year, "some additions were made to the number," and Badger himself baptized seventeen persons.[4] As reported by Badger in a notice published January 24, 1818, in the *Christian Herald*, these events were part of a larger wave of revivalism in Lima, Mendon, and the surrounding towns stimulated by a band of preachers under his leadership. "Within one year I have baptized about 100 in this region of the country," he declared.[5]

---

[3] "A Record of the Church of God at South Lima."
[4] Ibid.
[5] E. G. Holland, *Memoir of Rev. Joseph Badger* (New York: C. S. Francis & Co.; Boston: Benjamin H. Greene, 1854): 185.

In the months that followed, Badger consolidated this success by relocating to Norton's Mills and organizing a church society there. He then determined to organize the group in South Lima as a branch of the church in Norton's Mills. On June 17, 1818, he brought four members of the Norton's Mills group and two members of his band of preachers "to examine and receive candidates" for the South Lima church. The examiners (all of whom were male) "found ten who had given themselves to God and were willing to give themselves to each other." Seeing that they were all "in good standing" and that they "found a good union with each other," the examiners and candidates "all joined hands in sweet union ... before the Throne of Grace." Once the branch church was organized, "the Lord's work took a fresh revival" and membership grew. On August 19, 1818, the church received thirteen additional members. Again, most of these members were female. At the close of 1818, nineteen of the society's twenty-five members, or 76 percent, were women. Later, some of this imbalance was moderated. In 1819, eight out of fifteen new members were male. Nonetheless, females continued to outnumber males by at least three to two through 1825.[6]

The predominance of young people in general, and women in particular, in the evangelical church meetings and revivals of the Second Great Awakening is well established.[7] In this respect, the evangelical movement promoted a social pluralism that went beyond religion and geography. For the young people who organized the society in South Lima, church membership was not about asserting adult identities they had already established or acquired through external means. Without property themselves, and, in the case of the women who constituted the majority, without prospect of property ownership or political power in the future, these young people participated in church society not as heads of household with responsibilities for raising families but as dependent youth who had not yet assumed adult responsibilities. For these youth, participation in a society of peers was a way to forge and test adult identities and to do so with a degree of independence from existing patriarchal authority.

This combination of social liminality and independence from authority in turn shaped the character and quality of members' experiences within the society. As was common among evangelical societies, much of the recorded activity of the South Lima group focused on identifying and examining individuals for inclusion or exclusion as members. This practice had everything to do with identity formation. In the broadest sense, the point of examination was to determine who could legitimately be identified as Christians. The process might result in an identity as "an immoral person" or as "an ornament

---

[6] "A Record of the Church of God at South Lima."
[7] This was most fully established by Mary Ryan, *Cradle of the Middle Class: The Family in Oneida County, New York, 1790–1865* (Cambridge: Cambridge University Press, 1981) and has been confirmed for other upstate New York locations by Curtis Johnson, *Islands of Holiness: Rural Religion in Upstate New York, 1790–1860* (Ithaca: Cornell University Press, 1989) and Nancy Hewitt, *Women's Activism and Social Change: Rochester, New York, 1822–1872* (Ithaca, NY: Cornell University, 1984).

to the Church of God."⁸ Beyond resulting in official judgments, however, the examination process itself could be formative of internal identity for the person involved. Indeed, it could be said that this formative experience was the main objective of the process. To make a profound change in one's sense of self in the world was, after all, what it meant to experience conversion. Viewed from this perspective, the point of examining candidates for membership was to push individuals to change themselves and their identities through a ritualized practice of self-questioning and self-revelation.

Evangelicalism as an Educational Movement

The experience of mutual examination was formalized in the Methodist Church through a practice known as the class system. Chapter II of the *Doctrines and Discipline of the Methodist Episcopal Church* spelled out "the Nature, Design and General Rules" of Methodist societies, with direct reference to the tradition of weekly meetings developed by John Wesley himself in the mid-eighteenth century. According to the *Discipline*, a Methodist society was "a company of men having the form and seeking the power of Godliness, united in order to pray together, to receive the word of exhortation, and to watch over one another in love, that they may help each other to work out their salvation."⁹ Theoretically, the whole Methodist denomination was an interlocking network of such societies, from those constituted primarily of laypeople to those composed entirely of ordained ministers. Within this network, a class was the smallest, most intimate, and most basic unit of Methodism. As explained by the *Discipline*, "That it may the more easily be discovered, whether they are indeed working out their own salvation, each society is divided into smaller companies, called classes, according to their respective places of abode."¹⁰

Though Badger eventually disavowed Methodist affiliation, he did begin his career as a Methodist, and evidence suggests that members of the church society in South Lima practiced mutual examination in a manner much like that formalized by the Methodist *Discipline*.¹¹ As conceived in Methodism, the practice of mutual examination was essentially an educational process, with the class being the basic educational unit. Ostensibly, the only condition required for admission to a Methodist class was the desire to be saved from sin. To continue in society, however, members were expected to demonstrate evidence of their desire for salvation through their behavior. From

---

[8] Phrases quoted from "A Record of the Church of God at South Lima."
[9] *The Doctrines and Discipline of the Methodist Episcopal Church, Twenty-Second Edition* (New York: N. Bangs and J. Emory for The Methodist Episcopal Church, John C. Totten, Printer, 1824), 76.
[10] *Doctrines and Discipline*, 76.
[11] "A Record of the Church of God at South Lima" as compared against "Bloomfield Circuit Book, Genesee Conference, 1828–1880," CUDRMC; and "Early Members of Methodist Church, Honeoye Falls, Organized 1820," typed transcript from OMTH.

this perspective, class membership was simply the first step in an evangelical education. In effect, the *Discipline* was the curriculum guide for that education. It identified specific behavioral and learning objectives for Methodists. It outlined the steps that leaders and initiates should take to achieve those objectives. And it established procedures for assessing the results.

The *Discipline* identified three main sets of behavioral objectives. These general categories were "doing no harm," "doing good," and "attending to the ordinances of God." Under the category of "doing no harm," the *Discipline* censored a large number of behaviors such as "the putting on of gold and costly apparel"; "the laying up treasure upon earth"; "fighting, quarreling or brawling"; "drinking spirituous liquors"; "borrowing without probability of paying"; and "brother going to law with brother." Under the category of "doing good," the *Discipline* sanctioned acts such as "giving to the hungry;" "clothing the naked"; "visiting or helping them that are sick, or in prison"; "instructing, reproving or exhorting all we have any intercourse with"; "buying one of another, helping each other in business"; and "all possible diligence and frugality." Finally, under the ordinances of God, the *Discipline* directed members to attend to "the public worship of God," "the ministry of the word"; "the supper of the Lord"; "family and private prayer"; "searching the scriptures;" and "fasting or abstinence."[12]

Using these objectives as their standard, members of local Methodist societies confessed their faults and subjected themselves to criticism from others. A series of questions posed to initiates suggests the potential intensity of this experience. To test initiates' willingness to accept moral criticism, the *Discipline* directed that they be asked the following questions, each apparently aimed at pushing the point further: "Do you desire to be told of your faults?" "Do you desire to be told of *all* your faults, and that plain and home?" "Do you desire that everyone of us should tell you, from time to time, whatsoever is in our hearts concerning you?" "Consider! Do you desire that everyone of us should tell you whatsoever we think, whatsoever we fear, whatsoever we hear, concerning you?" "Do you desire that in doing this, we should come as close as possible, that we should cut to the quick and search your heart to the bottom?" And finally, "Is it your desire and design to be on this and all other occasions entirely open, so as to speak without disguise and without reserve?"[13]

In his memoir, Badger described the potential intensity of the class meeting with respect to his own life. His description clearly tied the experience to issues of identity. Once admitted to a class, members were expected to attend on a weekly basis. At each meeting they were to confess the sins they had committed since the group's previous meeting, the temptations they had met, how they had been delivered from those temptations, and the actions about which they remained doubtful. One member would take the lead, speaking about his

---

[12] *Doctrines and Discipline*, 77–80.
[13] *Doctrines and Discipline*, 84.

own state first, and then would ask the rest in order "as many and as searching questions as may be, concerning their state, sins and temptations." For Badger, this experience was primarily about finding his voice. The *Discipline* directed that members "speak, each of us in order, freely and plainly" regarding "the true state of our souls."[14] For some time, however, Badger found this directive difficult to follow. Meeting in a Methodist class week after week, with others who shared an interest in what it meant to be a Christian, he remained silent. Finally, however, he found the courage to speak. This was the first step toward his conversion.

Not every initiate survived this intense scrutiny. Some proved unable to find their voices, unwilling to submit to the authority of the group, or incapable of mastering themselves and their behavior according to the dictates of society. In his retrospective account of the early history of the South Lima church, Joseph Badger described one such case that illuminates the intensity of the struggle over identity that attended the experience of conversion. "In December of 1818," Badger wrote, "trials arose with Roxey Moon." The specific subject of the trials is unspecified and, in Badger's account, was as much a mystery at the time as it remains today. "She professed to have trials with certain members of the church," he wrote, but "refused to labor with them or to tell the church the cause of her dissatisfaction."[15] By this account, the dissension between Roxey Moon and the South Lima church was mutual, though Badger's concluding description of it was not. "Thus she left our meetings and returned to folly. ... As all exertions to reclaim her proved abortive, agree it was our duty to withdraw ourselves from her."[16] Thus, by the end of her thirteenth year, Roxey Moon had become both a founding member of a church and its first excommunicant. If not for a concurrent record of events left by another preacher, we might conclude that that was all there was to the story.

Discipline

Roxey Moon's expulsion from the South Lima church in December 1818 is the first trial of a Lima church member for which any reference survives. Whether this is because Roxey Moon in fact was the first person to be expelled from a Lima church is doubtful. She would not, in any case, be the last. Records of the trial and excommunication of members constitute a large part of the surviving paper evidence for Lima-area churches after 1820. Once it converted to Presbyterianism in 1820, the central church in Lima began putting members on trial for such charges as "unchristian conduct," "the sin of intemperance," "absenting themselves from the Lord's table," and having "embibed [sic] erroneous doctrines."[17] The South Lima church, meanwhile, continued to try and

---

[14] *Doctrines and Discipline*, 83.
[15] "A Record of the Church of God at South Lima."
[16] Ibid.
[17] Lima Presbyterian Session Records, passim.

expel members on a regular basis. The charges against Roxey Moon are vague in the historical record, but those against other members are somewhat clearer. In January 1820, for example, members were "constrained to withdraw ourselves from connection and fellowship with Sally Pain ... for submitting to imprudent conduct with a married man." Two years later the society agreed "to have no fellowship with Daniel Newman," having determined that he was "an immoral person." At about the same time, the Reverend Joseph Badger himself was put on trial for "immoral conduct" and forced to give up his local church position.[18]

Lima was not unusual in the extent and nature of its church trial activity. Although church trials and excommunications had a long history reaching back through the Reformation, their practice was significantly revived by evangelical churches in the Second Great Awakening. In his intensive study of another area of upstate New York, the historian Curtis D. Johnson documented a substantial increase in the number of church trials per 100 church members beginning in the mid-1820s and continuing through the mid-1840s. Rates of conviction or excommunication among trial defendants also increased.[19] This increased trial activity changed the meaning of church membership and the nature of church authority.

Until the late 1810s, church membership in Lima was essentially voluntary and largely a function of town residence and family affiliation. Official members of the town's original congregational society consisted of male heads of household who subscribed on behalf of themselves and their families. No religious test was required for membership and no disciplinary body enforced adherence to doctrine or attendance at worship. The goals of the society were broadly educational in content and enlightened in principle. Rather than examining closely the beliefs and practices of its members, Lima's central church took as its aim the general promotion of knowledge and virtue in the community through support of preaching and a central school.[20]

After it relinquished responsibility for schooling and lost its first settled minister in 1814, however, Lima's central church changed its focus. Under the leadership of its new settled minister, the Reverend John Barnard, the church adopted a new form of government and a new educational mission. Unlike his predecessor, the Reverend Barnard fulfilled the expectation of a lifetime pastorate, serving the congregation for forty years, from 1818 to 1857, and retiring in the community. In 1820 he convinced the congregation to adopt Presbyterianism and was elected clerk of the Ontario Presbytery, the denomination's regional body, holding that office for the remainder of his career.[21] More important than the fact of Barnard's denominational affiliation and

---

[18] "A Record of the Church of God at South Lima," passim.
[19] Johnson, *Islands of Holiness*.
[20] "Minutes, first Congregational Society in Charleston," passim, LPC.
[21] Lima Presbyterian Session Records; and Reverend Levi Parsons, *History of Rochester Presbytery from Earliest Settlement of the Country, Embracing Original Records of*

leadership, however, was his approach to pastoral duties. The Reverend Barnard presided over a cultural transformation of the central church in Lima. Instead of promoting the general education of the town as a whole, the church after 1820 concentrated on the moral education and religious discipline of its own members. This goal was pursued through the two-pronged strategy of individual moral scrutiny and remonstrance first, and then, if that failed, of church trial and excommunication.

Reverend Barnard was not alone in prosecuting this change in culture. The entire congregation participated in some way. As noted by the members of the Presbyterian Session who eventually excommunicated James Sterling, "there was but one dissenting voice" in the congregational vote "to adopt the Presbyterian Form of Government and Discipline."[22] Following that vote, any number of individuals cooperated in the implementation of the new discipline, whether by serving on the Session itself or by testifying before it as witnesses and complainants. In the relatively elaborate case of William K. Blasdell, for example, the Session heard "several complaints" before taking up his case and eventually charged that "common fame" accused him of "unchristian conduct." By the end of the trial in 1823, at least twenty-five persons had been directly involved in pressing the case. The trial resulted in the decision that Mr. Blasdell should be "suspended from the sacraments of the church until he shall give satisfactory evidence of repentance," a sentence "pronounced in the presence of the communicants in this church on the next Lord's day."[23]

In this and other cases, the church trial served as a means of enforcing common standards of decency and honesty. The specific matters of enforcement were not explicitly religious in character or directly connected to the life of the church. Rather, they concerned ordinary issues in the day-to-day life of the community as a whole, including matters of business practice and, more generally, the trustworthiness of a community member. This use of church trials was not unusual. Looking across denominations, Johnson found that in the 1820s, 44 percent of all charges brought in church trials in one rural county involved the behavior of church members in what he called "the public domain."[24] This proportion declined in the 1830s but recovered to a similar level in the 1840s. Among the charges included in this category were various forms of commercial wrongdoing and alcohol-related offenses.

The majority of church trials did not involve matters of moral behavior outside the church, however, but matters of religious thought and practice within the church. In Johnson's analysis, 56 percent of all charges in the 1820s and as much as 65 percent in the 1830s belonged to what he called the "ecclesiastical domain."[25] These included the espousal of doctrines deemed contrary to the

Ontario Association and the Presbyteries of Ontario, Rochester (former), Genesee River, and Rochester City (Rochester: Democrat-Chronicle Press, 1889), 76–77.
[22] Lima Presbyterian Session Records, October 17, 1822–January 2, 1823.
[23] Ibid., June 5, 1823.
[24] Johnson, *Islands of Holiness*, 189–190.
[25] Ibid.

church's faith and violations of church practice. In January 1824, for example, the Session of the Lima Presbyterian Church questioned John L. Adams and his wife Altheia regarding their "religious sentiments and their conduct." Based on this interview, the Session concluded that the couple had "embibed" a number of "errors" and had endeavored "to disseminate their errors" to other members of the church. For these violations of religious thought and practice, the Adams' were excommunicated.[26]

As described in the Session records, the defendants in this case undertook a rather deliberate campaign of opposition to the doctrines of the church. In this respect they differed from the vast majority of persons prosecuted on religious grounds. Most defendants charged with violations of religious thought and practice earned attention through inaction rather than action. Probably the most common charge of any kind made against church members was that they had withdrawn from normal church life. Repeated absence from worship and communion was a serious failure of Christian duty. It constituted a direct violation of many church covenants, which required that members pledge "to keep God's holy sabbaths."[27] If, after persistent remonstrance, a member did not resume attendance, this failure of duty was grounds for trial and dismissal. More than half the recorded cases of trial and dismissal from Lima's Presbyterian Church from the 1820s through the 1840s involved some version of this charge. In effect, this was the charge against James Sterling.[28]

Some of these instances may have been simple cases of disability or disinterest. For whatever reason, the member lost motivation or means for church participation. In one Lima case, for example, the communicant claimed lack of transportation.[29] In other cases, however, withdrawal from church life may have been a more pointed response to a grievance or complaint against the church or some of its members. David Warren Sabean has written insightfully about the historical significance of Christian Communion as a symbol of communal relations. Within the Christian tradition, the ritual of Holy Communion followed the confession and forgiveness of sins. It symbolized the reconciliation of people with Christ and with each other. In this context, to take communion in a spirit of grievance toward a fellow member of the community, or toward the church itself, was a violation of the sacrament. To refuse to participate in communion, by the same token, could express an inability to be reconciled with the church or its members.[30]

This insight into the possible meaning of a member's withdrawal from church life would seem to apply to the case of James Sterling. The sole dissenter in the congregation's decision to adopt the Presbyterian form of government in

[26] Lima Presbyterian Session Records, January 5, 1824.
[27] The "Confession of Faith" and "Covenant" are written out in the front of the Lima Presbyterian Session Records, Book #1.
[28] Ibid., January 2, 1823.
[29] Ibid.
[30] David Warren Sabean, *Power in the Blood: Popular Culture and Village Discourse in Early Modern Germany* (Cambridge: Cambridge University Press, 1984): 37–60.

1820, Sterling apparently ceased to participate in church life after this decision. Two years later, in October 1822, the Session took up his case, on the initiative of the Reverend Barnard, who had consulted the Presbytery on the issue. Following the Presbytery's advice, the Session as a body directed its members to "take further opportunities to converse" with Sterling and "endeavor to bring him a sense of his duty."[31] Three months later, members reported that they had "frequently and faithfully laboured with him but without effect" and that he "perseveringly refused to appear before the Session or acknowledge their authority over him."[32] As described here, Sterling's failure to participate in church life was far from passive. It was an act of determined resistance. Having concluded that this resistance was insurmountable, members of the Session voted to expel him from membership on January 2, 1823.[33]

Due to his refusal to appear before the Session, no record survives of Sterling's version of the conflict. Nonetheless, the Session's account of the episode and Sterling's own subsequent behavior illuminate certain dimensions of the issue from Sterling's perspective. First, it is clear that his grievance concerned the authority of the church itself. It was over adoption of the Presbyterian form of government that Sterling originally expressed his "one dissenting voice," and it was on the occasion of the congregation's vote to join the Presbytery that Sterling "did then avail himself of the opportunity to withdraw himself from our communion and fellowship."[34] From Sterling's perspective, this withdrawal was well within his rights as a founding member of the congregational society. The society's constitution stated that the signers agreed to come together to "enable us to Worship God in the Manner and Season Most agreeable to the Dictates of our own consciences."[35] It did not recognize a Presbyterian form of government or, for that matter, any religious authority beyond that of the congregational society itself. Nor did it make membership conditional on any form of religious test or participation. In fact, it specifically allowed for the withdrawal of members from the church in accordance with their consciences. Sterling's claim that the new Presbyterian Session had no authority over him thus had some warrant.

Sterling's actions after his exclusion from the church further indicate that freedom of conscience or, more specifically, freedom from religious examination was an important dimension of this conflict. According to the constitution of the congregational society, the procedure Sterling should have followed if he chose to withdraw from the central church was to show evidence of having joined another church that he believed to be "higher." At the time of his de facto withdrawal, the only alternatives to the central church were similarly evangelical in character, such as Badger's church in South Lima and

---

[31] Lima Presbyterian Session Records, October 17, 1822.
[32] Ibid., January 2, 1823.
[33] Ibid.
[34] Ibid.
[35] "The Form of the Constitution of the Charleston Congregational Society," written into the front of "Minutes, first Congregational Society."

the Methodist society in Norton's Mills. No evidence of his participation in these societies survives. Eventually, however, Sterling did join another church. When he did, he chose the Universalist Society of Lima, founded in the hamlet of North Bloomfield in 1825.[36] This choice indicates Sterling's resistance to the culture of religious examination common to many evangelical churches.

As in the case of the original congregational society, membership in the Universalist society was fundamentally voluntary. No religious tests were required for membership, and no religious authority was recognized in the constitution beyond that exercised by the members themselves. The constitution of the First Universalist Society of Lima specified only one criterion for membership. To become a member an individual had to sign the following statement: "We whose names are hereunto annexed do hereby freely and fully consent to be viewed and considered as legal members of the first Universalist Society of Lima, County of Livingston and State of New York."[37] This minimal criterion for membership and absence of religious tests fit the profile of Universalism beyond Lima. In general, Universalist churches were known as nonevangelical and tolerant of a wide range of religious beliefs. The covenant of a Universalist church in the town of Homer, New York, for example, stated that "we will not disfellowship or reject any brother or sister, merely on account of a difference of faith on particular points of doctrine."[38] To join a Universalist church was to take a stand against the culture of religious examination and conformity that characterized many evangelical churches.

The case of James Sterling shows how this culture of religious examination had changed the meaning of church membership and the nature of church authority in Lima. When Sterling first joined the congregational society in 1802, his eligibility as a member derived primarily from his town residence, his voluntary subscription, and his status as a male head of household with the resources necessary to contribute to the church's support. The authority of the church itself, meanwhile, derived directly from its members. Members governed church affairs in their capacity as household heads who had established a religious corporation in order to hold property in common, construct common buildings, and hire common preachers. In this respect, the church was essentially a patriarchal institution. Twenty years later, however, Sterling found that his identity as an original subscriber to the church and the senior male heir of an established local family were no longer a sufficient basis for maintaining church membership. The church now required that in order to maintain his membership he must subject himself to moral examination, conform to common patterns of religious thought, and reconcile himself to a new form of church government. This new form of government emphasized individual moral discipline and common religious practice as the ultimate standards of church membership. Its authority was no longer simply patriarchal.

---

[36] "Minutes of the First Universalist Society of Lima (1825–1884)," List of Subscribers, held as part of the "Records of the North Bloomfield School," LHS.
[37] Ibid., March 12, 1825.
[38] Johnson, *Islands of Holiness*, 98–99.

Transformations of Patriarchy

The gender dimensions of this shift in authority are highlighted by a closer look at Sterling's decision to join the Universalist Society of Lima. When Sterling became a member in 1825, he joined forty-three other local residents, all of them male.[39] This male dominance matches the profile of Universalist societies elsewhere but contrasts sharply with the majority female membership common to most evangelical churches at the time. According to Johnson, women constituted 60 percent of all those who joined evangelical churches in Cortland County, New York, before the Civil War. By contrast, 66 percent of the members of the First Universalist Church in Cortland were men. In Johnson's analysis, "the burst of Universalist activity in the 1830s' was a male-oriented minimalist response" to the evangelicalism of the Second Great Awakening.[40] In particular, Universalism responded to the culture of religious examination common to many churches with high levels of female membership and influence.

Most historians emphasize the importance of nineteenth-century evangelicalism in undermining patriarchal authority in American society. In this analysis, evangelical societies provided a space for women and children to forge identities outside the family structure and independent of the authority of male heads of household. At the same time, the discipline of evangelical church life cultivated a belief in the possibility of self-determination through individual moral discipline. Theoretically, in this new world, one's identity depended more on the recognition of morally righteous peers than it did on one's family, sex, or inheritance. *With respect to salvation*, men and women were equal. Moreover, *with respect to moral discipline,* both were subject to the same educational and corrective process. To the extent that men joined evangelical churches, they became subject to the discipline and influence of female members. As historians Mary P. Ryan and Johnson both found, many of the men who joined evangelical churches followed female family members.[41] Other men, by contrast, resisted female influence by withdrawing from church society or by forming Universalist churches.

If Sterling's case suggests one set of gender and authority issues at work in the Second Great Awakening, however, the case of Roxey Moon illuminates quite another. As in the case of James Sterling, Roxey Moon's withdrawal from church life seems to have been an active expression of grievance. By Badger's own account, "she professed to have trials with certain members of the church." Also as in the Sterling case, the surviving record includes no account of the conflict from Roxey Moon's perspective. Indeed, the lack of such an account is even more complete for Moon, as she "refused ... to tell the church the cause of her dissatisfaction."[42] The apparent inexplicability of

---

[39] "Minutes of the First Universalist Society of Lima," List of Subscribers.
[40] Johnson, *Islands of Holiness*, 98–99.
[41] Ryan, *Cradle of the Middle Class;* Johnson, *Islands of Holiness*.
[42] "A Record of the Church of God at South Lima," concerning events that occurred in December 1818, as (re)-written by Reverend Joseph Badger, 1825.

Moon's behavior is a provocative aspect of her case, especially given the circumstances under which the record of her church dismissal survives. These circumstances include Joseph Badger's own trial for "immoral conduct" in December 1821 and his formal withdrawal from the South Lima church in January 1822. The lengths to which Badger later went to obscure these events, and his near complete success in doing so, raise questions about the specific case of Roxey Moon and, more generally, about the power and authority of itinerant preachers and the nature of their relationships with largely female memberships.

The records of the South Lima church that survive today are records that Badger recreated in September 1825. Three years after his withdrawal from the church and departure from the area in 1822, Badger returned. Shortly after his return, according to the surviving record, the church chose to re-hire him and to have him prepare "a new record" and "to copy such parts of the old record into it as was important to be preserved."[43] Internal evidence suggests that in the process Badger made at least five significant alterations to the text.

The first alteration appears within the entry describing Roxey Moon's dismissal from the church in December 1818. Seven or eight words in length, it is a phrase or sentence that has been vigorously erased. "Thus she left our meetings and returned to folly," the entry reads. Then, [material whited out] "as all exertions to reclaim her proved abortive agree it was duty to withdraw ourselves from her."[44] By itself, this gap might not be noteworthy. Combined with a second, much larger gap, however, the disjunction is suggestive. Chronologically, the second gap is for a year-long period immediately following Roxey Moon's dismissal from the church in December 1818. It is introduced by a statement explaining, "Through the year 1819 the church remained prosperous and the trials fair. But the records were not properly kept as they were committed to brother John Titus who lived at a distance from the center of business."[45]

This reference to records imperfectly kept is one that Badger used again. According to the revised record, on January 23, 1822, the church "met for fellowship meeting and found the records had been imperfectly kept."[46] This statement seems to explain the absence of entries for the previous several months. Presumably, however, if the records had been properly kept, they would have included some reference to the trial of Joseph Badger, which occurred one month earlier, or to the circumstances of Badger's formal withdrawal from the South Lima church, which occurred four days later.

If not for a serendipitous discovery in the diary of another area preacher, Benajah Williams, the very fact that Joseph Badger was put on trial would be

---

[43] Ibid., September 3, 1825.
[44] "A Record of the Church of God at South Lima," concerning events in December, 1818, as (re)-written by Reverend Joseph Badger in 1825.
[45] "A Record of the Church of God at South Lima," concerning events in 1819, as (re)-written by Reverend Joseph Badger in 1825.
[46] "A Record of the Church of God at South Lima," concerning events in January 1822, as (re)-written by Reverend Joseph Badger in 1825.

lost. In a brief entry dated Wednesday, December 19, 1821, Williams reported from his home in West Mendon, "After family duties I called at an area church meeting, but as they were dissatisfied with my being there I withdrew. (They were about to try a preacher by the name of Joseph Badger for as it was said immoral conduct.)"[47] Even with the benefit of Williams' reference, the nature of the trial is unclear. Although often used to refer to sexual misconduct, the charge is not elaborated in Williams' account. Once the fact of Joseph Badger's trial is known, however, several other things are apparent. First, it is clear that Badger's withdrawal from the South Lima church in January 1822 was not voluntary. Whether the church formally requested that he leave or he managed to negotiate an apparently "voluntary" departure is unclear. Perhaps Badger agreed to leave in return for the "letter stating his good standing," which the revised record says he received. Perhaps, on the other hand, such a letter never existed.

Badger's 473-page biographical memoir, published thirty years later, is no help in clarifying the case. The memoir makes no mention of his church trial in December 1821, or of his withdrawal from the South Lima church in 1822. Nor, for that matter, does it note Badger's ostensible resumption of a pastoral relationship with the South Lima church in 1825. Published by a colleague of Badger's later life, E. A. Holland, *The Memoir of Joseph Badger* reads as a biography but includes long extracts from Badger's own autobiographical writing, journals, and letters. Many sections of the book provide detailed, month-to-month, week-to-week, even day-to-day accounts of Badger's preaching activities. The sections covering Badger's life from 1821 to 1825 include no such accounting. Holland makes a few references to Badger continuing his "local pastoral labors" in this period, and by that means leaves the reader with the impression that Badger's church affiliations in this period remained unchanged. A close look at the text, however, suggests that after 1821, Badger did not again engage in regular preaching in the Lima area until his effective retirement at the end of the 1830s. For the period from 1821 to 1825, Holland mentions only that Badger attended a conference in Connecticut in 1822, worked as an itinerant for a few weeks in Pennsylvania in late 1823, and served as chaplain to a death row prisoner in the Genesee region in early 1824, before resuming itinerant preaching in New York and Ohio in late 1825.[48]

Whether the case of Roxey Moon was directly connected with that of Joseph Badger is a matter of speculation. Perhaps the "immoral conduct" for which Badger was tried in 1821 was part of a pattern of behavior against which Roxey Moon had a grievance. Perhaps such a pattern dated back before Badger's arrival in the Lima area, to his abrupt departure from the town of Pittsford, or to his original migration from New England with his new and already pregnant first wife, married to him at the age of sixteen. Unfortunately, Roxey Moon herself remains silent on the matter. It is a noisy silence, but

---

[47] Benajah Williams' "Journals," Vol. I, December 19, 1821, SDL.
[48] Holland, *Memoir of Rev. Joseph Badger*, 224–277.

Discipline							69

it is silence nonetheless. In the revised record of the S. Lima church, Moon simultaneously spoke and refused to speak. She "professed to have trials" yet "refused to tell the cause of her dissatisfaction."[49] Ultimately, then, the only evidence connecting the dismissal of Roxey Moon with the trial of Joseph Badger is that of Badger's own actions when he temporarily returned to Lima in 1825 before leaving for Ohio. The date of this return, it should be noted, occurred less than a year after Roxey Moon's death in May 1824, at the age of nineteen.[50] During his brief stay Badger undertook a revision of the early records of the South Lima church. When he did, he made his own and Roxey Moon's trials a focus of revision. Even if this is the only evidence connecting the cases of Moon and Badger, it is enough to raise questions.

To begin with, it raises questions about gender dynamics within evangelical societies. On the one hand, these societies provided young women with a sphere of influence and identity that lay largely outside the patriarchal household and formal structures of corporate and political authority. On the other hand, within evangelical societies, these same young women participated in a new gender dynamic. In many ways, the culture of moral discipline and religious examination that characterized such societies heightened the significance of the individual, including the individual female. The same culture, however, also made its members dependent on its leaders for their new moral identities. In theory, evangelical men and women were equal in matters of morality and salvation. In matters of everyday church life, however, some people had more power and authority than others. Roxey Moon was not a person entirely without resources. Although her family was not wealthy by the standard of the town's leading landholders, the Moons' did own about eighty acres, enough to put them in the top 40 percent of local households with respect to property.[51] It is likely that in case of conflict, a young woman like Roxey Moon drew on her father's position in the community – that is, his patriarchal authority – to intervene in church affairs. In this way, a largely female membership at first succeeded in exercising moral discipline over their preacher. Later, however, the preacher effectively used the power of his putative office and his own personality to overturn this disciplinary judgment and impose a retroactive silence over members of the church. A young woman like Roxey Moon may at

---

[49] "A Record of the Church of God at South Lima," concerning events in December 1818, as (re)-written by Reverend Joseph Badger in 1825.
[50] "A Record of the Church of God at South Lima." The date of Roxey Moon's death is recorded in the back of the book next to her name in the running list of members of the church. No cause of death is identified.
[51] In 1818, the year Roxey both joined and withdrew from the S. Lima society, William Moon paid $5.88 in taxes on $1876.00 of real estate and $305.00 of personal estate, putting him in the top 38% of 223 taxpayers. Two years later, in 1820, Moon paid slightly less in taxes ($5.66) for 88 acres of land, 68 acres improved and 20 acres unimproved, and a house, making him the 90th highest taxpayer out of 245 that year. (Meanwhile, the Warners and Birchards owned hundreds of acres of land and paid $30–$45 a year in taxes.) Lima Tax Assessments for 1818 and 1820, OCRAIMS.

first have found her voice in the context of evangelical church life. In the end, however, she still could not be heard.

Moral Certification

The cases of Roxey Moon, James Sterling, and Joseph Badger highlight the larger significance of evangelical church discipline in society. Through the process of moral and religious examination, churches not only disciplined individual members, but infused church membership with a certain social meaning. When churches expelled members for acts of immorality or dishonest business practices, they at the same time effectively certified the good character of members who remained in good standing. In their decision to expel James Sterling, members of the Lima Presbyterian Church made this principle of moral certification explicit, declaring that as a consequence of their decision, "we do not consider ourselves as responsible for any of his conduct since the date before mentioned."[52] By implication, if Sterling had successfully maintained church membership, he would have carried a kind of moral credential. In fact, churches regularly issued formal certificates of good standing to members leaving town or seeking to join another church. In a rural society where individuals and families depended on local credit and the trusting exchange of goods and labor among neighbors, a certificate of good standing from an apparently respectable church could be financially as well as socially valuable.

The value of such a credential is further indicated by the lengths to which Badger went to establish a record of good standing in the South Lima church before moving to Ohio. In effect, Badger appropriated the social capital of the South Lima church to coin a (fraudulent) moral credential that he hoped would have currency in the wider world. At the same time, the fact that Badger largely succeeded in this effort illuminates a weakness in the model of society that evangelicalism helped create. The promise of evangelicalism lay in reconstructing the basis of social membership from one grounded in a specific patriarchal inheritance to one grounded in a more general education. Through successful initiation and examination in a discipline administered by a local church society, individuals could acquire a social credential with the potential to transfer from place to place. This credential in turn could enable individuals to forge new social capital – new networks of trust – with persons to whom they and their friends and families were otherwise unknown.

The problem was that effective regulation of such credentials was still limited by geography and history. Only people within a local area and with a local memory could be expected to know the seriousness with which a particular congregation undertook moral enforcement or to be aware of reasons to mistrust the legitimacy of a credential. This limitation was particularly acute with respect to itinerant preachers. Free from direct dependence on any one

---

[52] Lima Presbyterian Session Records, January 2, 1823.

congregation, an itinerant was also free from the regular scrutiny of a congregation, and thus potentially from moral oversight. Itinerants like Joseph Badger, who effectively eschewed not only local responsibility but formal affiliation with a denomination, might even prove to be agents of immorality who used the relative anonymity of itinerancy to escape the consequences of their actions. To regulate and supervise the moral certification of itinerants across locality required a complex denominational organization and system of enforcement such as that administered by the Methodist Episcopal Church. To those charged with administering it, that system was known as "the Methodist economy."

5

Bonding and Bridging – The Methodist Economy

> The Awakening's aspect of *organization* and *unity* can well be subsumed under the category of *movement* because its dynamism was made relevant to its recruits through local organization, and also because the unity that transcended localism is in the final analysis what gives a movement its continuity.
>
> Donald G. Mathews, "The Second Great Awakening as an Organizing Process," *American Quarterly*, 1969, 30[1]

> *Of the Presiding Elders, and of their duty...* 6. To oversee the spiritual and temporal business of the societies of his district.
>
> *Doctrines and Discipline of the Methodist Episcopal Church*, 1813, p. 32[2]

> After preparing some things for the comfort of my family about half past twelve started for my circuit....
>
> Benajah Williams, December 7, 1820[3]

Until he became known by some of the younger "boys" of his conference as an abolitionist in the late 1830s and early 1840s, Benajah Williams managed to stay clear of trouble with Methodism's many examining committees and its professional hierarchy.[4] Unlike some other preachers who took up itinerancy in the 1810s, Williams never actively cultivated an identity as a rebel. During his thirty years of service, he never questioned the authority of the Methodist church structure, for example, or flirted with joining another denomination, fomented a schism among his fellows, or experimented with going out on his own. Nor was he ever charged with misconduct of any kind. Benajah Williams

---

[1] Donald Mathews, "The Second Great Awakening as an Organizing Process, 1780–1830: An Hypothesis," *American Quarterly* 21:1 (Spring 1969): 23–43; quotation p. 30.
[2] *The Doctrines and Discipline of the Methodist Episcopal Church*, 16th edition (New York: Published by Daniel Hunt and Thomas Ware for the Methodist Connexion in the United States, J.C. Totten, Printer, 1813): 32
[3] Journals of Benajah Williams, Vol. I, p. 178, December 7, 1820, SDL.
[4] Journals of Benajah Williams, Vol. II, p. 717, n.d., but ca. 1843, SDL.

Bonding and Bridging

was an organization man. Rather than claim attention with combative statements or impulsive behavior, he kept his eye on specific goals and quietly set about achieving them. By the time he underwent what he described as an "inquisition" over his abolitionist activities in 1843, Williams had helped to organize a dozen circuits, numerous churches, several temperance societies, and the academy at Lima. In other words, he had thoroughly demonstrated his capacity to do the work of the Methodist economy.

This chapter details the distinctive organizational power and structure of the Methodist Episcopal Church. The Church was both geographic and hierarchic in structure. Geographically, it was characterized by a multi-level system of interlocking territorial units, from the local class and circuit, to the district, region, and nation. Hierarchically, the Church obliged an aspiring preacher like Williams to graduate through several levels of examination and territories of operation under the authority of appointed senior leaders, thereby increasing the currency of his credentials. Meanwhile, the Church itself expanded through a distinctive territorial strategy of encapsulation, division, and conquest. To fund this expansion the Church drew on small amounts of surplus capital generated by thousands of local exchange networks as well as on income generated by corporate capital consolidated at the national level. Economically, in other words, the Methodist Episcopal Church was simultaneously capitalistic and rooted in local production and exchange. In the language of Methodism, this distinctive multi-level system of mobilizing and organizing social and financial capital was known as the "Methodist economy." In the language of social capital theory, Methodism excelled at forging both "bonding" and "bridging" relationships.

Professional Hierarchy

An aspiring Methodist preacher learned to operate on several levels at once. At one level, his work was intensely local and personal. As a spiritual leader, a good preacher closely nursed the desire for salvation among individual seekers, fostered the expression of that desire in local church meetings, and promoted a general spirit of revival among people in a place. In large part, the success of a Methodist preacher depended on this intense local activity. At another level, however, the work of a Methodist preacher was purposely detached from any particular locality or people. A professional Methodist minister had no direct responsibility to a local church or community. To the contrary, he changed the location of his ministry every one or two years. This does not mean that he operated as a free agent. Rather, he moved from circuit to circuit as directed by other Methodist ministers who belonged to his "annual conference." An annual conference was a large territorial organization composed entirely of professional preachers who met once a year, each time in a different location. At these meetings, members examined each others' work and characters and made their next year's preaching assignments. They also admitted new members, decided changes in professional status, chose future leaders, and settled matters of remuneration. To excel in the Methodist system, a preacher not only had to be an effective spiritual leader, he also had to succeed at negotiating the politics of his position in this larger organization.

Benajah Williams took his first step toward negotiating such a position when he became a "local preacher" on what was known as "the Sweetland Circuit," near his home in Cazenovia, New York, in December 1816.[5] In the Methodist system, the route to professional status began at the local level and proceeded to larger levels of territorial organization. An aspiring Methodist first demonstrated his potential for the ministry in ordinary class activities, probably by becoming a class leader. Through his experience leading class meetings and speaking out in larger church assemblies, a serious Methodist might find himself "moved by the Holy Ghost to preach."[6] Recognized and encouraged in his aspiration by more senior leaders and existing preachers, he might then be presented as a candidate for "local preacher" at a quarterly meeting of his circuit.

A "quarterly conference" meeting included all the lay leaders and local preachers from the several towns and hamlets that made up a circuit, together with the two or three professional traveling preachers assigned to the circuit as a whole. This potential peer group examined candidates for the position of local preacher regarding their fitness for the work. According to the Methodist *Discipline*, such examinations were to focus on three main criteria: grace, gifts, and usefulness. Specifically, the *Discipline* directed examiners to ask aspiring preachers questions about their spiritual state: "Do you desire and seek nothing but God? And are you holy in all manner of conversation?" The *Discipline* then directed that examiners assess candidates' practical capabilities as preachers. "Have they gifts (as well as grace) for the work? Do they have a clear, sound understanding, a right judgment in the things of God?" Also, do they "speak justly, readily, clearly?" Finally, how successful or *useful* were the candidates as spiritual leaders? "Have they fruit? Are any truly convinced of sin, and converted to God by their preaching?"[7]

Assuming they judged a candidate worthy, the circuit leaders issued him a "license to preach," such as the one Williams received in 1816. This initial preaching credential had a limited jurisdiction. According to the *Discipline*, it took the following form: "N. M. has applied to us for liberty to preach as a local preacher in our circuit; and after due enquiry concerning his gifts, grace and usefulness, we judge he is a proper person to be licensed for this purpose; and we accordingly authorize him to preach."[8] As this text indicates, the jurisdiction of a local preacher was limited to the circuit from which he applied.

---

[5] Genesee Annual Conference Minutes, Tuesday, June 23, 1817, WNYCA. The manuscript minutes identify the circuit as the Sweetland Circuit, but the published summaries of the minutes list no circuit by that name. Its location is gathered from other biographical information, including that contained in Diane C. Ham, "Migration to Mendon," printed booklet, 1986, OMTH.

[6] *Doctrines and Discipline of the Methodist Episcopal Church*, 49.

[7] Ibid.

[8] Ibid., 74.

Though other circuits could decide to recognize a license on application, its official currency was restricted to the few townships that typically made up a preacher's home circuit. "Local" preachers were still essentially lay leaders in the Methodist system. They did not participate in the larger governing bodies of the Church. Nor did they earn regular salaries as part of the Methodist system of remuneration. To increase the currency of his credential, exercise influence in denominational governance, and earn a regular living as a Methodist minister, a local preacher had to leave his home circuit and become a "traveling preacher." In effect, the Methodist system had two leadership tracks: one for lay leaders, rooted in local social relationships, and the other for professional leaders, whose status and identity transcended locality. Becoming a traveling preacher was the equivalent of ordination in the Methodist system. It signified the transition from lay leader to professional.

To become a traveling preacher, a local preacher had to be recommended by his local circuit and apply for admission to the next level of Methodist organization, the annual conference. Benajah Williams acquired support from his home circuit quickly. Just six months after he received his initial license to preach in December 1816, his circuit recommended him to the Genesee Annual Conference as a candidate for the traveling ministry. At the next conference meeting in June 1817, a committee of professional ministers examined him for the work of itinerancy and for possible admission to the conference.[9]

Members of an annual conference weighed the decision to admit a new preacher carefully. To accept a new member meant assuming certain long-term obligations. Unlike most other Protestant denominations, the Methodist Church funded its professional ministers' salaries through a collective funding system, rather than depending on the congregations of individual local churches. In effect, each annual conference administered a mutual insurance system for their professional memberships, including guaranteed annual allowances, retirement incomes, and widows' benefits for families, all ensured by corporate capital funds. In making judgments about the admission of a new candidate, then, conference members had to consider the obligations he conferred on the group as a whole.

Among the qualities considered in this calculus were age and marital status. During the late eighteenth and early nineteenth centuries, when the church was first establishing itself in North America, Methodist leaders strongly recommended that candidates for the professional ministry be single at the time of admission and remain so for as long as possible, preferably for the duration of their careers. Free of family obligations, single young men would presumably be more zealous in their mission, more willing to put up with the hardships of itinerancy, and more able to subsist on the salaries they earned. Marriage, by contrast, would increase the claims on a professional preacher's time and loyalties, as well as on both the preacher's and the conference's financial resources. Early Methodist ministers apparently enforced this ethic of

[9] Genesee Annual Conference Minutes, Tuesday, June 23, 1817.

celibacy to some extent. Over time, however, this condition proved difficult to maintain. By the mid-1810s, the church had largely reconciled itself to marriage in the ministry, but the potential risks associated with family obligations continued to be a consideration in decisions about the admission of new members to the ministry.[10]

In 1817, when his circuit first recommended him "to travel" in the Genesee Conference, Benajah Williams was a twenty-eight-year-old husband and father of four children under the age of seven.[11] He thus posed a potential financial risk to the conference. In consideration of this fact, the committee recommended against accepting Williams as a traveling preacher right away in 1817. The members of the committee nonetheless recommended that the conference make use of his talents for a year in an unofficial role. As they often did in cases where they wanted to try out a candidate before making a commitment, the members voted that "the Presiding Elder" who had charge of the district "shall have liberty to employ him on a circuit" for a year. After serving in this way as a de facto traveling preacher, Williams again applied for formal membership in the conference. This time, in July 1818, the membership voted to accept him.[12]

With this vote, Benajah Williams took another step in the Methodist system of professional education and advancement. The promotion from local to traveling preacher increased the geographic range and currency of a minister's credentials. Williams' status as a professional preacher would now be recognized throughout the Genesee Conference. Promotion to the status of traveling preacher did not end the process of initiation into the profession, however. When members of the Genesee Annual Conference voted to admit Benajah Williams as a traveling preacher, they did so "on trial," an official probationary status that newly admitted ministers typically retained for two years.[13] As a probationary preacher, Williams assumed the full duties of a traveling preacher but traveled a circuit in conjunction with a more senior minister. Working with this superior, Williams continued to hone his skills as a professional.

Territorial Expansion

When Benajah Williams assumed the role of a probationary traveling preacher in July 1818, he took a position on the front lines of Methodist Church expansion in North America. The phenomenal growth of Methodism from the late

---

[10] Genesee Annual Conference Minutes, passim. For discussions of the norms regarding marriage in the Methodist ministry, see John H. Wigger, "Fighting Bees; Methodist Itinerants and the Dynamics of Methodist Growth, 1770–1820," in Nathan O. Hatch and John Wigger, eds. *Methodism in the Shaping of American Culture* (Nashville: Kingswood Books, Abingdon Press, 2001): 87–133, esp. pp. 112–120; also, Dee E. Andrews, *The Methodists and Revolutionary America, 1760–1800: The Shaping of an Evangelical Culture* (Princeton, NJ: Princeton University Press, 2000): 217–219.

[11] Williams' age, marital status, and ages of his children in 1817 are calculated from biographical information provided in Ham, "Migration to Mendon."

[12] Journals of Benajah Williams, Vol. I, inside cover.

[13] *Doctrines and Discipline*, 16th edition, 42.

eighteenth through the mid-nineteenth centuries is well known and often remarked upon by scholars. During a period in which virtually all Protestant denominations experienced significant growth relative to the size of the general population, Methodism stood out as particularly expansive. At the beginning of the Revolutionary era, the Methodist Church ranked a distant sixth in size among Protestant denominations in the British colonies. At the end of the Revolution, when many of its loyal British leaders and members had left, it had just 15,000 members. After its organization as a separate North American church in 1784, however, Methodism expanded quickly. Between 1784 and 1810, when the Genesee Conference was established, the North American church expanded by more than 1,000 percent to 175,000 members. During the 1810s, Methodism's rate of growth exceeded that of all other denominations, soon surpassing the Baptists and making Methodism the largest Protestant denomination in the United States.[14]

According to scholars, this achievement rested on Methodism's early success on four geographic fronts: its initial foothold on the Delmarva Peninsula on Chesapeake Bay in the late colonial era; its urban expansion in the coastal cities of New York, Baltimore, and Philadelphia during the Revolutionary period; its western expansion into Kentucky, Tennessee, and Ohio at the turn of the century; and its northern expansion into upstate New York during the first decades of the 1800s. Moving up the Susquehanna as well as the Hudson Rivers, Methodism reached well into the Finger Lakes region of central New York in the first decade of the nineteenth century and extended into the Genesee region in the decade of the 1810s.[15] Benajah Williams worked the leading edge of this expansion.

The phenomenal growth of the Methodist Church was the product of a distinctive geographic structure and a deliberate expansionist strategy. Methodism expanded through a strategy of territorial encapsulation, division, and conquest first developed by Methodist leaders in the 1790s. In 1810, when bishops of the Methodist Church carved out the boundaries of the new Genesee Annual Conference from parts of three existing conferences, they laid claim to territory that included virtually all of upstate New York north and west of the Catskill region and parts of Canada and Pennsylvania as well (see Figure 4). To the west the territory extended not only to Lake Erie but across the isthmus at Niagara to the settlement at Detroit and into Upper Canada. To the north the conference encompassed Lower Canada and the St. Lawrence region, and to the south it took in the Susquehanna River basin as far as

---

[14] Michael George Nickerson, "Sermons, Systems and Strategies: The Geographic Strategies of the Methodist Episcopal Church in its Expansion into New York State, 1788–1810" (Ph.D. dissertation, Syracuse University, 1988), 1; Edwin Scott Gaustad and Philip L. Barlow, *New Historical Atlas of Religion in America* (Oxford: Oxford University Press, 2001): 221 and 374.

[15] This summary of Methodism's geographical expansion in the immediate post-Revolution era is drawn from the combined work of Andrews, *The Methodists*; Wigger, "Fighting Bees"; and Nickerson, "Sermons, Systems and Strategies."

FIGURE 4. Territory of the Genesee Conference of the Methodist Episcopal Church, 1810–1824. The leading edge of Methodist expansion in the 1810s was the Genesee region of upstate New York. During the same decade, Methodism's rate of growth exceeded that of all other denominations, soon surpassing the Baptists and making Methodism the largest Protestant denomination in the United States. Boundaries shown here are approximate, reconstructed from the *Encyclopedia of World Methodism* (Nashville: Abingdon Press, 1974); the "Journal of the Genesee Conference," WNYCA, and "Conference Boundaries," MMC.

Wilkes Barre, Pennsylvania.[16] At the time, much of this territory was sparsely settled and only minimally under Methodist influence. The boundaries of the new conference represented not so much the parameters of the existing church but the intended reach of Methodism's next wave of evangelization.

Once the outer edge of the conference's activity had been defined, the encapsulated territory was divided for more systematic organization. Annual conferences were first divided into districts and then into circuits, with a "presiding

---

[16] Information on the boundaries of the Genesee Conference is compiled from maps in the *Encyclopedia of World Methodism* (Nashville: Abingdon Press, 1974); from a file on "Conference Boundaries" of the Oneida Conference, MMC; from *Minutes of the Annual Conferences of the Methodist Episcopal Church for the Years 1773–1828*, Vol. I (New York: T. Mason and G. Lane, 1840); and from Nickerson, *Sermons, Systems and Strategies*.

elder" assigned to oversee the work of all the circuits in a district. These divisions were essentially geographic rather than congregational. Presiding elders and traveling preachers were charged with covering a specific territory rather than with serving a particular group of people. At the first meeting of the Genesee Annual Conference in the summer of 1810, the fifty-seven traveling preachers who composed the membership organized their territory into three districts of nine or ten circuits each. Each of these districts and circuits in turn developed its own strategy for organizing the Church within its designated area. As preachers began working the territory and organizing new classes and societies within it, the density of the work intensified. To meet this intensified demand, members of the conference continually divided their territory into smaller units. By the time Benajah Williams became a traveling preacher in 1818, the number of districts in the conference had doubled from three to six and the number of circuits increased by nearly 100 percent, from twenty-eight to fifty-four. Eventually the conference itself would divide.[17]

As this early history of the Genesee Conference implies, Methodist boundaries were constantly changing. An important characteristic of Methodism was this geographic flexibility. At the local level, the map of Methodist activity changed from week to week, as preachers evangelized new neighborhoods and organized new societies. Just as important as change at the local level, however, was the constant reshaping of the Church at higher levels through district and conference organization. Circuit preachers did not act on their own, but developed their circuits in communication with "presiding elders," who made regular visits to the circuits in their districts. In this way, the Methodist system resembled that of a military organization. Presiding elders were like field commanders, sending their troops out to conquer new territory and at the same time collecting intelligence from the field to inform strategy at the next level of the system. At quarterly meetings of the district and annual meetings of the conference, presiding elders and traveling preachers reshaped their work through reassignment to new tasks and territories. Similarly, bishops traveled from district to district and from conference to conference to inform higher level decisions. Bishops shaped the Church by assigning presiding elders to new districts or by recommending changes in the *Discipline* or annual conferences. These recommendations would then be considered by delegates of the ministry nationally, at the next general conference meeting, held once every four years.

This interlocking geographic structure distinguished Methodism from other denominations. Through a comparative study of the diffusion patterns of five different Protestant denominations in New York State during the late eighteenth and early nineteenth centuries, the historical geographer Michael Nickerson determined that other denominations expanded in one of two main ways, through either *hierarchical* or *contagious* diffusion. Under a hierarchical structure, such as that of the Episcopalians, diffusion occurred when a

---

[17] *Minutes of the Annual Conferences*, 1818.

higher level authority sent a minister to serve a particular church community. Under a nonhierarchical structure, such as that of the Congregationalists or Baptists, diffusion occurred when existing churches multiplied on their own, through a process of division or reproduction, with the new churches issuing calls for preachers themselves. An important difference between these two models was the role of deliberation or strategy. In one model diffusion was planned as part of a larger church design. In the other model, diffusion was essentially spontaneous or "contagious." Methodism distinguished itself by combining these two strategies. Under its structure, regional-level organizations sent traveling ministers out to cultivate spontaneous reproduction in localities within their regions. In effect, Methodism expanded through a hierarchical system of locally contagious diffusion.[18]

In Nickerson's analysis, this hybrid system had a number of advantages over those of other denominations. First, Methodist leaders conceptualized a region as a whole rather than targeting specific localities within a region. This meant that they could deploy preachers in a way that enabled them to cover all of the territory in an established amount of time. Second, traveling preachers were identified with a region rather than with any one place. This meant that they could move to where they were most needed. Third, Methodist societies were largely self-sustaining. Once a traveling preacher cultivated a new church society, it developed its own lay leadership. The traveling preacher could then move on to new neighborhoods, returning only occasionally to provide direction and make connections with the larger organization. This meant that diffusion occurred more quickly than in other denominations. A fourth advantage of the Methodist system, according to Nickerson, was that leaders at every level had direct knowledge of the areas about which decisions were being made. At the local level, lay leaders made decisions that directly affected the local society, while at higher levels decisions were made by preachers and elders who regularly circulated through the whole affected territory. This meant that the organization could adapt quickly to changing conditions and new opportunities. It also meant that leaders could match the skills of individual preachers to the tasks that needed to be done.[19]

The Work of the Traveling Preacher

Benajah Williams' first official task as a traveling preacher was shaped in part by the rhythm of Methodist expansion. As a new probationary preacher in 1818, Williams joined what might be called the "second wave" of evangelization in the Genesee territory. During the first wave, most traveling preachers came from other conferences and growth occurred primarily in general membership. During the second wave, the conference produced its own cadre of professional leaders, thereby intensifying the evangelization of

---

[18] Nickerson, *Sermons, Systems and Strategies*, 340–347.
[19] Ibid., 127.

Bonding and Bridging 81

the territory. In the six years between 1810, when the Genesee Conference was first organized, and 1816, when Benajah Williams first became a local preacher, general membership in the conference increased by nearly 50 percent, from 10,693 to 15,166. Professional membership, meanwhile, increased by just 23 percent, from 57 to 70. Once local circuits began producing their own preachers like Williams, though, growth in the professional ministry caught up with that of the general membership. In just two years, from 1816 to 1818, the number of professional ministers in the conference increased by 50 percent, from 70 to 104. Benajah Williams was one of these new preachers.[20]

The timing of Williams' rise within this expansion shaped the location of his first assignment. As a local preacher from the Sweetland Circuit, near Cazenovia, New York, Williams entered the professional ministry from the eastern side of the Genesee Conference. Once he became a traveling preacher, however, he rode the next wave of Methodist expansion west. His first assignment was to the Bloomfield Circuit of the Genesee Conference, a territory that included the town of Lima and all the towns immediately surrounding it. This assignment put him at the center of the Genesee Conference territory, just east of the Genesee River.

The location of Williams' assignment in turn shaped the nature of his task. When he arrived in 1818, the Bloomfield Circuit had been a site of Methodist preaching and activity for at least five years. More recently, the Bloomfield Circuit had experienced a major surge in Methodist membership. According to the Minutes of the Genesee Conference, membership on the Bloomfield Circuit had increased by more than 50 percent in just one year, from 400 in 1817 to 616 in 1818. Williams' task when he arrived in 1818 was to build on this surge in membership.[21]

Williams' organization skills proved a good match for this task. In the near term, from 1818 to 1820, Methodist Church membership on the Bloomfield Circuit grew further, becoming the largest circuit in the district in both 1819 and 1820.[22] For the long term, Williams helped to establish an organizational basis for future Methodist institution building by founding the first Methodist chapel in the area, also in 1820.[23]

Williams' success in prosecuting these tasks in turn translated into further professional advancement. At the annual meeting of the Genesee Conference in July 1820, Williams finally achieved the status of "full connection" as a traveling preacher.[24] Among the benefits of this professional status was the right to share in the fruit of the Methodist system of collective

---

[20] *Minutes of the Annual Conferences*, passim.
[21] Ibid.
[22] *Minutes of the Annual Conferences*.
[23] "Early Members of Methodist Church, Honeoye Falls, Organized 1820," OMTH.
[24] Journals of Benajah Williams, Vol. I, inside cover.

funding for ministerial salaries. According to the *Discipline*, every traveling preacher was guaranteed a minimum annual salary standardized at the level of the national church. In 1820, Williams was eligible for an annual living allowance of $100 plus traveling expenses. His wife was eligible for an additional allowance of $100, and each of his children was entitled to an allotment pro-rated according to age ($16 apiece for children under seven and $24 apiece for children between seven and fourteen). Beyond this annual income, Williams and his family became eligible for retirement and widow and orphan benefits.[25]

To collect his allowance, a traveling preacher made claims on common funds from several different sources. As long as a preacher worked a circuit, the major part of his income was expected to come from "quarterage." Quarterage consisted of contributions of goods, services, and cash made by members of the various classes on a circuit and collected on a quarterly basis by specially appointed "stewards." At quarterly meetings, stewards totaled the amount contributed by class members and awarded shares to each of the traveling preachers on the circuit. In addition to quarterage, a traveling preacher drew income from more general "public collections" at open camp or church meetings, often held in conjunction with quarterly conferences. Typically, more than one preacher spoke at such meetings, which might extend over several days. According to the *Discipline*, proceeds from public collections went first to presiding elders and then to other traveling preachers with claims on their allowances. Finally, traveling preachers who did not meet their allowances from either quarterage or public collections presented their claims to the annual conference for shares of its corporate funds.[26]

Two sources of corporate funding in particular helped to bridge the gap between the incomes collected by preachers on their circuits and those officially allowed to them by the Church. Both corporate entities were national in scope but incorporated under the laws of individual states. The first of these enterprises, known as "the Methodist Book Concern," was a publishing house organized in 1789 and headquartered in New York City. The Book Concern published a wide array of books and tracts, including the Methodist *Discipline*, Methodist hymnbooks, and several Methodist periodicals, as well as some titles of general interest. It distributed its publications through presiding elders and traveling preachers, who sold them in their respective districts and circuits. The second corporate enterprise was a capital fund, known as "the Charter Fund," established in 1796 and administered out of Philadelphia. Initially created by "voluntary contributions" from "friends" of the Church, the Charter Fund invested capital in state securities. Proceeds from these

---

[25] *The Doctrines and Discipline of the Methodist Episcopal Church*, 20th edition (New York: N. Bangs and T. Mason, 1820): 176–178.

[26] *The Doctrines and Discipline of the Methodist Episcopal Church*, 22nd edition (New York: N. Bangs and J. Emory, 1824): 172–180.

investments, along with profits from the Methodist Book Concern, were then distributed to annual conferences in the form of dividends and interest for the relief of "distressed" preachers and their families.[27]

This was the theory, at any rate. In practice, the Methodist system was less than perfect. Annual conference minutes show that preachers regularly presented claims for one amount but received substantially less.[28] Not surprisingly, preachers often complained of such shortfalls. The historians John Wigger and Dee Andrews report several such complaints. After forty years of itinerancy, for example, the Methodist preacher James Quinn estimated that the church owed him $2,600 in unpaid salary and expenses. Another itinerant with a similarly long career calculated a shortfall of more than $6,400.[29]

In addition to these financial difficulties, Methodist preachers recorded other problems with the Methodist system. One problem was itinerancy itself. The same geographic flexibility that proved so advantageous when viewed from the perspective of the Methodist Church as a whole was not necessarily experienced that way by individual preachers and their families. Early rules specified that Methodist preachers should change their assignments as often as every six months. In Benajah Williams' time, the rotation was longer. Still, according to the Methodist *Discipline*, the church "shall not allow any preacher to remain in the same station more than two years successively," and the norm was to change assignments more often.[30] Williams' career adhered to this norm. At no time did he stay on the same circuit for more than two years, and in a number of cases he stayed only one. Altogether, he worked a dozen different circuits between 1818 and 1838, although he traveled only sixteen of those twenty years.[31]

Many Methodist ministers struggled with the tension between localized responsibilities to homes and families and translocal responsibilities to their profession. Soon after his promotion to "full connection" in the Genesee Conference, Williams "bargained for a house and lot with Mr. Sylbey" and established his family in an independent household in the hamlet of West Mendon. Having secured a home for his family, Williams then took up his next preaching assignment, this time on a new circuit much further west in the conference, almost to Niagara. As he took up his new assignment, he worried about maintaining his household and family. In his journals, he noted efforts to complete various "choars" and "family duties" before departing for his work as a circuit preacher. Keeping the family supplied with wood was one

---

[27] Ibid., 180–188; also, Emory Stevens Bucke, ed. *The History of American Methodism* (Nashville: Abingdon, Press, 1964), Vol. I, 453–454 and Vol. III, 149; and William Warren Sweet, *Methodism in American History* (New York: Methodist Book Concern, 1933), 150.
[28] Genesee Annual Conference Minutes, passim.
[29] Wigger, "Fighting Bees," 106 and Andrews, *The Methodists*, 214.
[30] *Doctrines and Discipline*, 22nd edition, 25.
[31] *Minutes of the Annual Conferences*, passim.

concern, and it probably figured among the tasks to which Williams referred on December 9, 1820, when he reported that he "started for my circuit" at "about half past 12," after "preparing some things for the comfort of my family."[32]

To some extent the Methodist system acknowledged the tension between professional and family responsibilities. Although the *Discipline* implied that the condition of itinerancy was semi-permanent, in practice, few preachers rode circuits their entire careers. Rather, most preachers traveled for several years and then reverted temporarily or permanently to the work of a more local preacher, deacon, or elder. This practice is apparent in the record of preacher assignments from year to year and in the indirect comments of preachers themselves.[33] Once a preacher put in some time as a circuit rider, he might decide or agree "to locate." In "taking a location," a preacher effectively gave up his claim to the common funds of the conference for the duration, although he retained his status as a professional preacher, which allowed him to continue to perform baptisms and marriages and collect fees for such services. According to some sources, a "located" preacher could in this way sometimes earn more than he would on a circuit or traveling assignment, as he was not obligated to forward any "surplus" from his labors to common funds. Temporary or permanent "location" was thus one way that Methodism acknowledged the tensions inherent in the role of an itinerant preacher.[34]

Another way that Methodism helped preachers negotiate this tension was through its provisions for "superannuated" or "worn-out" preachers. Technically, the term "superannuated" referred to a condition of retirement due to infirmity or age. In practice, however, the position of "superannuated" or "worn-out" preacher was not necessarily permanent. In the case of Benajah Williams and of other members of the Genesee Annual Conference, the status of superannuated preacher was awarded on an intermittent basis, as a kind of sabbatical. During his twenty years of service, Williams was superannuated four times – in 1822, 1823, 1828, and 1836. Presumably in these years Williams devoted himself to his family and household, thereby compensating somewhat for years in which he served on more remote circuit assignments.[35]

Now and then Williams also managed to integrate work and home life by bringing local and professional networks together for common ends. As a local householder in West Mendon, Williams participated not only in the larger Methodist economy but also in local Methodist society and in normal exchange and credit relations with neighbors. Among the neighbors and families with whom the Williams' developed such relationships were other local Methodists. In June 1820, for example, Williams recorded a ride with "brother

---

[32] Journals of Benajah Williams, Vol. I, 178, December 9, 1820.
[33] Genesee Annual Conference Minutes, passim.
[34] See Wigger, "Fighting Bees"; Andrews, *The Methodists*; and Nickerson, "Sermons, Systems and Strategies."
[35] *Minutes of the Annual Conferences*, passim.

Brake": "Took him in my one horse wagon with five bushels of grain and straw." Whether Williams was assisting Brake or Brake was assisting Williams is unclear. Nonetheless, the two cooperated in making two deliveries, including one to a Genesee River merchant. They then went on to lend both their labors to Methodist Church business. "Rode to Avon to Mr. Chappel, then to Lima, unloaded, & went to help raise the Methodist chapel in Mendon."[36] Thus Williams put local exchange networks to work for professional ends.

The Methodist Economy

In Methodist terms, Williams proved himself an effective agent of "the Methodist economy." The word "economy" in this sense meant something like "system," but it also captured a specifically Methodist idea. To understand this idea, it helps first to uncouple the word "economy" from its current, mostly financial, usage. In the eighteenth and early nineteenth centuries, the word "economy" could be used to refer to any collective enterprise. John Wesley himself invoked this sense of the word when he referred to the smallest band of spiritual seekers in Methodism as "an economy of young men." Employing the same idea at another level of organization, Methodist writers often referred to the operations of the Church as a whole as "the Methodist economy."[37]

According to the *Doctrines and Discipline* of the Church, the Methodist economy consisted of two parts, the "spiritual economy" and the "temporal economy." In making this distinction, Methodist writers drew on two intellectual traditions. On the one hand, they referred to a centuries-old concept of "divine" economy, that is, God's system of distributing salvation or grace. On the other hand, they referred to the idea of domestic or political economy, that is, the art or science of managing a household or nation-state.[38] Reflecting this distinction, the *Discipline* itself was divided into two sections. The first section, devoted to describing the spiritual economy, encompassed those aspects of the Methodist system aimed specifically at salvation. These included the articles of religion, the principles of Methodist discipline, and the methods by which members disciplined each other. The second section of the Methodist *Discipline*, devoted to describing the temporal economy, dealt with institutional organization. This included matters such as the boundaries of the annual conferences, the building of Methodist chapels, and the administration of the Church's corporate funds.[39]

---

[36] Journals of Benajah Williams, Vol. I, 121, June 9, 1820.
[37] The Wesley reference is from *The Oxford English Dictionary* (Oxford: Oxford University Press, 1971): 831. For the use of this phrase by other Methodist writers, see especially *The Doctrines and Discipline* and the pages of various Methodist periodicals, especially *The Christian Advocate and Journal and Zion's Herald*, N. Bangs and B. Badger, eds., New York.
[38] *The Oxford English Dictionary*, 831.
[39] *Doctrines and Discipline*, 22nd edition, 1824, Part II, "Temporal Economy," 155–190.

Methodist writers delighted in pointing out the connection between temporal and spiritual economy in the Methodist system. According to this logic, the Methodist economy was a way of organizing temporal society so as to achieve the greatest possible distribution of spiritual goods.[40] Traveling preachers were the linchpins of this connection. The mission of the traveling preacher was first to expand Methodist membership through spiritual awakening and, second, to integrate Methodists into the larger Methodist system.

Considered in its financial aspect, the Methodist economy embodied an interesting model of corporate capitalism. On the one hand, at regional and national levels, the Methodist system was expansionist and capitalistic. Preachers dedicated themselves to constant conquests of new territories and continual church growth. They also earned incomes from interest on capital markets and from profits on the sale of cultural goods in the form of books and other publications produced by a central publishing house. On the other hand, at the local level, the Methodist system was highly localized and rooted in household production and exchange. Preachers organized classes typically as small as ten people. They depended on localities not only to supply them with the goods that typically made up their quarterage, but also to organize the contributions of labor, goods, and cash that made church building possible.

What made the Methodist economy particularly effective was its integration of these multiple levels of social and geographic organization. A number of scholars have recognized the historical significance of nineteenth-century denominationalism in general, and of Methodism in particular, in connecting local communities with each other and with larger social structures. In a highly influential essay, Donald Mathews emphasized the character of the Second Great Awakening "as an organizing process" that was simultaneously intensely local and broadly national in its scope. Crediting Methodism with the innovative structures that made this process possible, Mathews described the Second Great Awakening as "a general social movement that organized thousands of people into small groups" and that simultaneously integrated those intimate religious communities into a larger whole, thereby helping to create a more integrated American society and culture.[41]

---

[40] Consider, for instance, the following examples from two lead editorials on the subject of "weekly class collections," published in the Methodists' national newspaper during the same month of 1829. "Has it not likewise been the economy of Methodism from the beginning to preach a free gospel to the poor and needy...?" *The Christian Advocate and Journal and Zion's Herald*, Vol. IV, No. 1 (September 4, 1829): 1. "It would be important to commence this work in an especial manner in all cities, towns and villages, as a prelude to its pervading the denser population in the country, until, at no distant period, all the dispersed and scattered children of Methodism should be brought under its influence throughout the land. ... Preachers and ministers of every grade have borne much of the executive burdens and hardships of the church, in relation not only to her spiritual but temporal economy," idem. Vol. IV, No. 3 (September 29, 1829): 1. For additional discussion of "weekly class collections," see Chapter 17.

[41] Mathews, "The Second Great Awakening as an Organizing Process," 30.

Mathews and others have emphasized the social and cultural dimensions of this organizing process, but clearly it had economic dimensions as well. Much has been written about the association between evangelicalism and economic development, particularly evangelicalism's association with market capitalism and manufacturing in the Northeast.[42] For the most part, however, this work focuses on the creation of a capitalistic culture of individual self-improvement, rather than on the actual movement of goods, labor, and capital through evangelical channels. One thing that stands out in a close study of the Methodist system is how it moved goods as well as the spirit. Just as it organized people into small groups and integrated them into larger societies, it also organized the products of their labors and integrated them into larger economies.

The significance of this integrative power lay in its capacity to facilitate coordinated action – to mobilize social and financial capital across localities for a common purpose. This was the difference between the kind of social capital forged by a free agent, like Joseph Badger, and that of a Methodist traveling preacher, like Benajah Williams. In the case of a largely unaffiliated – or possibly excommunicated – itinerant preacher like Joseph Badger, each newly evangelized territory or group operated largely on its own. The bonding relationships that members formed among themselves might well yield valuable social capital within a certain local network; but without a systematic structure for forging relationships with similar groups in other localities, that capital was unlikely to add up to much. The Methodist Episcopal Church, by contrast, was organized precisely to mobilize resources and facilitate action across localities and groups. The quarterly conference of a district and the annual conferences of a region convened precisely for that purpose. Annual conferences in particular, with their entirely professional memberships of 50 to 100 preachers or more, had the potential for coordinated action, for it was at this level that the Methodist Church held corporate status. An annual conference thus enjoyed the legal power necessary to hold funds in common and sponsor joint endeavors, such as the founding of a Methodist academy.

From the perspective of social capital theory, the Methodist economy provides a quintessential illustration of the distinction between two kinds of social capital called "bonding" and "bridging." Bonding relationships are dense, more or less permanent ties among insiders in an essentially closed community. Bridging relationships, by contrast, are "thinner" than bonding relationships, and less permanent, but extend connections outside the community.[43] The Methodist Episcopal Church excelled at forging both bonding and bridging relationships. Through a common organizational structure

---

[42] For a discussion of this literature, see Part III of this book.
[43] Robert Putnam discusses the distinction between "bonding" and "bridging" social capital in *Bowling Alone: The Collapse and Revival of American Community* (New York: Simon and Schuster, 2000), 22–23. He attributes the coining of these terms to Ross Gittell and Avid Vidal, *Community Organizing: Building Social Capital as a Development Strategy* (Thousand Oaks, CA: Sage, 1998).

and a common social discipline, it simultaneously stimulated the formation of intense local networks of trust and community and connected them to similar enclaves in other places. In the process, it accumulated substantial social and financial capital.

By 1830, when Lima residents bid for the site of the academy, the Methodist economy had arguably become the largest and most effective social organization in the country. It was this organization that Lima residents enlisted, and it was this power with which they eventually had to contend. Chronologically, the events that led to this joining of forces can be traced to the late 1810s, when Joseph Badger and Benajah Williams first worked the territory around Lima as itinerant preachers. Geographically, the launching point for this development was the hamlet of Norton's Mills or West Mendon, on Lima's northeastern border. During the decade from 1820 to 1830, local Methodists established a new Methodist circuit out of Norton's Mills, built a Methodist chapel in Lima, and hosted an extended series of revivals. These revivals in turn launched Lima's successful bid for the site of the academy. Benajah Williams' organizational skills and connections to the larger Methodist economy were crucial to these developments. Just as important, however, were the roots of these enterprises in the local economy.

6

Development – Evangelicalism and Capital Formation

> Let all our churches be built plain and decent; but not more expensive than is absolutely unavoidable; otherwise the necessity of raising money will make rich men necessary to us.
>
> *Doctrines and Discipline of the Methodist Episcopal Church*, 1813[1]

Becoming a Methodist was a temporal as well as a spiritual experience. A dedicated and well-situated member like Susan Sines would regularly be asked to contribute surplus goods and labor to the "quarterage" of traveling ministers. Occasionally, her household would also be asked to make more substantial contributions to capital projects such as the building of a Methodist chapel. Beyond funding the church itself, Methodists engaged in ordinary trade relations with each other. For men and women alike, a Methodist society could serve as an informal trade network of like-minded neighbors. Presumably a fellow church member could be trusted for honest dealing, timely payment, or a degree of forbearance when needed. If this expectation should be disappointed, the church could serve as an extralegal forum for mediating financial disputes, a practice outlined in detail in the Methodist *Discipline*.[2] Finally, for a few Methodists like Francis Smith, church membership conferred positions of leadership not only within the local church but in the larger economy. Among other men of influence, a church leader represented a capacity to mobilize people and resources. As both Methodism and the local economy grew in the Lima-Mendon area in the 1820s, so did the power of men in a position to make these connections.

This chapter explores the relationship between evangelical church organization and rural economic development through the example of early Methodism in the Lima-Mendon area. Increasingly, economists who study economic development in the present emphasize the significance of community organization and social capital formation for early development, especially in

---

[1] *Doctrines and Discipline of the Methodist Episcopal Church* (New York: J. C. Totten, 1813), 181.
[2] Ibid.

89

third-world contexts.³ In these accounts, informal social networks and female labor and trade often prove as important as formal labor relations or wage work. A close look at the Lima-Mendon case similarly suggests that informal social networks were important to early economic development, and that women played important roles in those networks. At the same time, the Lima-Mendon case shows how, when it came to corporate capital projects, the formal economic and political power of male property owners proved essential. Specifically, male credit-brokers were necessary to gain access to corporate power and to realize the value of surplus goods and labor from local households. In the process, they earned income for future investment and helped organize the local economy.

Female Leadership in Evangelical Networks

The people who first organized and funded the Methodist Church in West Mendon, on Lima's northeastern border, were male and female, rich and poor. A transcript of the church's membership at the time of its incorporation in 1820 identifies eighty-six "early members." Because the 1820 census identified only heads of household by name, it is difficult to know for sure to which household each church member belonged or how church members were related. In twenty-two (25%) of the cases, the surnames of church members do not match any of those in local census or tax lists. In another eleven (13%) of the cases, the surnames match those of more than one head of household. Nonetheless, by comparing the surnames of church members with those of local householders and taxpayers, it is possible to say a few things about the composition of the First Methodist Church in West Mendon in 1820.⁴

Early membership in the First Methodist Church was not patriarchal. Rather, the church started as a small group of mostly female members. Of the eighty-six people listed as "early" members of the Methodist Church in 1820, ten are further identified as having been "original" members of the church, before its formal incorporation. Eight of these "original" members were female (including Susan Sines), and two were male. The two men, John Fox and John Scramlin, were identified as heads of household in the census for that year. Otherwise, however, female dependents dominated early Methodist organization in Mendon. To some extent this condition continued after the

---

³ See, for example, Ross Gittell and Avid Vidal, *Community Organizing: Building Social Capital as a Development Strategy* (Thousand Oaks, CA: Sage, 1998). For an incisive, though now somewhat dated review of the literature, see Michael Woolcock, "Social Capital and Economic Development: Toward a Theoretical Synthesis and Policy Framework," *Theory and Society* 27:2 (April 1998): 151–208.

⁴ "Early Members of Methodist Church, Honeoye Falls, Organized 1820," OMTH. For the following analysis, the membership list has been matched against 1820 tax lists for the three towns of Lima, Mendon, and Bloomfield and against the original manuscript of the federal census of the United States for the same three towns in 1820, OCRAIMS. These sources will be referred to as "1820 Tax Lists" and "1820 Census."

church's formal incorporation. Even after the membership had expanded to eighty-six members in 1820, only thirteen (15%) were also identified as heads of household in either the federal census or local tax lists. Furthermore, only eight additional members had the same surnames as these known heads of household. As this suggests, the majority of the eighty-six total church members in 1820 – perhaps as much as 75 percent, certainly at least 50 percent – were the dependents of *non*member heads of household.

Some of these household dependents were the wives, mothers, or children of established heads of household in the area, but acted on their own. Mrs. Lydia Jackman, Mrs. Parish, Ahira Parkhurst, and Henry Lockwood, for example, all joined the church independently of the property-owning husbands and fathers who headed their families.[5] Other early church members were apparently unrelated to any local family. B. L. Buckingham, Lavinia Cargill, Hager Hallor, and Aurilla Jobes, for example, bore surnames that matched none of the heads of household identified in census or tax lists for Lima, Mendon, or other contiguous towns in 1820. Nor do they match those of any other church members. Most of these men and women were probably servants, tenants, laborers, wards, or apprentices. Their absence from such records was presumably a product of their marginal status within society itself.

Even though many individuals joined the church on their own, however, family networks were important to the growth of Methodism. As indicated by common surnames, the list of church members in 1820 included twenty-one family groups, which together represented fifty-six individuals, or 65 percent of the total membership. Within these family groups, mothers, children, and siblings often took the lead in church affiliation. Of the ten individuals identified as "original" members of the church, seven were eventually followed by other individuals with the same surname. A close look at this sample of early members provides some insight into the sequence of membership within families. In a few cases, a wife or daughter led a head of household into the church. John Sines, for example, followed Susan Sines into the church. Local cemetery records identify Susan as John Sine's wife.[6] Similarly, two men of the same surname followed Hannah H. Young into the church. One was her brother Andrew and the other was leading local landowner, Jacob Young, their father.[7] While these women brought heads of household into the church, some drew other dependent family members after them. Children followed their mothers into the church. Denton G. Shuart, for example, followed Betsy Shuart. According to local records, Denton was Betsy's teenage son.[8] In other cases, the nature of the relationship between members remains unknown. After Elizabeth Hanna became a Methodist, for example, another four

---

[5] Moses Jackman, Abraham Parish, Abell Parkhurst, and Jeremiah Lockwood of Mendon, respectively
[6] Diane C. Ham, "Migration to Mendon, 1791–1821," 35–36, OMTH.
[7] Ibid., 39–40.
[8] Ibid., 86–87.

individuals with the same surname joined the church. None of these individuals were named Isaac or Samuel, however, the only two heads of households by the name of Hanna to appear in local tax lists. Most likely, the four other members were Elizabeth's siblings or children.

These findings are consistent with those of other scholars who have studied family patterns among evangelical church members. Historian Dee Andrews has found similar patterns among Methodists going back as far as the 1760s in the Chesapeake region and to the 1780s in the cities of Baltimore, New York, and Philadelphia. According to her analysis, women typically formed a majority, often a large majority, of Methodist societies in these regions, and they often joined the church independently of their fathers or husbands, but in the company of other female family members.[9] From findings similar to these but from a somewhat later period in Utica, New York, Mary Ryan identified women as prime movers in shaping a new evangelical culture of the family. Specifically, Ryan saw the revivalism of the mid-1820s as effecting a transition "from patriarchal authority to maternal affection as the focal point of childhood socialization."[10] Tracing the associations and activities of women in the city of Utica and its surrounding countryside in the 1810s and 1820s, Ryan found that women financed evangelical ministry through their work in female missionary societies and perfected methods for converting their children through their work in maternal associations. In many cases, the children of these women became the new converts and church members of the 1820s.[11]

In the mostly rural contexts exemplified by Lima and Mendon and studied by Curtis Johnson, formal female missionary societies such as those studied by Ryan do not seem to have been present. Nonetheless, much the same pattern of female initiative, financial contribution, and family affiliation appear in early church records. Similarly, according to Johnson, neither church nor economic activities were as sex-segregated in rural Cortland County as they were in cities of the time. Nonetheless, women constituted 60 percent of church members across all denominations and a higher proportion of strongly evangelical denominations such as the Methodists.[12] Although these women did not generally organize separate missionary and maternal organizations, they did make substantial financial contributions to the ministry and successfully promote the conversion of adolescent children. As in the more urban environment studied by Mary Ryan, high rates of conversion and membership among women in the 1810s and 1820s were followed by high rates of conversion among youth in the late 1820s and early 1830s.[13] From this, one

---

[9] Dee Andrews, *The Methodists and Revolutionary America, 1760–1800: The Shaping of an Evangelical Culture* (Princeton, NJ: Princeton University Press, 2000).

[10] Mary P. Ryan, *Cradle of the Middle Class: The Family in Oneida County, New York, 1790–1865* (New York: Cambridge University Press, 1981): 102.

[11] Ibid., 93.

[12] Curtis D. Johnson, *Islands of Holiness: Rural Religion in Upstate New York, 1790–1860*, (Ithaca, NY: Cornell University Press, 1989): 53–55.

[13] Ibid., 61–66.

might conclude that much the same meaning inhered in the evangelicalism of rural and urban areas. Through evangelicalism women expressed independent hopes for the future of themselves and their children.

Methodist Membership and the Distribution of Wealth

The assertion of individual independence and the transformation of the family were not the only dynamics at work in the expansion of Methodism in the Mendon-Lima area, however. In a rural society still rooted in household production and structured by principles of inherited wealth, relations of family were also economic relations. Judging from the church membership list, Methodism appealed to individuals from all economic levels. This included a number of individuals from families who owned no property, many who came from property-owning families of middling and upper ranks, and several who were substantial landowners. A few of these more wealthy members were interrelated through marriage and business partnerships. These interrelated families shared not only an interest in Methodism but a stake in the future development of the Lima-Mendon area as a place.

Problems of identification make a complete analysis of the distribution of wealth among church members in West Mendon impossible. To some extent, however, the absence of evidence is itself evidence. The inability to match the surname of a church member in census or tax lists probably indicates that the church member did not belong to a property-owning family. In addition to these "invisible" church members, several others apparently lacked wealth. Three church members with the name Ostrander, for example, probably belonged to the family of Cornelius Ostrander, who appears as a head of household in the Mendon census. No one by the name of Ostrander appears in Mendon tax lists, however. From this juxtaposition of evidence, it can be concluded that the Ostrander family resided in Mendon, at least for a time, but did not own property. Altogether, twenty-seven church members (31%) apparently came from propertyless families.[14]

If nearly a third of Methodist church members had little or no wealth, at least half came from families who did own taxable property. Of eighty-six church members, thirty-seven can be assigned with confidence to specific taxpaying households, and another nine individuals can be assigned to one of two households, both of which owned property in 1820.[15] Altogether, at least forty-six of the eighty-six members (53%) are known to come from property-owning families. As a group, these property-owning families occupied the

[14] "Early Members of the Methodist Church," 1820, "1820 Tax Lists" for Mendon, and "1820 Census" for Mendon.

[15] In some cases, more than one possible match for church members exists, and their property status cannot be determined. It is not certain, for example, whether the two church members by the name of Parmele belonged to the family of Smith Parmele in Lima or to that of James Morrison Parmele of Mendon. Whichever the case, however, the Parmele families all owned substantial property.

middling and upper ranks of local society. Most owned property valued above the mean for taxpaying families as a whole. In 1820, the average value of property owned by all Mendon's 295 taxpaying households was $781.65, and the median value was $558. By contrast, among the taxpaying church families, the mean property value was $1,581.73, and the median value was $1,622. Only five of these families owned property valued at less than the mean for all taxpaying families in town.[16]

More important than wealth of the families from which church members came was the use these members were able to make of their families' resources. Although more than half of all church members came from property-owning families, most of these members were household dependents who lacked legal identity or formal control of household capital. Many of the women and other household dependents who joined Methodist classes regularly contributed to what might be called the "operating funds" of Methodism – the quarterage and public collections that helped pay professional preachers' salaries. These contributions commonly took the form of household and agricultural products such as butter, candles, or beef, and of labor and services such as shoe-mending, tailoring, or domestic service that might be supplied by women as well as men.[17] When it came to formal incorporation and capitalization of a local church building, however, Methodist leaders, like those of other denominations, depended on the networks and financial resources of a narrower group of people – the small number of church members who were themselves property-owning heads of household. Of the eighty-six church members, only eleven people fit this description.[18]

Several of these property owners were interrelated through marriage and business. Among them were three Smith brothers – Francis, Eldrick, and James; two Sines brothers, Peter and John; and three brothers-in-law, Peter Sines, Jacob Young, and John Scramling. At the heart of this network were the daughters and sons-in-law of Zebulon Norton, who, in 1791, purchased the large tract of land that included the mill site later known as West Mendon or Norton's Mills. By marrying Norton's daughters, John Sines, John Scramling, and Jacob Young each acquired shares of Norton's original tract.[19] The network

---

[16] Figures based on analysis of property holding for all households in the "1820 Tax Lists" for Mendon.

[17] Evidence of the kinds of goods contributed for quarterage of Methodist ministers comes from an account of such items kept by Benajah Williams in the Journals of Benajah Williams, SDL, Vol. II, pp. 541–546.

[18] "Early Members of the Methodist Church," analyzed against "1820 Tax Lists" for Lima, Mendon, and Bloomfield. As might be expected, finding members in tax lists yields mostly male matches, but the church included one property-holding female, a Lima woman named Hannah Gates, who owned an estate valued at $1,412. Of the ten remaining property holders, only one owned property valued at less than the average for all taxpayers in town; all the rest were above average with respect to wealth. For the group as a whole, property values ranged from a low of $420, in the case of a man named John Sanger, to a high of $3,490 for the household of Peter Sines. The mean value was $1,869 and the median was $2,005.

[19] Information on the marriages and landholdings from Ham, "Migration to Mendon," 34–35 and 39–40.

of property-owning church members and their connections to local mill sites did not end with Norton's progeny, however. In addition to their connection with the Norton family through marriage, the two Sines brothers were also connected to the Smith family through business. John Sines' brother, Peter, had owned and operated a mill site in the town of Lima. After Peter died in 1818, John entered into a partnership with Francis Smith that eventually led to the sale of the mill site to Smith.[20]

Links between female evangelical networks and male economic power have been noted by scholars before. In their studies of the Chesapeake region, seaboard cities, and commercial towns in Pennsylvania and New York, Dee Andrews, Anthony Wallace, and Mary Ryan all point out multiple instances in which the wives of important merchants, bankers, and landowners in a locality played prominent roles in early revivals and evangelical organization, with or without the company of their husbands.[21] Andrews has further noted that a shift in the composition of Methodist church societies often occurred as they expanded in size and became more concerned with capitalization and institution building. In their infancy, Methodist societies were almost always dominated by women. Commonly, eight of ten members were female. In the cities and the Chesapeake region during the period of the early Republic, such societies were also often inclusive of African Americans and the poor. Once a society became concerned with formal incorporation and church building, however, this profile changed. According to Andrews, the larger a Methodist society became, "the more it emulated the power relations of the larger world and barred women from positions of power."[22] This pattern can be seen in the Lima-Mendon case.

Why Rich Men Are Necessary

To establish its standing in the temporal world, a church depended on men of affairs. In the Lima-Mendon area, one man in particular helped Methodism lay a temporal foundation: Francis Smith. In his diaries, the Reverend Benajah Williams made frequent reference to Smith as a "brother" with whom he consulted and spent time. As a traveling minister, Williams bore responsibility for cultivating lay leadership and for overseeing its exercise. In this capacity, Williams promoted Smith for the position of "local Preacher" on the Bloomfield Circuit in 1820 and observed Smith's work in class meetings and Sunday worship. On a Sunday in December 1820, for example, Williams reported that he "heard Br Francis Smith [preach] at the old school house." The text, according to Williams' notes, was "ye will not come unto me that ye

---

[20] Information on the lives, properties, and death dates of the Sines brothers from Ham, "Migration to Mendon," 35–36 and in the 1819 and 1820 "Tax Lists" for Lima.
[21] Andrews, *Methodists*, 100–105; Ryan, *Cradle of the Middle Class*, 102–103; and Anthony F. C. Wallace, *Rockdale: The Growth of an American Village in the Early Industrial Revolution* (New York: W. W. Norton, 1972): 22–37 and 101–113.
[22] Andrews, *The Methodists*, 112–122; quotation, p. 120.

might have life." Apparently, Smith performed well. "We had a precious time under preaching," Williams commented. "God was in our class meeting."[23] Over the next decade Williams made many other references to visiting Smith and consulting him over local church business. In 1825 Williams named one of his children "Francis Smith Williams."[24] Between 1820 and 1830, the two men worked closely to promote Methodism in the area.

Without any surviving evidence composed by Francis Smith himself, or even much in the way of indirect evidence about him and his family, it is difficult to know how to interpret his leadership in the West Mendon Church or his subsequent role in local Methodist institution building. We cannot know, for example, what attitude Smith assumed in his preaching, whether he was paternalistic or empathic, literal or inspired. We do know that Francis Smith's importance to local Methodism did not lie only in his spiritual leadership, however. It also derived from his position in the local economy. As a local landowner and businessman as well as a Methodist, Smith would prove to be a valuable agent of capitalization for the church. In 1820 he took the lead in raising funds for the construction of the first Methodist chapel in Mendon. Several years later, in 1827, he and his family were instrumental in raising funds for a second Methodist chapel in Lima. In 1830, when Lima residents raised a successful bid for the site of a Methodist academy, the Smith family again played a leading role.

To succeed in raising funds for capital projects, it helped to have capital oneself. Local tax records show that in 1820 Francis Smith had four sets of local property holdings in the three contiguous towns of Lima, Mendon, and Bloomfield, including shares in two mill sites.[25] With these holdings, Smith and his family were well-posed for the promotion of economic development. Ownership of a mill site substantially increased the value of a landowner's property holdings. For centuries, simple water mills had provided a means for landowners to earn commercial incomes from fixed capital. With such mills, landholders could convert raw logs and cereal crops into marketable lumber and grain. These processed goods could then be accumulated, stored, and transported to commercial markets elsewhere. There they would be exchanged for goods, cash, or other forms of liquid capital. In this way, a mill site turned the product of a farmer's agricultural labor into money, adding to the wealth he held in land.[26]

This was just the beginning of a mill site's value, however. A mill enabled a landowner to realize income not only on the product of his own labors, but on that of his neighbors as well. In medieval Europe, the primary producers of

---

[23] Journals of Benajah Williams, Vol. I, p. 177, Sunday, December 3, 1820.
[24] Ham, "Migration to Mendon," 171–172.
[25] Ibid.
[26] On the early history and significance of mills, see Fernand Braudel, *Civilization and Capitalism, 15th to 18th Century* (New York: Harper and Row, 1979), Vol. I: *The Structures of Everyday Life: The Limits of the Possible*, 353–362 and Vol. III: *The Perspective of the World*, 544–548.

agricultural goods were peasants or tenants, who surrendered substantial portions of any goods they milled as rent or tillage to the landlord who owned the mill. In the Hudson and Mohawk Valley regions of eastern New York State, a version of this manorial system continued well into the nineteenth century. As late as the 1840s, tenants in Dutchess, Schoharie, Otsego, and Delaware Counties paid annual quit-rents in the form of agricultural produce to proprietors like the Livingstons, van Cortlandts, and Coopers, with whom they held lifetime leases.[27] In western New York, by contrast, the sale of large tracts of lands seized after the Revolutionary War transformed the tenancy system into a more market-based agricultural economy. The speculators who purchased land from the state resold it on terms that effectively maintained their proprietary claim to annual income from the land, even as they redefined the nature of the relationship between the proprietor and the farmer. Instead of holding land leases, men of modest means contracted with speculators to purchase landholdings under long-term mortgage agreements. These agreements still required that farmers surrender a share of the product of their labors to the proprietor in the form of land payments, but they offered the prospect of eventual land ownership.[28] As in the past, mills provided landowners with the mechanical means necessary to realize income from the "surplus" labor and goods of others, although the landowners did so in the capacity of land sellers rather than in that of landlords.

In a tenancy system, the mill owner's claim to a share of farmers' produce derived from his ownership of the land and came to him by custom or contract. Similarly, under the mortgage sales agreements common to early land speculation, a mill owner enjoyed extraordinary leverage over farmers as their primary creditor in a situation where farmers had few alternative means of trade. In a situation where farmers owned their land outright, however, or purchased it with less extortionate mortgages from their own family, friends, or connections, the position of the mill owner changed. It was no longer ownership of the land but access to markets that gave a mill owner claim to the product of farmers' labors. Even when farmers owned their land outright, they still depended on local mills to process goods, and often also on local mill owners to transport and sell those goods on the market. In exchange for such services, a mill owner took a share of income from producers' goods. Now the mill owner earned income as a processor/merchant rather than as a landlord or speculator. In effect, the market liberated capitalism from the land. It enabled mill owners like the Smiths to earn income from farm labor even in the absence of substantial landholdings of their own.

---

[27] Thomas Summerhill, "Farming on Shares: Landlords, Tenants, and the Rise of the Hope and Dairy Economies in Central New York," *New York History* 76:2 (April 1995): 125–152; Sung Bok Kim, *Landlord and Tenant in Colonial New York: Manorial Society, 1664–1775* (Chapel Hill: University of North Carolina Press, 1978).
[28] Neil Adams McNall, *An Agricultural History of the Genesee Valley, 1790–1860* (Philadelphia: University of Pennsylvania Press, 1952): 32–65.

To gain this income, however, a mill owner had to win the trade of his neighbors. As it did not come to him by manorial custom or mortgage contract, trade had to be developed. This is where Smith's position in the local economy and his position in the local Methodist church came together. Social networks were important for the development of trade. When Francis Smith formed a business partnership with the Sines of Mendon, he extended the Smith family's trade networks in the Lima-Mendon area. Over the next ten years, Smith and his family expanded their business, drawing trade from the three towns of Lima, Mendon, and Bloomfield and developing the hamlet at North Bloomfield into a multi-mill settlement sometimes referred to as "Smithtown."[29] The Smiths' owed this accomplishment to Methodism as well as to the mills themselves. As a local Methodist preacher, Francis Smith helped the traveling ministry develop the Bloomfield Circuit. This involved rotating among the Methodist classes in his area, exhorting new members, and providing regular Sunday preaching. As just one of several local preachers on the circuit, Francis Smith was charged with visiting a portion of its territory. In 1820, this commission included the towns of Lima and Mendon as well as a portion of the town of Bloomfield. Through his visits, Smith cultivated relationships with fellow Methodists, some of whom became clients of his mills. He also raised funds for the quarterage and capital projects of the church.[30] He thus promoted the growth of his trade at the same time as he promoted the growth of the Bloomfield Circuit.

The construction of the first Methodist chapel in West Mendon jumpstarted this relationship. When local Methodists set about "raising" the chapel in 1820, Francis Smith took the lead in collecting subscriptions for the project. This role immediately put him in the position of creditor with respect to the church's subscribers. It also stimulated trade between Smith and his neighbors. When subscribers pledged to contribute to a building project, they often stated both the cash value of their pledge and the goods or services with which they expected to make payments, such as "$5 in team work," "$50 in produce," "$6 in cash," or "one pair fine boots." In some cases, the goods or services might be directly applicable to building construction, such as pledges of "lathe" or "painting."[31] In other cases, the value of the subscription would have to be realized through trade. The role of the collector in this situation was not only to collect the pledges but to render them useful for building. This

---

[29] Mabel Furner Jencks, "Lima 1788–1964: Outline of the History of Lima Written for the 175th Anniversary Celebration" (n.p., 1964): 39.

[30] An understanding of the operations of Methodist circuits generally, and of the Bloomfield Circuit in particular, is derived from the Journals of Benajah Williams; the "Bloomfield Circuit Book, Genesee Conference, 1828–1880," CUDRMC; and from a number of other Methodist circuit books held by MMC, MAHC, and WNYCRA.

[31] These specific quotations come from the subscription for the construction of the Methodist Church in Lima, 1827–1829, transcribed and kept in the "Methodist Church" file, LTH. A portion of the same subscription list was published in an undated and unattributed newspaper article, circa 1950, on p. 79 of "Avon Scrapbook #4, LCHO.

he could do in one of two ways. He could exchange the pledges with other local households for the materials and labor actually needed for construction. Or, in the case of marketable produce such as grain, he could convert goods into cash by trading them on the market. This option was facilitated for Smith by his capacity to process produce at his mill and incorporate the trade into his business. In any case, however, the collector effectively absorbed the subscriptions into his own accounts and served as a broker in the building process. For these brokerage services he earned a customary fee, or rate of interest, on his collections.[32] The construction of the chapel in West Mendon thus contributed to Smith's economic power both by adding directly to his income and by extending his trade relationships.

These relationships extended not only to people within the church but beyond them to other people in the local area. When Francis Smith raised and collected subscriptions for construction of the Methodist chapel, he did not limit his solicitations to fellow Methodists. A surviving receipt shows, for example, that in 1823 Matthew Warner paid a $5 pledge to Francis Smith "for construction of the Methodist chapel in Mendon."[33] Warner was not a Methodist. Nor did he reside in Mendon. Rather, he was a leading member of the congregational society in Lima. He was also a member of the leading landholding family in Lima and an important local political leader. In soliciting support from Matthew Warner, Francis Smith asserted his position as a fellow property owner and man of influence. Building the Methodist chapel helped to solidify this status.

Even as church building proved valuable to the Smiths, the Smiths proved valuable to Methodism. Officially, the Methodist Church regarded the construction of church buildings with ambivalence, precisely because such capital projects tended to make the church solicitous of wealthy members. Francis Asbury, the founding father of North American Methodism, warned church leaders as early as 1796 that the building of preaching houses was fraught with difficulties, for "you will make rich men necessary and they will rule you and impede your discipline if you are not well aware."[34] By 1813, this warning had been codified in Methodist doctrine. "Let all our churches be built plain and decent; but not more expensive than is absolutely unavoidable," the *Discipline* specified; "otherwise the necessity of raising money will make rich men necessary to us."[35] Nonetheless, as Asbury and other Methodist leaders acknowledged privately and demonstrated in their own careers, when it came to church building, "rich" men *were* necessary to Methodism, as to any other

---

[32] This description of how the subscription collection process worked is based on examination of numerous subscription records in archives and historical collections throughout the states of Vermont and New York.

[33] According to a surviving bill and receipt signed by Francis Smith, Warner pledged and paid a modest $5 for the "construction of the Methodist chapel in Mendon." "Bill and receipt from Francis Smith to M. Warner," May 28, 1823 (Wrb 113), Warner Papers, LHS.

[34] Quoted from Asbury correspondence in Andrews, *The Methodists*, 159.

[35] *Doctrines and Discipline*, 181.

denomination.³⁶ This necessity lay not only, or perhaps even primarily, in the funds that such men contributed to church building themselves, or even in the legal and political standing they provided. Rather, it lay in the leverage that men of wealth exercised in local economies. Not only did mill owners like the Smiths have the mechanical means to convert surplus labor and goods into capital, they also had the influence necessary to command and collect pledges of support. Without them – specifically, without the leverage necessary to command goods and labor of others and to convert goods and labor to use – church building would be, if not quite impossible, certainly much less successful.

Evangelicalism and Economic Development

Many scholars have studied the apparent association between evangelicalism and economic development in the late eighteenth and early nineteenth centuries. A number of these studies focus on the demography of church membership.³⁷ Beyond counting the numbers of capitalists and laborers who participated in evangelical religion, most studies emphasize the ideological dimensions of conversion. From this perspective, the economic significance of evangelicalism lay primarily in how it shaped the way people thought about the shift from household to capitalist production, from family to wage labor. In his classic study of the British working class from 1790 to 1830, for example, the historian E. P. Thompson argued that the culture and practice of Methodism was crucial in shaping the responses of artisans, dispossessed peasants, and textile workers to the transformation of the British economy. Both the individual discipline and the social organization of Methodism were important in this respect. The discipline helped to provide workers with a sense of agency and order in otherwise unsettled conditions, while the social organization of the church provided a system of mutual support and, occasionally, a base of resistance to economic change. Methodism, in other words, was an essential historical component in forming the consciousness of the English working class.³⁸

Influenced to some degree by Thompson's work, scholars of the Second Great Awakening in the United States have developed somewhat similar lines of interpretation. For the most part, however, they have emphasized the logic of evangelicalism from the perspective of the capitalist, rather than from that

---

[36] Andrews, *The Methodists*, 159–161.
[37] Wallace, *Rockdale*; Paul E. Johnson, *A Shopkeeper's Millennium: Society and Revivals in Rochester, New York, 1815–1837* (New York: Hill and Wang, 1978); Ryan, *Cradle of the Middle Class*; Andrews, *The Methodists*, 155–183; and John H Wigger, "Fighting Bees: Methodist Itinerants and the Dynamics of Methodist Growth, 1770–1820," in Nathan Hatch and John H. Wigger, eds, *Methodism and the Shaping of American Culture* (Nashville: Kingswood Books, 2001): 87–133.
[38] E. P. Thompson, *The Making of the English Working Class* (New York: Vintage Books, 1966 [1963]).

of the laborer. In their studies of Rockdale, Pennsylvania, and Rochester, New York, for example, Anthony F. C. Wallace and Paul E. Johnson interpreted the evangelicalism of the Second Great Awakening as providing capitalist shopkeepers and mill owners with a cultural tool for maximizing the production of labor.[39] According to this analysis, the culture of individual discipline and improvement promoted by evangelicalism absolved capitalists of responsibility for workers' welfare. In the new, market-based culture, workers' welfare depended on their own efforts and characters, rather than on their superiors' fulfillment of obligations inherent in relationships of mutual dependence. At the same time, evangelical culture increased the leverage of capitalist owners over their workers, as church membership and its associated discipline increasingly became a qualification for employment.

To some extent, these conclusions reflect the general demography of sites scholars have chosen to study. Most studies focus on commercial towns or cities, where mechanics and shopkeepers composed high proportions of the population. Few comparable studies of rural areas have been done, in part because the sources necessary for systematic analysis of economic relations are not as available for rural as for urban areas before 1840.[40] The Lima-Mendon case provides an opportunity to examine the relationship between evangelicalism and economic development in a rural context, albeit with typical source limitations.

Without directly challenging findings from urban studies, the Lima-Mendon case suggests that a focus on the relationship between capital and labor is insufficient to explain the connection between evangelicalism and economic development. For starters, there is a problem of chronology. In the Lima-Mendon case, evangelical activity *preceded* the employment of large numbers of wage laborers in manufacturing. Early mills were about exchanging the product of agricultural labor – not about wage labor or factory-style production. The development of factory-style mills that employed numbers of mill workers in the Lima-Mendon area occurred in the period from 1827 to 1837, while evangelical activity originated in the period from before 1820. A second problem is one of demography. A third of the members of the Methodist church in 1820 were from propertyless families, and may well have worked as domestic or agricultural laborers. The majority of early Methodists, however, were from agricultural households with above-average landholdings. They were, in other words, neither wage laborers nor merchant capitalists, but members of farm families who owned their own means of production. Eventually, evangelicalism may have helped some local manufacturers shape a culture of wage work, but it does not make sense to explain the origins of evangelical activity in this context primarily in terms of the relationship between capital and labor.

---

[39] Wallace, *Rockdale*; Johnson, *A Shopkeeper's Millennium*.
[40] The 1820 census includes a basic count of the number of people involved in agriculture, commerce, and manufacturing, but specific occupations are not identified, making the results difficult to interpret. Urban studies for periods before 1840 often rely on city directories, a source that does not exist for rural areas.

Still, it cannot be denied that Methodism and economic development were closely intertwined in the Lima-Mendon case. The falls on Honeoye Creek were a significant source of water power and a frequent incubator of new economic activity. They were also a site of early Methodism. A number of the same people took the lead in both early Methodism and early development. This may have included Zebulon Norton, the original owner of the West Mendon mill site and an early miller and merchant of local grain, who died in 1815. It certainly included Smith Weeks, the first professional Methodist preacher in the area, who, according to local histories, built a long frame building in West Mendon in 1815 from which he ran a "cloth-dressing establishment." It also included Norton's son-in-law, Jacob Young, who in 1821 purchased the Weeks' operation and developed it as a carding and fulling mill.[41] In the years immediately following completion of the chapel at West Mendon in 1823, Methodist mill owners at both the West Mendon and North Bloomfield sites invested in expanded mill operations. Zebulon Norton's grandson, Lyman Norton, built a new mill at the West Mendon site (known as Norton's Mills) in 1824 before selling out to go west. At the same time, the Smith family enlarged its mills at the North Bloomfield site (later known as Smithtown).[42]

This pattern of give and take between Methodism and economic development challenges us to look further for theories of connection between evangelicalism and the capitalist transition. The Lima-Mendon case suggests three such relationships. The first is that evangelicalism contributed to the formation of capital as well as to the formation of a capitalist culture. Although no personal financial records survive to detail the impact of the Smith family's Methodist fundraising activity on their household finances, the method of fundraising and the chronology of events suggest a link between this activity and subsequent capital investment. By raising subscriptions and brokering trade for local church building, Francis Smith commanded surplus goods and labor from his neighbors, converted that surplus into useable corporate capital, and accumulated a share of the surplus for his own household. This fundraising activity added to the Smiths' income and capital not only through the commissions they earned directly on such collections, but also by stimulating further trade with fellow Methodists and other local residents. With the surplus earned from trade and collections, the Smiths then went on to invest in further mill development. Considered in this light, the economic significance of Methodism lay not in the ideology of conversion, but in the formation of capital itself.

---

[41] Information on Weeks' and Young's associations with these establishments from Ham, "Migration to Mendon," 39–40 and 95–96. These early establishments were not factories, but more like shops or trade stores. They did not produce goods themselves but performed services for independent household producers. In the case of a carding and fulling mill, for example, domestic producers took raw wool to the mill to prepare it for spinning at home, and then returned with woven cloth for fulling or finishing.

[42] Information on the history of mills in the area drawn primarily from Diane Ham, "Mills," and Mabel Jencks, "Lima," with corroboration and detail from miscellaneous other sources.

A second relationship, closely related to the first, is that evangelicalism contributed to the organization of local economies. It is likely that women as well as men contributed to this organizing process. As historians Laurel Thatcher Ulrich and Joan Jensen have shown, rural women at the beginning of the nineteenth century commonly directed labor and trade in certain aspects of household production. Especially during the Revolution and the War of 1812, international trade embargoes stimulated women's involvement in domestic textile production, but women's economic activity could also include extensive dairy operations and the manufacture of other domestic goods.[43] Women employed the labor of other women in various stages of production, traded the product of their labors as well as labor with other households, and maintained formal or informal accounts of such transactions.[44] In some cases, women managed wider trade networks than did male heads of household.[45] Surviving records for the Lima-Mendon case do not permit a precise analysis of female economic activity, but they do show that women contributed to preacher support in their own names.[46] Beyond that, the case provides interesting grounds for speculation. Given the patterns that Ulrich detailed for other places, it is possible that in the mid-1810s the Norton women constituted a textile production network, and that Smith Weeks, the Methodist preacher, processed their goods at his "cloth dressing establishment." In any case, rural women as a rule contributed to the production of goods and accumulation of household wealth that made church building possible. From this perspective, the connection between female evangelicalism and male economic power was mutually reinforcing. Men and women played important roles in the organization of production and trade necessary for both economic development and church building.

But there is more to economic growth than the formation of capital and the organization of trade. In order for surplus labor and goods to amount to much, they have to come from multiple households. Economic development requires, in other words, a kind of collective economy. The manorial system was one model for such a collective. In that system, landlords claim shares of production from multiple households based on their ownership of land. Corporations provide another model of collective economy. In that model, individual households accumulate their own household capital but voluntarily contribute surplus labor and goods to corporations in pursuit of common aims. For ordinary men and women living in the 1810s and 1820s, church

---

[43] Joan M. Jensen, *Loosening the Bonds: Mid-Atlantic Farm Women, 1750–1850* (New Haven, CT: Yale University Press, 1986); Laurel Thatcher Ulrich, *A Midwife's Tale: The Life of Marta Ballard, Based on Her Diary, 1785–1812* (New York: Vintage, 1991); idem., *The Age of Homespun: Objects and Stories in the Creation of an American Myth* (New York: Random House, 2001).

[44] Ulrich, *Homespun*.

[45] Ulrich makes this particularly clear in her analysis of contacts between Martha Ballard and other households in *A Midwife's Tale*, 92–93 and 111.

[46] Journals of Benajah Williams.

and school societies were the primary means of corporate action. Through the familiar practice of church organization, men and women forged a sense of corporate identity and collective purpose. They then projected a common future and pledged the financial capital necessary to make that future real. The third, and perhaps most important, economic effect of evangelicalism, in other words, was the creation of social and financial capital on which subsequent acts of corporate community building and economic development could draw. Among these acts was the founding of what became the largest educational institution in New York State for a time, the Methodist-sponsored Genesee Wesleyan Seminary of Lima.

PART II

SCHOOLS AS AGENCIES OF POLITICIZATION

7

Between Markets and the State – Venture Schools and Academies

> It is propos'd, THAT some Persons of Leisure and publick Spirit, apply for a CHARTER, by which they may be incorporated, with power to erect an ACADEMY for the Education of Youth, to govern the same, provide Masters, make Rules, receive donations, purchase Lands, & c. and to add to their Number, from Time to Time such other Persons as they shall judge suitable....
>
> Benjamin Franklin, *Proposals Relating to the Education of Youth in Pensilvania*, 1749[1]

During the dramatic political changes of the early republican era – a period in which political agency was initially property-based but eventually expanded to encompass universal white male suffrage – schools were important agencies of civic engagement and politicization. In 1790, most schooling in the United States occurred without direct state intervention, either on the market, as the businesses of entrepreneurial teachers, or under the sponsorship of churches and voluntary associations, as subscription schools. In 1840, by contrast, some form of state-sponsored schooling had been established in every northern state. In the interim, states experimented with various ways of "encouraging" education. In many states, academies were the first schools – even before common schools – to receive state support. To understand why this might be so, it helps to consider what academies meant in the context of early republican culture. In their independence from established church authority and their responsiveness to popular demand expressed through the market, they embodied certain revolutionary principles. At the same time, as corporate institutions, academies represented more than the private interests of a few individual teachers. They were the product of voluntary initiative and coordinated social action. Given this combination of revolutionary independence and demonstrated social capital, many states chose to provide their first support for education in the form of subsidies to such

---

[1] Benjamin Franklin, *Proposals Relating to the Education of Youth in Pensilvania* (Phildaelphia: Franklin and Hall, 1749), facsimile reprint (Philadelphia: University of Pennsylvania, 1931): 6–7.

schools. In doing so, they also effectively tied the constituencies who supported those schools to the larger political economy. Historically and theoretically, in other words, academies mediated between markets and the state.

This chapter explores the academy idea as it developed in British North America in the early republican era, and as it was embodied by specific institutions in New York prior to 1828.[2] Academies emerged in the mid-eighteenth century in a context of thriving venture school markets and disestablishment politics. In colonial cities and towns, as in Britain itself, a growing commercial class of craftsmen, shopkeepers, merchants, and middling farmers expressed increasing popular demand for instruction in a range of English and practical subjects on a pay-as-you-go basis. Entrepreneurial schools and teachers of all kinds responded to this popular demand. In the process they put competitive pressure on the tradition of classical education and the existence of Latin grammar schools, which had often enjoyed established church and/or government support. Academies responded to this competitive education market, bringing the kinds of instruction offered by Latin grammar schools and English venture schools together in one place. At the same time, academies reflected the politics of colonial independence and religious disestablishment. During the Revolutionary period, religious dissenters and advocates of political independence directly challenged established authority by rejecting colonial affiliations with the established Church of England, including the Church's sponsorship of leading educational institutions. In their place, new institutions, or newly transformed institutions, were founded on disestablishment terms. Academies came to embody those principles. A close look at the practice and principles of academy organization in this period illuminates the norms on which residents of Lima drew in founding their own institution in 1830, as well as those from which they departed.

Definitions and Distinctions

To understand the educational landscape into which the academy at Lima eventually emerged requires a high tolerance for conceptual chaos. Current distinctions among elementary, secondary, and higher education are not very useful for understanding late eighteenth- and early nineteenth-century schooling, because many institutions offered all these levels of instruction. Most academies enrolled at least a third of their students in elementary subjects, even as they also instructed students at a level equivalent to collegiate study. Neither is subject matter a reliable institutional marker. Although distinctions

---

[2] This chronology focuses on British North America. If French and Spanish colonial territories are included, the date of the first academy could arguably be extended back to at least 1727, with the founding of the Ursuline Academy of New Orleans, though the nature of the charter issued in that case is unclear and may distinguish it somewhat from the sense in which academy is defined here. On the Ursuline Academy, see Clark Robenstine, "French Colonial Policy and the Education of Women and Minorities: Louisiana in the Early 18th Century," *History of Education Quarterly* 32:2 (Summer 1992): 193–211.

between Latin or classical courses and English study existed, these distinctions did not map neatly onto institutions, as many schools offered a wide variety of subjects depending on the demands of students and the skills of instructors. Nor do school names provide much in the way of guidance. None of the terms used to identify schools in this period had settled definitions, and both the number of terms and the variations in their use were great. Given these inconsistencies, historians seeking to distinguish among institutions have developed their own classification systems.

Surveying the range of schools operating in the United States in the late eighteenth and early nineteenth centuries, historian Kim Tolley identified four broad categories of schools based on the nature of their sponsorship rather than on the level or content of instruction. These four categories are church schools, town schools, venture schools, and academies.[3] "Church schools," as the term implies, were schools that operated under the auspices of a church or parish. These included charity or mission schools dedicated to serving poor children and/or designated populations (i.e., Native Americans or African Americans), often in cities, as well as church-sponsored pay schools for children of all classes. Often ministers took in students on a fee basis to augment their salaries as preachers. To the extent that the ministers themselves were subject to governance by a church hierarchy (in the case of Anglican parishes) or a local church council (in the case of congregational churches), so were the schools they operated. The original "brick school" in Lima functioned on these terms. "Town schools," by contrast, were governed by elected political officials. In the eighteenth and early nineteenth centuries this meant governance by the property owners who were eligible to vote and assume office. Like the district schools that operated in Lima under New York's common school laws after 1815, these schools were funded by some combination of taxation, in-kind contributions, and supplementary rate bills or fees.

Both church and town schools could offer instruction in higher level subjects as well as in basic reading, writing, and arithmetic, and many did. In the early colonial period, the dominant model of schooling beyond the elementary level was that of the classical grammar school. Schools that followed this model instructed male students in the study of Latin grammar, with perhaps some attention to mathematics and Greek. Many such schools were funded in part through taxes or tithes and taught by ministers, although some classical schools operated on an entrepreneurial basis and a few received colonial charters. In Massachusetts, colonial laws required that towns of a certain size maintain a Latin grammar school at local expense. Historians have found, however, that by the mid-eighteenth century these laws were more often defied than enforced, as parents demanded a greater share of tax support for common English instruction of students of all ages and both sexes. As a practical

---

[3] Kim Tolley, "Mapping the Landscape of Higher Schooling, 1727–1850," in Nancy Beadie and Kim Tolley, eds. *Chartered Schools: Two Hundred Years of Independent Academies in the United States, 1727–1925* (New York: Routledge/Falmer, 2002): 19–43.

matter, only larger cities or wealthy towns like Boston and Northampton, Massachusetts, had the client base and political constituency necessary to maintain distinct Latin schools at public expense.⁴ Most schools that offered classical instruction did so in conjunction with teaching basic English subjects, in which the majority of students enrolled.

A "venture school," as defined by Tolley, was an entrepreneurial school that operated as the household business of an individual teacher and his or her family. Venture schools depended entirely on tuition for support and were shaped directly by market supply and demand. The difference in character and clientele between a town-sponsored Latin school and a venture school is famously illustrated by the case of Benjamin Franklin. Franklin early demonstrated the aptitude and inclination for serious study, which his father, who was a chandler, initially encouraged by sending him to Boston's Latin grammar school. Despite Franklin's rapid progress through the Latin curriculum, however, his father soon determined that he could not afford to continue his son's classical education. The problem was not the cost of grammar school itself, but that of college, which would be necessary before Franklin could earn a decent return on his father's investment. Even then, as his father noted, many a college-educated man earned a mean living. After less than a year of study, then, Franklin's father withdrew him from the Latin school and sent him to a "school for Writing & Arithmetic" kept by a well-regarded independent teacher, Mr. George Brownell. There, Franklin improved his writing before being placed in an apprenticeship.⁵ Mr. Brownell's school, which Franklin attended for just a few months during the winter of 1715–1716, was a venture school. It was, in other words, a household trade or business that Brownell operated on entrepreneurial terms. Unlike the teachers at Boston's Latin school, Brownell did not report to a committee of municipal overseers. Nor did he earn a salary set by the city and guaranteed by local taxes.⁶ Rather, he depended for his living on student fees paid directly by parents.

According to Franklin's description, Mr. Brownell was known primarily for teaching writing and arithmetic, but he may have taught other subjects as well. In 1743, for example, the *Philadelphia Gazette* included advertisements for several venture schools, including one for Mr. Charles Fortesque, who

... offers to teach at his home in the alley commonly called Mr. Taylors, the Latin Tongue, English in a Grammatical Manner, Navigation, Surveying, Mensuration, Dialling,

---

⁴ On Latin Schools in Boston and Northampton, see William J. Reese, *The Origins of the American High School* (New Haven, CT: Yale University, 1995): 1–15; David Tyack and Elisabeth Hansot, *Learning Together: A History of Coeducation in American Public Schools* (New York: Yale University Russell Sage Foundation, 1990): 13–27; and Kathryn Kish Sklar, "The Schooling of Girls and Changing Community Values in Massachusetts Towns, 1750–1820," *History of Education Quarterly* 33:4 (Winter 1993), 511–542.

⁵ Benjamin Franklin, *The Autobiography* (New York: Vintage Books, 1990): 9.

⁶ Ibid. For a description of how the Boston Latin School operated, see Reese, *Origins*, 1–15.

Geography, Use of the Globes, the Gentleman's Astronomy, Chronology, Arithmetic, Merchants Accounting, etc. The above to be taught at night school as well as Day.[7]

As this advertisement indicates, the subject matter and even the timing of instruction depended on student demand and could include anything from classics, to English grammar, to sciences and applied studies.

Many – perhaps most – eighteenth-century venture schools enrolled both male and female students, though certain schools did specialize in education of one sex, especially those designed for children of the upper classes. Coeducational enrollment did not necessarily mean coeducational classes, however. Tolley quotes an advertisement for Robert Leeth's school in the *New York Gazette-Weekly Post Boy* in 1751, which offered instruction to both sexes in "two handsome Rooms, with Fire-places, the one for the Boys and the other for Girls."[8] In this case, the instruction of female students probably occurred under the direction of Leeth's wife or another female member of the family, while he and/or his sons or other male assistants instructed the male students. Female teachers also operated their own schools, sometimes in the household of a husband or father, and sometimes as heads of household in their own right.[9]

Eighteenth-century venture schools drew students from a wide range of social class backgrounds, sometimes separately and sometimes on a mixed basis. Certain schools catered to social elites, emphasizing, for example, the manners and social connections that could be acquired by young women at exclusive households. Other schools catered to servants, clerks, and other workers by offering basic and applied subjects during early morning or evening hours. At the same time, venture schools also provided the dominant school experience for children of the urban middle classes, which in the eighteenth century consisted primarily of mechanics and craftsmen.

The historian Carl Kaestle has demonstrated this point with respect to New York City in the 1790s. Tracing the families of students who attended one of the city's 91 known venture schools in 1796, Kaestle found that the school enrolled a relatively wide variety of students with respect to both religion and social background.[10] From his analysis, Kaestle concluded that venture

---

[7] Cited in Edward Potts Cheyney, *History of the University of Pennsylvania, 1740–1940* (Philadelphia: University of Pennsylvania Press, 1940): 14.
[8] Tolley, "Mapping," 24.
[9] In his comprehensive study of New York City schooling in the 1790s, Carl Kaestle identified 31 female teachers of venture schools in 1796, as compared with 60 male teachers for the same year. Carl F. Kaestle, *The Evolution of an Urban School System: New York City, 1750–1850* (Cambridge, MA: Harvard University Press, 1973): Table 3, p. 39.
[10] Ibid., pp. 41–55. At one end of the spectrum, the families of 40% of the students identified owned no real estate and slightly less than half of these (or 18% of the total) owned neither real nor personal property. In these cases, the heads of household included a mariner, a widow, an oyster picker, a shoemaker, and a tobacconist. At the other end of the spectrum, the father of one of the students was an Episcopalian grocer with real estate valued at 2,800 British pounds and an additional 200 pounds of personal estate. With respect to religion, the majority of students identified were from families who were either Dutch Reformed or

schools (which he called "independent pay schools") effectively *were* the common schools of the city in the early republican era. By this he meant several things: that most urban children who attended school in this period attended venture schools; that they did so on a mixed-class basis; that venture schools were the dominant school experience for the common or middle class person; and that they taught common subjects. Extrapolating from precise enrollment data for 19 of the 91 known venture schools in 1796, Kaestle estimated that venture schools enrolled a total of 4,760 students, or 47 percent of an estimated 10,043 children between the ages of 5 and 15 in the city's population that year, a large proportion considering the sporadic school attendance patterns of children in this era.[11]

It was in this context of flourishing venture schools that the academy of the late eighteenth and early nineteenth centuries emerged. An "academy," as defined by Tolley, was an incorporated institution that operated under the authority of a state charter and was governed by a self-perpetuating board of trustees. Although still highly dependent on student fees, these schools also held title to some form of corporate property that provided financial support beyond that of tuition. They thus enjoyed a degree of insulation from the market as compared with venture schools. To the extent that academies are defined as corporate institutions, their origins can be dated fairly precisely to the period after 1750. According to most accounts, the first such institutions in the British American colonies were the Academy of Philadelphia, chartered in 1751, and New Bern Academy of North Carolina, first chartered in 1764. In New York, the first was Kingston Academy, founded in 1774, with others following soon after the Revolution. Since these institutions endured and left records, they provide a basis for considering what the term "academy" meant at the time.

An Amalgamation of Schools

In the Philadelphia case, the idea of an academy is famously laid out in Benjamin Franklin's plan for the institution, which he published in 1749 on behalf of the organizing trustees as *Proposals Relating to the Education of Youth in Pensilvania*. Perhaps the most elaborate statement of the academy idea ever written, Franklin's *Proposals* highlights two characteristics of academies: corporate governance and curricular breadth. With respect to the benefits of

---

Episcopalian, but the list also included a Presbyterian and a Catholic, indicating a degree of religious diversity that exceeded that of church-based charity schools at the time. Given that the teacher in this case was himself Episcopalian, owned real estate valued well above 1,000 pounds, and charged at the upper end of the (albeit still modest) tuition scale for all teachers reporting that year, this profile of venture school students would presumably be biased, if at all, toward propertied families. Certainly, the families of cartmen, mariners, and day laborers were underrepresented at this school. Nonetheless, the results suggest that a mix of children attended venture schools.

[11] Ibid., Table 10, p. 52.

corporate governance, the document was explicit. After a few introductory paragraphs suitably lauding the value of education to society and civilization, the organizers went on to state their practical objectives:

> It is propos'd, THAT some Persons of Leisure and publick Spirit, apply for a CHARTER, by which they may be incorporated, with power to erect an ACADEMY for the Education of Youth, to govern the same, provide Masters, make Rules, receive donations, purchase Lands, & c. and to add to their Number, from Time to Time such other Persons as they shall judge suitable.[12]

As indicated here, a central benefit of incorporation was the power it conferred to acquire corporate property – that is, to receive donations, purchase lands, and erect a building. The *Proposals* themselves were drafted precisely for these purposes, as Franklin explained in his autobiography. Having distributed his pamphlet to inhabitants of the city for free, Franklin waited until he supposed "their Minds a little prepared by the Perusal of it," and then "set on foot a Subscription for Opening and Supporting an Academy."[13] Once sufficient pledges had been collected, the organizers hired a house, engaged masters, enrolled students, and began searching for a piece of real estate to purchase for a more permanent home for the institution. Incorporation served as a tool for accomplishing these practical tasks.

With this authority over financial matters came authority to determine the structure of the institution and the content of instruction. In the *Proposals*, Franklin and his associates outlined a list of studies for the projected academy, including the subjects of penmanship, writing, drawing, English grammar, and arithmetic usually taught at urban "writing schools" such as the one Franklin himself had attended as a boy; advanced English subjects such as geography, history, composition, and rhetoric taught in English grammar schools; classical languages characteristic of Latin grammar schools; and modern languages, bookkeeping, geometry, astronomy, and other applied subjects often taught at urban venture schools and considered useful for merchants, navigators and surveyors. As indicated by this list, the organizers of the Academy of Philadelphia conceived of the institution as offering a broad range of instruction. In his autobiography, Franklin described the academy as a sort of umbrella organization for the operation of multiple "schools." According to his account, when the first board of trustees had drafted and signed a constitution and had hired the first masters, "the Schools opened."[14] Similarly, a few years later, when a large existing building had been purchased and refitted for the academy, the facilities were divided into different rooms "for the several schools," including, among others, "a Free School for the Instruction of poor children."[15] The image that emerges is of a single building

---

[12] Franklin, *Proposals*, 6–7.
[13] Franklin, *Autobiography*, 114–116.
[14] Ibid., 114.
[15] Ibid., 115.

housing an association of schools and schoolmasters, each with its own area of emphasis and expertise.

This image puts an interesting spin on a characteristic that has long been associated with academies: their curricular breadth. Historians of education and biographers of Franklin have often emphasized the attention to nonclassical study in the *Proposals*. The document includes an extended discussion of the importance of learning English composition and of the relative value of classical and modern languages for various occupations. In Franklin's analysis, all foreign languages were to some degree "ornamental" accomplishments, while English, arithmetic, and other English subjects were necessary studies, not to be neglected in favor of the classics. Given the ornamental character of foreign languages, Franklin concluded that students should not be compelled to learn Latin and Greek, but neither should any be excluded from studying them. From these passages and from his ultimately unsuccessful attempt to name an English master head of the school, Franklin is typically portrayed as an educational reformer, critical of the emphasis on the classics that had traditionally dominated the higher branches of education.[16] This characterization of Franklin is entirely warranted. For the purpose of understanding the origins and common characteristics of early academies, however, the important point is not the extent to which the institution Franklin proposed departed from the traditional classical school, but the extent to which the academy described by Franklin was an amalgamation of existing school models, including charity and venture schools as well as Latin and English grammar schools.

This idea of an academy as an amalgamation of schools is illustrated by the correspondence of a minister named William Andrews who opened a Latin grammar school in Schenectady, New York, in 1771. Writing sometime shortly thereafter to Sir William Johnson, a colonial agent, Andrews explained:

> I lately took the Liberty of acquainting You, that I had opened a Grammar School in this Town, and since that, I have determined on forming it into an Academy, and propose giving Instruction in Reading, Writing, Arithmetic, Geography and History to those who may be designed to fill the Stations of active Life, exclusive of those who may be taught the Learned Languages – Bookkeeping, and Merchants accounts to fit them for Business, and the Mechanic Arts.[17]

In Andrews' terms, transforming a grammar school into an academy involved adding subjects of instruction and prospective students. The expanded institution would offer not only instruction in the learned languages, but English subjects (reading, writing, arithmetic, geography, and history) and applied subjects (bookkeeping and merchants accounts). By distinguishing between those students destined "for active life" and those who pursued the "learned languages," Andrews also highlighted his assumption that an academy would

---

[16] See, for example, Carl Van Doren, *Benjamin Franklin* (New York: Viking Press, 1938; republished, Penguin Books, 1991): 189–194.

[17] Cited in George Frederick Miller, *The Academy System of the State of New York* (Albany, NY: J. B. Lyon, 1922): 15.

attract a broad clientele. It would enroll not only children of proprietors and professionals but also those of merchants and mechanics.

For the most part, academies bore out this idea, at least according to their advertisements. Trustees of the academy in New Bern, North Carolina, for example, advertised a wide array of subjects in 1775, including: "the English, Latin or French Tongue; ... also Writing, Arithmetic, Algebra, Trigonometry plain and spherical, Astronomy, Navigation, Surveying, Geography, the use of Globes, or any other Part of the Mathematics, [and] the Italian Method of Bookkeeping."[18] Early academies in New York presented similar lists. In 1785, for example, Clinton Academy in East Hampton, Long Island, advertised instruction in reading, grammar, rhetoric, composition, penmanship, arithmetic, navigation, geography, French, Latin, and Greek. Similarly, the founders of Erasmus Hall Academy in Flatbush, also on Long Island, described their school in 1785 as consisting of two departments under two masters, classical and English, with the English master offering instruction in the applied subject of bookkeeping as well as in grammar, arithmetic, and history.[19] Commensurate with the idea of the academy laid out earlier by Benjamin Franklin and his associates, these institutions represented an amalgamation of Latin, English, and venture school models, although on a more modest scale than that initially contemplated in Philadelphia.

In practice, academies turned out to be even more solicitous of nonclassical students than their advertisements indicated. As described by historian Nathalie Naylor, all three of Long Island's early academies enrolled both male and female students, and the vast majority of pupils studied English subjects. At Clinton Academy in 1796, for example, just 7 of a total of 92 pupils studied the classics, while 72 enrolled in common school subjects. Erasmus Hall, by comparison, apparently achieved a greater degree of emphasis on higher subjects, reportedly enrolling 33 of its 104 students in the classical department in 1804, although only 12 of the 33 actually studied Latin and Greek that year. Similarly, at Union Hall in Jamaica, Long Island, in 1792, the vast majority of 50 total pupils studied common school subjects, with many designated as "reading only." Only two studied foreign languages and three "the higher branches of sciences." By 1801, Latin scholars had increased to 14 of 94.[20]

These facts suggest the practical realities that sustained the academy idea. Viewed from a financial perspective, the wide-ranging curricula of academies were not anomalous but essential. Major cities like Boston, New York, and Philadelphia might have sufficient clientele to support specialized Latin grammar schools, but for towns any smaller, the viability of an institution depended

---

[18] Mary Ellen Gadski, *The History of the New Bern Academy* (New Bern: Tryon Palace Commission, 1989): 17.
[19] Nathalie A. Naylor, "'The Encouragement of Seminaries of Learning': Early Academies on Long Island, New York" (Paper presented at the History of Education Society Annual Meeting, Toronto, Canada, 1988): 6 and 9.
[20] Ibid., 6–7 and 10–11.

on an eclectic mix of subjects and students. In this respect, academies were similar to venture schools. Indeed, as the historian George Frederick Miller concluded in his 1922 study of academies in New York, the emergence of academies in the mid-eighteenth century can be attributed in part to the influence of venture schools:

> ...private institutions, free to experiment and to broaden their curriculums to meet popular demands, seem, on the basis of similarity, to have been the forerunners of academies. They were independent [of direct church or governmental control]; their existence was determined by their popularity; they sought pupils of all grades; and they undertook to give instruction in any subject for which there was a demand.[21]

In effect, venture schools reshaped the dominant model of higher schooling in the late eighteenth century. In Boston, for example, over a forty-year period from 1727 to 1767, grammar school enrollments declined by 16 percent while venture school enrollments increased by 241 percent. Meanwhile, the population increased by just 19 percent.[22] Through their success in attracting a wide variety of students to study a wide variety of subjects on a market basis, venture schools forced established schools and teachers to broaden their sense of mission. The academy was one result of this competitive market pressure.

Religious Disestablishment

Another factor that influenced the emergence of academies in the late eighteenth century was the politics of colonial independence and religious disestablishment. The American Revolution put an end to established church authority in the United States, not only at the federal level, where it was explicitly precluded by the Bill of Rights, but within individual states. Before the Revolution, nine of the thirteen colonies established religion in the form of direct tax aid to churches.[23] In New York and the five southern colonies of Virginia, Maryland, North Carolina, South Carolina and Georgia, tax aid supported the Anglican Church, an institution of British rule. In the New England colonies of Massachusetts, Connecticut, and New Hampshire, tax funds supported churches in the Congregational tradition, itself born of Puritan religious dissent. The Revolution effected an immediate elimination of the established church in all the Anglican states but Virginia, where it took a decade. The change occurred somewhat later in the Congregational states of New England, where the last vestiges of established church support ended in 1833.[24]

---

[21] Miller, *Academy System*, 16.
[22] Jon Teaford, "The transformation of Massachusetts education, 1670-1780." *History of Education Quarterly* 10:3 (Autumn 1970): 287-307.
[23] The exceptions were the iconoclastic New England colony of Rhode Island, often credited with first institutionalizing the concept of religious liberty, and the heterogeneous mid-Atlantic colonies of Pennsylvania, New Jersey, and Delaware.
[24] Massachusetts was the last state to abolish tax support for established churches, in 1833. Connecticut ended tax aid for established churches in 1818. New Hampshire continued the

The disestablishment of church authority had a direct effect on education. New laws and constitutional provisions often implicitly or explicitly referred to education as part of their statements of the principle of religious liberty. Georgia's constitution, for example, stated that "all persons ... shall not, unless by consent, support any teacher or teachers except those of their own profession," while New Hampshire's provided that no person "shall ever be compelled to pay towards the support of the teacher or teachers of another persuasion, sect or denomination."[25] In addition, several states actively reconstituted existing educational institutions under disestablishment principles.

The case of the Academy at New Bern, North Carolina, illustrates this point. Twice chartered as a "public school," in 1764 and 1766, and then re-chartered as an "academy" in 1784, the institution at New Bern had roots in a church-sponsored pay school started by an independent teacher named Tomlinson in 1763. From the beginning, Tomlinson enjoyed moral, if not financial, support from the rector of the local Anglican church, as well as some assistance from an Anglican mission organization. In addition, his school soon acquired financial support from the colonial government. In 1764, an initial subscription produced 200 pounds for a building and a preliminary charter.[26] Then, in 1766, when the school building had been largely completed, the institution's sponsors applied to the legislature for a new charter providing additional funds for operations. As part of the new charter, the legislature specified that in exchange for enrolling a certain number of poor scholars annually for free, the school would receive annual income from a liquor excise tax.[27]

This support was shaken, however, by the politics of the Revolution. The 1766 charter had specified that the master of the school at New Bern should be of the Anglican faith. As Revolutionary sentiment developed in the mid-1770s, however, both the rector of the local Anglican church and the schoolmaster were forced to resign due to their association with the colonial government, and the schoolmaster went into temporary exile outside the country. When the war concluded, one of the first acts of the newly constituted legislature of the state of North Carolina was to move the headquarters of the government from New Bern to Raleigh. One of its next acts was to revise New Bern's school charter. The new charter embodied two significant changes: It eliminated direct government support of school operations from the liquor excise

---

practice but allowed the possibility of exemption to any Christian in 1819. For a precise enumeration of various establishment and disestablishment provisions in each colony and state, see John K. Wilson, "Religion under the State Constitutions, 1776–1800," *Journal of Church and State* 32:4 (Autumn 1990): 753–764. For a deeper philosophical and historical discussion of the meaning of religious liberty and how it emerged in the colonial and U.S. contexts, see Chris Benneke, *Beyond Toleration: The Religious Origins of American Pluralism* (Oxford: Oxford University Press, 2006); and William Lee Miller, *The First Liberty: Religion and the American Republic* (New York: Knopf Press, 1985).

[25] Wilson, "Religion under the State Constitutions," 755 and 757.
[26] Gadski, *New Bern*, 3–9.
[27] Gadski, *New Bern*, 9.

tax, and it dropped any reference to the Anglican Church. In addition, the 1784 charter was the first to officially use the term "academy" to refer to the institution.²⁸ Thus, in the case of New Bern, use of the term "academy" was directly linked to religious disestablishment.²⁹

Similarly, in New York, official use of the term "academy" was associated with the politics of colonial independence and religious disestablishment. The first corporate institution to adopt the term "academy" in New York was Kingston Academy (1774), located in the town that served as the first headquarters of New York's revolutionary government and the residence of the government's chief revolutionary leader, George Clinton. Otherwise, official use of the term "academy" was a postwar development. During the first session of the newly constituted New York State legislature in 1784, Governor George Clinton called the legislators' attention to "the neglect of the education of youth" that had occurred during the war and recommended that they attend to "the Revival and Encouragement of Seminaries of Learning."³⁰ In the near term, the legislature responded by forming a corporation known as the Regents of the University of the State of New York, with the power to establish, oversee, and promote the organization and operation of schools and colleges. This included Kings' College, the colonial institution that by the same act of 1784 was renamed Columbia College. In keeping with the principle of religious disestablishment that characterized state formation in this period, the law directed that both the trustees of the college and the Regents of the university represent multiple religious denominations.³¹ The law thus amounted to a rejection of previous Anglican control of King's College (now Columbia) and of the general practice of placing the highest institutions of learning under the authority of an established church. Henceforth, the state would be expected to operate on a principle of nonpreference with respect to religious affiliation in education.

Of course, this did not mean that professional ministers and church networks did not continue to exercise influence on individual institutions. For one thing, the founding of a "literary institution" required considerable local initiative, leadership, and support, the roots of which were often found in church organization. The law establishing the Board of Regents initially implied that

---

[28] Ibid., 25.
[29] In this light, the fact that Philadelphia, the most ethnically and religiously diverse city in the British American colonies, was the first to adopt the term "academy" in an official charter is not surprising. In his autobiography, Franklin explained that in order to attract and maintain support from individuals of diverse church affiliations, the original charter for the building bought by the academy specified that trustees represent different denominations, i.e., one Baptist, one Presbyterian, one Anglican, one Moravian. Although this ecumenism developed in relation to the school building more than to the educational program, it carried over to the academy's charter, which specified that the academy building remain open to the use of multiple denominations. Franklin, *Autobiography*, 115.
[30] Miller, *Academy System*, 19.
[31] Ibid., 20.

the Regents themselves would serve as a sort of supra-board of trustees, obviating the need for schools to obtain separate charters or form separate corporate boards. In practice, however, the kind of corporate financing a school required proved unlikely to occur without some structure of corporate governance at the local level. Thus, in 1787, the legislature reorganized the Regents of the university on somewhat different terms, delegating to them the power to issue corporate charters to individual institutions. In this way, the state preserved some of the *form* of traditional church sponsorship, without its substance. In fact, the 1787 law explicitly forbid Regents-chartered academies from requiring a religious test or oath of their teachers.[32]

Early academies founded under the new Regents law provide a basis for considering how this combination of church precedents and disestablishment principles worked out in practice. The first academies to acquire corporate status under the Regents were two schools on Long Island, Erasmus Hall in Flatbush and Clinton Academy in East Hampton, both chartered in 1787, immediately following passage of the revised Regents law. Within five years, the Regents had chartered a third academy on Long Island, Union Hall in Jamaica. As described by the historian Nathalie Naylor, support for all three of these early academies responded to ministerial initiative. Beginning in 1784, the minister of the local Presbyterian church in East Hampton raised 935 British pounds and supervised construction of a three-story brick academy building, which opened for students as Clinton Academy the following year. By the time its founders applied for a charter under the new Regents law in 1787, then, the school had completed two years of successful operation under ministerial leadership. Similarly, Erasmus Hall in Flatbush benefited from the leadership of a Dutch Reformed minister, who apparently already had experience operating a "parsonage school" in the same town. In 1786, a total of thirty-nine subscribers pledged enough to cover a third of the initial costs of constructing a large two-story "public school" building for instruction in "all the branches of learning usual in academies." Remaining costs were met through a combination of church land sales and long-term debt assumed by trustees of the academy under a charter acquired the following year.[33] In both these cases, the academies were clearly rooted in church schools. What the Regents law provided was a means of separating the schools from direct church control and establishing them under their own corporate charters and boards of trustees.

The case of Union Hall, chartered a few years later in 1792, presents an interesting variation on this pattern of ministerial leadership and local subscription support. Commensurate with its name, Union Hall was the product of collaboration among three towns (Jamaica, Flushing, and Newton) and three denominations (Episcopal, Presbyterian, Dutch Reformed). In 1791, a group of ministers and citizens from the three towns launched subscriptions

---

[32] Ibid., 21.
[33] Naylor, "Encouragement," 4–8; quotation, p. 8.

to erect an academy for the purpose of "diffusing knowledge and useful learning." Declaring "the importance and utility of Seminaries of Learning to be instituted in all places convenient," they launched a set of subscriptions for the erection of an academy in Jamaica, centrally located among the three towns.[34] In this case, the Regents law provided a genuine alternative to the individual church affiliation common among similar schools in the past. Given a means of establishing corporate organization without direct church control, promoters of the school could draw support across denominations, making the resulting school ecumenical in ways that paralleled the Board of Regents itself.

In this respect, educational development in the United States during the late eighteenth and early nineteenth centuries paralleled that in Europe at much the same time. In Britain and in France, as in North America, a rising middling class of craftsmen, shopkeepers and merchants increasingly sought alternatives to the forms of education traditionally supported by the aristocracy and controlled by an established church. According to comparative historian Margaret Archer, however, reformers in Britain and France pursued different strategies for achieving this goal. In France, the growing bourgeoisie seized political power directly and forcibly removed educational institutions from direct church control. In Britain, by contrast, the commercial class lacked the formal political power necessary to seize control directly. Instead, they used their growing wealth to pursue a "substitutive" strategy of supporting venture schools on the market. By comparison, the United States represents a hybrid of British and French strategies. As in Britain, a growing commercial class supported a thriving educational market in many towns and cities in colonial North America. In addition, however, Americans seized direct control of certain institutions during the Revolution, reorganizing and reestablishing them on disestablishment principles. In New York, access to corporate power through general incorporation laws, such as those administered by the Board of Regents, facilitated this strategy.[35]

Permanence and Stability

In effect, the incorporation of academies provided an alternative to the organizational structure and authority that an established church had once provided. Without such a substitute structure, the governance and support of schooling would be entirely subject to the market. It would depend, in other words, on venture schools. In this context, what distinguished academies was not the content of their instruction or the composition of their enrollments;

---

[34] Ibid., 12.
[35] Margaret S. Archer, *Social Origins of Educational Systems* (London: Sage Publications, [1979] 1984). For a fuller account of Archer's work and a more detailed version of the comparative international argument summarized here, see Nancy Beadie, "Education, Social Capital and State Formation in Comparative Historical Perspective: Preliminary Investigations," *Paedagogica Historica* 46:1/2 (2010), 15–32.

it was their physicality and their relative stability. Especially in the earliest period of academy development, what most often motivated townspeople to apply for an academy charter was demand for an academy building. Whether in Philadelphia in the 1750s, North Carolina in the 1760s, the upper Hudson Valley of New York in the 1770s, or Long Island in the 1780s, organizers initially cooperated in organizing an academy in order to capitalize the acquisition of real estate and the purchase or construction of a school house. This emphasis was reflected in the language organizers used to describe their institutions. In New Bern, Kingston, and East Hampton, organizers initially referred to their project as "the public school house," a phrase that highlighted the contrast with schooling in private households that otherwise constituted the norm of school experience. Similarly, use of the term "hall" in the names of several early academies reflected the importance of physical facilities. For New York such institutions included not only Erasmus Hall of Flatbush (1787) and Union Hall of Jamaica (1792), but also Farmer's Hall of Goshen (1790). As the term suggests, trustees who held title to charters for these institutions were first and foremost trustees of the buildings, which might also serve other community purposes.[36]

Sometimes, what the academy buildings housed were venture schools. Initially, for example, trustees of Union Hall assumed no responsibility for the salary or supervision of the academy's principal teacher. Specifying that the master obtain his compensation from "the profits arising from the tuition of scholars," they effectively interpreted their roles as those of building caretakers who provided a hall to house a school that otherwise operated on entrepreneurial terms.[37] Schools operating on these terms did not always achieve such continuity, however. In the case of Union Hall, for example, the first schoolmaster lasted only a year, followed by a spate of teachers with very short-term tenures. By 1797, when the institution stabilized, the trustees had assumed more direct responsibility for teacher salaries and collection of student fees. Under these terms, they finally managed to attract a master who stayed in his position for a number of years.[38]

From the perspective of a particular locality, the relative instability of the open market was a compelling reason to organize an academy. As a general rule, an academy achieved greater continuity and permanence in a particular location than did a venture school. This relative stability was a direct consequence of an academy's corporate status and physical structure. Venture schools, as the household businesses of individual teachers, were potentially mobile institutions. If the market for a venture school proved insufficient to

---

[36] In Philadelphia, the academy took over a hall initially built to house the audiences of traveling preachers, a tradition the institution continued by agreement with the building's original trustees. In Goshen, at the intersection of two major turnpikes east of the Catskills, Farmer's Hall no doubt housed assemblies of farmers as well as of students.
[37] Naylor, "Encouragement," 12.
[38] Ibid., 13–14.

support a teacher's household, then the teacher could simply relocate, and many did. Teaching was a highly peripatetic occupation in the late eighteenth and early nineteenth centuries, and both male and female teachers often moved many times over the course of a career in search of a stable market and adequate income.[39] Academies, which also depended heavily on tuition for teacher salaries and operating funds, were similarly subject to the vagaries of market demand – including competition from venture schools. In the case of a corporate institution, however, the board of trustees still held title to an academy building and property in a particular location. Given their corporate entitlements and responsibilities, they were likely to find a way to continue the school, whether by adjusting to the existing market; recruiting new teachers on different terms; or securing additional financial support in the form of loans, benefactions, or subscriptions. In the case of corporate institutions, in other words, fixed capital ensured a degree of permanence despite the vagaries of market demand.

Capitalization of independent corporations in this way became a strategy for institutionalizing and stabilizing education in the context of market competition and the absence of established church support. The Lima residents who organized to establish an academy in their town clearly had this kind of permanence and stability in mind. In addition to subscriptions valued at more than $10,000, their bid included a ten-acre building site and the offer of a large adjoining farm. Together, the land and subscription funds provided the means to erect a permanent structure and acquire corporate status. In this way, Lima residents drew on a long tradition of academy building in their state. At the same time, by enlisting the power of the Methodist Episcopal Church to organize such an institution, residents departed from the disestablishment principles that had shaped the meaning of the academy in British North America generally, and New York specifically, since the mid-eighteenth century. This departure was part of a larger shift in policy and politics in New York around 1828. To understand and appreciate the nature of this political change requires close consideration of state educational policy and politics in New York prior to 1828, as well as of the sources of political change between 1828 and 1830, when the academy in Lima was founded. Illuminating those policies and political dynamics is the project of the next five chapters.

---

[39] For a discussion of this issue, see Kim Tolley and Margaret A. Nash, "Leaving Home to Teach: The Diary of Susan Nye Hutchison, 1815–41," in Nancy Beadie and Kim Tolley, eds. *Chartered Schools: Two Hundred Years of Independent Academies in the United States, 1727–1925* (New York: Routledge/Falmer, 2002): 161–185.

8

Political Economies of Schooling – Academies and Common Schools

> Through the greater part of Europe .... the endowment of schools and colleges makes either no charge upon that general revenue, or but a very small one. It every where arises chiefly from some local or provincial revenue, from the rent of some landed estate, or from the interest of some sum of money allotted and put under the management of trustees for this particular purpose.
>
> Adam Smith, *Wealth of Nations*, 819[1]

> For a very small expence the public can facilitate [for] almost the whole body of the people, the ... most essential parts of education ... by establishing in every parish or district a little school, where children may be taught for a reward so moderate, that even a common labourer may afford it; the master being partly, but not wholly paid by the public.
>
> Adam Smith, *Wealth of Nations*, 843[2]

In the decades following the Revolution, New York experimented with a number of methods of providing legal and financial support for education. Like other states, New York directed its first central state support for education primarily to colleges and academies, only later developing a systematic basis for supporting common schools. Eventually, however, New York distinguished itself from other states by establishing a dual system of state support for education: one for common schools and one for academies. In addition, New York's system was distinctive in that it provided regular annual disbursements to schools and academies from centralized state funds rather than relying entirely on local funding or on special state appropriations. This distinctive political economy of schooling in turn facilitated changes in prevailing models of school

---

[1] Adam Smith, *An Inquiry into the Nature and Causes of the Wealth of Nations*, ed. by Edwin Cannan (New York: Random House, 1994 [1776]), Book V, Chap. 1, Part III, Article II, p. 819.
[2] Ibid., 843.

support at the local level – from land-based to capital-based methods of endowment, and from proprietary to associational models of school organization. This shift in prevailing models of school support is illustrated by two different academies founded in the Lima vicinity in the post-Revolutionary period: Canandaigua Academy, founded in 1795; and Middlebury Academy, founded in 1819. This chapter describes how the political economy of schooling changed in New York during this period with reference to these two examples.

Two Different Models of Academy Organization

Canandaigua and Middlebury Academies differed from each other in a number of ways, starting with their locations and the dates of their founding, and extending to the model of academy education they provided. Chosen in 1789 as the headquarters of the huge Phelps and Gorham Purchase, the town of Canandaigua developed as the seat of Ontario County and the launching point for settlement and trade in the new western territories. This meant that it became the headquarters for land transactions, the site of the county courts, and the locus of a state appointment system that at the time attached considerable importance to county-level positions. It would be, in other words, a place where professional men, men of influence, and men of ambition gathered and did business – including lawyers, justices, newspapermen, financiers, politicians, and merchants. In this context, the founding of an academy made sense. The all-male academy at Canandaigua would provide a training ground for future agents of commerce, law, and politics.

This model of academy education matches the profile that scholars have drawn of academies generally during the early republican era. In his study of New England academies in the period from 1780s to 1820s, the historian J. M. Opal associated the founding of academies with the commercial transformation of the rural North. Located in commercial villages and promoted by a commercial elite, academies, in his analysis, both forged and diffused a new culture of competitive individualism and social ambition.[3] Similarly, in his comprehensive geography of academy founding in New York State before the Civil War, Edward Herring O'Neil found that the vast majority of academies were established neither in major urban centers, such as New York City, nor in backwoods locations, as earlier scholarship had sometimes suggested, but in places that he called "crossroads towns," which served as nodes of communication and trade for their surrounding countryside. O'Neil also described three different periods and patterns of academy founding, distinguished by the dominant modes of transportation in each

---

[3] J. M. Opal, "Exciting Emulation: Academies and the Transformation of the Rural North, 1780s–1820s," *Journal of American History* 91: 2 (September 2004): 445–470.

era. During the first period, before 1825, the founding of new academies primarily followed the paths of navigable natural waterways and improved roads and turnpikes. Between 1825 and 1841 most new academy towns were located on newly developed canals. After 1841 they tended to develop along newly constructed railroads.[4] The town of Canandaigua embodied the concept of a crossroads town in the first of these periods. Located at the northern tip of Canandaigua Lake where it met the Genesee Road, the town site had always been a major settlement site for Native Americans on the old Iroquois trail and would continue to be a transportation node on what became the major state-improved road running east to west across the breadth of New York State.

In 1795, however, Canandaigua's significance as a commercial town was still somewhat speculative. At the time of the academy's incorporation, the town of Canandaigua was far and away the furthest west of any academy town in New York and the most remote from established areas of white settlement. It was also hardly yet much of a town, having only achieved legal status in 1791 and completed construction of its first public building in 1794.[5] When Phelps and Gorham planted their headquarters at Canandaigua in 1789 and chartered an academy there in 1795, they asserted a strategic claim. They declared their intent to capture politically and culturally a territory that they so far barely occupied. Considering the early date of the academy's founding and its far western location, Canandaigua could be said to have pioneered the concept of a crossroads academy town. It would remain the only chartered academy anywhere in western New York until Middlebury Academy was founded in 1819.

Like Canandaigua Academy, Middlebury was the furthest west of any academy in the state at the time it was chartered. The Middlebury site originally belonged, like Canandaigua, to the huge area of western New York opened to land speculation in the period immediately following the Revolutionary War. As a result of early financial failure on the part of Phelps and Gorham, however, the sites of Canandaigua and Middlebury ended up in two different tracts of land owned by two different groups of speculators, developed through two different transportation networks, and governed under two different political authorities. Although they would later be subdivided further, most of the territory east of the Genesee River, where Canandaigua was located, was acquired by the Poultney group and belonged to Ontario County (organized in 1789) while the territory west

---

[4] Edward Herring O'Neil, "Private Schools and Public Vision: A History of Academies in Upstate New York, 1800–1860" (unpublished Ph.D. dissertation, Syracuse University, 1984).
[5] On the history of Canandaigua see George S. Conover, ed. *History of Ontario County New York* (Syracuse, NY: D. Mason & Co., 1893); and n.a. *History of Ontario County New York* (Philadelphia: Press of J. B. Lippincott & Co., 1876 [reprinted by W. E. Morrison & Co., Ovid, New York, 1976]).

of the Genesee River, where Middlebury was located, was acquired by the Holland Land Company and organized as Genesee County (in 1802).⁶

Within these respective land sale systems and political networks, the towns of Canandaigua and Middlebury occupied very different positions. While Canandaigua developed as the seat of Ontario County and a center of commerce, law, and politics for the whole Poultney territory, the town of Middlebury developed no such importance in Genesee County or the Holland Land Company system. As such, the academy at Middlebury represented something of a departure from the general pattern of academy founding during the early republican era. Hidden in the rolling hills well south of the Genesee Road and west of the Genesee Valley, Middlebury occupied the margins of the most fertile and desirable agricultural lands of the region. Neither a county seat nor a stop on a significant transportation route, it lay roughly along the diagonal between the Holland Land Company's main headquarters in Batavia, to the northwest, and its satellite headquarters in Bath, to the southeast, but it was not on the main turnpike that connected those two towns. Nor did it have a significant waterway. In short, the site of Middlebury lacked both the natural resources necessary to attract major developers in the first round of land sales and the political resources necessary to attract significant state investment in transportation improvements. It was not a crossroads town. (See Figure 1 for town locations.)

These differences of commercial promise and political prominence in turn shaped the origins and characters of the academies in Middlebury and Canandaigua. For Oliver Phelps and Nathaniel Gorham, who took a lead in organizing the original endowment for Canandaigua Academy, the incorporation of such an institution was part of a larger vision of what it meant to establish the political and cultural capital of a new western territory. Like other major proprietors and land speculators in other parts of the state at the time, they saw the establishment of religious and educational institutions partly as their duty and partly as a wise promotional move. Just as the building of a state road or county courthouse could increase property values in a town, so the founding of an academy could help generate land sales by asserting the future significance of the town and a consequent return on present investment. At about the same time as Phelps and Gorham acquired the charter for Canandaigua Academy in 1795, the proprietor, William Cooper, adopted the same logic to organize an academy in Cooperstown, several counties to the east.⁷ In both cases, the founding of a state-chartered academy symbolized a

---

⁶ Donald W. Meinig, "Geography of Expansion, 1785–1855," in John H. Thompson, ed. *Geography of New York State* (Syracuse, NY: Syracuse University Press, 1966): 140–171; Neil Adams McNall, *An Agricultural History of the Genesee Valley, 1790–1860* (Philadelphia: University of Pennsylvania Press, 1952): 11–16; and Orasmus Turner, *History of the Pioneer Settlement of Phelps and Gorham's Purchase and Morris' Reserve* (Rochester, NY: W. Alling, 1851).

⁷ Alan Taylor, *William Cooper's Town: Power and Persuasion on the Frontier of the Early American Republic* (New York: Alfred A. Knopf, 1995): 209–213.

town's centrality in a proprietary system of land ownership and social and political order.

Acting more than two decades later, the founders of the academy at Middlebury pursued a similar promotional purpose, but in a much different context. In 1809, a settler/investor by the name of Silas Newell purchased a tract of land from Joseph Ellicott, agent of the Holland Land Company, in what was then part of the town of Warsaw, in Genesee County. Variously described as a carpenter, brick-maker, tavernkeeper, and wool manufacturer, Newell apparently operated as something of an all-around entrepreneur in an area that came to be known as Newell's Settlement.[8] With modest-sized landholdings of 400 acres, Newell was never a major land speculator or proprietor. Nor does he appear among the early town leaders and first officers of Middlebury when it divided off from the town of Warsaw and organized as a separate town in 1812 and held its first town meetings several years later.[9] Nonetheless, it was on Newell's land that residents constructed a substantial brick structure known as the academy in 1817, land that he signed over to the academy for the sum of $1 when organizers applied for a state charter the following year.[10] As a result of these efforts, Middlebury Academy became in 1819 the first academy to be chartered west of the Genesee River or, for that matter, west of Canandaigua.[11] In founding Middlebury Academy, residents acted less to solidify a claim to centrality in a larger economic and political system than to make a bid for influence that it lacked on other grounds. Lacking the wealth, political prominence, and geographic advantages of proprietors like Phelps, Gorham, and Cooper, landowners in Middlebury staked their future on education.

To some extent this contrast between Canandaigua and Middlebury Academies and their sponsors reflects a historical shift in the social geography and culture of academies in the North. Historian of education Doris Malkmus distinguishes between a "genteel" tradition of academy education of single-sex academies characteristic of urban areas of the Northeast during the early national era and what she calls a "productionist" culture of coeducational academies in small towns and rural areas of western New York, Pennsylvania, and the Midwest after 1820. In the genteel tradition, academies represented and promoted the gendered manners and society of a proprietary class of landed and leisured men and women. By contrast, academies that belonged to a productionist rural and small town culture drew students from families where both men and women were expected to engage in productive work and contribute to a household economy.[12] On the surface, at least, the

---

[8] Rhoda B. Warren, *History of the Town of Middlebury* (Wyoming, NY: Town of Middlebury Historical Society, 1995): 10–12.
[9] Ibid., 12.
[10] Indenture between Silas Newell and Academy Trustees, 1818, Box 1, MAC.
[11] See footnote 2.
[12] Doris Malkmus, "Capable Women and Refined Ladies: Two Visions of American Women's Higher Education, 1760–1861" (unpublished Ph.D. dissertation, University of Iowa, 2001).

contrast between the all-male Canandaigua Academy and the coeducational Middlebury Academy matches Malkmus' distinction. Reflecting their different contexts, Canandaigua and Middlebury also represented two different models of corporate capitalization and two different political economies of schooling.

A Land-Based Model of School Support

During the first two decades after the Revolution, New York experimented with several different methods of supporting education. The first of these was a land-based system of school support. In 1782, still in the midst of the Revolutionary War, New York Governor George Clinton and the legislature cooperated to promote "the establishment of schools and seminaries" by reserving portions of any newly acquired public lands for "gospel and school lots." In 1784, at the close of the war, the legislature reiterated and extended this policy, dedicating 690 acres of each township in newly acquired "public" lands for the support of schools. At this point, the type of schooling to be supported was unspecified. Two years later, in 1786, however, the legislature distinguished between support for ordinary common schooling and support for higher learning, directing that one lot in each township of new land be dedicated to "the promotion of literature" and another for schools and the gospel.[13]

In the years immediately following the end of the Revolutionary War, several huge tracts of previously unappropriated (Indian) land within New York's boundaries opened for sale. First, in 1786, the state auctioned several thousand acres of land in the Cherry Valley region of the state, known as the Otsego Patent, north of the Catskills. Then, in 1788, as part of a boundary settlement between the states of Massachusetts and New York, the land speculators Oliver Phelps and Nathaniel Gorham purchased from Massachusetts "the right to extinguish Indian title" to virtually all the territory that would become western New York.[14] This included land that would later constitute the town of Canandaigua, as well as that which would become the sites of Middlebury and Lima.

Other major land sales followed. In all these cases, according to law, the state retained portions of the disposed land for educational purposes. What remained unclear, however, was exactly how such land would be converted to school support. Over the decade of the 1790s the legislature and the Regents experimented with various strategies for converting land into actual income for schools.[15]

---

[13] George Frederick Miller, *The Academy System of the State of New York* (Albany, NY: J. B. Lyon Company, 1922): 19–30 and 66–68.
[14] Meinig, "Geography of Expansion"; McNall, *An Agricultural History*; Turner, *History of the Pioneer Settlement*.
[15] Meinig, "Geography of Expansion"; Miller, *Academy System*, 27–28 and 66–68; David Murray, "An Introductory Sketch," in Franklin B. Hough, *Historical and Statistical Record of the University of the State of New York during the Century from 1784–1884* (Albany, NY: Weed, Parsons & Co. for the State of New York, 1885): 29–30.

The founding of the academy at Canandaigua was a product of this early land-based system of endowment. According to local histories, the original endowment for the academy consisted of 6,300 acres.[16] Such a huge figure is implausible except as representing the whole of the gospel and school lots reserved for the support of education in the entire Phelps and Gorham Purchase. Since Phelps and Gorham purchased the rights to their original tract of land in 1788, very early in the development of the state's system of support for education, and since they purchased these rights from Massachusetts, rather than from New York, many of the details regarding the control and management of gospel and school lots had yet to be worked out. Instead of surrendering reserved lands to state control, Phelps and Gorham apparently used them to endow an educational corporation known as Canandaigua Academy. What the original academy charter represented, in other words, was a means of controlling and managing the lands that would have been reserved by the state under existing law. Presumably, any proceeds or income earned on the lands would be appropriated to the support of education in the territory's various towns, once those towns had been organized and settled.

As both Phelps and Gorham and the state itself soon discovered, however, the logic of a land-based system of educational endowments was limited by the conditions of a newly opened territory. Beyond providing a site for academy building, land could not itself finance an institution. Only through rent or managed production could it produce the income necessary for building construction or for hiring academy teachers. In a land-rich, labor-poor economy, however, the demand for land to rent and the prospects for significant yield were low. For the endowment of Canandaigua Academy, as for Phelps and Gorham personally, such returns proved elusive. To meet the high cost of debt service on the funds necessary to acquire the lands in the first place, Phelps and Gorham almost immediately were forced to divest most of their holdings.[17] Similarly, the conditions that created cash flow problems for speculators constrained the income-generating capacity of land-based endowments. Five years after receiving a state charter for the academy at Canandaigua, the trustees of the corporation, who included Phelps and Gorham themselves, had yet to support the operation of any school from the endowment.

Much the same problem confronted by Phelps and Gorham and the trustees of Canandaigua Academy existed for the state as well. Despite the fact that New York had dedicated large amounts of land to the support of schools and academies, these lands proved unable to provide a stable source of income for education. In recognition of this fact, the legislature experimented with other forms of school support, including special appropriations and literary lotteries. The first such effort was a special appropriations bill in 1792 that

---

[16] Conover, ed. *History of Ontario County* (1893): 225–229; *History of Ontario County* (1876): 78–82.
[17] McNall, *An Agricultural History*, 14; Turner, *History of the Pioneer Settlement*; Meinig, "Geography of Expansion," 141–142.

directed 1,500 pounds for each of the next five years to the support of academies.[18] Meanwhile, at the common school level, New York tried a hybrid arrangement combining special state appropriation and local taxes. In 1795, and for each of the next five years, the state appropriated a sum of $100,000 in support of common schools and required that localities match their share by raising a sum equal to one-half the amount they received from the state in the form of local taxes. Both the academy and common school provisions expired after their five-year terms, however, to be replaced by yet another method of funding education. In 1801, the state began conducting a series of "literary lotteries," designating $82,500 of the proceeds for the support of common schools and $12,500 for the support of academies.[19] These lotteries seem to have been limited in number and effect, however, and were eventually outlawed entirely. At the beginning of the nineteenth century, in other words, New York had experimented with three different methods of providing state support for schools, none of which had proved stable or reliable. Both the special appropriations laws of the 1790s and the lotteries of the early 1800s depended on special acts of the legislature that could be discontinued or rescinded at any time. Although reserved lands seemed to promise longer term support, this promise went largely unrealized due to the limited demand for the rental of such lands.

In the case of Canandaigua Academy, as in that of most other academies and of the state itself, the problems of land-based systems of endowment were eventually addressed by turning to other sources of funding. Convening in 1800, the trustees of Canandaigua Academy launched two subscriptions – one aimed at raising the means to construct an academy building and another aimed at producing income for operations. After a year or two of sponsoring a venture school in temporary quarters, the trustees finally opened an academy in a dedicated building in 1803. In keeping with the ambitions of landowners and the presumed prominence of the town, the new facility was substantial. With a footprint of 2,500 square feet and a height of three stories, the physical plant compared favorably with those of other academies at the time. Beyond the building itself, Canandaigua Academy also retained title to substantial landholdings and other income-producing property. Together these assets

---

[18] "An Act to encourage Literature by Donations to Columbia College, and to the several Academies in the State, Passed 11th April, 1792" *Laws of New York*, 15th Session, Chap. 64 (Albany: State of New York): 479–480. This funding proved temporary. It is not clear what the source of this funding was. Although the specified appropriations may have been met by income from the rental of designated lands, they were paid out of general funds, making their continuance over the long term subject to shifting politics and financial fortunes in the state. When the original appropriations bill expired in 1797, it was not renewed, and for the remainder of the decade the state apparently discontinued the distribution of funds to academies. For a discussion of early funding of academies, see Miller, *The Academy System*, 23–26.

[19] Fletcher Harper Swift, *A History of Public Permanent Common School Funds in the United States, 1795-1905* (New York: Henry Holt and Co., 1911): esp. 349–360; and Miller, *The Academy System*, esp. 23–26 and 66–71.

made Canandaigua among the most highly capitalized academies in the state in the early nineteenth century, excepting only the wealthiest institutions in Albany and New York City.[20]

In the end, most of the initial capitalization of the academy in Canandaigua, as in the case of virtually every other school in the state, came from local sources, specifically from the practice of raising local subscriptions. Moreover, perhaps partly in response to the Canandaigua case, the Regents made this practice of local capitalization a matter of official policy. In 1801, they specified that as a condition of receiving a Regents charter, an academy's sponsors must demonstrate "that a proper building for that purpose hath been erected and finished and paid for."[21] They further required that the corporation hold title to the site of the academy building and to income-producing property yielding a minimum of at least $100 a year in 1801 (and a maximum of 4,000 bushels of wheat), and that the institution's charter specify that the principal of this endowment could never be diminished or appropriated.[22] In effect, the Regents institutionalized the principle that schools should be capitalized through voluntary funding and local initiative.

Principles of Political Economy

With this policy, New York effectively conformed to the principles of political economy outlined by Adam Smith in *The Wealth of Nations*. Writing the part of that monumental work devoted to the financing of public works and institutions, Smith discussed specifically the "expense of the Institutions for the Education of Youth." Reflecting the reality of schooling at the time, Smith made clear that he expected the greater part of such instruction to occur on the market, with the fees that scholars paid the master furnishing a revenue sufficient to meet the expenses of the institution. Consistent with his historical reputation as a promoter of free market principles, Smith also emphasized his conviction that dependence on student fees and the "rivalship of competitors" fostered the best work from teachers. According to him, endowments and subsidized salaries were bound to diminish the application of teachers to their work. In Smith's analysis, the direct exchange of fees for instruction constituted "natural revenue," while the endowments of English universities produced corrupted institutions in which professors felt little obligation either to students or to any superintending authority.[23]

Even as he insisted on the superiority of market-based methods of school funding, however, Smith also recognized two exceptions to his normative rule, one for higher learning and the other for the education of the common people.

---

[20] Conover, *History of Ontario County* (1893), 225–229; *History of Ontario County* (1876), 78–82. For comparisons with other institutions, see Hough, *Historical and Statistical Record*, 594–595 and passim.
[21] Miller, *The Academy System*, 23–24.
[22] Ibid.
[23] Smith, *Wealth of Nations*, 819–846.

With regard to higher learning, Smith allowed that without some form of subsidy, certain subjects, including ancient languages, the sciences, and higher branches of philosophy, would not be taught at all. Accordingly, he also outlined the preferred terms of support for endowed institutions. Specifically, he noted that even where the reward of the master did not arise from "natural revenue," or direct fees for instruction, his support need not be a charge on the *general* revenue of society (i.e., the state) but could and most often was derived from "some local or provincial revenue," from land rents, or from capital investments managed by trustees, that is, endowments.[24] In Smith's account, then, market-based venture schools were the preferred mode of education and education funding, supplemented, if necessary, by a local tax or corporate endowment. Only on top of these other sources of revenue, as a supplement to other funding, and only for those subjects and forms of schooling incapable of subsisting on entirely on market fees, should institutions be a charge on the general revenue of society, and then only a small charge.

Similarly, with respect to the education of the common people, Smith insisted that the primary source of school funding should come from tuition fees, even as he allowed that some form of public subsidy might be necessary. In Smith's analysis, the education of the common people required more public attention than that for people of rank and fortune. Not only did common people have fewer financial resources to devote to education than did those of rank and fortune, but they had less time and opportunity for such education. Unlike families of wealth and status, who were able to organize their households around extending their children's educations even unto the eighteenth or nineteenth year, children of commoners had to quit their educations as soon as they were old enough to work. Once employed, moreover, these youth had little opportunity for further learning. Cognitively, the occupations of common people were unlikely to stimulate the mind or to allow the time for study. These limitations concentrated the need for instruction in reading, writing, and arithmetic of children of this class at an early age. They also made public support for such education a relatively efficient investment. For a very small expense, the public "can facilitate, encourage and even impose" basic education "upon almost the whole body of people." Again, what Smith had in mind was a public subsidy, not a replacement for tuition fees. Public funds would reduce rates to a level so moderate that even a common laborer could afford them. The master would be paid "partly but not wholly by the public," because a master paid wholly, or even principally, by the public "would soon learn to neglect his business."[25]

Consistent with these principles, New York at the beginning of the nineteenth century left the vast majority of schools to survive on a market basis, with what revenue they could generate from tuition and fees. What limited support the state provided was offered on a supplementary basis in the form

---

[24] Ibid.
[25] Ibid., 843.

of matching funds or per pupil subsidies. At the academy level, the Regents required after 1801 that any institution applying for Regents status and funding already be substantially capitalized from local sources. Any additional funds the Regents had available – whether from quit-rents, special appropriations, or lotteries – were distributed to chartered Regents academies on a per pupil basis, according to the total number of students attending the institution, and were designated specifically for the support of teacher salaries.

At the common school level, the principle of distribution for state funds varied over time. During the five-year period of the first, temporary special appropriation bill for common schools, from 1795 to 1800, the state distributed funds to localities throughout the state on a matching basis with local taxes, according to the size of the local population. Once this special appropriation expired in 1800, however, so did that distribution system. Under the lottery provisions that followed, the primary recipients of state funds for common schools were a small number of urban charity schools rather than local common schools. Most communities and households, in other words, were left to their own devices for securing common education after 1800.

Eventually, however, New York settled on a new strategy of school support that provided stable support for both common schools and academies on a systematic basis. In 1805, New York established a centralized endowed fund "for encouragement of common schools" using 500,000 acres of reserved land. It then directed that the surveyor general sell the lands and that the state comptroller invest the proceeds until the annual income on the fund reached at least $50,000. Once this level had been attained, "the interest annually arising shall be distributed and applied for the support of the common schools in such manner as the legislature shall direct."[26] Among the investments the comptroller made to generate this interest income were the acquisition of bank stock and the advancement of mortgage and manufacturing loans.[27] The new system, in other words, shifted state school support from a land-based to a capital-based model.

The resulting system of support for education synthesized several elements of New York's past experiments with school funding. When the Common School Fund approached maturity in 1812, the legislature began passing laws to direct the distribution of its income, which first occurred in 1815. Specifically, the legislature directed that localities match their share of income from the fund with an equal sum raised by local taxes, much as the state had done with earlier special appropriations for common schools. The legislature then organized a separate endowed fund for the support of academies. The Literature Fund, established in 1813, followed the same principles of capitalization as the Common School Fund. When that fund matured in 1816, the

---

[26] Swift, *A History*, 353.
[27] Ibid.; Miller, *The Academy System*; and John Anthony Muscalus, *the Use of Banking Enterprises in the Financing of Public Education, 1796–1866* (Philadelphia: University of Pennsylvania Press, 1945).

legislature delegated to the Regents the authority to distribute income from this fund to academies on a per pupil basis, just as it had with earlier special appropriations. In this way, New York established a distinctive two-tiered system of support for common schools and academies. For decades this system set the standard for state support of schools in North America.

New York's Distinctive Two-Tiered System of School Support

As compared with other states, New York's school funding provisions were distinctive but not anomalous. Most states in this period *either* allowed for local tax support of schools *or* established centralized state literature funds. No other state combined these provisions in quite the way New York did. In the well-known case of Massachusetts, for example, state laws required that localities organize common schools and also, if the towns were of a certain size, some form of grammar education. They left up to the locality, however, how the school would be funded – whether through local taxes or by rate bills to parents. Moreover, Massachusetts did not organize a state-level fund for the support of schooling until 1834. Connecticut, by contrast, had a generous state-endowed fund that supplied supplemental school monies to localities that applied for its use. Known simply as the "school fund," the Connecticut endowment produced an income that localities could use to support either common schools or academies, as they chose.[28] In practice, the monies were often used to support academies, leaving the funding of common schools entirely up to local provision.

Both the New England states of Massachusetts and Connecticut were exceptions, however, in that they continued to provide tax support for established local churches for decades after the Revolution. Connecticut did not finally eliminate local tax aid for established churches until 1818. Massachusetts, meanwhile, continued such support until 1833. In this context, the funding and administration of common schools could be left to local towns and churches, which themselves enjoyed tax support. Viewed in this light, the appropriate basis of comparison for New York's system of school support was not New England but other states where the Anglican Church had been disestablished during the Revolution. These states, all of them in the South, similarly relied heavily on venture schools for much of the education offered during the early Republican period. Also like New York, southern states such as Virginia in 1810, South Carolina in 1811, and North Carolina in 1825 established what they called "literature funds" for the support of designated institutions, which could include both academies and charity schools.[29]

New York was one of only three states, and was the earliest and most successful of these, that established separate endowed funds for both

---

[28] Swift, *A History*, 23–25 and 228–237; also see Harvey S. Reed, "The Period of Academy in Connecticut, 1780–1850," (Ph.D. dissertation, Yale University, 1942).

[29] Swift, *A History*, 98–106.

academies and common schools. Indiana established a "county seminary fund" as early as 1816 to support academy-like institutions. Not until the 1830s, however, did it organize comparable funding for common schools, and not until 1851 was such funding truly productive. Similarly, Pennsylvania's early land-based endowments benefited primarily academies and charity schools, with separate common school funding not established until the 1830s.[30] Virtually all states, other than Massachusetts, established some sort of endowed education fund by the end of the 1810s or the early 1820s. New states set up funds as they achieved statehood with land reserved by the federal government for that purpose.[31] New York remained distinctive, however, in providing separate funds for both common schools and academies and in regularizing the distribution of funds to both sets of schools on an annual and systematic basis.

By making school funding at both levels both annual and systematic, and thus to some extent predictable, New York exerted an important stabilizing influence on education. Ultimately, New York's model of support for education represented a hybrid of methods tried by other states, drawing both on the congregational tradition of local tax-based support of schools common in New England and on the practice of capitalizing independent corporate institutions prevalent in the South and in the traditionally disestablishment state of Pennsylvania. At the same time, New York went further than other states in subsidizing education in corporate institutions. Taking advantage of the large acquisition of new territory in the aftermath of the Revolution, it used this land to endow public support of education, much as did the new states of the Northwest Territories. Unlike states like Ohio, however, New York did not leave the appropriation of such lands entirely up to the locality, but consolidated their control at the state level, eventually selling them to capitalize state-level endowments for schools. In this way, New York's system of support for schooling made the transition from a land-based to a capital-based system of school support.

A Capital-Based Model of School Support

Among the institutions admitted to the Regents system in the period immediately following the maturation of New York's Literature Fund was Middlebury Academy, chartered in 1819. Although similar in some ways, the organization and financing of Middlebury Academy proceeded in a different order than that of Canandaigua Academy, and with somewhat different results. According to local histories, in 1817 Newell launched a subscription for construction of the brick academy building, heading the list with the largest single pledge, a sum of $600. Once the building was completed in 1817, organizers recruited a

---

[30] Ibid., 383–386.
[31] Ibid., 98–106.

teacher and began enrolling students in the school.³² They then began contemplating an application for a state charter for the institution from the Regents. To receive a state charter, sponsors of an academy had to meet certain requirements regarding endowment and property ownership. In accordance with these specifications, organizers designated an initial set of trustees, secured a deed from Newell for the property on which the academy building stood, and compiled a list of subscriptions or promissory notes payable over a term of twenty years as a form of endowment.³³ As contrasted with Canandaigua, in other words, and in compliance with Regents policy after 1801, the construction of a building and the commencement of school operations in Middlebury preceded rather than followed state incorporation.

These differences in the organization and capitalization of the two academies point to other differences in the models of academy founding the two institutions represent. Initially, at least, the founders of Canandaigua Academy operated on what might be called an aristocratic or proprietary model of institution building. In the context of the 1790s, men like Oliver Phelps and Nathaniel Gorham may well have imagined themselves as latter day lords of large proprietorships, like those in New York's Hudson Valley. Such proprietorships gave families like the Livingstons and the Van Rensselaers control not only over large amounts of landed wealth and natural resources, but also over the labor, produce, and political loyalties of the tenants who worked the land, effectively reviving old world patterns of land-based fealty in a new world context. Using their landed wealth and their claim on dependent labor and resources, the proprietors in return assumed both the responsibility and obligation to establish social institutions such as churches and schools.³⁴ To some extent, at least, Phelps and Gorham's initial endowment of Canandaigua Academy and subsequent roles as academy trustees fit this model.

By contrast, the founders of Middlebury Academy, acting more than two decades later, followed what might be called an associational model of organization. Although Silas Newell certainly figured prominently in the founding of the academy, his role seems to have been more that of a contractor than that of a proprietor. He did end up granting land to the institution, but only the one or two acres necessary to meet the state's requirement that the academy hold title to its building and building site. He did take the lead in the first round of pledges for building construction, but he did not end up being part

---

[32] Rhoda B. Warren, *A History of Middlebury in Commemoration of America's Bicentennial* (Wyoming, NY: Middlebury Historical Society, 1984 [1975]); idem, *History of the Town of Middlebury*, 19–21.

[33] "Indenture," 1818.

[34] On the practice and culture of proprietorship in New York during the colonial, early republican, and antebellum periods, respectively, see Sung Bok Kim, *Landlord and Tenant in Colonial New York: Manorial Society, 1664–1775* (Chapel Hill: University of North Carolina Press, 1978); Taylor, *William Cooper's Town*; and Thomas Summerhill, *Harvest of Dissent: Agrarianism in Nineteenth-Century New York* (Urbana: University of Illinois Press, 2005).

of the institution's subsequent governance. The first trustees of the institution instead consisted of other local residents, most of whom made cash pledges as part of the second round of subscriptions for the academy's endowment. In this way, the initial financing and incorporation of Middlebury Academy depended as much on community organization as on the actions of an individual proprietor.

In 1819, when the designated trustees submitted the charter application, the list of local subscriptions numbered fifty-six and totaled $3,845 in value.[35] Over the next seven years, the institution collected fifty-seven additional notes totaling $5,200.[36] According to state reports, these notes together were eventually valued at $7,768 in "additional property" that, when combined with the building and building site, contributed to an overall capitalization level of $13,721.[37] Although this figure put Middlebury Academy substantially behind Canandaigua – whose total assets were in the same year valued at more than $30,000 – it did put Middlebury Academy in the top 20 percent of all Regents-chartered academies in operation that year.[38] Middlebury's endowment consisted primarily of long-term promissory notes, however, while Canandaigua's consisted primarily of real estate.

Once the academy received its state charter, in 1819, it became eligible for shares of state funds distributed through the State Board of Regents. In fact, Middlebury received two types of funding from the Regents: a one-time special appropriation of $1,000 made at the time it received its charter in 1819, and a systematic allocation of income from the state Literature Fund, distributed on a per pupil basis. For the first two years of its operation under the Regents, Middlebury received small allotments of $50 on this basis, but in 1822 it received $237.50, a figure that could pay the full salary of a senior female teacher or more than half that of a senior male teacher at the time. By providing a relatively stable and predictable form of annual per pupil funding, the New York system facilitated the founding and operation of schools on an associational rather than a proprietary model.

The men who organized the institution at Lima would adopt elements of both the Canandaigua and Middlebury models of academy organization, even as they also perfected certain innovations on those models. Drawing on more than thirty years of experience with an associational model of community building in their town, local leaders initiated their bid for the Methodist-sponsored academy by raising a subscription for more than $10,000 from more than 160 local households. At the same time, a few of these local leaders asserted some of their own proprietary influence by offering substantial

---

[35] List of promissory notes, Middlebury Academy, MAC. The list extends through the 1830s. The first 56 pledges all date from 1819 and total $3,835.
[36] Ibid.
[37] *Report of the Regents of the University of the State of New York* (Albany: State of New York, 1838).
[38] Ibid.

amounts of their own lands as part of the bid for the academy, including a large income-producing farm held by the town's leading landholder at the time, Asahel Warner. Even as they built on previous models of academy founding, however, organizers of the academy at Lima capitalized on a changing social, economic, and political context. In particular, the organizers of the academy at Lima took advantage of the new economy of evangelical religion perfected by Methodists in the 1810s and 1820s and the new politics of schooling that developed in New York after 1825.

9

Education and Civic Engagement – Schools and Politics

> Voted that the publick money be paid as far it will go on the master's wages and the Remainder Be made upon the School list.
>
> Minutes of Lima School District No. 4, October 30, 1819[1]

> Resolved that one half of the public money be appropriated to defraying the charges of the summer school.
>
> Minutes of Lima's School District No. 4, March 1826[2]

The group that convened the spring meeting of Lima School District No. 4 in March 1826 certainly knew that it broke with tradition. After choosing as moderator a first-time officeholder but established resident, William Gray, and taking the usual vote to hold summer school for four months starting in May, the group took the unprecedented step of specifying "that one half of the public money" be used to defray charges for summer school. That this move was not innocent is indicated both by previous practice and by the response that followed. For years trustees had made their assumptions regarding the proper allocation of common school funds explicit. Under the ongoing leadership of men like John Phillips, who had helped to organize the district in the first place, money received from the town's school commissioners always went toward paying the salary of the master who ran the winter school. Even if members of the district had somehow forgotten that this was the practice, however, they soon had the opportunity to remember it. Two weeks following the March meeting, the district reconsidered its decision at a special meeting moderated by Phillips. In place of the original resolution, participants substituted a new one. This resolution directed that the public money received from the town commissioners be appropriated "exclusively to the winter school." For now, the rebels had lost their cause. From the perspective of just a few years later, however, they were harbingers of a changing politics of schooling.

---

[1] Minutes of Lima School District No. 4, October 30, 1819, LHS.
[2] Ibid., 1826.

This chapter explores the politics of schooling in the 1820s, on the cusp of political change. To send a child to school in New York in the 1820s was simultaneously a foregone conclusion and a political act. More than any other aspect of society, schooling reached into the households of individual families and connected them to the larger political economy of the state. Unlike banks or insurance companies – state-chartered institutions in which most men had little if any direct financial stake or experience – schooling laid claim to the productive labor and financial resources of virtually every rural household, as well as to its children. At the same time, schooling involved families in political decisions about the allocation of public funds. Unlike turnpikes or canals – state-sponsored enterprises in which many households had an interest but few had any influence – local schools were directly subject to the influence of individual families. Each child between the ages of five and fifteen whom a household sent to school earned the local district an additional share of public money distributed by the state and matched by town-level taxes.[3] These funds then ended up in the hands of neighbors, who met to decide to which teachers and to whose children they would be allocated. In this way, schooling gave virtually every family a stake in decision making about the distribution of public funds. It also forged a connection among households of diverse locations and experiences. Consciously or unconsciously, households across the state came to share a common set of benefits from, and demands on, the state. Schools in this way became agencies of civic engagement and politicization. In the process, of course, they also became sites of political conflict.

What led to the particular conflict over the allocation of public funds in Lima's school district no. 4 in 1826 cannot be fully known. Most likely it was an interaction among individual circumstances, changing norms of schooling, and competing political principles. As a relatively new father in 1826, William Gray probably sought a share of public money to educate his own child. At the same time, he and his associates may have intended to lodge a general protest against the district's established leadership and older patriarchal norms, or a more specific complaint against the schoolmaster chosen to teach the preceding winter. Perhaps the March meeting expressed some of the resentment against local political elites that would ignite in the anti-Masonic movement in that area of western New York later that year. On the other hand, Gray and his associates may have acted primarily as taxpayers concerned about the most effective use of public funds. The public money that the district received would go three times as far in summer as it would for the winter school. After all, winter and summer schools were not simply held in different seasons. They were different kinds of schools. They hired different teachers, served different students, and operated on difference principles. As a result, they mobilized different constituencies and implied different politics.

---

[3] "An Act for the Support of Common Schools, Passed April 12, 1819," *Laws of New York*, 42nd Session, Chap. 44 (Albany: State of New York, 1819): 186–208.

Norms of School Keeping

In the early decades of the nineteenth century, rural common schooling was at least as embedded in matters of household economy as it was in the political economy of the state. To keep common schools going, local families followed certain norms and traditions. These traditions had more to do with the cycle of the seasons than with any notion of public policy. When fall came, the heads of local families met to assess the condition of the school house for the approaching winter. In October 1819, for example, the residents of school district no. 4 in Lima began their meeting by voting "that the schoolhouse be repaired."[4]

Having addressed the condition of the school house, the fall meeting moved on to deciding the date and duration of the winter term. Although the physical structure of a school house might survive from one year to the next, the school itself was essentially created anew each season. In 1819, for example, residents "voted that we have a school fore [four] months to begin the 15th day of November next."[5] As this phrasing indicates, trustees did not so much administer an existing school as call one into existence on an annual basis. In this way of operating, a school was not a permanent institution but a kind of "event" held at a certain time of year. Given this conception, a district could decide to "have" more than one school a year. Most districts had two schools, one in the winter and one in the summer. These two schools operated under largely parallel meeting structures. One set of meetings occurred each fall, in late September or early October. At this meeting the district decided on the terms of the winter school. The other set of meetings occurred each spring, in late March or early April. At those meetings, the district established plans for the school to be held in the summer. In April 1820, for example, the residents of Lima's district no. 4 voted "that we have a woman school to commence on the first Mondy [sic] in may [sic] and continue four months and longer if the trustees see fit."[6]

In this usage, it made at least as much sense to talk about a woman school held in the summer as to talk about a summer school taught by a woman. Scholars have long known and amply detailed the distinct and gendered characters of winter and summer schools. They trace this gendered division of labor back to the early colonial period in New England. There it had roots in the tradition of dame schools, in which some women provided a combination of day care and primary reading instruction for their own and other children in their homes. As far back as the 1670s, some New England towns paid such women to provide this service to poor and orphaned children as well as to paying neighbors. Eventually, this practice developed into a more formal two-tiered system of town-supported schooling in which women taught

---

[4] Minutes of Lima School District No. 4, October 30, 1819.
[5] Ibid.
[6] Ibid., April 11, 1820.

basic literacy skills to young children in the summer and male school masters taught higher subjects, including Latin grammar, to older male children in the winter. Historians Joel Perlmann and Robert A. Margo found evidence of such two-tiered arrangements as early as 1702 in Connecticut. They suggest that the practice became prevalent enough to be familiar by 1750 and that it became the norm in New England by 1820. During the same period, the practice migrated with New Englanders to other northern states, becoming particularly common in the state of New York.[7]

Lima's school district no. 4 adopted this two-tiered system of summer and winter schooling from the beginning of its operation under state law and may well have had such a system in place before the first common school laws went into effect. In January 1815, the first year that district trustees recorded arrangements for schooling under provisions of the law, they voted that "we have school to begin the middle of May and to keep fore [sic] months to be taught by a Woman."[8] The district would continue the tradition of hiring a woman for summer and a man for winter for at least the next twenty years.

One common element of this two-tiered system, wherever it existed, was a substantial gap in the wages paid male and female teachers. In 1820, the first year the trustees of Lima's school district no. 4 identified teachers by name and recorded salary rates, they employed a woman name Harriet Partridge to keep the summer school at a rate of eleven shillings per week. During the same year, the district employed a man named Thomas Caulkins to keep the winter school at a rate of $14 a month. Assuming a New York exchange rate of eight shillings to the dollar, Harriet's wages worked out to about $1.38 per week or $5.95 per month. This female-to-male wage ratio of 42.5 percent closely matches the ratio that scholars have found for labor generally in the mid-Atlantic region, for farm labor specifically in New York, and for teachers in the Northeast.[9] It was the major reason that winter schools were more expensive to operate than summer schools.

The wage gap was not the only reason that winter schools were more expensive, however. In addition to wages, teachers also received board. Once the district decided to hold a school for a specified term, it proceeded to determine how the various costs of the school would be assessed. One of the first things a district decided was the value of board for the teacher. In October 1819, for example, school district no. 4 immediately followed its decision to have a winter school with a vote "that the Board of the master be estimated at $1 and 25 cents per week."[10] Board could also be differentiated by sex and season of employment. Throughout the 1820s, the trustees of Lima's school district no. 4 estimated the value of board at 75 cents per week for the female teacher of

---

[7] Joel Perlmann and Robert A. Margo, *Women's Work?: American Schoolteachers, 1650–1920* (Chicago: University of Chicago Press, 2001): 18–26.
[8] Minutes of Lima's School District No. 4, January 9, 1815.
[9] Perlmann and Margo, *Women's Work?*, 54–59.
[10] Minutes of Lima School District No. 4, October 30, 1819.

the summer school. By comparison, the value of board for the male teacher of the winter school was typically set at one dollar or more per week.[11] Since the difference in board costs was smaller than that for wages alone, the inclusion of board actually improved the salary ratio for women, bringing the total male-to-female salary ratio for teachers in 1820 to 50 percent. Nonetheless, the greater value of board supplied to male teachers added to the higher total cost of the winter school for the district.

Not only the amount but the terms of board also could vary by season and sex and status of the teacher. Board was an integral and not insignificant part of a teacher's salary, amounting to anywhere from just under a third to more than a half of total wages, depending on the teacher. By including board as part of a teacher's salary, a district thus effectively reduced the cash liability of local households for the cost of teacher wages. For this reason, districts generally preferred that teachers board with local families. In those instances when the teacher managed to make other arrangements, residents expected certain allowances regarding teacher payment. These special allowances were more likely to apply to married male teachers, however, than they were to single women. In 1823, for example, residents of school district no. 4 first "Voted that the master board round the district, the board at one Dollar per week." They then proceeded to specify the conditions under which they would make an exception. "If the master board himself, he is to take his pay in such things as his family wants, such as grain and pork."[12]

In addition to higher wages and higher board costs, the expenses of winter school included heating. As historians of rural schooling in other settings have noted, no item consumed more attention in school district minutes than that of providing wood for the school house stove.[13] In Lima school district no. 4, every fall meeting included at least one vote on this matter, sometimes two or three. As with board, the district determined the value of a cord of wood as a basis for figuring what each family owed for schooling its children. In September 1820, for example, the district voted that "wood be estimated at one dollar per cord." It then went on to determine the amount of wood each family would have to supply per child. In 1820, a household owed the district three-quarters of a cord of wood for each child it sent to school that winter.[14] Often the district took additional votes specifying the conditions under which the wood was to be provided. As the minutes regularly repeated, wood was to be "cut fit for the fire" and delivered to the school house at the start of the winter term, with trustees occasionally commissioned to measure the wood once

---

[11] Ibid., passim. In one year, 1819, the district set the board rate for the winter school at $1.25. In the 1820s, however, a general decline in the economy depressed both board and wage rates below 1819 levels.
[12] Ibid., September 17, 1823.
[13] For example, see Wayne E. Fuller, *The Old Country School: The Story of Rural Education in the Middle West* (Chicago: University of Chicago Press, 1982): 48–53.
[14] Minutes of Lima School District No. 4, September 26, 1820.

it arrived.[15] Those who did not provide wood as specified incurred a charge for services that others – who had wood and labor to spare – might receive some credit for supplying. Or, as one clerk put it, "If enny one fails delivering the wood by the time they shall pay such pay as we pay the teacher."[16] Families were expected to supply wood at a rate of three-quarters of a cord for each member of the household sent to school. Given an estimated enrollment of twenty-two students, the wood for winter heating added $16.50 to the total cost of keeping the winter school.[17] Altogether, with wood, board, and wages included, total expenses for winter school were about three times those of summer school.

Sources of School Funding

The business of supplying wood and board linked the labor and produce of every child's household into the cycle of sustaining common schools. Beyond heating the school house and feeding the teacher, local school families also supplied the major part of teacher wages directly from their households' "surplus" goods and labor. As directed by the revised and consolidated common school law of 1819, the trustees of each school district paid the wages of teachers out of the public money "so far as such moneys shall be sufficient for the purpose." The residue would then be collected "from all such persons as shall be liable" to pay for instruction, that is, the heads of households who sent children to school.[18] Thus, in October 1819, residents of school district no. 4 "voted that the public money be paid as far as it will go on the master's wages" and that "the Remainder Be made upon the School list."[19] A "school list" was a record kept by a common school teacher of each of the households sending children to school. Specifically, as spelled out in the 1819 common school law, the list contained "the name of each person liable to pay for instruction" and "the number of days each such person shall be liable to pay for instruction."[20] Charged to the head of each household, this liability applied to every child, ward, apprentice, servant, and boarder the household sent to school. As the clerk of school district no. 4 explained on more than one occasion, "whoever boards a scholar that goes to school shall be considered holden" (1824) and "if

---

[15] Ibid., i.e., third Wednesday in September 1829.
[16] Ibid., last Wednesday in September 1822.
[17] Ibid., passim. For figures on school enrollment, see Report[s] of the Lima School Commissioners recorded in "The Lima Town Book, 1818–1840," LHS, passim. The first such report recorded in the Town Book is dated 1825. For the period from 1825 to 1835, total enrollment in district no. 4 ranged back and forth between 44 and 62 students a year. There is no way to know how the enrollment broke down between summer and winter schools. Here I have estimated winter school enrollment at half the lowest total enrollment reported.
[18] "An Act for the Support of Common Schools, Passed April 12, 1819."
[19] Minutes of Lima School District No. 4, October 30, 1819.
[20] "An Act for the Support of Common Schools, Passed April 12, 1819."

Education and Civic Engagement

enny one in the district take in enny one that does not belong to the district, they are accountable for them" (1823).[21]

This, then, was the other end of the cycle of school keeping. At the close of each year, usually at the March meeting, when most tax lists were made out, the trustees calculated the amount each household owed for wood, board, and teacher's wages. As a part of this task, school officials regularly identified and made allowances for families too poor to pay school costs. In 1819, for example, the district voted that Alexander Craig "be exempted from paying his school Bill and be made up in the Bill on the rest of the District." This vote formalized what had previously probably been an informal arrangement. It followed the provisions of the revised school law of that year, which empowered trustees "to exonerate the payment of the wages of such teachers, or the residue aforesaid of such wages, all such poor persons, within their district, as they shall think proper; and to collect the whole of the said wages, or the whole of the residue thereof aforesaid, from all such other persons as shall not be so exonerated therefrom."[22] Since the law also required that the trustees "certify" their decision to "exonerate" certain persons from school costs, the school district clerk thereafter regularly recorded such votes. Having identified those persons to be exempted from paying school bills, the trustees added up the money they "had in hand from town and county taxes," subtracted it from the teacher's total salary, calculated the amount each family owed for the remainder of the teacher's wages, and assessed the amount each household should be charged for tuition or credited for supplying wood and boarding the teacher.[23]

The official collector for the district would then go around to each household and negotiate with each family a way of balancing its accounts. In keeping with the norms of a social or barter economy, this negotiation might well result in an exchange of goods or labor as well as cash. To settle accounts, the collector effectively assumed responsibility for his neighbors' debts to the district. Ultimately he would be liable for paying over the cash equivalent of any payments he received. In the meantime, however, he made his own deal with each of his neighbors, accepting either cash, goods, or labor of value to him or the district. This might include grain. In 1823, for example, school district no. 4 apparently collected some portion of the school bill in wheat, voting that it be "sold for one dollar per bushel or stoared till it will fetch it."[24] Occasionally, the district might accept a specific item of use to the school. In 1821, for example, the district voted "that the pay that is comming [sic.] from the Widow Church for her last winter's schooling" be accepted in the form of "a pair of handirons."[25] For these services, official collectors for schools,

---

[21] Minutes of Lima School District No. 4, third Wednesday of September, 1824, and September 17, 1823.
[22] Ibid., October, 30, 1819.
[23] Ibid., and passim.
[24] Ibid., September 17, 1823.
[25] Ibid., March 27, 1821.

churches, and towns commonly received a kind of commission. The common school law allowed for five cents on every dollar for collectors' fees.[26]

Overall, then, districts covered the costs of common schooling with a combination of public subsidies and per pupil fees. The terms of funding differed, however, for winter and summer schools. When the trustees of school district no. 4 hired Thomas Caulkins to teach winter school for three months at a rate of $14 per month in 1820, they assumed that any public money the district received would go toward his salary. For that year, the trustees reported drawing $32.52 in public money from the town of Lima and $3.80 from the town of Livonia, all of which was "in our hands to pay said Caulkins with." This sum of $34.32 left just $7.68 of Caulkins' $42 in wages to be collected by other means. In accordance with common practice, the trustees "made out a rate Bill for the residue of his wages."[27] When it came to operating a winter school, in other words, the cost of employing a teacher was subsidized by public funding.

When it came to hiring teachers for summer school, by contrast, no such public subsidy existed. Instead, trustees assumed that the full cost of summer school would be born by the households that sent their children to school. To cover the cost of Harriet Partridge's wages in 1820, the trustees simply "collected the pay of the district and paid her."[28] As a result of these different funding methods, summer and winter schools operated on essentially different principles. Because the winter school received a subsidy of public funds, it was subject to decisions by taxpayers and to oversight by district and town-level officials who might or might not have had children in school. The summer school, by comparison, drew all its financial support from the households who sent their children to school. It thus responded more directly to parental demand.

Rural School Demand

One indicator of the demand for schooling is the length of school terms. In 1815, the first year that New York's state common school laws went into effect, and thus the first year of formal district reporting, Lima's school district no. 4 held school for a total of eight months during the year. This included four months of summer school beginning in the middle of May and four months of winter school beginning in the middle of November. At the time, the state specified just three months as the length of time a district had to operate a school in order to be eligible for a share of public funds. Meanwhile, no state requirements existed for school attendance, because attendance was entirely voluntary in New York and other states until the late nineteenth century. From the very beginning of state involvement in school funding and regulation, in

---

[26] "An Act for the Support of Common Schools, Passed April 12, 1819."
[27] Minutes of Lima's School District No. 4, April 11, 1820.
[28] Ibid.

other words, residents and parents in school district no. 4 demanded much more schooling than the state required.

The high level of demand for common schooling as early as 1815 suggests that local common schools did not begin *de novo* that year, when the state officially recognized them, but built on existing schools and school constituencies. In the case of Lima's school district no. 4, the trustees of the newly established district chose to house its school in an existing facility previously used for instruction by an itinerant Baptist minister. They also hired the daughter of a local widow who had previously taught children in her home to teach summer school. Meanwhile, the school in Lima's village center, known officially in 1815 as school district no. 9, occupied the existing brick school house, constructed in 1803 under the auspices of the local congregational society.[29]

School district records also show that local financial investment in common schools went far beyond that directed or required by law or supported by the state. In 1825, for example, Lima's school district no. 4 received a total of $19.32 in public funds. Meanwhile, the total cost of teacher wages was $64.00. The remaining $44.68 in wages was collected by rate bills assessed to "whoever boards a scholar that goes to school."[30] Altogether, public funds covered 30 percent of the total cost of teacher wages, while the remaining 70 percent came from nonpublic sources, that is, tuition or rate bills (Table 1). This high proportion of teacher wages covered by nonpublic sources again indicates the high demand for common schooling among families.[31]

Town-level records show that the high demand apparent for school district no. 4 was not exceptional among districts in the town of Lima. In fact, with respect to the length of the school year, district no. 4 was near the bottom of the range in 1825 with eight months of schooling. Other districts, especially the more commercial districts no. 3 and no. 9 near the village center, held school for as many as ten or ten and half months a year (see Table 2).[32] In addition, town-level records provide data on attendance rates for school districts in Lima. These records identify the number of children between the ages of five and fifteen residing in each district and the number of children taught in each district school. From these two sets of figures, a rough indication of the rate of school attendance for each district can be determined. These data show that, already in 1825, common school attendance was essentially universal in the town of Lima. In fact, the number of children taught substantially exceeded the number of children aged five to fifteen, making the attendance

---

[29] The story of the "Brick School House" is reconstructed from the "Minutes of the Charleston Congregational Society," LPC, and recounted in Chapters 2 and 3 of this book.
[30] Minutes of Lima's School District No. 4, September 1825.
[31] Minutes of Lima's School District No. 4. For a fuller discussion of the tuition-based funding on which common schools in general and Lima's school district no. 4 in particular depended, see Nancy Beadie, "Tuition-Funding for Common Schools: Education Markets and Market Regulation in Rural New York, 1815–1850," *Social Science History* 32: 1 (Spring 2008): 107–133.
[32] "Lima School Commissioners' Report," 1825, in "Lima's Town Book, 1818–1840."

TABLE 1. *Sources of Funding for Teacher Wages, Lima School District No. 4, 1825*

Cost of teacher wages	
Cost of male teacher for four-month winter term	$48.00
Cost of female teacher for four-month summer term	$16.00
Total cost	$64.00
Sources of funding	
Public funds from Lima (state funds plus local school taxes)	$16.67
Public funds from Livonia (for portion of the district in next town)	$2.65
Total public funds	$19.32
Additional money collected from the district by rate bill	$44.68
Ratio of public funds to total funds spent on teacher wages	0.30

Source: "Minutes of Lima's School District #4, 1814–1854," Lima Historical Society, Tenny Burton Museum, Lima, New York.

rates higher than 100 percent for every district but one. These high attendance rates probably reflect several factors, including the common rural practice of sending very young children (under the age of five) to school and of continuing to enroll older children (especially males) for a few months a year even in their late teens.[33] It may also be that at this early stage of school reporting, some children were counted twice (for example, if they attended both summer and winter schools). Even taking these factors into account, however, it is clear that attendance rates across districts were very high in 1825, once again indicating the high demand for common schooling among rural households.

This high level of demand for common schooling continued and even increased during the next two decades. Although the length of summer and winter terms varied occasionally, the overall trend was toward a longer school year, from seven to eight months in the 1820s and ten months by 1830 (see Table 3).[34]

This increase in the length of the school year occurred in the summer term. In 1820, the trustees of school district no. 4 hired Thomas Caulkins to keep winter school for just three months, the minimum time required by the state for a district to keep a qualified school if it wanted to receive a share of public funding. Meanwhile, during the same year, the district voted to hire Harriet Partridge to teach summer school for a period for four months, "and longer if the trustees see fit."[35] Of course, four months of summer school taught by

---

[33] On age norms for school enrollment in the Northeast see Carl F. Kaestle and Maris Vinovskis, *Education and Social Change in Nineteenth-Century Massachusetts* (Cambridge: Cambridge University Press, 1980): 50–71.
[34] Minutes of Lima School District No. 4.
[35] Ibid.

TABLE 2. *Length of School Year and Rates of Attendance by School District, Town of Lima, 1825*

School District #	# Months in Session	# of Children Taught	# of Resident Children Ages 5 to 15	Ratio of Children Taught to # of Children Ages 5 to 15
Whole districts				
3	10	97	82	1.18
5	8	75	53	1.42
6	9	52	42	1.24
7	9	71	57	1.25
8	8.5	70	53	1.32
9	10.5	99	90	1.10
Partial districts*				
4	8	58	48	1.21
10	8	41	41	1.00
16	8	7	8	.88
19	8	22	7	3.14
TOTAL		592	481	1.23

* These districts drew children across town lines, receiving funds from more than one town. The enrollment figures reported are for the students from Lima households only.
Source: "Lima School Commissioners' Report, 1825," in "Lima's Town Book, 1818–1840," Lima Historical Society, Tenny Burton Museum, Lima, New York.

TABLE 3. *Length of School Year, Lima School District No. 4, 1815–1835*

Year	Total # Months In Session	Length of Winter Term (in months)	Length of Summer Term (in months)
1815	8	4	4
1820	7	3	4
1825	8	4	4
1830	10	4	6

Source: Information compiled from "Minutes of Lima School District #4, 1814–1854," Lima Historical Society, Tenny Burton Museum, Lima, New York.

a woman could be secured for two-fifths of the cost of hiring a male teacher for just three months in winter, not including the additional costs of heating. Moreover, as parents bore the full cost of summer school teaching, a decision to extend the number of months the school was in session imposed additional burdens only on those who chose to enroll their children for the full length of the summer school term. Nonetheless, the fact that the district considered offering more than four months of summer school suggests that parental demand for summer school exceeded that for winter school.

That demand continued to increase in subsequent years. After experimenting for a few years with three- or three-and-a-half-month winter terms, the district stabilized the length of the winter school at four months in 1823. At the same time, it gradually lengthened the summer term further. By 1830, the district regularly employed a female teacher to keep school for six months in the summer while continuing to hire a male teacher for just four months in the winter.[36] Over the course of the decade, in other words, the trustees made substantially more schooling available in summer than winter.

A greater demand for summer than winter school made sense, given the different populations that summer and winter schools served. Summer schools enrolled young children of both sexes for instruction in basic literacy expected of virtually everyone. Winter schools, by contrast, enrolled somewhat older youth, especially older males, who alternated school attendance with agricultural labor or other forms of employment. To these students winter schools offered not only continuing instruction in basic English literacy but also some classical and advanced English instruction not expected of everyone. No study yet provides generalized data on school enrollment by both age and sex for the period before 1840, let alone a comparative breakdown for summer and winter schools. Nor does surviving evidence allow such an analysis in the Lima case. Two broad trends are suggestive in this regard, however. First, studies have shown that before 1840, schools in the Northeast experienced relatively high rates of enrollment among young children ages four and under, especially in rural areas, with a possible surge in such "infant" enrollment beginning in the 1820s.[37] These children certainly would have attended summer school. In addition, scholars have concluded that literacy rates for girls equaled that of boys in the Northeast by 1820, and that this parity resulted from increased school attendance.[38] Although some girls may have attended winter schools,

---

[36] Minutes of Lima's School Distrct No. 4, passim.
[37] Kaestle and Vinovskis, *Education and Social Change*, 50–71.
[38] An incisive summary of scholarship on the history of female literacy in the Northeast in this period is provided by Kathryn Kish Sklar, "The Schooling of Girls and Changing Community Values in Massachusetts Towns, 1750–1820," *History of Education Quarterly* 33:4 (Winter 1993): 511–542. Sklar makes the point there that schooling may have been important for gains in female literacy. This supposition departs from some earlier scholarship, which emphasized that the rise of schooling did not have a significant influence on literacy rates, since nearly universal literacy had been achieved in the Northeast before common school systems were established. This scholarship focused on male literacy, however, relied primarily on extrapolations from 1860 census data and underestimated the extent and significance of schooling *before* the organization of state common school systems. See Lee Soltow and Edward Stevens, *The Rise of Literacy and the Common School in the United States: A Socioeconomic Analysis to 1870* (Chicago: University of Chicago, 1981). Finally, this earlier body of scholarship does not sufficiently explain southern literacy rates, which were substantially lower than northern rates even among whites, and which showed a more persistent gender gap. Recent scholarship on southern cases suggests that schooling may have been particularly important for literacy acquisition for girls in the South, especially for poorer girls. See James E. Murray, "Literacy Acquisition in an Orphanage: A Historical-Longitudinal Case Study," *American Journal of Education* 110: 2 (February 2004): 172–195. Perlmann and Margo, *Women's Work?* (pp. 61–64), also provide a brief comparative discussion of gender and literacy rates north and south.

it is likely that many girls attended common school only in summer terms.[39] Meanwhile, poor families were less likely to extend their children's schooling beyond the level of basic English language literacy taught by summer schools. Together these age, gender, and class norms suggest that summer school was a more universal school experience than winter school. While virtually all children attended summer school, girls and poor children were less likely to also attend winter school.

Political Principles

In this context, decisions about whether to award public funds to summer or winter schools had a certain social and political meaning. When residents of Lima's school district no. 4 decided to direct all their public money to the winter school, they effectively decided to allocate public funds to the school that was most expensive and least universal. Since not every child attended winter school, this meant that not every school family benefited from public funding. Families who only sent children to summer school received no benefit from public school funds even if they paid local school taxes on their property and even if their children's attendance at summer school helped to earn the district a share of public school funds. These circumstances may have been particularly aggravating to someone like William Gray, who in 1826 had recently inherited a farm and become a new taxpayer. At the time, his only child was a daughter aged six or under who would have attended summer school.[40]

As problematic as district no. 4's funding policy appears from an equity perspective, it did make sense according to other principles. Local residents

---

[39] In her study of girls' schooling in Massachusetts, Sklar quotes a set of guidelines for female school attendance from the town records of Northampton dated 1801. These guidelines specified that all female students, up through the age of 14, should attend summer schools, whether they sought basic instruction in reading or instruction in writing and the higher branches. It is clear from Sklar's study that Northampton would have tended toward greater sex segregation than other towns; nonetheless, the Northampton example suggests that a norm of excluding women from winter school altogether did exist in some places. Sklar, "Schooling of Girls," 520.

[40] William Gray is listed in the manuscript federal census for Lima in 1830 as a male head of household between the ages of 30 and 40 with one male child under the age of 5 and one female child between the ages of 5 and 10. In 1826 he would have been between the ages of 26 and 36 with one female child under the age of 6. In the same census a woman named Martha Gray, between the ages of 50 and 60, also appeared as a head of household. I am surmising that this Martha Gray was the widow of Simeon Gray, who appeared in the 1820 census as a head of household age 45 and up. Manuscript Census of the United States for the town of Lima, Ontario County, New York, 1820, OCRAIMS, and Manuscript Census of the United States for the town of Lima, Livingston County, New York, 1830, LCHS. In the 1820 tax assessment, Simeon Gray is listed as having an estate of 111 mostly unimproved acres valued at $1043.00, a valuation that put him slightly below the median of assessed householders in town. Lima Tax Assessment, 1820, OCRAIMS. William Gray, meanwhile, was listed in the 1820 census as a married householder between the ages of 16 and 26 with no children. He was not listed in the tax assessment for that year. Unfortunately, no tax assessments survive for Lima after 1821, so it is not possible to determine his status precisely for 1826.

and state officials alike assumed that families bore primary moral and financial responsibility for educating their children. State funds helped families and localities make traditional household resources go further than they otherwise would, but no one in the 1820s imagined that public funds would cover the whole of school costs. Given that public funds would cover only a portion of the cost of schooling, and given that families would have to cover the remainder, school officials effectively decided to direct the funds to the school with the highest per pupil expenses – that is, to the school whose costs would be the most difficult for parents to bear on their own. In this way of thinking, the fact that summer schools were more affordable than winter schools meant that they did not *need* public subsidies as much as winter schools.

Ultimately, the justification for this way of thinking lay not only in notions of financial efficacy, however, but in patriarchal norms and principles of government. Within Anglo patriarchal tradition, the state was justified in subsidizing two forms of instruction at opposite ends of the social and political spectrum. At one end of the spectrum, the state had a compelling interest in the liberal education of future political leaders. Arguably the entire society benefited if such men were schooled in the history and theory of good government, taught examples of exemplary leadership from the past, socialized into a culture of public virtue and sacrifice, and initiated into a polite society of honor and civic engagement. Thus states subsidized academies and colleges to provide advanced instruction to mostly male children of independent families. At the other end of the spectrum, states and municipalities had a compelling interest in subsidizing basic education for the poor. In a society in which property-owning heads of household assumed responsibility for the welfare, education, and correction of all dependents – including not only wives and children but also laborers, servants, slaves, wards, and apprentices – it made sense for higher authorities to be concerned about the widows, orphans, and roving poor who lived outside a household system of governance. Arguably it was in the interest of the entire society, as well as in that of the poor themselves, that children from this class be familiarized with texts of religious obedience, schooled in moral virtue, instructed in basic skills of reading and measure, and initiated into the norms of deference necessary to get them a place in a proper household in the future.[41] Thus states and municipalities subsidized charity schools to provide basic literacy instruction for poor children of both sexes.[42]

[41] For a thorough and incisive analysis of scholarship on the history of patriarchal thought and practice in the West, with special attention to issues of education, see Pavla Miller, *Transformations of Patriarchy in the West, 1500–1900* (Bloomington: Indiana University Press, 1998). I am indebted to Miller's work and to Kim Tolley, who suggested I read Miller's book, for encouraging me to sharpen my thinking about connections between patriarchal social norms and state educational policies in this case study.
[42] F. H. Swift, *A History of Public Permanent Common School Funds in the United States, 1795–1905.* (New York: Henry Holdt and Co., 1991); and idem, *Federal and State Policies in Public School Finance in the United States* (New York: Ginn and Company, 1931). For a summary of changes in state school funding policies from the colonial era to the present, see Nancy

Between these ends of the class spectrum, the state provided little or nothing. As long as rural common schools achieved nearly universal attendance without it, why should public funding extend to summer schools? With the introduction of the first common school laws, which occurred in New York from 1812 to 1815, this logic began to change. Nonetheless, older social norms and assumptions lived on at the local level in the distinction between winter and summer schools. In 1824–1825, for example, Lima's school district no. 4 hired a man named Lord Sterling to teach the winter school. A younger brother of James Sterling (the self-imposed exile from the Congregational church who had lately converted to Universalism), Lord Sterling may or may not have shared his sibling's stubborn adherence to older forms of church organization or his preference for the principle of freedom of conscience over the practice of evangelical moralism. Nonetheless, his employment as schoolmaster reinforced certain patriarchal norms. At age forty-five in 1825, Lord Sterling had not yet acquired a portion of his father's estate, as had his older brother, but as the younger son of a well-established and propertied family from Connecticut, he probably had the advantages of an advanced education. If so, he offered the district considerable educational advantages for the price. As a middle-aged man and a head of household from a moneyed family, however, he seems an exceptional choice for schoolmaster in a minor rural school district.[43] One could imagine a younger farmer with weaker financial connections and no sons, like William Gray, feeling some resentment over surrendering his hard-earned cash and produce to a member of one of the wealthiest families in town – all so that aspiring sons of other families might have the advantage of instruction from someone with classical training.

In her comparative study of schooling for girls in Massachusetts, Kathryn Kish Sklar discovered similar conflicts over the funding of winter and summer schools. The character of the conflicts varied, however, with that of different towns. On one end of the spectrum, the wealthy town of Northampton refused to direct any town funds to support either basic English education or "the schooling of girls" in summer schools, despite a formal complaint and civil suit by members of the town. Instead, the selectmen of that town insisted on reserving all public funds for the support of a Latin grammar school for boys. At the other end of the spectrum, the poorer town of Sutton raised no school funds through taxation, paying for its schools entirely through rate

---

Beadie, "The Limits of Standardization and the Importance of Constituencies: Historical Tensions in the Relationship between State Authority and Local Control," in *Balancing Local Control and State Responsibility for K–12 Education: 2000 Yearbook of the American Education Finance Association* (Larchmont, NY: Eye on Education, 2000), 47–91.

[43] In 1820, James Sterling was listed in the county tax assessment as owning an estate of 178 mostly improved acres valued at $3,904, a valuation that put him in the upper 10% of assessed households. Unfortunately, no data on wealth and status of Lord Sterling are available until 1850. At that time he was a 70-year-old man with an estate valued at $5,000, a valuation that put him in the top 30% of householders, though he had probably already settled several children. Lima Tax Assessment, 1820.

bills to families who sent their children to school. This town devoted all such funds to the support of a summer school for the basic education of children of both sexes, refusing to raise any taxes for a Latin grammar school, despite being fined for this failure by the state.[44]

Sklar's study focuses on a somewhat earlier period in Massachusetts than the events in the Lima case, and the organization of public funding was not the same in the two states.[45] Nonetheless, her study provides valuable comparative insight into the situation in Lima. In particular, Sklar's study highlights the political dimensions of decisions about summer school funding. In Lima, as in Sklar's Massachusetts towns, conflict over summer schools did not turn on the gender of the teacher per se, or even on the value of female schooling. What concerned certain members of district no. 4 as well as the selectmen of Northampton was not whether "women's schools" should exist, but whether public funds should be used to fund them. This was a political question.

Gender and the Politics of Schooling

Gender was inextricably bound up in the politics of schooling in the 1820s and 1830s. Even as residents of school district no. 4 adhered to certain patriarchal norms regarding the allocation of public school funds, the balance between winter and summer terms shifted. Although the initial impetus for longer summer school terms probably lay in a desire to increase the amount of schooling available to families at the lowest possible cost, it had the additional effect of expanding the presence of women in common school teaching. Eventually, this expanded presence translated into a change in status for female teachers and women's schools, and in a change in the politics of schooling at the state level.

The status of common school teachers was defined in part by the terms of common school law and in part by the social norms of the local school districts. As directed by the state, local school commissioners issued an annual report to the county that distinguished between the length of time "any school was taught" in each district and the length of time in each district that school was taught "by an approved teacher." To become an "approved" teacher meant to be certified by local school inspectors. As early as 1819, the state allowed that a certified teacher could be either male or female. The "Act for support of the Common Schools" directed school inspectors to examine a candidate to determine whether "he, or she, (as the case may be) has a good moral character and is in all other respects qualified to teach a common school."[46] Nonetheless, judging from the combined evidence of town and district records, Lima school

---

[44] Sklar, "The Schooling of Girls."
[45] What counted as public funds in Massachusetts at that time was local taxes and rate bills. No state-funding or state-administered system of county taxes existed in Massachusetts at this time as it did in New York after 1812.
[46] "*An Act for the Support of Common Schools*, Passed April 12, 1819," *Laws of New York* (Albany: State of New York, 1820), Forty-Second Session, Chap. CLXI, Section 18, p. 197.

Education and Civic Engagement

officials initially understood the concept of "approved teacher" as gendered. For the year 1825, all ten of Lima's school districts reported a significant split between "the whole length of time any school has been kept in the district" and "the length of time school was kept by an approved teacher."[47] In school district no. 4, this split corresponded exactly to the number of months the district kept summer and winter schools.[48] At this point, local officials understood the concept of "approved" teacher as applying to males.

Over the next ten years, however, this understanding changed. Instead of showing a split between the total time school was in session and the time it was taught by an approved teacher, districts began reporting identical figures in the two categories. Initially, just a few districts took this step. But by 1830, seven of eleven districts reported employing an approved teacher for the entire time school was in session.[49] Together with more detailed evidence from school district no. 4, these data suggest that school officials changed their conception of who could be an approved teacher. For the years 1825, 1826, 1827, and 1828, the length of the winter school term in district no. 4 matched exactly the number of months the district reported employing an "approved teacher." In 1829, however, the district began reporting that it employed an approved teacher for all eight to ten months that school was in session, even as it continued to hire female teachers for summer school.[50] Instead of assuming that approved teachers were by definition male, officials had begun accepting both males and females as "approved."

What happened by the end of the 1820s, then, was a two-pronged change in the norms of common school teaching. Gradually and somewhat fitfully over the decade, residents enlarged the scope and significance of female teaching, from four months a year in the early 1820s to six months a year in 1830, a standard that would prevail into the following decade. During the same period, officials also changed the way they thought about certified teachers. Before the late 1820s, a certified teacher was by definition a male teacher. Beginning in the late 1820s, the meaning of certified teacher expanded to encompass women as well as men.

This change marked a political shift as well as a change in social norms. In her study of local school funding in Massachusetts, Sklar concluded that the structure of local decision making was an important factor in determining whether a town supported summer schools. In Northampton, decisions about how schools should be funded were made by the town selectmen. Elected by male property owners, this small number of officials typically came from the wealthiest families. Their decisions, in turn, reinforced older patriarchal norms of authority and governance. Assuming that heads of household would

---

[47] "Report of the Commissioners of Common Schools," Lima, New York, 1825, recorded in "Lima Town Book, 1818–1840."
[48] Minutes of Lima's School Distrct No. 4, September 1824.
[49] Report[s] of the Lima School Commissioners recorded in "The Lima Town Book, 1818–1840," passim.
[50] Minutes of Lima's School Distrct No. 4, passim.

take care of education for dependents, they reserved the use of public funds for the grammar education of males destined to become future heads of propertied households. In Sutton, by contrast, school decision making was left entirely to the parents of children who attended school. Instead of funding schools through taxes, Sutton funded them entirely through rate bills. While this practice disadvantaged the poorest parents, it also empowered families of middling means. Given the power to decide how to use their own school funds, these parents concentrated on providing basic English education for youth of both sexes.[51]

In Lima, the structure of decision making also affected support for summer schools. Under New York State law, eligibility to vote in school district meetings was restricted to freeholders and inhabitants of the district who were "liable to pay taxes."[52] This meant that in Lima, as in Northampton, property owners made the decisions about how public funds would be used. In Lima in 1820, 63 percent of the heads of household listed in the federal census were assessed local taxes and thus eligible to participate in school decision making.[53] Through the 1820s in school district no. 4, property owners directed public funds exclusively to support the winter school. Despite a lack of public funds for summer school, however, parents demonstrated growing demand for the kind of instruction summer schools provided, supplying enough funding to extend the length of summer school terms. In effect, parents changed the meaning of common schooling through acts of voluntary funding. Voting with their purses and their children's feet, they shifted the balance of common schooling away from advanced instruction for future male heads of household toward basic English instruction for children of both sexes.

Eventually, public funds followed this demand. Although William Gray failed in his initial attempt to direct a share of the district's public funds to the summer school in 1826, the district approved a similar decision a few

---

[51] In their study of the "feminization" of common school teaching, Perlmann and Margo dispute Sklar's focus on town support of summer schools as an indicator of female access to common schooling. They suggest, no doubt correctly, that winter schools taught by male teachers did sometimes include girls as well as boys, and thus that a lack of support for summer schools does not necessarily indicate a lack of support for girls' schooling (though it apparently did signal such an absence in the case of the town of Northampton). Perlmann and Margo, *Women's Work?*, 23. This important caution against using the Northampton, Massachusetts, case as the basis for a general comparative indicator should not obscure several larger points of significance illuminated by Sklar's study, however, specifically her findings regarding the social and political contexts that favored community support for female schooling.

[52] In fact, the 1819 "Act for the Support of Common Schools" specified that if any person not liable to pay taxes "shall vote in any district meeting," that person should be fined ten dollars.

[53] Lima Tax assessment, 1820, and Manuscript Census for Lima, 1820. Differences in methods and timings of the census and the tax assessment would explain some of this discrepancy. In addition, some householders not listed in the tax assessments were adult offspring of property owners who had not yet settled their estates on their children. Nonetheless, the data suggest that about a third of householders were not represented in school decision making.

years later. In 1829, the same year that the district first reported employing an "approved" teacher for both summer and winter terms, voters decided to "retain one quarter of the public money to be applied in paying the summer school bill." Although not as large a share as the half of the district's public funds sought by Gray three years earlier, this provision survived to become a new norm in the district. For the five remaining years for which the district recorded the allocation of funds by school term (through 1834), it devoted a quarter of the public funds to paying the summer school teacher.[54]

This apparently minor change in one district's school funding practices was actually part of a much larger transformation of politics and political economy in New York State. Between 1820, when district no. 4 hired Harriet Partridge to teach summer school for four months or more "as the trustees see fit," and 1829, when the district first devoted a share of public funds to summer school teaching, the sociology of the electorate in New York State changed fundamentally. Beginning with a constitutional revision in 1821–1822 and continuing with a further constitutional amendment in 1825–1826, the state abolished property qualifications for white males for state and county elections and made many offices subject to popular election that had not been elective before. As a result, the state electorate went from comprising 40 percent of the adult white male population to nearly universal white male suffrage in just five years.[55] Following these electoral reforms, New York undertook a major revision of its legislative code in 1827–1828 to reflect a more populist political culture. One result of these revisions was a change in the rules for allocating public school funds. Under the revised statutes, the law directed trustees of each common school district to divide the public funds it received into portions, not exceeding four in number, and apply one of the portions to each quarter or term during which a school was kept in the district. The state now effectively required that every district allocate some public money to summer as well as winter schools. In voting to direct one-quarter of public funds to the summer school in 1829, district no. 4 complied with these new state requirements. Through engagement in local school decision making, in other words, ordinary citizens like William Gray participated in a broader shift toward a more populist politics at the state level and achieved a more equitable distribution of public funds in local schools. Schools, in this way, were agencies of politicization.

---

[54] Minutes of Lima's School District No. 4.
[55] L. Ray Gunn, *The Decline of Authority: Public Economic Policy and Political Development in New York, 1800–1860* (Ithaca, NY: Cornell University Press, 1988): 67–71.

10

Diffusing Intelligence – Education and the Formation of the Liberal State

> If it is important that the inhabitants of the same country shall be bound together by a community of interests and a reciprocation of benefits; that agriculture should find a sale for its productions; manufactures a vent for their fabrics; and commerce a market for its commodities, it is [the state's] incumbent duty to open facilities and improve navigation.
>
> DeWitt Clinton, 1815[1]

> The more elevated the tree of knowledge and the more expanded its branches, the greater will be its trunk and the deeper its root.
>
> DeWitt Clinton, Annual Message of the Governor, 1827[2]

There's no way to know whether the men who took the lead in organizing the academy at Lima were once supporters of DeWitt Clinton. Nonetheless, it is clear that the political fortunes of Clinton and of local leaders like Asahel Warner were closely tied. As governor in 1827, DeWitt Clinton effected a set of policies that significantly expanded state support for schooling in New York. Local leaders capitalized on these changes when they founded the academy at Lima in 1830. It was not only the consequences of such policies that linked the fortunes of Clinton with those of men like Asahel Warner, however. It was also the political conditions under which they took the actions they did. After the structure of state politics was fundamentally altered by the populist suffrage reforms of 1821–1826, politicians at all levels were forced to develop a new method of establishing political influence. Drawing on a common set of

---

[1] This famed passage from DeWitt Clinton's *Memorial* is reproduced, among other places, in Nathan Miller, *The Enterprise of a Free People: Aspects of Economic Development in New York State During the Canal Period, 1792–1838* (Ithaca, NY: Cornell University Press, 1962): 42. Miller cites the original as "Memorial of the Citizens of New York," New York Canal Laws, I, 123.

[2] DeWitt Clinton, "Annual Message of the Governor," 1827, *State of New York Messages from the Governors*, Charles Z. Lincoln, ed. (Albany, NY: J. B. Lyon Company, State Printers, 1909), Vol. III, 158–159.

Diffusing Intelligence

ideas and experiences in Freemasonry, state leaders like DeWitt Clinton and local leaders like Asahel Warner responded to this new political context in similar ways. Specifically, as governor, Clinton articulated a vision of the new liberal state that connected ideas of individual liberty with those of public liberality through increased state funding for common schools and academies. In the process, he created a "community of interests" and "reciprocation of benefits" among local leaders like Asahel Warner, rural communities like Lima, and urban merchants and financiers.[3]

This chapter explores the significance of education in the formation of this new liberal state. Specifically, it suggests that education was at the heart of coalition building at both local and state levels during the politically chaotic 1820s. This analysis reverses the usual lens for considering the relationship between education and the state. Most accounts of the rise of state support for mass education focus on the state as the central actor in the creation of mass education systems. In Lima, as in much of the rural North, however, voluntary demand and support for schooling far exceeded anything required by the state in 1820. Indeed, it could be argued that in the early decades of the nineteenth century, social and financial support of *education* exceeded that of the state itself. From this perspective, the significance of increased state support for schooling in the 1820s was more political than financial. It converted the already considerable social capital commanded by schools into political capital for the state.

Education and Politics in DeWitt Clinton's Career

It is difficult to know anything about how party politics operated at the local level during the early nineteenth century. Surviving poll lists from before 1860 are rare, and electoral totals at the town level from before 1830 cannot be found for any but a few exceptional years.[4] Even when such information does exist, it does not necessarily tell us much. One vote total for Lima does survive for 1823. It shows the Lima electorate evenly split between candidates for state senator, as most other towns in the county were.[5] We also know that in 1838 the local leader and academy organizer Asahel Warner was listed among the leaders of the "democratic republicans" at the county level.[6] However, this

---

[3] These phrases are quoted from Clinton's *Memorial*. See footnote 1.

[4] Beginning in 1830, official election totals for state-level offices were reported in Edwin Williams, *The New York Annual Register* (New York: J. Leavitt, 1830–1840). The Register also included some totals from previous years, including 1828. Some years, however, the Register reported totals for the county rather than the town level. County newspapers are another source of electoral totals and can be found for earlier years, but this reporting is also inconsistent and the newspapers themselves do not survive for every year. At the local level, poll lists for the town of Lima survive only for the 1860s and 1870s, and for 1900.

[5] *Livingston County Journal*, Vol. III, No. 31, November 14, 1823, LCHS.

[6] A September 1836 newspaper account identifies Asahel Warner, Melancthon Brown, Alexander Martin, and E. A. Sumner as representatives from the town of Lima to the county convention of the Democratic Republicans. The newspaper itself was clearly a pro-Jackson newspaper at that time, though two years earlier, under previous ownership, it had been an anti-Jackson

association with Jacksonianism dates after the Morgan affair of 1826 and the resulting anti-Masonic movement had fundamentally realigned state politics, particularly in western New York. We cannot assume from this information anything about politics in Lima in DeWitt Clinton's time.

If Clinton somehow failed to win votes from leading men in Lima, it wasn't for lack of political acumen. DeWitt Clinton was something of a political alchemist and, as some have said, a political phoenix. More than once his political career appeared to be dead, only to undergo a stunning revival. Although the 1821 constitutional convention had been largely the work of his political opponents, for example, and had led indirectly to his loss of the governor's office in 1822, Clinton ultimately came to be associated with the new constitution's essentially populist principle, winning back the office as an advocate of universal suffrage and a candidate of the "People's Party" in 1824. Similarly, although he was something of a patrician in many ways and had been the Grand Master of the Masons for the State of New York for fourteen years, Clinton not only managed to retain his credibility and his office through the Morgan affair and the rise of anti-Masonry in 1827, but he also successfully cast his political opponents as agents of "the Mason Party."[7]

The success of the Erie Canal, with which Clinton was so strongly associated, had a lot to do with his capacity for political regeneration. It may also be true, as one historian has remarked, that the experience of defeat inspired Clinton's most imaginative political acts.[8] Certainly it was his vision for the Erie Canal, and his efficacy in promoting it, that turned Clinton's defeat for reelection as mayor of New York City in 1815 into a successful bid for governor of New York two years later – just as canal construction got underway. It was also indirectly the Erie Canal that rescued him a decade later, after he had lost the governorship. In 1824, as the canal neared completion, Clinton's opponents dismissed him from the Board of Canal Commissioners, a position he had held without pay since the board's initial organization. Capitalizing on this experience as a victim of the spoils system, Clinton affiliated with the People's Party and rode the backlash back into the governor's office later that same year.[9]

---

paper. Livingston Register Vol. XI, No. 38, September 6, 1836, GVHC. According to *The New York Annual Register* for 1836 (see footnote 4), the town of Lima voted for the Whig candidate for governor (Seward) in 1834 over the Jacksonian candidate (Marcy), 213 to 185 (54% for Seward). This vote was much closer than for Livingston County as a whole, however, which voted for Seward 3,217 to 1,961 (62% for Seward). Again in 1840 the county as a whole voted against the Jacksonian candidate.

[7] For a detailed account of Clinton's political career, see Evan Cornog, *The Birth of Empire: DeWitt Clinton and the American Experience, 1769–1828* (New York: Oxford University Press, 1998). For an even more detailed account of Clinton's later career in the context of the politics of the 1820s, see Craig Hanyan with Mary L. Hanyan, *DeWitt Clinton and the Rise of the People's Men* (Montreal: McGill-Queen's University Press, 1996).

[8] For a succinct summary of Clinton's character and political strengths and weaknesses, see Dixon Ryan Fox, *The Decline of Aristocracy in the Politics of New York* (published Ph.D. dissertation, Columbia University, 1919): 344–347; also pp. 194–205. For a detailed account of Clinton's involvement with the Erie Canal, see Miller, *Enterprise*.

[9] Cornog, *Empire*, 145–157.

More than the canal itself, however, it was Clinton's genius for political economy that explains the ease with which he made the transition from patrician to populist. Clinton saw and articulated, perhaps earlier and better than anyone else, how certain public expenditures could create not only new common wealth but new political capital. Much of this understanding partook of the old practice of "creating interest," in which constituencies were rewarded with the allocation of public benefits. But there was more to Clinton's understanding of politics than this simple quid pro quo. The genius of Clinton's approach to politics was to make the distribution of public benefits not simply discretionary but systematic. Beyond cobbling together supporters through the exchange of individual favors and loyalties, Clinton sought to join the interests of multiple groups and constituencies together through the practice of political economy. He aimed, in other words, at creating common interests through systemic public works.

This was an idea exemplified by the Erie Canal, but its implications went far beyond the canal. When Clinton made his oft-quoted remarks about the importance of binding a country's inhabitants together in a "community of interests" and "reciprocation of benefits," he was arguing for public investment in internal navigation.¹⁰ At least as important to his vision of distributive politics, however, was state support for education. Biographers and historians often note Clinton's avid interest in scientific and literary organizations, as well as his leadership in various educational institutions. Among the organizations in which he took a lead were the New York Historical Society, the Literary and Philosophical Society, the American Academy of Fine Arts, the Free School Society of New York City, and – perhaps more important than any of these – the Freemasons. By all accounts, Clinton took great pride in his learning and scientific knowledge, a pride that verged on pomposity and was sometimes a subject of satire. Less commented on are his associations with a number of public measures in support of education and his ideas about the significance of education in the political economy of the state.¹¹

The men who took the lead in organizing the academy at Lima had roles in Clinton's vision. It is not that Clinton took any particular interest in Lima as a

---

¹⁰ These phrases from Clinton's "Memorial" belong to the most widely cited passage of Clinton's writings. The passage is reproduced, among other places, in Miller, *Enterprise*, 42–43; and Cornog, *Empire*, 115.

¹¹ The original account of Clinton's intellectual pride, dilletantism, and pomposity appears in Fox, *Decline*, 194–220. A more friendly account of the significance of Clinton's literary and scientific activities appears in Thomas Bender, *New York Intellect: A History of Intellectual Life in New York City, from 1750 to the Beginnings of our Own Time* (Baltimore: Johns Hopkins University Press, 1987): 48–88. Still, Bender's focus is on New York City and on Clinton's activity in various educational and cultural organizations headquartered there. Although Bender, Fox, Cornog, and others note that Clinton was a great promoter of education, they do not examine closely his role in systematic school legislation. The chief exception to the way Clinton's educational interests are presented is Edward A. Fitzpatrick, *The Educational Views and Influence of DeWitt Clinton* (New York: Teachers College, Columbia University, 1911). This book provides a valuable blow-by-blow account of Clinton's writings

place. Nor was it that Lima's leading men were personally known to Clinton, at least as far as we know. Rather, the leading men of Lima participated in Clinton's vision by acting out a shared idea of their roles in a broader enlightenment project often referred to as the "diffusion of intelligence." That this idea was indeed shared is indicated by their common experience. Like Clinton, local Lima leaders Asahel Warner and Justin Smith were longtime Freemasons. In fact, as Grand Master for the State of New York in 1816, Clinton signed the charter for Lima's Masonic Lodge, of which Warner and Smith were founding members.[12] Based on their common history as Freemasons and their subsequent actions, we can say that Clinton and men like Warner and Smith shared certain ideas about their roles as leaders.

Freemasonry and the Promotion of Education in the United States

As it emerged in Britain in the 1710s, Freemasonry was a fraternal movement of learned gentlemen with a common interest in science, a nostalgic relationship to medieval guilds, and a fascination with ancient mysteries and even magic. Through commercial and colonial networks it quickly spread throughout the world, including the American colonies, where it took root in the 1730s and flourished in the Revolutionary era. Always associated with Enlightenment thinkers and ideas, including, most famously, Isaac Newton, Freemasonry assumed a new significance in the United States. Freemasons in the post-Revolution United States self-consciously organized themselves around the selection and cultivation of virtuous and enlightened leaders for the new republican state. During the Revolutionary era the sociological profile of Masonry also changed. New Masonic lodges rejected associations with aristocratic social ranks and promoted the idea of equality among members. Although the wealth and social standing of Masons as a group always remained substantially above that of the population as a whole, during the Revolution and post-Revolutionary periods Masonic membership broadened. The new, self-described "Ancient" lodges invoked older guild associations and included higher proportions of artisans and retail shopkeepers than did previous "Modern" lodges, whose membership was dominated by men from the mercantile and professional classes.[13]

---

and activities on education. It does not examine these views and activities in any kind of political context, however.

[12] According to miscellaneous records and references held by the Lima Historical Society, Asahel Warner was one of three men who organized the first local lodge in 1809, though it appears that this first lodge may have been located elsewhere in the county (the other two men listed are not traceable as residents of Lima) and that the first lodge to be located in the town of Lima was organized in 1815. Asahel Warner, Smith Weeks, and Justin Smith are listed as the first officers of this new lodge. The official charter for this lodge, which is included in the surviving materials, is dated 1816 and signed by DeWitt Clinton. "Mason Scrapbook," Lima New York, LHS.

[13] Steven C. Bullock, *Revolutionary Brotherhood: Freemasonry and the Transformation of the American Social Order, 1730–1840* (Chapel Hill: University of North Carolina Press, 1996).

Although most often remembered for their secrecy and mysterious rituals, Masons in the United States had a decidedly public agenda. Central to this agenda was the promotion of learning and education, a link that Clinton, as an important Masonic leader in the 1790s, helped to establish and articulate. This commitment to learning and education operated at several levels. The first of these was the education of members themselves. As described by historian Steven C. Bullock, Masons not only favored a degree of learning among the men they chose to accept as members, but they understood the rituals of the organization in pedagogical terms. Through these rituals, Clinton explained in a 1793 address, Masons "impress" their lessons "with a greater force upon the mind." To ensure the efficacy of this pedagogy, moreover, the Masons effectively organized a form of teacher training in which traveling agents of the organization, known as "lecturers," drilled members in the texts of Masonic rituals and the meaning of Masonic symbols. Among the ideas cultivated by these means were the value of virtue and the virtue of learning itself. DeWitt Clinton, in particular, celebrated the roots of Freemasonry in scientific learning and defined the mission of Freemasonry in educational terms. In his 1793 address, Clinton credited the "scientific and ingenious men" who founded the fraternity with the aim of sharing the secrets of the arts and sciences with the world and of bringing "the means of instruction to all ranks of people."[14]

According to Bullock, this emphasis on learning and education represented a post-Revolutionary shift in Masonic culture. It also brought an educational emphasis to Masonic ideas about the role of its members as leaders in republican society. Masons at every level of organization began portraying themselves as promoters of education and learning in society and as sponsors of educational activities and institutions, including libraries, public schools, and museums. Bullock recounts instances in which particular Masonic lodges housed and financed schools and libraries and referred to lodges themselves as seminaries of learning and places where the sciences were taught. More broadly, Masonic leaders and lodges by the 1820s began associating themselves with the *policy* of encouraging "schools and the advancement of knowledge" and of promoting "the general diffusion of education." As an orator at the consecration of Maine's grand lodge said in 1820, "To no order in society is the encouragement of schools and the advancement of knowledge more valuable than to the Fraternity."[15]

The historical significance of Freemasonry derived from the way it coupled this enlightenment vision with an extensive and effective organizational structure. At every level of Masonic membership, from certification as an "Entered Apprentice" to the award of the "Fellow Craft" and "Master's"

For the Revolutionary era change in membership and ideology among American Masons, see especially pp. 109–133.
[14] Clinton's 1793 address to the New York Masons is described at length in Bullock, *Brotherhood*, 139–147.
[15] Bullock, *Brotherhood*, 148.

degrees, men were initiated into the historic traditions, structures, and values of Freemasonry. These included ideals of nonsectarian civic virtue and disinterested public service, as well as a vision of a republican leadership based on talent and merit rather than on birth or connection. Through the experience of sponsorship, initiation, and advancement as members, Masons were confirmed in their roles as social and political leaders who exercised power and influence for the common good. Men like Asahel Warner and Justin Smith, who assumed positions of leadership both within Freemasonry and in society at large, presumably came to see themselves as agents of Masonic enlightenment within their own locality. In Lima, Asahel Warner in particular clearly regarded Freemasonry as central to his identity. A member of the order since at least 1809, and quite possibly before, he built a Masonic meeting room into the attic of his home.[16] His leading role in virtually every local education and community building project from the early 1800s until his death in the late 1840s also suggests a self-conception consistent with Masonic visions of leadership. From the founding of the first church society in 1801 to the construction of the brick school house in 1803, from his service with Justin Smith in 1815 as one of the town's first three common school commissioners to his leading role in organizing the academy in Lima in 1830, Warner acted as one who assumed that his status as a major landholder conferred on him certain prerogatives but who exercised that role in ways commensurate with Masonic enlightenment ideas about the importance of education and the value of civic and intellectual improvement.

At the same time as Freemasonry inculcated certain ideas of leadership among its members, it also connected them with a wide-ranging network of like-minded fellows beyond their locality. Masons were strongly acculturated to the idea of belonging to a universal and affectionate brotherhood that extended across place and time. As first developed and elaborated by Masons in British colonial society, who came largely from the mercantile and professional classes, these ideas of universal brotherhood clearly facilitated political and business activity in an international context.[17] In the early republican United States, the same brotherly relations served a similar function in local, state, and national contexts, facilitating the formation of personal connections and networks between urban and rural society, and between coastal and interior locations.[18] Although originating primarily in coastal cities, Freemasonry expanded considerably into the interior during the late eighteenth and early nineteenth centuries. Between 1790 and 1806, the number of lodges in New York State increased from about 10 to about 100, with new lodges meeting primarily outside New York City. By 1825, the number of lodges in the state had increased to nearly 500, with most in the interior of the state, including the

---

[16] Thanks to Fran Gotscik, member of the Lima Historical Society, for arranging for me to see this lodge room, which still survives.
[17] Bullock, *Brotherhood*, 229.
[18] Ibid., 224.

Diffusing Intelligence

new lodge founded in Lima in 1816.[19] This gave New York the largest number of Masonic lodges of any state at the time and may in part be explained by the role Masonic networks played in New York politics.

The Significance of Freemasonry in New York State Politics

Everywhere in the United States Freemasons participated in politics, but for some places and levels of officeholding Masonic membership was more important than for others. At one meeting of the grand lodge in Raleigh, North Carolina, in 1797, 70 percent of the attendees held or had held high state office, and another 10 percent would gain such office in the following decade, according to Bullock. This meeting occurred in the state capital during the legislative session and thus no doubt included an exceptionally high number of state officeholders. Outside such highly political contexts the proportion of Freemasons who were officeholders was lower but still impressive. Bullock's analysis of lodge memberships in Lexington, Kentucky, from 1794 to 1810 and in Geneva, New York, from 1807 to 1819 showed that in both cases nearly half of the lodges' members held political office at the village, county, state, or national level.[20] In the Geneva case, more than a tenth of these offices were those of state or national legislators.

There is some evidence that in New York, at least, the political significance of Freemasonry was greater for men from rural areas than for those in larger towns and cities. In her extensive study of county officeholding in Genesee County, New York, the next county west of Lima, Kathleen Kutolowski found that in the 1820s Masonic membership was more strongly associated with county officials who came from small towns and rural areas than with those from the leading towns of the county.[21] These findings are complemented by Bullock's analysis of places of residence for members of four different lodges during the first decades of the nineteenth century. Anywhere from a third to more than half of the members resided in places outside the town in which the lodge was located. For one of two lodges in Geneva, New York, itself a county seat, the proportion of out-of-town members was as high as 63 percent.[22]

That membership in a Masonic lodge should have been so important to men living outside the state capital or county seat makes sense when one considers the way in which offices above the town level were filled in New York State. Under New York's somewhat distinctive Revolutionary era constitution, most county-level offices were filled by state-level appointment. In such a system, membership in a multi-level fraternal network of public-minded men made

---

[19] Ibid., 187–188.
[20] Ibid., 223.
[21] Kathleen Smith Kutolowski, "The Social Composition of Political Leadership: Genesee County, New York, 1821–1860" (unpublished PhD. dissertation, University of Rochester, 1973): 185–187.
[22] Bullock, *Brotherhood*, 231.

sense as a strategy for acquiring power at the county or state level. It may also have made particularly good sense for men in small towns and rural areas who did not have the opportunity to become acquainted with men of power through other forms of association. In the case of Lima's Asahel Warner, it is not entirely clear whether he brought Freemasonry to the task of being nominated and elected to state office, or whether he became a Mason as a result of that service, but the chronology of surviving evidence is suggestive. Warner began his first term as state assemblyman in 1807. The earliest surviving reference of his activity as a Mason dates from 1809.[23] As this date precedes that of the founding of the first lodge in Lima, Warner must have first joined a lodge elsewhere, such as the state capital or the county seat in Canandaigua.

All this suggests the organizational as well as the affective power of Freemasonry for inculcating a shared vision of leadership among men from diverse geographical locations and at various levels of office. This capacity transcended differences of political faction or party. In her study of county-level officeholders in Genesee County, Kutolowski found that the proportion of Clintonians and of his Bucktail opponents who were Masons before 1826 were roughly equal, 46 and 48 percent, respectively.[24] These data suggest that Freemasonry successfully achieved a degree of nonpartisanship. It also suggests how politics may have worked in a period of weak party organization. Given a common education in republican leadership and enlightenment values, men of similar experience may have acted in concert even in the absence of deliberate organization. More specifically, a shared vision of leadership forged through Freemasonry made it possible for men like DeWitt Clinton and Asahel Warner to respond to political crisis in parallel ways despite their lack of personal acquaintance, their differences of political status, and what probably were opposing party affiliations at the state level.

The crisis of political leadership experienced by Asahel Warner and DeWitt Clinton in the 1820s was initiated by the constitutional revision of 1821. The new constitution fundamentally transformed politics in New York State in several ways. First, the new constitution significantly altered suffrage qualifications. Under the original state constitution of 1777, New York restricted suffrage to male freeholders. It also defined two standards of property holding depending on the office for which electors were voting. For local offices and the office of state assemblyman, an elector had to own taxable property worth at least 20 pounds or lease a tenement at a rate of 40 shillings per year. According to later estimates, this standard encompassed 78 percent of adult male citizens in 1821.[25] For the offices of governor and state senator, electors had to own taxable property worth at least 100 pounds, a standard

---

[23] "Mason Scrapbook," Lima, New York.
[24] Kutolowski, "Political Leadership," 150.
[25] These estimates seem to have originated with Franklin B. Hough, *Census of the Electors of the State of New York* (Albany, 1857) as cited by Chilton Williamson, *American Suffrage: From Property to Democracy, 1760–1860* (Princeton, NJ: Princeton University Press, 1960): 197. Williamson then became the source for later citations, such as in Richard McCormick,

that included 38 percent of adult male citizens. Both these standards were changed in the constitutional revision of 1821. After the new constitution was ratified in January 1822, New York defined a single electorate for both local- and state-level offices. It also extended suffrage to all adult white males who paid taxes to the county or state, served in the militia, or contributed labor to maintain the highways. At the state level, the new provisions resulted in a significant expansion of the electorate. In the governor's race of 1824, twice as many electors participated as had in 1820. According to historians, the proportion of the population eligible to vote at all levels of government increased to 90 percent of adult white males.[26]

The new constitution would not have had nearly the impact it did, however, if it had not also abolished the state-level Council of Appointment. Under the old constitution, a small number of officials at the state level held the power to appoint an immense number of officials at the county level, including sheriffs, judges, justices of the peace, militia officers, and constables. This arrangement fostered a particular pattern of political organization that scholars have variously referred to as "patronage" or "personal" politics. To attain office, an individual had to be known personally, or by personal recommendation, to men of standing at the state level.[27] This was the structure that made Freemasonry particularly important in New York politics following the Revolution. Under the new 1821 constitution, however, the logic of such alliances was largely broken. The new constitution made many offices elective that had previously been filled by the state Council of Appointment. This change substantially altered the dynamics and direction of political affiliation and organization throughout the state. A man seeking office at the county level now had to look less to his political superiors for sponsorship and more to his inferiors. Add to this the fact that one's inferiors now included a whole new set of previously ineligible voters, and the problem of political organization in the 1820s becomes clear. Not only had many offices now become elective, but the electorate had expanded, and the basis for cultivating support from this larger group of voters had not yet developed.

Scholars of political history refer to the period between 1821 and 1827 as one of profound political confusion and transition in New York State, especially in its western regions.[28] As one newspaper editor put it in 1822, the new

---

The Second American Party System: Party Formation in the Jacksonian Era (Chapel Hill: University of North Carolina Press, 1966): 113, and McCormick became the source for later citations yet, such as in L. Ray Gunn, *The Decline of Authority: Public Economic Policy and Political Development in New York, 1800–1860* (Ithaca, NY: Cornell University Press, 1988): 71.

[26] McCormick, *Party System*, 113.

[27] For a particularly illuminating description of how patronage politics worked in New York before the constitution of 1821, see Alan Taylor, *William Cooper's Town: Power and Persuasion on the Frontier of the Early American Republic* (New York: Alfred A. Knopf, 1995), esp. pp. 231–49. See also Fox, *Decline*.

[28] The most illuminating description of this political chaos appears in Kutolowski, "Political Leadership." See also McCormick, *Party System*, 113–114 on the significance of abolishing

state constitution of 1821 had "broken up the political deep" and "set afloat a mass of matter that will require time to find its proper level."²⁹ For Lima, these already significant changes in existing political structures were compounded by simultaneous changes in local political geography. In 1821, just before the constitutional convention, the legislature created two new counties in the western region and altered some town boundaries. In what may well have been a deliberate gerrymander, Lima became part of a new county and simultaneously lost territory. The lost territory included some of the most valuable land owned by the Warners, thereby dividing their property-based influence between two different towns and counties. The new county of Livingston, to which Lima now belonged, was dominated by the Wadsworths, a family of land agents and large-scale landowners who represented a different political network than that which governed Canandaigua and Ontario County.³⁰ With these changed conditions, the Warner family in particular lost political power. The last year either Asahel or his brother Matthew Warner served in a state-level office was 1822. In this respect, Asahel had much in common with the erstwhile Governor DeWitt Clinton. Both lost power and confronted a changed political world in which the path to reconstructing political power was unclear. For Clinton, the exile from office proved temporary. For Warner, retirement from office (though not from politics) proved permanent. Nonetheless, for both the political dilemma was much the same. Ultimately, the two men would respond to this dilemma in parallel ways.

Education and the New Liberal State

Clinton's response to the political dilemma of the 1820s began with embracing the expansion of suffrage, including a number of new provisions that would further increase the size of the electorate. Specifically, "the People's Party" took shape around the issue of making the choice of presidential electors subject to popular election rather than to the vote of the legislature, as had

---

the Council of Appointment; and Fox, *Decline*, 229–270 on the issues and debates surrounding adoption of the 1821 constitution.

²⁹ *Spirit of the Times*, October 25, 1822. Cited in Kutolowski, "Political Leadership," 127. Kutolowski quotes the Bucktail newspaper editor's comments at length in support of her claim that "the six years following the passage of that new constitution can best be characterized by factional confusion, flux, and upheavel."

³⁰ Given the advantages and attention that the Wadsworths and the town of Geneseo received at state hands in 1821 and 1827, both under Clinton's governorship, it is highly likely that the Wadsworths affiliated with the Clintonians in the 1820s. So far, however, though the Wadsworths figure prominently in various historical treatments of politics and economy in western New York during this time period, I have not succeeded in finding any discussions of their political activities and affiliations in this early time period. Members of later generations of the family assumed even more prominent roles in state politics and thus seem to have overshadowed the political activities of earlier generations. Nail Adams McNall, *The First Half-Century of Wadsworth Tenancy* (Ithaca, NY: Cornell University Press, 1945); Alden Hatch, *The Wadsworths of the Genesee* (New York: Coward-McCann, Inc., 1959).

been the case theretofore. More broadly, as a candidate of the People's Party in 1824, Clinton came to advocate a number of electoral reforms, including some originated by his opponents, that would broaden the franchise and the number of offices open to popular election beyond what had already been effected in the 1821 constitutional revisions.[31] By the time of the governor's race of 1824, Clinton had adopted an essentially populist platform, at least with respect to suffrage.

Just as important as the reforms themselves was the rationale Clinton articulated for the continued expansion of the franchise. Once he had won the gubernatorial election of November 1824 and regained office in January 1825, Clinton framed the logic for the additional electoral reforms he advocated. He did this first by grounding his own authority in the popular will, presenting himself as "having been elected to office, not by a party, but by the people."[32] He then proceeded to articulate the principles on which suffrage should turn. "Without the right of suffrage liberty cannot exist," Clinton began. And yet, under the existing provisions, suffrage was conditional. While no longer confined strictly to property holders, it still depended on payment of taxes, performance of military duty, or labor on the highways, and thus on the actions of tax assessors, road masters, and militia officials. The problem with such provisions was not only that they "exclude(d) a great body of citizens from the elective franchise" but that they did so on a contingent basis. "The rights of a citizen ought not to be held at the pleasure of others, but should be fixed and unchangeable," Clinton declared.[33] They should, in other words, *inhere in the individual* rather than depend on circumstance.[34] Clinton thus articulated an essential principle of political liberalism – individual liberty.

Even more interesting is how Clinton used this idea of individual liberty to justify a more liberal state government. Drawing on standard early national rhetoric, he posed the familiar problem of the survival of the republic. Now that the representative system is well understood, Clinton stated, "it will

---

[31] Cornog, *Empire*, 145–157.
[32] DeWitt Clinton, "Annual Message of the Governor," January 4, 1825, *Messages of the Governor* (Albany): 55.
[33] Ibid., 58.
[34] The shift to this idea that liberty should inhere in the person of the individual, rather than in the person's condition or status, had profound implications for how suffrage and citizenship were conceived and administered in the nineteenth century – a topic worthy of a whole separate essay. By positing the inherent quality of civil liberty, political leaders indirectly posed the question of whether the capacity to exercise civil liberty really DID inhere in ALL individuals. Predictably, men of the time decided that it did not – that certain classes of persons (i.e., blacks and women) did not have this inherent quality. In this way, the shift to a more individualistic concept of liberty solidified and made explicit race and gender restrictions on citizenship and suffrage that had not been explicit before, when suffrage was based on ownership of property. And indeed, as Rowland Berthoff documented extensively some years ago, the question of whether blacks and women had such inherent qualities was an explicit and extensive topic of conversation in the constitutional conventions of the mid-nineteenth century. See Berthoff, "Conventional Mentality: Free Blacks, Women, and Business Corporations as Unequal

be our own fault if its duration prove not as permanent as its blessings are inestimable." He then went on to outline the means of preventing such an eventuality. After a brief review of the tendency to corruption and oppression characteristic of monarchies, Clinton asserted "man becomes degraded in proportion as he loses the right of self-government." Given this fact, "every effort ought to be made to fortify our fine institutions," Clinton continued:

> and the great bulwark of security is to be found in education; the culture of the heart and head; the diffusion of knowledge, piety and morality. ... Upon education we must therefore rely for the purity, the preservation and the perpetuation of republican government. In this sacred cause we cannot exercise too much liberality.[35]

Of course, the idea that the security of the republic depended on knowledge and virtue was not new. Nor was the idea that the state should provide some support or "encouragement" for education. For Clinton, active sponsorship of schools and learning societies and of public funding for education at both the municipal and state levels went back to the early days of the republic in the 1790s. For New York, state support of education began with the creation of the Regents system of incorporation for academies and colleges in the 1780s, continued with the establishment of a permanent common school fund in 1805, and was followed by the organization of the similar fund for support of academies in 1813. What is interesting about Clinton's remarks is not the fact that he advocated state support of education. What is noteworthy is how he connected ideas of individual liberty and public liberality. Clinton embraced the expansion of suffrage and then used that expansion to justify a more expansive role for government.

More precisely, Clinton argued for increased state support for education.[36] As it turned out, such increases had to wait until the electoral reforms had been achieved. Taking up the issue again two years later, in January 1827, Clinton noted that the right to vote was now established on a permanent basis, as a condition inherent to each white male person's status as citizen. In Clinton's analysis, this achievement of universal white male suffrage required increased investment in education. "After all," Clinton stated, "the great bulwark of republican government is the cultivation of education, for the right of suffrage cannot be exercised in a salutary manner without intelligence."[37]

Clinton's plan for fostering such intelligence included increased funding not only for common schools but for higher schooling as well. Rhetorically, at least, the education of teachers played an important role in the logic of this argument. With nearly 8,000 schools in operation, many teachers lacked the requisite qualifications for teaching and few had the capacity to teach

---

Persons, 1820–1870," *Journal of American History* 76: 3 (December, 1989): 753–784; and David N. Gellman and David Quigley, eds. *Jim Crow New York: A Documentary History of Race and Citizenship, 1777–1877* (New York: New York University Press, 2003).

[35] Clinton, "Annual Message, 1825," 59–60.
[36] Ibid., 61.
[37] DeWitt Clinton, "Annual Message of the Governor," 1827.

Diffusing Intelligence

beyond the rudiments. To address these problems, Clinton recommended that each county establish a central school "on the monitorial plan" for "the education of teachers" and for "other momentous purposes connected with the improvement of the human mind." By way of example, he cited the model of the New York High School organized two years earlier. Lest the viability of such an institution be thought peculiar to New York City, Clinton noted that "enlightened and public spirited citizens in Livingston County were organizing a similar school."[38]

Clinton did not limit his statement of support for higher education to the training of teachers, however. He went on to articulate the general value to society of promoting institutions of higher study. The positive influence of such institutions derived not only from the education of teachers but from their impact on other individuals who became leaders. Independent of their "intrinsic merits and their diffusive and enduring benefits," higher institutions "give to society men of improved and enlarged minds." Feeling "the importance of information on their own experience," these individuals "will naturally cherish an ardent desire to extend its blessings."[39] The benefits of higher learning extended well beyond those who actually pursued higher study themselves, in other words. Although the number of people attending colleges and academies or who participated in scientific and literary societies was small, those who did participate were likely to be agents of education and scientific improvement in their own localities, thus diffusing the benefits of intelligence throughout the state:

Science delights in expansion as well as in concentration, and after having flourished within the precincts of academies and universities, will spread itself over the land, enlightening society and ameliorating the condition of men. The more elevated the tree of knowledge and the more expanded its branches, the greater will be its trunk and the deeper its roots.[40]

In short, the interests of society lay both in the horizontal expansion of common schooling and in the vertical building of higher learning. This idea that learning and improvement could be diffused through the education of enlightened leaders for all levels of government was the American Masonic ideal rendered as public policy.

Increased School Funding and the "Reciprocation of Benefits"

Clinton did not stop at articulating this idea, however. On April 13, 1827, the idea was instantiated in "An ACT to provide permanent funds for the annual appropriation to Common Schools, to increase the Literature Fund, and to Promote the Education of Teachers."[41] This legislation directly accomplished

---

[38] Clinton, "Annual Message, 1827," 160.
[39] Ibid.
[40] Ibid., 160–161.
[41] "An ACT to provide permanent funds for the annual appropriation to Common Schools, to increase the Literature Fund, and to Promote the Education of Teachers," Passed April 13,

two main things. First, it significantly increased the amount of funding available for distribution to both common schools and academies. With respect to common schools, the act directed that the common school fund be augmented by the balance due on a substantial existing state loan and by $100,000 in shares of bank stock owned by the state. With respect to academies, the act directed that the state comptroller sign over to the Literature Fund a total of $150,000 in bonds and mortgages held by the state's canal fund. This amounted to more than four times the fund's existing capital, the largest single increase to the state's Literature Fund ever made, then or later. Second, the 1827 education act officially altered the terms on which state funding for higher institutions would be distributed. Instead of prorating the distribution of income from the state Literature Fund according to the number of students pursuing a classical course of study at each institution, as the Regents had done previously, the 1827 act directed the Regents to distribute funds according to the number of students who pursued *either* classical studies *or* "the higher branches of English education," or both.[42] This provision marked an important turn in the practice of state support for higher schooling. Henceforth, state funds for higher schooling would go not only to support classical education for the sons of professionals and gentlemen who aspired to collegiate education and membership among the political elite; they would also go to support a scientific or higher "English" education for sons and *daughters* of middling farmers, merchants, shopkeepers and craftsmen who sought employment as teachers, or as clerks and agents in the growing number of commercial occupations that defined the new middle class.

In addition to the increase in funding and the change in policy accomplished directly by these provisions, the 1827 education law had several indirect consequences. One consequence was a significant expansion of academy education in the state. Once income on the new funds became available in 1828, the Regents substantially increased the number of institutions to which they granted Regents status, thereby making them eligible for shares of the state's Literature Fund. In 1828 alone, the Regents chartered eleven new academies, nearly four times the number it had ever chartered in a single year before. Not only the number but the type of institutions expanded. The eleven institutions granted Regents charters in 1828 included several that would have been denied Regents status under previous policy. They included three female institutions and the first Methodist academy to acquire Regents status – an institution located in Cazenovia, 100 miles east of Lima. The following year, in 1829, the Regents chartered another six institutions, including two county high schools, one of which was the Livingston High School of Geneseo. Also chartered by the Regents in 1829 was a novel experiment in the town of Whitesboro, New York – an institution called the Oneida Institute of Science and Industry, sponsored by antislavery activists and associations, which admitted both black

---

1827, *Laws of the State of New York*, 50th Session, Chap. 228 (Albany: E. Croswell, Printer to the State, 1827): 237–238.
[42] Ibid., 237.

and white students. One practical consequence of the 1827 education act, in other words, was that the distribution of and access to state-supported higher schooling was broadened in several ways – with respect to geography, subject matter, sex, class, religion, and even race.

Another indirect consequence of the 1827 education law was that school funding became even more strongly connected to capitalist economic development. This occurred in several ways. The most obvious of these was the capitalization of the common school fund with shares of bank stock. This method of capitalization tied the availability of state school funds directly to the expansion of the money supply and to interest on banks loans and other forms of bank credit.[43] Already in 1819, nearly a third of the annual income on New York's common school fund came from dividends on bank stock. The 1827 education law increased this form of capitalization by nearly 40 percent.[44] Similarly, the 1827 education law increased the capital of the Literature Fund through the consignment of bonds and mortgages owned by the state's canal fund. Many of these bonds and mortgages were held on lands originally owned by the state and sold to raise funds for canal construction. Indirectly, then, the Literature Fund benefited from state investment in internal navigation and, more specifically, from the conversion of state land into investment capital. Or, to put the same point another way, the aims of education and the interests of local school communities were tied to those of bankers, merchants, manufacturers, and land speculators with financial stakes in certain forms of economic development. In this way, the 1827 school law effectively forged the kind of connection that Clinton had once called "a community of interests" and a "reciprocation of benefits."

This method of school funding represented a somewhat different idea of the political economy of education than that articulated by Adam Smith. In Smith's *Wealth of Nations*, the subject of education appeared in a section on the "expense" of public works and institutions. For Smith, the question was how much of a draw or drain schooling made on common wealth. As the practice of political economy developed in New York in the 1810s and 1820s, however, education actually became a producer of wealth in a real, though somewhat peculiar way. Education was an end or value that motivated and justified the creation and investment of capital and the production of new wealth. To use Smith's terms, the end or value of education "put into motion" productive labor.[45] This productive capacity developed at two levels: at the state level and at the local level. At the local level, the social value of education

---

[43] New York was not the only state that adopted this funding technique. According to the historian John Muscalus, the use of banking enterprises to finance public education was a common practice in states during the period from 1796 to 1866. In his book, he provides a state-by-state account of how this technique was used. John Anthony Muscalus, *The Use of Banking Enterprises in the Financing of Public Education, 1796–1866* (Philadelphia: University of Pennsylvania Press, 1945).

[44] Ibid., 34.

[45] Adam Smith, "Of the Expense of the Institutions for the Education of Youth," and "Of the Expense of Institutions for the Instruction of People of All Ages," Book V, Part III, Articles 2

motivated the creation of common wealth for local institutions. At the state level, the social value of education justified state investment in economic development. In this political economy, education and production did not occupy opposite sides of a ledger, one for the accumulation of wealth and the other for expenditures. Rather, they were complementary endeavors, each stimulating the other. The more the state invested in economic development, the more it promoted the "diffusion of intelligence" through schools. Similarly, the more local communities invested in schools, the more they stimulated state investment in economic development. A second consequence of the 1827 school law, then, was to advance a change in the logic of political economy with respect to schooling.

This logic of the new liberal state had political as well as economic dimensions. As Clinton clearly understood when he first framed the phrases "community of interests" and "reciprocation of benefits," economic interests were also political interests. To the extent that the new political economy of schooling succeeded in strengthening the connection between state benefits and local constituencies, it provided a tool for meeting the political challenges of the 1820s. Men with economic power and enlightenment ideals but waning political influence, like Asahel Warner, could seize the opportunity presented by expanded state benefits, use their economic power to forge coalitions among new and old constituencies, and bid for a share of state benefits for their local communities, thereby increasing their own political standing. In the process, they also helped to create a larger "community of interest," or political capital, for the new liberal state.

To forge this political capital and respond to the political crisis of the 1820s, state and local leaders like Clinton and Warner invoked a shared Masonic vision of the diffusion of intelligence. That Clinton and Warner drew on Masonic enlightenment ideas at this particular moment is somewhat ironic, however. Even as he delivered his annual message promoting the new Education Act in January 1827, Clinton was busy trying to figure out how to respond to an increasingly powerful attack on Freemasonry. In October 1826, a provocateur and resident of western New York by the name of William Morgan threatened to publish the rites of the Masons and was kidnapped. In the ensuing months, the failure of authorities either to locate Morgan or to find and charge his abductors began to look like a coverup and stimulated an anti-Mason backlash. By the spring of 1827, a number of towns throughout the state, but especially in western New York, had passed resolutions banning the election of Masons to local office. The town of Lima lay near the geographic heart of this anti-Mason movement, where long-standing Masons and political leaders like Warner were its chief target. In the fall of 1827, an anti-Masonic political party formed and successfully ran its first candidates

and 3, *An Inquiry into the Nature and Causes of the Wealth of Nations*, Edwin Cannan, ed. (New York: Random House, 1994): 819–845 and 846–875.

for state office.⁴⁶ By 1830, anti-Masonry had achieved substantial power in the New York legislature, with members of the anti-Mason party occupying fifty assembly seats and seven senate seats, and an anti-Mason candidate nearly taking the governor's office. Evangelical religion played an important role in this politicization process. Yet, it was precisely in this charged political context that the western regional body of the Methodist Church and local residents under the leadership of Masons like Warner forged a coalition to found a Methodist institution at Lima.

⁴⁶ Many accounts of the Morgan affair and anti-Masonic movement exist. See, for example, Ronald P. Formisano and Kathleen Smith Kutolowski, "Antimasonry and Masonry: The Genesis of Protest, 1826–7," *American Quarterly* XXIX: 2 (Summer 1977): 139–165; and, more recently, C. Bullock, *Revolutionary Brotherhood*, 277–319.

11

Education and Coalition Building

> Motion made and withdrawn that every person coming forward for office or admission be asked whether he belongs to the Masons.
> Minutes of the Genesee Conference of the Methodist Church, July 26, 1828[1]

> Motion submitted and seconded that no one be admitted to any connection with the Conference who is member of the Masons ... and that existing members must renounce their association with Masons....
> Minutes of the Genesee Conference of the Methodist Church, June 24, 1829[2]

> Lima offers $11,650. ... The site proposed is a pleasant lot of ten acres, at $50 per acre, which with the privilege of purchasing 100 acres or less immediately adjoining at $30 per acre is secured by Bond.
> Report of the Seminary Committee, Genesee Annual Conference, July, 1830[3]

How a coalition of local households led by Asahel Warner, Augustus Bennett, Ralph Smith, Erastus Clark, Henry Grout, and Frederic House came together to forge a bid to found a Methodist academy in Lima is a question worth examination. At first glance, the interests of landholders like Bennett and Smith, of merchants like Clark and Grout, and of a craftsman and builder like House may seem obvious. Moreover, anyone who knew anything about the history of Lima would expect Warner to play a leading role in the founding of such an institution in that town. On the other hand, the interest of someone like Warner in this specific project should not be taken for granted. He was not, after all, a Methodist. Moreover, he was a Mason. Though historically Masons had been friendly to evangelical religion generally, and even to Methodism specifically, by 1830 Methodists in western New York had officially

---

[1] Minutes of the Genesee Conference of the Methodist Church, July 26, 1828, Journal of the Genesee Annual Conference, WNYCA.
[2] Minutes of the Genesee Conference, June 24, 1829.
[3] Report of the Seminary Committee, Genesee Annual Conference, July 1830, Account Book #178, GWSC.

Education and Coalition Building

condemned Freemasonry. Nor should the support of other Lima residents be assumed. After all, not everyone in Lima was enamored with the evangelical project and culture that Methodism represented. This was just the sort of issue that led to the excommunication of James Sterling from the local Presbyterian church in 1823 and to the organization of the local Universalist Church in 1825. Yet both Sterling and the Reverend John Barnard, the Presbyterian minister who expelled him, subscribed to the academy project – for $100 and $50, respectively.[4] Though their status in the community may have made them each a likely candidate for the role of local booster, it does not explain how each overcame what appear to be obvious objections to the founding of a Methodist institution in their town.

In other words, the coalition of Methodists and non-Methodists who brought the academy to Lima should not be treated as a foregone conclusion. Within four years of winning the site of the Methodist academy, and within two years of the institution opening its doors, forty-one Lima residents would complain to the state legislature about the sectarianism of the institution.[5] Presumably the potential for such conflict existed from the start. The fact that differences of religion and politics were transcended, however temporarily, for the purpose of founding an educational institution is an achievement to be investigated, not a common place to be assumed. This chapter explores the significance of local institution building in the context of religious and political conflict. Specifically, it argues that the significance of corporate educational institutions like the academy at Lima lay precisely in their capacity to create common interests and mobilize corporate capital across localities and political and religious divides.

Boosterism Defined

From one perspective, the question of how and why local households came together to bid for the location of a Methodist academy in the town of Lima holds no mystery at all. Scholars have amply documented the quintessentially American combination of boosterism and denominationalism that characterized the founding of many nineteenth-century educational institutions. These accounts often emphasize the small size and frontier-like conditions of booster college towns, particularly in states of the old Northwest such as Ohio and Illinois, but also in the western regions of the mid-Atlantic and southern states. In the case of Illinois College, for example, early landowners in the town of Jacksonville successfully courted an agent of the American Home Missionary Society to win the site of the institution in 1828, at a time when the population

---

[4] Lima Subscription List, Subscription Book, 1830–1837, Account Book #102, GWSC.
[5] "Memorial from sundry inhabitants of Lima, in the county of Livingston, remonstrating against the further incorporation of the Genesee and Wesleyan seminary at Lima, dated January 7, 1834," No. 51, *Documents of the Assembly of the State of New York* (Albany, NY: E. Croswell, printer to the state, 1834).

of the town numbered as few as 400 people. As understood by most historians, the logic of such ventures from a local perspective was primarily financial, though the cultural capital that resulted was essential to realizing the value of the effort. The founding of a literary institution would presumably enhance the prospects of a locality generally, and of its leading property owners specifically, by attracting respectable settlers, drawing investment from outsiders, stimulating commerce, and increasing land values. In places and times of extensive land speculation, in particular, the founding of an academy or college was regarded as a shrewd real estate move.[6] From this perspective, the founding of an academy in Lima was part of a broader phenomenon.

Still, when the particularities of the Lima case are considered closely, further explanation is required. Lima was not a frontier town in 1830. Although small by some standards, its population of 1,764 was typical of what would be considered a mature farming town through much of the nineteenth century. In this respect it differed from the town of Jacksonville, Illinois, with its 400 people in the same year, a population more typical of what would be considered frontier conditions in this period. Given its small geographic size and agricultural economy, Lima was actually quite densely occupied for the time at sixty-two people per square mile.[7] Though real estate still changed hands and owners no doubt welcomed opportunities to re-sell at higher values, the time had long passed when large tracts of land were available and whole networks of families would arrive and settle together as had the Warners, Bristols, Nortons, and Birchards in the 1790s. By the 1820s and 1830s, that kind of opportunity belonged to new territories in states such as Michigan, Ohio, Indiana, and Illinois. Lima did not become the site of the academy because a few speculators sought to settle the first families on their lands.

Nor was Lima's economy undeveloped. Already in 1820, local tax assessments identified 56 percent of Lima's 21,093.76 acres of taxable lands as "improved." Overall, the average per capita land value for Lima was $208.35 in that year, a fairly high figure in relation to surrounding towns. By comparison, the assessment for the similar-sized town of Mendon, just to the north, identified only 32 percent of its 20,600 acres of assessed land as improved and had an average per capita land value only half that of Lima's at $110.27. Meanwhile, the much larger town of Bloomfield to the east had a per capita

---

[6] A classic account of the booster college phenomenon appears in Daniel Boorstin, *The Americans: The National Experience* (New York: Vintage Books, 1965): 152–161. Boorstin recounted the case of Illinois College (p. 155), a case that owes much of its attention by historians to the 1890s autobiography of the articulate Yale graduate, Julian Sturtevant, who served on its original faculty and eventually as its president. The Illinois College case and the boosterism that helped create it are intensively treated by Don Harrison Doyle in his excellent study: *The Social Order of a Frontier Community: Jacksonville, Illinois, 1825–70* (Urbana: University of Illinois Press, 1978).

[7] As compared with other towns in the surrounding area, Lima was geographically quite small at approximately 28.5 square miles in 1830, and somewhat smaller than it had been in 1820 before the redistricting of towns and counties that occurred in 1821. See Appendix Table 3.

Education and Coalition Building

land value of just $143.91 in 1820.[8] Unfortunately, tax assessments for Lima for later in the decade do not survive.[9] Even by later standards, however, Lima's 1820 real estate values were well above those associated with frontier conditions. According to more than one model of nineteenth-century economic development, its level of agricultural improvement and per capita land values were characteristic of a commercial farming economy, a status that economic historians distinguish both from an extractive economy and from several categories of limited or nonexistent development.[10]

This is not to deny that speculation was involved in Lima's bid for the academy; to the contrary, the Lima case helps to illuminate the very meaning of the word. Rather, the point is to introduce some precision into an analysis of the booster phenomenon. Lima's successful bid for the academy involved complex land deals and manipulations of credit that contributed directly to increased wealth for certain men as well as to economic change for the town as whole. The consequence of this activity was not, however, to initiate a process of local economic development but to facilitate a transition from one level of economic development to another.

Class Interests

The coalition of local residents who promoted this development crossed religious and political lines but shared certain economic interests. Lima's official bid for the academy included $11,650 in subscriptions, a ten-acre building site

---

[8] For data on which these comparisons are based see Appendix Table 1.

[9] Unfortunately, Livingston County, to which Lima belonged after 1821, has not saved early tax records.

[10] Unfortunately, systematic and comparative economic data are very difficult to obtain for the period before 1850, when the federal census began collecting such information. In order to place Lima within a range of economic conditions I have compared the limited data available for Lima in the earlier period with models of development focused on the later period. I refer here in particular to the model of economic development presented by Linda Pritchard in "Religious Change in a Developing Region: The Social Context of Evangelicalism in Western New York and the Upper Ohio Valley During the Mid-Nineteenth Century" (unpublished Ph.D. dissertation, University of Pittsburgh, 1980). Pritchard's model delineates ten categories of economic development using data from both the federal population census and from the agricultural and industrial censuses for the years 1840, 1850, and 1860. Although based on data from a later period than is the focus of this study of the Lima case, Pritchard's study does provide a model for placing Lima in a range of possible economic conditions. According to the criteria for categorizing economic development presented in her table 3.4, pp. 108–109, Lima best fits the sixth level of development, the commercial farming category. For data on which these comparisons are based see Appendix Table 3. In addition to placing Lima with respect to Pritchard's model of economic development based on population density and land values, it is possible to compare Lima with other places with respect to its proportion of improved land. By this criterion, Lima also seems to represent a fairly advanced commercial farming economy. See, for example, the comparison of four Massachusetts towns in Christopher Clark, *The Roots of Rural Capitalism: Western Massachusetts, 1780–1860* (Ithaca, NY: Cornell University Press, 1990): 286; and Pritchard, "Religious Change," Table 2.2, p. 67. See Appendix Table 2.

at $50 an acre, and an offer of up to 100 acres of adjoining land at $30 per acre. Of the 166 total subscriptions, 115 came from Lima households, 35 from the town of Avon to the west, 5 from the town of Livonia to the south, and 2 from the town of Bloomfield to the east. Nine additional subscriptions came from Methodist sources somewhat further afield, including 5 from Rochester, 1 from Caledonia, and 3 from the nearby town of Henrietta. At the top of the list in terms of the amount of money subscribed were Asahel Warner for $600, followed by four subscriptions of $500 each from Ralph Smith, holder of the land proposed for the Seminary site; Frederic House, a local Methodist builder; and Erastus Clark and Henry Grout, two leading merchants in the town of Lima.[11]

At every level of investment, the bid included subscriptions both from established local leaders, usually landowning farmers, and a newer, often more mercantile, local leadership. Among the 115 local subscribers in 1830 were 8 men who had subscribed nearly 30 years earlier to the project of organizing the town's Congregational Society and building its brick school house.[12] Although not a large number in absolute or proportional terms, the subscriptions of these eight individuals do suggest an impressive continuity of community leadership over time. Simple age and morbidity, let alone geographic mobility, would seem to mitigate against greater representation.

At the same time that these longtime local leaders renewed their commitment to local community building, the list of subscribers to Lima's academy bid also included some newer leaders. Beginning in 1826, when the last of the electoral reforms expanding suffrage went into affect, a subtle shift in the names of those elected to town office and in the status of their positions occurred. The somewhat mysterious George W. Little, referred to in one place as a doctor but never listed as a head of household in census or tax records for the town of Lima, first appeared in the town roster in 1825 in the modest role of common school inspector. The following year, in 1826, he ascended to the role of town clerk, an office he held continuously through 1832. Other men whose political influence rose about this time include Ransom B. Lyon and Smith Parmelee. A longtime local Methodist, Lyon first became "constable and collector" for the town in 1827, a post to which he and then his son Luther were regularly elected through at least 1833. Parmelee, meanwhile, a farmer with a large family and a 160-acre farm, had resided in the town of Lima since at least 1820 and had begun appearing in the town records then in the modest role of commissioner of highways. In 1828, however, he suddenly rose to the position of town supervisor, an office to which he continued to be elected for the next four years.[13] As 1828 was the year that anti-Masonry began to be an organized political force, it is likely that Parmelee's increased influence was

---

[11] Lima Subscription List, Subscription Book, 1830–1837. The nine subscriptions from Methodist sources are discussed more specifically in the next chapter.
[12] Ibid. and "Minutes of the First Congregational Society."
[13] "Town Book, 1818–1840," passim, LHS; census and tax lists.

fostered by shifting politics. Nonetheless, he and other new community leaders joined longtime local leaders to bid for a Methodist academy.

This mix of established local residents and a rising generation can be further seen in the persistence rates of subscribers relative to the total population. As other scholars have noted, U.S. society in the nineteenth century was characterized by a high degree of geographic mobility. Only a small portion of the population continued to reside in the same location from one decade to the next. Typically, somewhere between a quarter and a half of the heads of household listed in one census can be matched against heads of household listed a decade earlier or a decade later for the same town.[14] Persistence rates for the town of Lima in the early antebellum period fit within this pattern. Of the 295 heads of household listed in the 1820 census, 96 appeared again as heads of household in the 1830 census, a figure that results in a persistence rate of just under 33 percent. In some ways, this figure understates the degree of stability among families that continued to reside in a town after the death or relocation of the head of household. If surviving relatives are taken into account, the persistence rate for 1820 to 1830 for Lima increases to 50 percent. In addition, the redrawing of Lima's town boundaries in 1821 resulted in a loss of population for reasons other than change of residence.[15] Nonetheless, the 33 percent persistence rate provides a basis for comparison with other places and with subgroups in the population. As might be expected, persistence rates among local subscribers to the academy were somewhat higher than for the population as a whole. Of the 94 Lima residents who subscribed to the academy project and also appeared in the federal census in 1830, 40 had also appeared in the 1820 census, for a 43 percent persistence rate. Thus, the population of subscribers represented more stability than the population as a whole, but this stability still amounted to less than half the population: 4 out of 10 subscribers were established local residents, while 6 out of 10 were new.[16]

A similar balance between old and new is apparent with respect to age. Predictably, the average age of academy subscribers in 1830 was somewhat higher than for heads of household as a whole. Wealth generally increases with age, making those in a position to pledge surplus goods and resources to community building somewhat older than those who were not. Although the proportion of male heads of household between the ages of forty and fifty

---

[14] Doyle, *The Social Order of a Frontier Community*, 95–96 and Tables 1–9, pp. 261–265. Doyle reports a persistence rate of 27% for the town of Springfield, Illinois, between 1850 and 1860. He also provides a breakdown of persistence rates for occupational subgroups within the population, and for different levels of wealth. Among the wealthiest town residents, persistence from 1850 to 1860 was as high as 60%. Among the poorest, it was as low as 18%. Summarizing the work of scholars, he cites a persistence rate of 40–50% as a norm, though this covers a wide range of places, time periods, and methods of calculation.

[15] Persistence rates were calculated through a name-by-name match of heads of household from the federal census for 1820 and 1830 using microfilm copies of the federal manuscript census, OCRAIMS (for 1820) and LCHO (for 1830).

[16] Ibid., and Lima Subscription List, Subscription Book, 1830–37.

were roughly equal among subscribers and nonsubscribers (approximately 24%), a higher proportion of subscribers than nonsubscribers were between the ages of fifty and sixty, and sixty and seventy (17% each for subscribers; 11% and 9%, respectively, for nonsubscribers). Meanwhile, the proportion of male heads of household between the ages of twenty and thirty, and thirty and forty were higher for nonsubscribers (30% and 18% as compared with 22% and 15% for subscribers).[17]

Despite these demographic incongruities, subscribers did include a number of relatively young men. Among these were progeny of long-established (and landed) families. Others, however, were more recent arrivals. Interestingly, this latter group seemed to consist of more merchants and craftsmen than farmers. William Dean and Ebenezer Sumner each operated groceries, as indicated by a list of those who paid local liquor excise taxes. Each also had a financial partner of similar age but longer local tenure who also subscribed to the academy project: Erastus Clark of Clark & Dean, and Henry Grout of Grout & Sumner. All were in their thirties. Aldridge Wiley was a local wagon maker and Charles Ingersoll was a leather worker and merchant who, according to a newspaper ad, manufactured saddles, valises, bridles, harnesses, and travelling bags at his own "stand" in Lima village, while also carrying stoves and boots and shoes of "eastern manufacture." Other relatively young men who subscribed to the project also represented nonagricultural occupations, though they were not new residents of the area. These included the builder Frederic House, recently relocated to Lima from the town of Livonia, the tavernkeeper Jasper Marvin, and the chairmaker Samuel Burpee, all men in their thirties who had been heads of household in the area since at least 1820. In addition, they included the young lawyer Melancton Brown, still in his twenties, who, though not a head of household in 1820, probably grew up there as the son of one of the Brown brothers who had lived in Lima for decades.[18]

Together this suggests that Lima's bid for the academy represented a coalition between well-established farm families, including both their older and younger members, on the one hand, and a newer and/or younger group of nonagricultural households, including merchants, craftsmen, and professionals, on the other hand. Or, to put the hypothesis somewhat more simply, the coalition represented Lima's commercial class – both agricultural

---

[17] Ibid. Age ranges determined from the manuscript copy of the federal census for Lima for 1830.
[18] Sources of information on occupation include "Book of Commissioners of Excise at Lima, 1830–1859," LHS; Matthew Warner Papers, 1797–1844, LHS; Mabel Furner Jenks, "Lima, 1788–1964: Crossroads of Western New York, Outline of the History of Lima Written for the 175th Anniversary Celebration, July 18, 1964," Pamphlet printed by the Lima Recorder, 1964; Fran Gotcsik, "Lima Village History" and "A Short History of Lima, New York," papers authored in the 1980s, LHS; and advertisements published in the county newspapers including the *Livingston County Journal* (1823–1825), the *Livingston Register* (1824–1828 and 1834–1840), the *Livingston Republican* (1837+), and *the Livingston Democrat* (1835–1837), LCHS.

and nonagricultural. Unfortunately, incomplete records make a thorough test of this hypothesis impossible. Where available, the church affiliations, real estate holdings, and occupations of subscribers have been identified. However, the availability of this information is uneven. With respect to religion, for example, Methodist membership information is more scattered than that for Presbyterians. The number of Methodists identified thus probably significantly underestimates their representation in the population. Even for the more well-documented Presbyterians, information on membership must be drawn from multiple sources, including church minutes, session books, and subscriptions, none of which are comprehensive for the years in question. Similarly, data on the occupations and real and personal wealth of local residents are available on a systematic basis only for the years 1820 and 1850. For the intervening period, including the years when the academy was financed and built, such information must be drawn from a miscellany of probate records, private papers, newspaper advertisements, and local histories. Altogether, reasonably sound information on occupation can be found for just under half the subscribers, and on church affiliation for just over half the subscribers, with both sets of data available for a much smaller proportion of the total population. Given these inconsistencies, a thorough sociological analysis of the significance of various characteristics of academy subscribers relative to the rest of the population cannot be done.

Nonetheless, a few things can be said. First, it is clear that members of the Lima Presbyterian Church were well represented among subscribers. At a minimum, 49 of the 115 local subscribers, or 43 percent, and 73 percent of the subscribers whose church affiliations could be identified were members of the Presbyterian Church.[19] In one sense this is not surprising, since the Presbyterian Church remained the dominant religious institution in Lima long after the town had become the site of a major Methodist academy. According to summary statistics for the town of Lima reported in the federal census for 1850, the Presbyterian church, though only one of five churches located in the town at the time, still represented 1,000 of the 2,300 total "church seats" in Lima, a proportion that, interestingly enough, also works out to 43 percent.[20] From this perspective, the number of Presbyterians among subscribers to the academy is what one would expect given their representation in the population as a whole. From another perspective, however, the number of subscriptions from Presbyterians is noteworthy. It makes clear – as later petitioners would claim in their protest to the state legislature – that initial capitalization of the academy did not come primarily from Methodist sources. The local bid for the academy certainly included subscribers with Methodist church affiliations,

---

[19] Membership in the Presbyterian Church determined from multiple record books and lists, including "Minutes, First Congregational Society of Charleston, beginning 1802"; "Lima Presbyterian Records, beginning 1804," LPC; "History of Early Church Sessions, 1820–1831"; Lima Presbyterian Session Records, 1831–1841," and "Lima Presbyterian Session Records, 1842–1866," LCHO.

[20] Manuscript schedule of the federal census for Livingston County, 1850, LCCO.

including several at the top of the list, such as Frederic House, Ralph Smith, and Augustus Bennett, and others from regular participants in the work of the Bloomfield circuit. Nonetheless, the list also included a significant number of Presbyterians, many of them leading members of that church, starting with its longtime minister, John Barnard.

With respect to occupation, the limited data support the observation that nonagricultural occupations were well represented among subscribers. At a minimum, the primary occupations of at least 21 of the 115 subscribers (18%) were nonagricultural: 6 craftsmen, 7 merchants, 4 service providers, and 4 professionals.[21] Although this may seem a small proportion of the total, it is likely that it represented a very high proportion of all residents in such occupations at the time. In the federal census for 1820, just 6 persons were identified as "engaged in commerce" in the town of Lima, a figure that represented just 2 percent of all households. Surrounding towns such as Bloomfield and Mendon reported even smaller proportions of their households involved in commerce in 1820, 1 percent or less.[22] Commercial activity certainly increased during the 1820s. Nonetheless, there was a limit to how many commercial households a small town of less than 2,000 people could support in 1830. Among the subscribers to the academy project, by comparison, 7 persons can be positively identified as merchants. In addition, other persons might be identified as "involved in commerce," depending on how the term is interpreted. Comparisons regarding craftsmen and manufacturers are even more difficult to make. Although incomplete information for 1830 makes it impossible to say anything definitive about the proportion of local craftsmen's households who subscribed to the academy project, it is reasonable to conclude that it was more than 50 percent.

Finally, the available data support the expectation that subscribers were wealthier than nonsubscribers. Unfortunately, the proportion of Lima households in 1830 for which information on wealth is readily available is small. This is because the latest surviving tax lists date from a decade before. Just sixty total households, or 19 percent of all households listed in the 1830 Lima census, also appeared in the tax lists for 1820. Nonetheless, even among these sixty households, a gap existed between the wealth of those who subscribed to the academy in 1830 and those who did not. The twenty-seven households that did subscribe to the academy project had a median total estate value of $2,760. Meanwhile, the thirty-three households that did not subscribe to the academy project had a median total estate value of just $1,454. In other words, the median value of subscribers' estates exceeded that of nonsubscribers' estates by 90 percent. These differences in turn were reflected in the relative size of the estates. Subscribers owned a median of 135 acres – 80 percent more than nonsubscribers, who owned a median of 75 acres.[23]

---

[21] Identification of occupations based on multiple sources described in footnote 17.
[22] Manuscript schedules of the 1820 federal census, OCRAIMS.
[23] Ibid. Total acreage, improved acreage, and real estate values calculated from 1820 county tax records for the town of Lima, OCRAIMS. I would like to thank Mary Jo Lanphear of the

Overall, the limited available data support the hypothesis that subscribers to the academy represented a rural commercial class consisting of well-established farm families on the one hand, and a newer group of professionals, merchants, and craftsmen, on the other. Subscribers crossed boundaries of religious denomination and occupation in order to support the academy, but they shared above-average levels of wealth and land ownership. The question, then, is how to interpret this information. At a minimum, one might conclude that subscribers had a common class interest in the academy project. Beyond this minimal presumption, one might speculate about the significance of the academy project in the historical formation of this class interest. A shared class interest may in part have preceded the academy project, but it may also have been forged through the academy project itself. Taking this line of analysis a bit further, one might be tempted to make a claim of motivation based on this evidence – that is, that the men who subscribed to the academy project did so in pursuit of their class interest – that through the act of subscribing to the academy they hoped, expected, or connived to achieve a class advantage. This advantage could be either economic or socio-cultural in character. It could encompass expectations of direct personal gain and of local economic growth. It could also include the prospect of advancing a more general commercial culture of mobility and thus also of self-definition pursued through education.[24]

Political Brokers

Even if one assumes a shared class interest among subscribers, the question of *how* a sense of shared interest and common purpose was forged, and by whom, remains. No doubt each of the men involved in founding the academy in Lima had a somewhat different account of how the project developed. Descendents of Augustus Bennett apparently got the idea that his role in the origins of the institution was that of benefactor. A 1930s newspaper article published on the occasion of the academy's 100th anniversary began by reminding readers that the grounds where Genesee Wesleyan Seminary stood "were given by Augustus A. Bennett, well-known lawyer of western New York," a fact rarely recalled "save by his descendents." It then goes on to surmise from the combined evidence of the seminary's coeducational enrollment and the subsequent business success of one of Bennett's daughters, an alumna of the institution, that Bennett was motivated in this act as "an early advocate of higher education for women." The fact that Bennett lived in Avon, the next town to the west, rather than in Lima, presents a puzzle for this account. The author of the article sidesteps this issue by suggesting that Bennett may at one time have lived in Lima. In her account, the story of Genesee Wesleyan is not one of local boosterism but of "pioneers in the education of women."[25]

Ontario County Archives and Records Center and Taylor Kokjohn for assistance that made possible these calculations.
[24] See Chapters 16 and 18 for further development of this idea.
[25] Augusta S. Anderson, "Pioneers in the Education of Women: Genesee Wesleyan Seminary Site Given by Noted Attorney of Last Century Whose Legal Successes and Final Strange

Other records tell a somewhat different story. It is clear that Bennett at one time held title to some portion of the land on which the seminary was built. By his own account, however, he held the title jointly with a partner, elsewhere identified as Ralph Smith. Moreover, it appears that at the time the site of the academy was chosen, the two had held title to the land only briefly, perhaps less than a year. They forged a partnership to acquire the land, it seems, precisely for the purpose of including it in the bid for the academy. Once Lima "won" that bid and constructed the academy building, Bennett and Smith signed the deed for a 10-acre building site and 25 of the 100 acres of adjoining farm land over to trustees of the institution.[26] They did not simply "give" the land to the academy, however, but received a number of subscriptions in exchange, including their own, valued at $150 and $500, respectively, and those of several of Bennett's neighbors. Altogether, the total value of the subscriptions they received exceeded the recorded value of the land by some $200 or 14 percent.[27] In addition, the eventual allotment of 25 acres of the adjoining farm to the seminary left about 75 acres available for subsequent re-sale. In July of 1831 Bennett acquired exclusive title to a parcel of this land from Smith. He then subdivided it into lots that were purchased by Methodist ministers and others who built homes and boarding houses near the institution over the course of the 1830s.[28]

It is not entirely clear what the nature of the financial relationship was between Bennett and Smith, how they divided the subscriptions, or how much they made on the re-sale of various parcels and lots. According to Bennett's vague accounting, he and Smith "paid out 2 or 3000 dollars" for the whole building site and adjoining farm.[29] Assuming they re-sold the remaining 75 acres of farmland at a rate no less than they offered the land to the seminary (surviving evidence suggests that Bennett sold at least some of the lots at a

Disappearance Cast About His Name a Glamor (sic) That Was Slow to Fade," LCHO. Unfortunately, the files include no identification of the periodical in which the article was published and from which it was clipped. Evidence internal to the article indicates that the date of its publication was probably 1930 or 1932.

[26] Bennett's somewhat selective account of this transaction was provided by him in a letter to Isaac Bronson, dated December 6, 1831, Folder 10, Box 44, BFP. The folder in which the letter is preserved is labeled, "Asahel Warner, Lima, 1821–44." The Bennett letter and the Warner materials of which it is a part will be discussed further in Chapter 17. The fact that Bennett's partner was Ralph Smith, and the amount of land signed over to the institution, are recorded in records of the seminary, specifically Account Books #178, "Minutes of the Board of Trustees," and #102, "Day Book" (Subscriptions 1830–1840), GWSC.

[27] An account of the subscriptions signed over to Bennett and Smith is recorded in Account Book #102, GWSC. It was also verified against the record of individual subscriptions in Account Book #59, "Payment Book" (Subscriptions 1830–1840), GWSC. Additional discussions of subscriptions and payment arrangements will appear in subsequent chapters.

[28] I am grateful to Martha and John Sempowski for the information regarding Bennett's subdivision and re-sale of this land. They kindly shared a written copy of this information, which had been compiled by their son, Greg Sempowski, in January 1989 as part of his search into the history of their Lima house and land, part of the original Smith and Bennett holdings.

[29] Augustus Bennett to Isaac Bronson, December 6, 1831, BFP.

substantially higher rate), they stood to make at least a 50 percent profit on their original investment.[30] It is likely, in other words, that far from being a benefactor of the seminary, Bennett made money from the project. To the extent that he became involved in the original land purchase precisely in order to profit from the change in land values likely to result from locating the seminary there, Bennett's actions can be said to represent the very definition of market speculation.

The involvement of Ralph Smith in Lima's bid for the seminary presents its own puzzle. In the federal census for both 1820 and 1830, Ralph P. Smith is listed as a resident of the town of Reading in Steuben County, a circuitous distance from Lima.[31] There is some reason to believe that he was a relative and perhaps a financial backer of Frances and Eldrick Smith, who were both well-established local Methodists and mill owners with solid records as local householders, taxpayers, and churchmen back to at least 1820. However, this cannot be confirmed. Smith appears in the journals of the Benajah Williams as a resident of Lima in 1827 and 1828, and as a subscriber to the Lima Methodist church in 1828 and to Lima's bid for the academy in 1830, but he does not appear in any other local records except in 1832, when the Bloomfield Circuit put him on trial for a series of charges related to his role in financing the construction of the Methodist chapel in Lima.[32] By all appearances he arrived in Lima to take advantage of certain business opportunities and left when he got what he came for.

The question of whether men like Bennett and Smith are best understood as serious Methodists, feminist social reformers, or ordinary land speculators misses an important point, however. By focusing on individual motivation, the author of the 1930s article about Bennett imposed an idea of philanthropy on the Genesee Wesleyan case that did not yet exist in 1830. The prospect of individual capitalists endowing institutions to promote their own favorite

---

[30] Bennett and Smith offered the farm land to the seminary at a rate of $30 per acre. At that rate, they could re-sell the remaining 75 acres for a minimum of $2,250. Evidence indicates, however, that Bennett managed to re-sell individual house lots of an acre or less at $78 and $82 apiece in 1834 and 1836, respectively, or between two to three times the rate originally offered to the seminary. At the same time, Bennett and Smith received subscriptions valued at $1,460 in payment for the 10-acre building site and 25 acres of farm land signed over to the seminary. Meanwhile, Bennett's vague statement regarding what he paid for the land, combined with other evidence, casts doubt on the claim that Bennett and Smith paid $2–3000 for the land in the first place. With all this information combined, it seems reasonable to conclude that they made at least $2,000 on their original investment. [Information on re-sale prices of individual lots comes from a title search for a particular house lot conducted by Greg Sempowski (see footnote 27).]

[31] Index to U.S. Federal Census Record, 1820 and 1830.

[32] References to Ralph Smith appear in Journals of Benajah Williams, Vol. II, 1825–1846, p. 274, SDL; "Historical Record of Methodist Episcopal Church at Lima," ca. 1800 to 1881, WNYCA; Avon Scrapbook #4, p. 79, LCHO; and Minutes of Quarterly Conference, April, 1832, "Bloomfield, NY Circuit (Methodist Episcopal) Circuit Book, 1829–1880," microfilm copy, Accession #6190, CUDRMC.

causes and organizations was an idea born of the post–Civil War era and of the industrialization and concentration of capital that the war itself helped to effect. Often referred to as "the Gospel of Wealth" after the essay by that name written by the postwar industrialist, Andrew Carnegie, this idea presumed a distinction between the creation of capital and the use of capital that the men who subscribed to the academy project would have found somewhat strange.[33] For the men from Lima and the vicinity who subscribed to the academy project, there was no pre-existing capital to be captured for the purposes of education or social reform. Capital was a product rather than a precursor of the academy project. Moreover, this capital never belonged to one or two individuals. In a very real sense it was a social creation.

Understood from this perspective, Bennett's most important role in founding the academy was not that of individual financier but of political mediator. According to the 1930s chronicler of the Bennett family, Augustus Bennett and his many siblings had grown up as Methodists under the influence of their father, with something of a Methodist chapel located on the premises of their East Avon farm.[34] If true, this historical affiliation could help to explain some or all of the subscriptions from Avon as well as Bennett's role as an agent in the project. Numbering thirty-five and totaling $1,072, Avon's subscriptions represented more than a fifth of the subscribers included in Lima's bid and nearly 10 percent of the dollar value of its offer.[35] No doubt, Bennett played a role in soliciting subscriptions from his town. Surviving records for the Bloomfield Circuit of the Methodist Church lend support to this account. In August 1829, the quarterly meeting of the circuit was held in the town of Avon. Augustus Bennett was not identified as present at the meeting, but someone named William Bennett, probably a son or nephew of Augustus, was identified as an "exhorter."[36] A year later, in July 1830, when the circuit met in the town of Lima, Augustus Bennett was present and named to the role of "steward" for the circuit, a position essentially focused on the solicitation of pledges and collection of funds.[37] As this appointment occurred just three weeks prior to the annual meeting of the conference where Lima would compete for the site of the academy, it is likely that Bennett's role and presence at the meeting were stimulated by the effort to mobilize support for the project. As a Methodist and leading man in the town of Avon, Bennett would have had the social and political capital necessary to induce other residents of his town to subscribe to the institution. Even more importantly, as a lawyer involved in other land deals in Livingston County, Bennett had the capacity to broker coalitions between Methodists and non-Methodists.

---

[33] Andrew Carnegie, *The Gospel of Wealth and Other Timely Essays* (New York: The Century Co., 1901).
[34] Anderson, "Pioneers in the Education of Women."
[35] List of original Lima subscribers, Account Book #102, GWSC.
[36] Minutes of Quarterly Conference, Avon, August 8, 1829, "Bloomfield, NY Circuit Book. "
[37] Ibid., July 3 and 4, 1830, "Bloomfield, NY Circuit Book."

Moreover, Bennett, though a Methodist, was, like Warner, a leading local Mason. Without imputing too much importance to Freemasonry per se, the influence of leading Masons in the founding of a Methodist institution at *this* particular time and in *this* particular place warrants further consideration. The founding of the academy in Lima in 1830 occurred during the height of anti-Mason activity in western New York, and the town of Lima was located near the heart of anti-Mason sentiment.

Denominational Politics and Political Anti-Masonry

Historically, relations between Freemasonry and religion generally, and Methodism in particular, had been fairly good at both the local and state levels before 1827. According to historian Steven C. Bullock, Methodist ministers often sought Masonic membership to ease the difficulties of itinerancy with the benefits of translocal fraternal ties.[38] This seems to have been the case in Lima. The three men identified as founding members and officers of the local Masonic lodge in 1815 included not only Asahel Warner and Justin Smith but also Smith Weeks. Weeks was a Methodist minister – the first Methodist circuit preacher known to work and reside in the Lima vicinity. In 1817 he also became the first man elected and the second, after Justin Smith, to serve as master of the local Masonic lodge.[39] The Smith family, meanwhile, would be closely associated with Methodism in the hamlet of Honeoye Falls from at least 1818. Although Justin Smith was not among the family members named in the 1820 membership list for the Honeoye Falls Methodist Church, and was at one time listed as a Congregationalist, he appeared as a leading subscriber to the Methodist church in Lima in 1828.[40] Perhaps he did so more as a Mason than as a Methodist. According to Bullock, it was common during the 1820s for Masons to conduct cornerstone ceremonies for the construction of new churches, and Smith's 1828 pledge was for $50 "in stone from my quarry."[41] Whether he would have advertised his Masonic identity at that late date is doubtful. Nonetheless, the fact that Smith, Weeks, and Warner were founding officers of Lima's Masonic lodge suggests that cooperation across Methodist and Masonic lines ran deep in Lima.

---

[38] Steven C. Bullock, *Revolutionary Brotherhood: Freemasonry and the Transformation of the American Social Order, 1730–1840* (Chapel Hill: University of North Carolina Press, 1996): 177.

[39] Emmett E. Hawkins, *Freemasonry in Livingston County, State of New York* (Caledonia, NY: Keith Press, 1983): 10–18.

[40] "Minutes, First Congregational Society in Charleston, beginning January 6, 1802," LPC; "First Methodist Episcopal Church, Honeoye Falls, Organized, 1820"and "Early Methodist Church, Honeoye Falls, Mendon, circa, 1820," OMTH.

[41] Bullock, *Revolutionary Brotherhood*, 150–153. File, "Methodist Episcopal Church in Lima," LHO. This file of notes from the minutes of the Methodist Episcopal Church in Lima (which was torn down in 1957) includes a partial listing of the subscribers. Unfortunately, the original documents do not seem to survive. A similarly partial listing from the original building subscription is reproduced as part of a brief history of the church in an undated and unattributed newspaper clipping apparently published on the occasion of the building's demolition in 1957, Avon Scrapbook #4, p. 79, LCHO.

Although it is impossible to know exactly how the broad political attack on Freemasonry after 1826 played out at the local level, surviving evidence suggests that the story in Lima was interesting. For starters, local Methodists on the Bloomfield Circuit were among the first to formally pressure the leadership of the Methodist Church to take a stand against Freemasonry. At the annual meeting of the Genesee Conference in Ithaca, New York, in 1828, the Bloomfield Circuit was one of four circuits to present petitions on the issue. The petitions were presented in conjunction with a resolution requiring that every candidate for office or admission to the ministry declare whether he was a Mason. According to contemporary sources, a majority of Methodist ministers in the Northeast were Masons at one time.[42] Perhaps for that reason, the 1828 resolution was withdrawn from consideration, but the issue persisted. In 1829, at the first meeting of a newly defined Genesee Conference, now consisting entirely of western districts, an anti-Mason resolution passed. The new resolution not only forbid Masons from becoming Methodist ministers in the future, but required that existing Masons publicly renounce their membership.[43] Presumably Methodists from the Bloomfield circuit supported such a resolution as they had the year before.

Methodists were not the only anti-Mason activists from the vicinity of Lima to participate in such agitation. In February 1827, the town of Bloomfield, on Lima's eastern border, sent representatives to one of the earliest regional meetings of anti-Masonic activists in the town of Lewiston, New York, near Buffalo. Through subsequent gatherings in LeRoy and Utica the following years, the Lewiston meeting became the incubus of the state's Anti-Mason Party. According to historian William Bruckney, the early stages of anti-Masonry were animated primarily by evangelical sentiment and networks. Regional bodies of evangelical churches in western New York, including Presbyterian synods and Baptist associations as well as Methodist conferences, responded to pressure for action on similar timelines and with similar results. Bruckney notes that Baptists pursued the most strident anti-Masonic course and provided the movement with some of its most important early leaders. Again, the area immediately surrounding Lima was a locus of this agitation. The first joint meeting of Baptist associations regarding anti-Masonry occurred in the town of Livonia, just south of Lima, in October of 1828.[44]

Over the next two years, anti-Masons continued to organize as a movement, with similar effects on the politics of other denominations. Baptist associations first adopted formal resolutions requiring the renunciation of Masonic membership in 1829 and experienced a schism over the issue in 1830.

---

[42] Minutes of the Genesee Conference, July 26, 1828. As late as 1826, according to Bullock, a Masonic newspaper in Boston claimed that the majority of Methodist ministers in the New England Conference were Masons. Bullock, *Revolutionary Brotherhood*, 177.

[43] Minutes of the Genesee Annual Conference, June 24, 1829.

[44] William Bruckney, "Religious Antimasonry: The Genesis of a Political Party," (unpublished Ph.D. dissertation, Temple University, 1976): 304, 131–150, 160; passim.

Presbyterians proceeded somewhat more cautiously, beginning in 1828, by appointing a committee to study the situation. Perhaps as a result of this more cautious approach, the synod adopted a resolution much like those adopted by other church associations in 1830, but without an accompanying schism. Meanwhile, political operatives took advantage of the sentiment coalescing both within and across denominations to create the anti-Mason political party. By 1830, organized anti-Masonry was at the height of its power in New York State and had become a major political movement.[45] Methodists became a powerful force in that movement. In that context, the newly defined Genesee Conference decided to solicit bids from towns in western New York for the site of a Methodist educational institution.

Education and Coalition Building

Given the strength of anti-Mason sentiment and activity throughout the area immediately surrounding Lima, the fate of Lima's own Masonic lodge is noteworthy. According to official Masonic sources, Union Lodge no. 45 of Lima was the only lodge in Livingston County, one of the few in western New York, and one of just forty-two (out of 450) in the whole of New York State, that continued to operate and hold meetings during the whole of the period of anti-Mason feeling and activity, from 1826 to 1850. Most of the lodges in the area "turned in their charters," but the lodge at Lima "kept hers." Among those that lost their charters was the lodge in Avon, which, according to its official history, dated back to 1804 but was "washed out of existence in 1827" due to public indignation over the Morgan affair. In 1835 the warrant for Avon's Masonic charter was formally revoked by the state organization, and a new lodge was not reconstituted in Avon for another thirty-five years. In the meantime, Masons from the town of Avon, such as Augustus Bennett, and from other surrounding towns, including Livonia, Geneseo, and Mendon, attended the lodge in Lima.[46] Lima's distinctiveness in this regard is further reinforced by election returns. Although the anti-Mason candidate for governor won a majority of votes in Lima in 1830 as he did in every other town in Livingston County, his margin was smaller there than in all but one of the county's twelve towns. While receiving as much as 89 and 91 percent of the vote in some towns, 78 percent in Avon, 70 percent in Livonia, and 74 percent in the county as a whole, the anti-Mason candidate received just 61 percent of the vote in Lima.[47] In Lima, in other words, the anti-Mason movement was not as strong or effective as it was in surrounding towns.

---

[45] Ibid.
[46] Emmet E. Hawkins, *Freemasonry in Livingston County, State of New York* (Caledonia, NY: Keith Press, 1983): 10–18.
[47] Town by town breakdowns of the vote for Governor in 1830 are printed in Williams Edwin, *The New York Annual Register* (New York: J. Leavitt, 1832): 50.

In this context, Lima's bid for a Methodist academy, and the role of leading Masons like Warner and Bennett in forging it, make a certain political sense. To the extent that anti-Masonry represented an attack on established local elites, the survival of Masonry in Lima and the relative weakness of anti-Masonry suggests that for whatever reason – simple longevity, personal appeal, social accommodation, economic dominance, political acumen, or some combination thereof – established leaders from the early republican era in Lima endured longer than their counterparts in other western New York towns. Despite significant setbacks in the 1820s, when they lost authority, political office, influence, and territory to new forms of social and religious organization, expanded suffrage, and political realignment, local Masons like Warner and Bennett could still draw on reservoirs of social and financial capital to assert local leadership. Rather than retreat in the face of substantial evangelical consensus and organized political opposition, they forged a coalition with local Methodists to undertake a new collective project. From this perspective, Warner's decision to assume the financial lead in a bid for a Methodist academy could be seen as courting his opposition. Indeed, the opportunity may have appealed to him partly on that basis. In his study of Jacksonville, Illinois, historian Don Harrison Doyle suggested that booster projects derived their logic precisely from conditions of conflict. "Boosterism defined a strong, tangible incentive to community harmony while it disciplined internal conflicts," Doyle observed.[48] Borrowing from this observation, it is not hard to imagine longtime leaders and local Masons Warner and Bennett appealing to neighbors to put aside religious differences, social divisions, and political conflicts to found an institution that would surely benefit all.

---

[48] Don Harrison Doyle, *Social Order*, 64.

12

Denominational Politics and Institution Building

> Moved and carried that a committee be appointed to take into consideration the propriety and expediency of dividing this conference.
>
> Minutes of the Genesee Conference of the Methodist Church, 1828[1]

> Moved that a committee be appointed to obtain information and report to the Conference at its next session preparatory measures for the erection of a Seminary within the bound and under the direction of this Conference.
>
> Minutes of the Genesee Conference of the Methodist Church, 1829[2]

> Attended a meeting of the citizens of Lima on the propriety of petitioning the Genesee Conference at its next session to locate a proposed Seminary in the village of Lima.
>
> Benajah Williams, March 8, 1830[3]

The decision to found a Methodist academy in western New York was a product of political conflict both within and outside the denomination. In the summer of 1828, in the context of the battle over Freemasonry, the professional preachers who represented the western half of the Genesee Conference succeeded in effecting a division of the conference that their eastern colleagues had rejected the previous year.[4] Under the 1828 agreement, everything east of Cayuga Lake became part of the newly named Oneida Conference (see Figure 5). The Genesee Conference, meanwhile, retained all the territory west of Cayuga Lake, that is, the remaining Finger Lakes; all of the Genesee country, including the developing cities of Rochester and Buffalo; and much of the southern tier of New York State.[5] In making this division, leaders of the

---

[1] Minutes of the Genesee Conference, June 24, 1829.
[2] Minutes of the Genesee Conference, June 24, 1829
[3] Journals of Benajah Williams, Vol. 2, March 8, 1830, p. 266, SDL.
[4] At the annual meeting of the Genesee Conference in 1827, the motion "that a committee be appointed to take in consideration the propriety of dividing the conference" was "not carried." Minutes of the Genesee Annual Conference, June 14, 1827.
[5] At the annual meeting of the Genesee Conference in 1828, it was "moved and carried" that "a committee be appointed to take into consideration the propriety and expediency of dividing

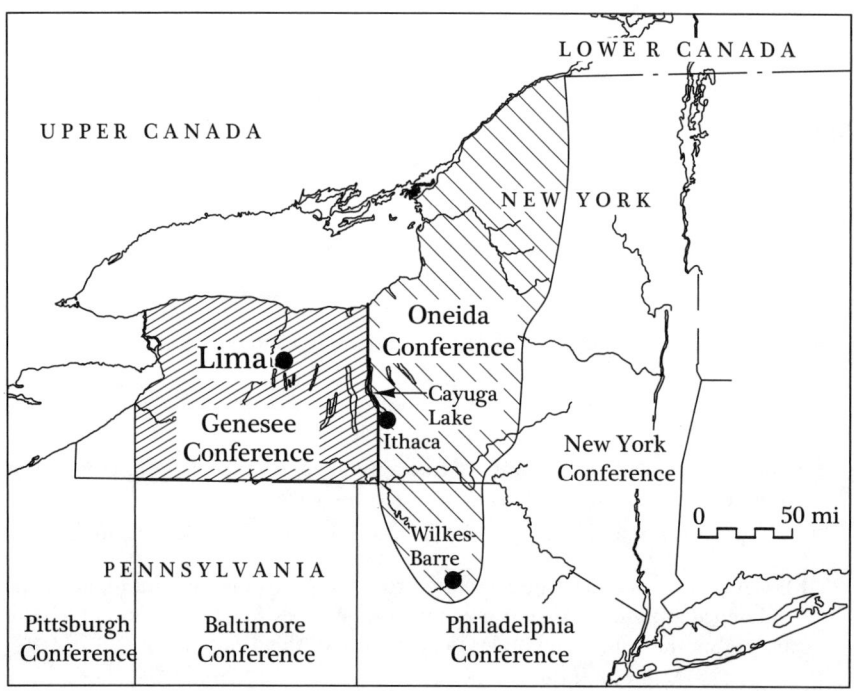

FIGURE 5. Territory of the Genesee Conference of the Methodist Episcopal Church, 1829. Agitation over Freemasonry in western New York led to a formal division between the eastern and western regions of the Genesee Conference of the Methodist Church in 1828 and to the decision to institutionalize the new regional identity of the conference by founding a Methodist educational institution within its bounds in 1829. Boundaries shown here are approximate, reconstructed from the *Encyclopedia of World Methodism* (Nashville: Abingdon Press, 1974); the "Journal of the Genesee Conference," WNYCA, and "Conference Boundaries," MMC.

Genesee conference recognized the growing cohesion and influence of western New York in state-level politics. They then went on to take the first step toward capitalizing on this influence. At the first meeting of the re-defined conference, in 1829, members voted to establish an educational institution within the conference bounds.

this conference." At the same meeting the committee reported back that "the Conference is too large" and recommended that it be divided at Cayuga Lake. Minutes of the Genesee Conference, July 26, 1828. Additional information regarding the boundaries of the conferences compiled from maps in the *Encyclopedia of World Methodism* (Nashville: Abingdon Press, 1974); from a file on "Conference Boundaries" of the Oneida Conference, MMC; and from information on districts and circuits of the various conferences in the published *Minutes of the Annual Conferences*.

This chapter considers the political significance of Methodism and Methodist institution building in the early nineteenth century. Generally speaking, denominational influence and control of educational institutions was weak in the decades immediately following the Revolution. In the context of religious disestablishment, the success of an educational institution depended far more on local than on denominational support. By 1830, however, the influence of denominationalism generally, and of Methodism in particular, had begun to increase. Methodism owed its increasing influence in part to the new source of political leverage provided by the anti-Masonry movement and in part to its distinctive capacity for mobilizing social and political capital across multiple localities and levels at once. Institution building both solidified and exploited this organizational power. In the language of social capital theory, Methodism's peculiar interlocking network of regional, state, and local units enabled it "to mediate between local people and political parties and legislators,"[6] thereby turning social capital into political capital.

Denominationalism in Education

Scholars have long considered the relative significance of denominationalism in the founding and shaping of nineteenth-century educational institutions. Much of the scholarship focuses on degree-granting institutions – that is, colleges. Although some scholars have seen the prevalence of denominational colleges in the United States as the result of rampant sectarianism, others have downplayed the importance of denominational initiative in the founding of such institutions.[7] In his study of Baptist colleges, David Potts

---

[6] Theda Skocpol, "The Toqueville Problem: Civic Engagement in American Democracy," *Social Science History* 21:4 (Winter 1997): 455–479; quotation from p. 470.

[7] The original study documenting extensive denominational sponsorship of U.S. collegiate institutions was Donald G. Tewksbury, *The Founding of American Colleges and Universities Before the Civil War: With Particular Reference to the Religious Influences Bearing Upon the College Movement* (New York: Bureau of Publications, Teachers College, Columbia University, 1932). Tewksbury emphasized that religion was the controlling interest of antebellum institutions (p. 55), a characteristic that he viewed unfavorably. He argued that denominational sectarianism produced an irrationally high number of antebellum institutions and resulted in very high failure rates. Tewksbury's specific findings as well as his general attitude were picked up by subsequent scholars, including, most famously, Richard Hofstadter and Walter P. Metzger in *The Development of Academic Freedom in the United States* (New York: Columbia University, 1955); and Daniel Boorstin, *The Americans: The National Experience* (New York: Vintage Books, 1965).

In the 1970s and 1980s, however, scholars began to develop a different perspective on antebellum higher education. See David Potts, "American Colleges in the Nineteenth Century: From Localism to Denominationalism," *History of Education Quarterly* 11 (Winter 1971): 363–380; idem, "'College Enthusiasm!' as Public Response, 1800–1860," *Harvard Educational Review* 47 (February 1977): 28–42; and James McLachlan, "The American Colleges in the Nineteenth Century: Towards a Reappraisal," *Teachers College Record* 86 (December 1978): 287–306. These articles emphasized the significance of localism rather than denominationalism in the founding of such institutions and were inclined to see their prevalence as a response to popular

recounted the founding stories of a number of institutions spanning the period from the 1810s through the 1850s. The ministers involved in the earliest of these initiatives, such as the founding of Colby College in Waterville, Maine (1812), operated more or less as free agents, launching their own projects and forging their own alliances to solicit the financial and political support necessary to acquire land, construct buildings, and acquire charters. Drawing on the tradition of venture schools and the norms of evangelical preaching, these ministers effectively constructed a basis for their own individual employment. Only later, in the 1820s and 1830s, did formal Baptist education societies and associations assume any kind of sponsoring role with respect to such institutions. Even then, according to Potts, these societies were often small, local groups, composed primarily of Baptist laymen with their own booster stakes in local development. Because of the highly decentralized structure of the Baptist Church, Baptist educational institutions in this period did not generally originate as strategic efforts initiated by formal denominational bodies.[8]

---

demand. Then, in 1982, historian Colin Burke published *American Collegiate Populations: A Test of the Traditional View* (New York: New York University Press, 1982), a comprehensive re-analysis of the original Tewksbury thesis in conjunction with a vast compilation of relevant data. He found, among other things, that contrary to the Tewksbury/Hofstadter data and interpretation, denominational institutions had not increased at a rate out of proportion to that of their congregants, and that they had actually failed at lower rates than had state or secular institutions.

More recently, several scholars have revived interest in the history of religious and denominational influence in the history of U.S. higher education. In some cases, this renewed interest seems to involve a revival of the emphasis on sectarianism as a shaping force in the founding and governance of institutions. See George M. Marsden, *The Soul of the American University: From Protestant Establishment to Established Non-belief* (New York: Oxford University Press, 1994): 68–78; also, John R. Thelin, *A History of American Higher Education* (Baltimore: Johns Hopkins University Press, 2004): 43–45 and 60–63. It is not entirely clear whether a renewed emphasis on denominationalism and sectarianism reflects more a failure to fully engage the critique of that perspective represented by Potts et al. or a shift to the use of more rhetorical sources of evidence. (It is inexplicable that Marsden cites Tewksbury but not Burke's comprehensive re-analysis of the Tewksbury thesis. Similarly, though Thelin cites Burke, he inexplicably suggests that the new scholarship revising Tewksbury's analysis of college failure rates depends on "a relatively small statistical sampling." In fact, Burke's statistical analysis includes a complete count of every U.S. college known to be chartered in the antebellum era. In other words, it does not involve a sample at all, but a complete population.) In other cases, the new focus on religion provides welcome attention to the intellectual history of higher education, i.e., Julie Reuben, *The Making of the Modern University: Intellectual Transformation and the Marginalization of Morality* (Chicago: University of Chicago Press, 1996); Douglas Sloan, *Faith and Knowledge: Mainline Protestantism and American Higher Education* (Louisville, KY: Westminster John Knox Press, 1994). For a review of the literature, see Linda Eisenmann, "Reclaiming Religion: New Historiographic Challenges in the Relationship of Religion and American Higher Education," *History of Education Quarterly* 39:3 (Fall 1999): 295–306.

[8] David Potts, *Baptist Colleges in the Development of American Society, 1812–1861* (New York: Garland Publishing, 1988).

Denominational Politics and Institution Building

Other denominations founded educational institutions through more formal organizations and on the basis of more strategic considerations. The American Home Missionary Society was a joint voluntary association of Congregationalists and Presbyterians organized in 1826 with the goals of expanding Protestant Christianity, promoting social order, and employing surplus ministers "in the West," outside its home territory of New England.[9] Under its aegis, a number of educational institutions were founded. The fact that such institutions had the formal backing of a missionary organization did not ensure support from more local church organizations, however. In the previously cited case of Illinois College, of Jacksonville, Illinois, the missionary agent who negotiated with local boosters ostensibly had a commission from the Missouri Presbytery as well as from the American Home Missionary Society, but this understanding broke down almost immediately.[10] Although the institution received substantial financial support from the society – more than most institutions received from sponsoring denominations – its local church support was subject to conflict between Presbyterians and Congregationalists, and between different Presbyterian factions. As compared with the Baptist example, then, the denominational component of this enterprise was less localized and more "missionary" in character. Church funding and influence came more from outside than inside the region.

In other cases, regional church bodies such as presbyteries and synods assumed more direct sponsorship of educational institutions within their own jurisdictions. Even for more centralized denominations, however, this sponsorship could be tenuous. The origins of the first Lutheran institution in the United States, for example, lay in a bequest for the purpose in the 1790s by a retired minister. Only after two decades of delay and conflict, however, was Hartwick Seminary (later College) founded in Oneonta, New York, as an official project of the Lutheran Synod.[11] Similarly, as reported by historian Bruce Leslie, denominational support for what became the Lutheran-sponsored Franklin and Marshall College of Pennsylvania was often limited. Initially funded in the early 1830s from a combination of state and local sources, Marshall College of Mercersberg for a time enjoyed considerable success as a German Reformed institution. After a decade of operation, however, denominational in-fighting undercut support from congregants. Eventually, the Pennsylvania Synod decided to move the college and merge it with Franklin College of Lancaster. Once again most of the money for the move came from the locality, and governance remained divided within the denomination and between

---

[9] On the founding of the American Home Missionary Society see Sidney Ahlstrom, *A Religious History of the American People* (New Haven, CT: Yale University Press, 1972): 457. For an excellent summary of factors shaping its organization, see Don Harrison Doyle, *The Social Order of a Frontier Community: Jacksonville, Illinois, 1825–70* (Urbana: University of Illinois Press, 1978): 23–32.

[10] Doyle, *Social Order*, 21–23 and 47–51.

[11] Harry Kreider, *History of the United Lutheran Synod of New York and New England* (Philadelphia: Muhlenberg Press, 1954): 38–40 and 52–56.

the denomination and the locality. Not until the post–Civil War period did the synod assume full legal control and responsibility for the institution.[12]

Together, this scholarship suggests that the nature and extent of denominational influence and control over educational institutions varied not only by denomination but also over time. Although ample precedent for some sort of church affiliation certainly existed in 1830, formal sponsorship of "literary institutions" by denominational organizations would be more common after that date. Similarly, although some older scholarship emphasized the sectarianism of antebellum colleges, most scholars now conclude with Potts and Leslie that denominational governance was relatively weak before the Civil War. They point out that earlier denominational support was often fickle at best, divided by intradenominational conflict or dependent on the initiative of an individual preacher or a church layman, rather than on that of an organized denominational body. With respect to financing in particular, nondenominational support typically proved much more important than denominational funding. Most chartered educational institutions, whether denominational or not, depended heavily on local financing for their initial capitalization and on tuition from students of diverse religious persuasions for their operating funds. Under these conditions, they could not afford to be too sectarian.[13]

If this was true for colleges, it was at least as true for academies. For a number of reasons, academies were much less likely to be sponsored by denominations than colleges. Although few studies consider the characteristics of academies on a systematic basis, those that do indicate that only a small proportion of academies were denominationally sponsored, ranging from less than 10 percent in some states, including New York and Ohio, to just under 30 percent in other states, such as Illinois.[14] By comparison, Colin Burke's comprehensive study puts the proportion of antebellum colleges with

---

[12] W. Bruce Leslie tells the founding story of this institution in his study of four Pennsylvania colleges, *Gentlemen and Scholars: College and Community in the 'Age of the University,' 1865–1917* (University Park: Pennsylvania State University Press, 1992): 15–20.

[13] This point about the limits of sectarianism imposed by the need to attract students and funding from diverse sources seems to be the consensus view, even among those who have returned to emphasizing the significance of interdenominational competition as a driving force in the founding of new institutions. See Marsden, *The Soul of the American University*, 68–96. One thing that changed in the postbellum era was that the power and endowment support of individual industrial capitalists made institutions less dependent on the small contributions and tuition of a wide range of people, and more subject to the influence and views of a few men and their appointees. For an excellent analysis of how a concentration of wealth could correspond to a concentration of denominational control and influence, see not only the Potts and Leslie works cited above, but David Potts' outstanding study of the history of a Methodist institution, *Wesleyan University, 1831–1910: Collegiate Enterprise in New England* (New Haven, CT: Yale University Press, 1992), especially his chapter on "Denominational Support and Influence," pp. 83–117. There he convincingly establishes that the peak years of denominational influence and control of the institution were 1870–1890.

[14] Because of New York's distinctive system for supporting and regulating academy education, it provides the most systematic and accessible data for the study of academies. For this reason, New York academies have until recently been more systematically studied than academies in other states. On New York academies see George Frederick Miller, *The Academy System*

denominational sponsorship at 82–87 percent.[15] With respect to the institutions that were denominationally sponsored, moreover, many of the same variations in the extent of church control existed for academies as for colleges. In her study of academic education for women in New York, Ohio, Indiana, and Illinois, Doris Malkmus identified a shift to evangelical models of academy education after 1830. Despite their evangelical emphasis, however, these

of the State of New York (New York: Arno Press, 1969); Edward Herring O'Neil, "Private Schools and Public Vision: A History of Academies in Upstate New York, 1800–1860" (unpublished Ph.D. dissertation, Syracuse University, 1984); Kathryn Kerns, "Antebellum Higher Education for Women in Western New York State" (unpublished Ph.D. dissertation, University of Pennsylvania, 1993); Nancy Beadie, "Female Students and Denominational Affiliation: Sources of Success and Variation among Nineteenth-Century Academies," American Journal of Education 107:2 (February 1999): 75–115. For recent studies of academies that go beyond New York and New England, see Nancy Beadie and Kim Tolley, eds. Chartered Schools: Two Hundred Years of Independent Academies in the United States, 1727–1925 (New York: Routledge Falmer, 2002); Margaret Nash, Women's Education in the United States, 1780–1840 (New York: Palgrave/MacMillan, 2005); and Doris Malkmus, "Capable Women and Refined Ladies: Two Visions of American Women's Higher Education, 1760–1861" (unpublished Ph.D. dissertation, University of Iowa, 2001).

In her study of antebellum higher education for women, Doris Malkmus compiled a comprehensive and valuable annotated list of antebellum academic institutions in four states. From these lists, which Malkmus annotated with information on sponsorship when available, it is possible to calculate the number and proportion of academies known to be denominationally sponsored. Eliminating institutions founded specifically as universities or colleges, and recognizing that the sources of data and period covered varied from state to state, this calculation puts the proportion of all chartered academies with denominational sponsorship at 28% for Illinois, 18% for Indiana, 7% for Ohio, and 2% for New York:

Denominationally Sponsored Academies as Proportion of All Academies Chartered by State Based on Data Compiled by Doris Malkmus

State	Years	# Academies Total	# Denominational	% Denominational
New York	1787–1843	208	5	2.4%
Ohio	1797–1861	256	17	6.6%
Indiana	1816–1859	145	26	17.9%
Illinois	1818–1871	230	65	28.2%

Figures are calculated from Tables 2, 3, 4 and 5 in the Appendix of Doris Malkmus, "Capable Women and Refined Ladies: Two Visions of American Women's Higher Education, 1760–1861" (Unpublished Ph.D. dissertation, University of Iowa, 2001): 297–320.

[15] Burke, American Collegiate Populations, 22. See table below.

Proportion of Denominational Colleges among All Liberal Arts Colleges in Operation by Decade

Decade	1800s	1810s	1820s	1830s	1840s	1850s
Proportion	84%	82%	83%	86%	85%	87%

institutions were not necessarily denominationally sponsored or under direct church control. Baptist academies, for example, were likely to be the efforts of town founders and to function primarily as local institutions.[16]

Given the existing practice in 1830, in other words, there was little reason to expect strong denominational control of the academy at Lima. However, a close look at the particularities of the Genesee case confounds expectations. Although the product of intense local effort, Genesee Wesleyan Seminary was not primarily a local academy. More than any other school in the state, it was a regional institution. That regional scope derived directly from denominational sponsorship. When it came to mobilizing capital for institution building, in other words, Methodism was not just any denomination.

One person who may have appreciated the significance of denominational sponsorship from both local and denominational perspectives was Benajah Williams. As a traveling Methodist preacher with nearly fifteen years of professional experience in the Church in 1830, Williams certainly knew how Methodism operated. He had, in fact, helped to create the Methodist system in western New York. As a newly licensed preacher in the late 1810s, he had been part of the first wave of Methodist church builders in the western territory. He had also worked with community leaders in Lima and its vicinity before, including especially the Smiths, but also, less directly, the Warners. On his very first assignment as a licensed professional, he had helped to raise the first Methodist chapel in the area in the hamlet of West Mendon with the help of funds from both the Smiths and the Warners, and had settled his family nearby. Since then, he had worked many other circuits in western New York, from Batavia to Niagara. Now, for the first time since the beginning of his career, he had been assigned to the Bloomfield circuit. In that capacity, he attended meetings both of local residents and of Methodist ministers to discuss the founding of the new Methodist academy. As one of few men present for both sets of deliberations, he knew as much as anyone about the prospects for Methodist institution building in Lima.

Not even Benajah Williams could predict the future, however. In 1830, the Methodists were just beginning to consolidate their gains from decades of territorial expansion in North America. They now dominated church membership in more counties of the United States than any other denomination.[17] Culturally and financially, Methodism had also grown. In the 1820s, the Methodist Book Concern had significantly expanded its operations; by 1830, its chief publication, the *Christian Advocate and Journal*, had the

---

Note that Burke's figures are not directly comparable to those derived from Malkmus' data in that his figures are for denominational colleges as a proportion of all colleges in concurrent operation by decade, rather than as a proportion of all new institutions founded. As many institutions continued from one decade to the next, Burke's figures would not capture changes in the types of new institutions founded over time.

[16] Malkmus, "Capable Ladies," 145.

[17] Edwin Scott Gaustad and Philip L. Barlow, *New Historical Atlas of Religion in America* (New York: Oxford University Press, 2001): 221.

Denominational Politics and Institution Building

largest circulation of any periodical in the country.[18] With respect to formal education, the Methodist Church was also entering a new era. In 1820, the General Conference had recommended the establishment "as soon as practicable" of "literary institutions" under the control of the Church's regional conferences.[19] Since then, one such institution had been established in New York. That was the academy in Cazenovia, admitted to the Regents in 1828.[20] Meanwhile, the first degree-granting Methodist institution in the country, Wesleyan University of Connecticut, would be founded in 1831. In 1830, in other words, Methodism was just beginning to make its influence felt. Methodist strategies for founding educational institutions, securing state charters, raising capital funds, and recruiting students were young. It is thus unlikely that even a well-informed observer like Benajah Williams could have predicted in 1830 that in less than a decade the Methodist academy at Lima would be the largest in the state, or that in the interim it would be the object of considerable interest and conflict in the state legislature.

Institution Building

Methodist leaders in western New York took steps toward capitalizing on this growing influence at the first meeting of the newly redefined Genesee Conference. On June 24, 1829, the fifty to sixty professional preachers who constituted the membership of the Genesee Conference voted to appoint a committee "to obtain information and report to the Conference at its next annual session preparatory measures for the erection of a Seminary within the boundaries and subject to the direction of this Conference."[21] This decision was a direct outgrowth of the recent conference division. One consequence of the division of territory was that the relatively new Methodist academy in the town of Cazenovia, New York, was now located within the boundaries of the Oneida Conference. Trustees of that institution, awarded Regents status in 1828 as "the Seminary of the Genesee Conference," were anxious to continue sponsorship by the western districts of the state. Toward that end, they

---

[18] The history of the Methodist Book Concern is described in Emory Stevens Burke, ed. *The History of American Methodism*, Vol. III (Nashville: Abingdon Press, 1964). On the relative circulation and influence of Methodist periodicals, see R. Laurance Moore, *Selling God: American Religion in the Marketplace of Culture* (New York: Oxford University Press, 1994): 18–19.

[19] William Warren Sweet, *Methodism in American History* (NY: Methodist Book Concern, 1933): 211.

[20] An earlier Methodist institution, Wesleyan Academy, located in New York City, was chartered in 1819. "An Act to incorporate the Wesleyan Seminary, Passed April 13, 1819," *Laws of New York*, 42nd Session, chap. 198 (Albany, NY: Weed, Parsons & Co., 1820): 249–251. It was chartered directly by the state legislature, however, and never received a charter from the Regents. Nor is it clear for how long the academy actually enrolled students. By 1821 the building had become the headquarters of the Methodist Book Concern. Burke, *History of Methodism*, p. 149.

[21] Minutes of the Genesee Annual Conference, June 24, 1829.

officially renamed the institution "the Seminary of the Oneida and Genesee Conferences."[22] Whether members of the western Genesee Conference ever intended to continue this arrangement is questionable, however, given that at their very first meeting they voted to take steps to found an institution of their own. Read with reference to this context, the emphasis of the 1829 resolution seems to be at the end of the sentence, on the phrase declaring that the new institution would be "within the boundaries and subject to the governance of *this* Conference."[23]

As this resolution suggests, the founding of Genesee Wesleyan Seminary was not an ad hoc effort by a few Methodist laymen or a preacher acting on his own. The five men appointed to the Seminary Committee represented the strategic leadership of that body. They included four current and one past presiding elder for each of the conference's four districts at the time: the Genesee, Ontario, Steuben, and Buffalo districts. Their collective experience in this role made them particularly well suited for their task. As presiding elders they were responsible for implementing conference policy, for assessing needs and opportunities within their respective territories, and for determining the assignment of personnel and the organization of work to address conditions in the field. Moreover, under the distinctive Methodist system of church organization, they rotated assignments. The presiding elder of the Genesee district in 1829 had the previous year served in the same capacity in the Buffalo district, and vice versa.[24] Theoretically, at least, the practice of rotation enabled presiding elders to assess objectively the advantages and disadvantages of various denominational strategies, without the conflict of interest represented by a personal or professional stake in a particular location. In this way, Methodism, perhaps more than any other Protestant denomination, had the capacity to make the decision to sponsor and locate an educational institution the product of deliberate strategic choice.

This does not mean that such decisions were apolitical or uncontested. To the contrary, the decision to found a seminary within the bounds of the Genesee Conference in 1829 was a direct outcome of the intradenominational conflict occasioned by the anti-Masonry movement and the resulting conference division. For Methodists, however, the decision to found an academy carried particular strategic significance. The location of an educational institution was both more deliberate and more important for Methodism precisely because its professional preachers did not have permanent locations. From the perspective of the professional ministry, the academy was *the* official location of Methodism within the conference territory.

---

[22] Minutes of Genesee Annual Conference, 1828.
[23] Ibid., 1829.
[24] Members of the committee were listed in the Minutes of the Genesee Annual Conference, 1829, as Abner Chase, Glezen Fillmore, Loring Grant, Asa Abell, and John Copeland. Their positions at the time and their previous and subsequent assignments can be found in the published *Minutes of the Annual Conferences*.

Denominational Politics and Institution Building

To recognize this fact is to begin to glimpse how the founding of a Methodist institution could have political significance not only within the denomination but in the state as a whole. At the time Genesee Wesleyan was founded, New York State's traditional stance toward denominational governance of academic institutions was in the process of change. Before 1828, the Regents adhered to a policy of awarding Regents status and public funds only to institutions whose charters made them independent of control by any one denomination.[25] After 1828, as a result of policies initiated under DeWitt Clinton, that changed. The first denominational institution to benefit from this change in policy was the Methodist academy at Cazenovia.[26] Although the number of denominational academies operating under Regents authority in New York thereafter remained small, those few denominational institutions would prove to be among the largest and most successful institutions in the state, and among the most effective at winning state funds. Most of those few institutions would be Methodist, and the largest would be Genesee Wesleyan.[27] Together, the constituencies of those institutions represented a significant political force.

Methodism owed its success at institution building to its distinctive structure, which made it uniquely effective at organizing support both within and across localities.[28] Of course, different agents within the structure had different accounts of how that institution building proceeded. According to Asa Abell, one of the five presiding elders appointed to the original Seminary Committee, the founding of Genesee Wesleyan was entirely the work of the conference leadership. In a "Brief History of Genesee Wesleyan Seminary"

---

[25] The one exception is the Lutheran-sponsored Hartwick Seminary, chartered by the Regents in 1816. Hartwick was included by the Regents in its academy system, though it probably operated more as a college aimed at the preparation of ministers. Franklin B. Hough, *Historical and Statistical Record of the University of the State of New York* (Albany, NY: Weed, Parsons & Co., 1885): 365 and 639–640.

[26] The first step toward this shift in policy actually occurred in 1825, when DeWitt Clinton recommended that the power to grant new charters for academic institutions no longer be exercised solely by the Regents. ["Perhaps ... the authority of the regents of the university ought to be only recommendatory; and the incorporation power exclusively vested in the legislature, as a more safe depository than a single body," Clinton suggested.] DeWitt Clinton, "Annual Message of the Governor," January 4, 1825, *Messages of the Governor* (Albany): 62. In general, this was a step toward a less restrictive charter policy, since legislators had an interest in granting charters to constituents. Right away in 1825, the legislature granted charters to several institutions that would not have received them under previous Regents policies, including the seminary at Cazenovia, the first female academy, and the first public high school. "An Act to Incorporate the Seminary of the Genesee Conference," Passed April 6, 1825, *Laws of New York* 48th Session (Albany: E. Croswell, Printer to the State, 1825), 125–7; "An Act to Incorporate a Female Seminary in the Village of Canandaigua, Passed April 14, 1825," ibid., 239–241; and "An Act to Incorporate the High School of New-York," Passed April 4, 1825, ibid., 107–108. This shift in policy was then solidified in 1827–1828 funding legislation, which generally promoted a more liberal policy toward the types of institutions and students supported by state funds. Thereafter, the seminary at Cazenovia and some other new institutions were granted Regents charters. Hough, *Historical and Statistical Record*, 598–599.

[27] Beadie, "Female Students and Denominational Affiliation."

[28] This distinctive structure is discussed at length in Chapter 5, The Methodist Economy.

composed by Abell in 1843, the names of local leaders like Augustus Bennett and Asahel Warner are barely mentioned, and those of Frederic House and Ralph Smith are eliminated entirely, despite their central roles in mobilizing the local financial capital necessary to get the academy built. Also entirely absent from Abell's account is the name of Benajah Williams, the preacher who may have contributed more than anyone to generating enthusiasm for the academy project in Lima and the vicinity. In Abell's account, the founding of Genesee Wesleyan Seminary was the work of people with the power necessary to make decisions official, rather than of those who made such decisions possible.[29]

Other sources tell the story of how that decision-making power was acquired. There is no doubt that ministers like Asa Abell, Loring Grant, and Glezen Fillmore carefully crafted the resolutions and negotiated the intra-denominational politics behind the decisions to divide the conference and to found a new conference seminary. Loring Grant in particular, who served as presiding elder of the Genesee District of the Conference in both 1829 and 1830, appears to have been an effective political agent within the Methodist hierarchy. He was one of eighteen professional ministers from the original Genesee Conference, and one of seven from the western districts, to be elected as representatives to the national meeting of the Methodist Episcopal Church in 1828, where the decision to divide the conference was officially made.[30] The fact that he presided over the Genesee District during the whole of the period when the Seminary Committee was appointed and did its work also was significant. As it turns out, all five of the towns that competed for the site of the seminary were from circuits within that district. This indicates a tacit agreement regarding the general location of the future institution, a close association with the bishop who made circuit assignments, a careful drawing of district boundaries, and/or a heavy hand in managing the work of the committee. If Benajah Williams' judgment can be trusted, all of these ways of working the system would be in character for Loring Grant.[31]

---

[29] "Brief History of the Genesee Wesleyan Seminary from A.D. 1830 to 1842," Account Book #178, GWSC.

[30] The ministers elected to attend the General Conference are listed in Minutes of the Genesee Annual Conference, 1827.

[31] Benajah Williams regarded Loring Grant as a man without integrity. In a rare critical comment, Williams expressed direct criticism of Grant in his journal. This occurred in the same journal entry in which Williams reported that the seminary would be located in Lima (July 29, 1830). Despite (or because of?) his active cultivation of support for the academy on the Bloomfield Circuit over the previous year, Williams was re-assigned in 1830 to the Prattsburgh Circuit in the Steuben District "some distance from home, and a very hard list," a decision he attributed to "the influence L.G. P. E." (Loring Grant, Presiding Elder), "moved by a spirit of enmity" and "prejudice." The prejudice Williams believed dated from a "certain trial" in which Williams happened to be involved "& in which trial he [Grant] took a great interest & which terminated contrary to his wishes, & as he supposed, to his discredit, though he meant it for evil." Journals of Benajah Williams, vol. II, 1825–1846, p. 274, SDL. Later events in Lima support Williams' view of Grant.

Still, as Williams himself understood, this kind of machination at the top of the Methodist hierarchy could only go so far toward the real work of institution building. When it came to a brick and mortar project such as the organization and construction of a Methodist chapel or the founding of a conference academy, the activity of local preachers and Methodist laymen was crucial. It was at the level of the local circuit that professional preachers cultivated the spiritual identities of individuals as evangelical Christians and their social identities as committed Methodist constituents.

Circuit Work

A close look at events at the circuit level shows how the skilled work of professional and lay leaders could foster conditions that made Lima's bid for the academy possible and its selection as the site reasonable in 1830. The August 1829 quarterly meeting of the Bloomfield Circuit, which included Lima, was the first to occur after the Genesee Conference decided to found an academy within its bounds. Although the minutes of the meeting do not make reference to the academy project, they do suggest that the area around Lima was ripe for Methodist institution building. At the August meeting, lay and religious leaders voted to hold a camp meeting on the circuit on the 8th day of September.[32] The decision to hold a summer camp meeting was certainly not unusual for Methodist circuits, but neither was it routine. Surviving circuit books for other areas of upstate New York suggest that members were often encouraged to attend camp meetings but less often expected to host one.[33] In 1829, however, the Bloomfield circuit may have been regarded as ready to do so. At the time, the circuit reported 700 members "in society," by far the largest number reported by any circuit in the district.[34] Moreover, the Bloomfield numbers had been similarly high and at the top of the district for at least the past four years. For 1827 and 1828, the figures were 639 and 620, respectively.[35] Although circuits varied in geographic size and thus were not directly comparable, the numbers do indicate the relative prominence of

[32] Ibid.
[33] Typically a camp meeting was held in conjunction with the annual conference meeting in whichever district, on whichever circuit, and in whichever town that meeting occurred. This ensured an ample supply of clergy and enough attention from surrounding communities to sustain the event. Other area circuit books examined include "Record of Scipio Circuit, 1826–1856"; "Johnstown Circuit, 1839–1867"; "North Lansing Circuit Church Records, 1837–1878"; and "Old Seneca Circuit Book, 1825–1847"; MCSUL.
[34] The numbers of people "in society" on the various circuits of the Genesee Conference were recorded in the published "Minutes of Conferences for 1829, Genesee Conference," *Minutes of the Annual Conferences of the Methodist Episcopal Church for the Years 1829–1839* (New York: T. Mason and G. Lane for the Methodist Episcopal Church, 1840): 30–31. The other nine circuits in the district reported less than 500, with two reporting numbers closer to 100.
[35] "Minutes for 1827, Genesee Conference," *Minutes of the Annual Conferences of the Methodist Episcopal Church for the Years 1773–1828* (New York: T. Mason and G. Lane for the Methodist Episcopal Church, 1840), 535–537; ibid., 1828, 568–570.

the Bloomfield circuit within the Genesee Conference in 1829. It was, by all appearances, a site of great awakening.

This level of religious activity was no accident. Often the language used to describe the Second Great Awakening suggests that it was the product of chaotic and inexplicable forces. Most famously, Whitney Cross described upstate New York during this period as the "burned-over district," an analogy suggesting a case of spontaneous combustion that raged out of control.[36] A close look at the chronology of events in a particular location, however, illuminates the combination of skill and organization that underlay such events. In the case of the Bloomfield Circuit and of Lima in particular, the activity that contributed most directly to the events of 1830 started in 1827. For the first time that year, Methodist leaders recognized the church at Norton's Mills, otherwise known as West Mendon or Honeoye Falls, as a distinct "station" and assigned a professional minister, the Reverend John Parker, to preach there on a regular basis. According to official Methodist Church history, Parker also occasionally preached that year in Lima village at the town hall. As a result of this attention, a separate Methodist church soon took shape in Lima. In the language of official Methodist history, the Lima church was "regularized" in March 1828 "and the class south of the village was transferred to the new organization."[37] Methodism developed in Lima, in other words, as a direct consequence of the strategic reorganization and re-assignment of personnel.

The presence of organized Methodism in the village of Lima began small but soon grew. A list of founding members of the Lima church when it was "regularized" numbers only nine – six women and three men. Between the spring of 1828 and the end of the year, however, membership in the Lima church grew to seventy people. This was the time that Ralph Smith and Frederic House first appeared in local Methodist records. Benajah Williams identified Ralph Smith among those to whom he sold books and other items in the spring of 1827. Smith and House were also listed by Williams as subscribers to an unnamed periodical sometime either in late 1827 or 1828.[38] House at this time was apparently an active Methodist. He was listed in the official church history as one of the original nine members of the Lima church in the spring of 1828.[39] Smith's religious status, by contrast, was (and would remain) ambiguous. The two men nonetheless would play significant roles in the continuing development of local Methodism. In late 1828 a site for a Methodist chapel was chosen just "out of town," according to the official history, on a hillside on the street leading west toward the town of Avon.[40] According to other sources, 120 subscribers

[36] Whitney Cross, *The Burned-Over District: The Social and Intellectual History of Enthusiastic Religion in Western New York, 1800–1850* (New York: Harper and Row, 1965 [orig., 1950]).
[37] "Historical Record of Methodist Episcopal Church at Lima," Record Book of the Lima, Livingston County Church ca. 1800 to 1881, WNYCA.
[38] Journals of Benajah Williams, vol. II, pp. 141–155 and pp. 162–171.
[39] "Historical Record of MEC at Lima."
[40] Ibid.

pledged a total of $1,800 for the construction of the Lima church in 1828. Although surviving records include only a small sample of the subscription list, the few known subscribers included Ralph Smith for "$50 in produce" Justin Smith for $25 "in stone at my quarry," and Frances Smith at "$20 in lumber or ground axes."[41] The builder was Frederic House.[42]

In the summer of 1829, then, at the time that the newly reorganized Genesee Conference appointed the Seminary Committee and the local Bloomfield Circuit voted to hold a camp meeting, organized Methodism was just a year old in Lima village and Lima's Methodist chapel was just approaching completion. By comparison, Methodism had taken root as early as the mid- to late 1810s in several hamlets in the vicinity, such as that of East Avon, where Augustus Bennett resided, the hamlet of South Lima on the border of Livonia, and, most substantially, at the mill-site on Honeoye Falls, near Lima's northeastern border, now known as West Mendon. In this context, it could be said that between the spring of 1828 and the summer of 1829, when the chapel was completed, Methodism moved from the margins of the town of Lima toward the center.

This progress of spiritual events was part of a broader historical and geographic dynamic. In her study of religious change and economic development in western New York and the upper Ohio Valley in the mid-nineteenth century, Linda Pritchard analyzed the relative strength of evangelical and nonevangelical religious groups under various economic conditions. Comparing counties characterized by different levels of economic development, Pritchard found that while some historical observers and scholars associated early nineteenth-century evangelicalism with frontier or subsistence farming, this apparent strength was only relative to the virtual absence of nonevangelical churches in such contexts. Overall, the total number of church members, whether evangelical or not, was lower under frontier or subsistence conditions than in other areas. Nor did Pritchard's findings support the claims of other historians who associated evangelicalism with industrializing economies. The level of economic development most strongly associated with evangelical religion, as it turns out, was that of commercial farming. "Evangelical denominations held a higher average per capita number of seats in Commercial Farming counties than in counties of any other type," Pritchard concluded.[43]

When considered in relation to a particular case such as that of Lima and its vicinity, Pritchard's findings suggest a possible model for the historical and geographical development of evangelical religious organization across space and time. On the Bloomfield Circuit at least, it appears that Methodism developed first on the margins of farming towns, in hamlets characterized by limited or mixed development, and over time moved to the commercial heart of

---

[41] Methodist Episcopal Church in Lima." See footnote 10.
[42] "Bloomfield Circuit Book," 1832.
[43] Linda Pritchard, "Religious Change in a Developing Region: The Social Context of Evangelicalism in Western New York and the Upper Ohio Valley During the Mid-Nineteenth Century" (unpublished Ph.D. dissertation, University of Pittsburgh, 1980), quotation p. 310.

the local farming economy. Pritchard herself implies the possibility of such movement in her overarching description of evangelical organization across various settings: "Evangelicalism rode the wave of economic development," she stated, "cresting in its initial stage of commercial farming, but breaking over and fully penetrating the more advanced settings."[44]

That such a dynamic developed should not be surprising in the case of Methodism, since the denomination was organized precisely to pursue such a strategy. The whole Methodist system of circuits, stations, districts and conferences was designed first as a means of financing missionary work in undeveloped areas, second to methodically incorporate newly developed areas into the larger Methodist system, and finally to concentrate and tap the resources of more established areas to finance further territorial expansion. This systemic strategy also helps to explain Pritchard's further finding that among the "complex weave of religious groups" in commercial farming areas, Methodism was an especially "outstanding fiber."[45]

Reformation

No doubt, the camp meeting that took place on the Bloomfield Circuit in September of 1829 helped to lay the groundwork for Lima's bid for the Methodist academy. In itself, however, a one-time event like a camp meeting would not achieve the reorganization of individual and social life at which professional preachers like Benajah Williams aimed. As Williams once explained with respect to work on a neighboring circuit: "if reformation breaks out in any place it [must] be attended to and not neglect other parts of the list. We frequently lose much by not having time to tend to the reformation. Others come in and take away the lambs."[46] In the winter following the camp meeting in the fall of 1829, Williams and his fellow preachers and lay leaders on the Bloomfield Circuit carefully tended the lambs in their midst, circulating continually through the hollows and hamlets of Avon, Mendon, Bloomfield, Livonia, and Lima, fostering waves of conversions and cultivating a series of revivals that Williams imagined as a general "reformation" in 1830.

This work involved more than one level of activity. At the most intimate level a preacher visited and prayed with individuals and families in their homes. These visits included, according to Williams, "not only the members of the society" but any unaffiliated sinners or atheists a preacher encountered by travelling on the road and going from house to house. In this day-to-day work, a preacher sought to engage others in conversation "on the subject of religion," make them sensible of the perilous states of their souls, and bring them to the next step in seeking salvation. This next step typically involved some overt expression of spiritual yearning on the part of the individual. From

---

[44] Ibid., 306.
[45] Ibid., 310.
[46] Journals of Benajah Williams, Vol. 2, June 2, 1827, p. 90.

the "peddlar of factory clothes" he met at the home of a church family in the town of Livonia in January 1830, for example, Williams succeeded in eliciting a promise to "pray for himself three times a day for four weeks."[47]

Beyond engaging in individual spiritual counseling, an effective Methodist preacher kept up a continual round of appearances in small groups. In this work, a preacher encouraged group expressions of spiritual yearning, from which he might then lead some to take a step toward more regular religious activity and organization. In July 1827, for example, Williams, his fellow Methodist preacher Reverend John Parker, and their two wives attended a prayer meeting about a mile out of the village of West Mendon, at a site he described as a "wicked, a very wicked place." Having begun "good work" in that way, some participants "stayed in that were serious" and helped to organize a class meeting.[48] From such beginnings an effective preacher might eventually build a more general reformation. In addition to prodding groups of people to undertake more regular religious activity by appearing at local prayer and class meetings, a minister preached and exhorted at more open church assemblies. In effect, the home and class visits laid the groundwork for larger church meetings. On such occasions Williams hoped to attract "large" and "attentive" congregations and to experience a "liberty in speaking." Such liberty or "freedom" in speaking indicated that "the spirit of God attended to the word" and might ultimately provoke a more general reformation, as apparently developed in and around Lima in the first months of 1830.

Beginning the first of January in 1830 and continuing for two months, Williams recorded a usual round of activities but with a sense of mounting excitement. At a special "watch night" in the Lima church at New Year's, "eight or ten mourners approached the altar" to testify, with two experiencing immediate conversions.[49] In the month or two that followed, Williams preached in Lima, Avon, and Mendon to congregations he described as "unusually large and attentive." On January 17 he remarked that "the good work of the Lord is going on in this place" and prayed that it might continue. Some days later, at a place he identified as "Burley Hollow," he preached to what he described as a "large and attentive congregation." According to Williams, he had "great freedom" in speaking, and the "spirit of God attended the word," apparently to good effect. "A certain deacon begged the privilege to speak when I got through," Williams reported. "He said he had lived seventy years and had heard a great deal of preaching and had seen many great reformations; and some of them great and powerful; but never had he seen the way pointed out so clear as it had been that evening."[50] Throughout the circuit, it seems, people were responding to the Word. In the Lima church on the first Sunday of February and later that evening in the east part of town, Williams noted

---

[47] Ibid., January 7, 1830, p. 256.
[48] Ibid., July 1, 1827, pp. 97–98.
[49] Ibid., January 1, 1830, pp. 253–254.
[50] Ibid., January 1830, pp. 253–260, passim; and January 28, 1830, p. 260.

"we were favoured with the presence of God. Several of late have been converted in this place. Others are serious and our prospects are good." Similarly, in Avon on February 14, Williams noted that "the house was crowded" and declared that that "the good work of the Lord is still prospering in this place." Nine days later, at the west falls in Mendon, on Lima's northeastern border, Williams wrote, "We are looking for a reformation in this place. O Lord may we not be disappointed."[51]

"Reformation" was clearly the ultimate aim of Williams' work as he conceived it. This term implied much more than individual conversion. A "reformation" involved not only the conversion of individuals, but the transformation of society, of a "place." This was spiritual, but also social work. The goal was not only to change the character of individuals but the nature of social relations. In Methodist parlance the aim was to bring people "into society." At an event such as the one at Burley Hollow, Williams hoped first to make his hearers "thoughtful," and then to get them to stay for class. In class they could explore their thoughts in a disciplined way with fellow seekers. Together these members of society would establish new ways of talking, new norms of interaction, and new ways of being in the world. The more people a circuit preacher succeeded in motivating to create this new society, the more he succeeded at reformation. It was through social organization that reformation occurred.

Beginning in the winter of 1830, lay leaders on the Bloomfield Circuit like Augustus Bennett and Frederic House helped to convert this spiritual work and resulting social capital into a bid for the site of the Methodist conference academy. It should be emphasized, however, that this was a lay project. At the local level, it was not a project of the church itself. Throughout 1829 and the early 1830s, the seminary was never mentioned in the quarterly meeting minutes of the Bloomfield Circuit. Similarly, in his journals, Benajah Williams reported events associated with the bid for the seminary with studied disinterest. Thus on Monday, March 8, 1830, Williams recorded attending a "meeting of the citizens of Lima on the propriety of petitioning the Genesee Conference at its next session to locate a proposed Seminary in the village of Lima." His only further comment was that "the meeting was respectable and interesting."[52]

How exactly the local bid for the academy developed in the four months between the meetings of March 1830 and the end of July, then, when the Genesee Conference met in Rochester to choose a site, is obscure. A few things are known, however. One is that Lima's bid for the academy included a number of subscribers from Avon (35), five from Livonia, and two from Bloomfield – all towns on the Bloomfield Circuit.[53] Another is that Augustus Bennett of Avon attended the July 3 quarterly meeting of the Bloomfield Circuit just three

---

[51] Ibid., February 23, 1830, p. 264.
[52] Ibid., March 8, 1830, p. 266.
[53] "List of original Lima Subscribers," Account Book #102, GWSC.

Denominational Politics and Institution Building

weeks before the conference session in Rochester, and that he was named at that time to the position of circuit steward.⁵⁴ The last is that as support for Lima's bid for the seminary accumulated, professional and lay leaders at the July 3 quarterly meeting voted "that Bloomfield Circuit join Rochester in holding a camp meeting ... and that there be a committee of three to correspond with a like committee from Rochester...."⁵⁵

To hold a camp meeting in Rochester in the summer of 1830 was to ride the wave of rural evangelicalism to the next level of economic development. It was also to participate in the most intense (and intensely studied) revival of the Second Great Awakening.⁵⁶ During that revival in Rochester, in July of 1830, members of the Genesee Conference decided on Lima as the site of their new conference seminary. More importantly, it was at that meeting that leaders of the conference effectively solidified a regional constituency. In ensuing years, the institution would mobilize that constituency to win specific legislative actions, polices, and benefits. It would, in other words, effectively convert the associative power of Methodism into political capital.

---

⁵⁴ "Bloomfield Circuit Book," 1830.
⁵⁵ Ibid.
⁵⁶ I refer to the Finney revivals, commonly understood as having achieved a climax in the City of Rochester in the fall and winter of 1830–1831. The most well-known account of this cycle of revivals is Whitney Cross, *Burned-Over District*. The revivals in Rochester in 1830–1831 were then given focused attention by Paul E. Johnson, *A Shopkeeper's Millennium: Society and Revivals in Rochester, New York, 1815–1837* (New York: Hill and Wang, 1978). Johnson focused on the class and economic dimensions of the Rochester revivals. In her 1980 dissertation, Linda Pritchard tested some of Johnson's findings comparatively and came to different conclusions, discussed in detail in the next chapter. A number of other historians have also focused on the Finney revivals both within and outside of Rochester and have attended to other aspects of their social and political meaning, particularly the gender dimensions of evangelicalism and their significance in class formation. See Mary Ryan, *Cradle of the Middle Class: The Family in Oneida County, New York, 1790–1865* (Cambridge: Cambridge University Press, 1981); and Nancy Hewitt, *Women's Activism and Social Change: Rochester, New York, 1822–1872* (Ithaca, NY: Cornell University Press, 1984).

PART III

EDUCATION AND ECONOMIC TRANSFORMATION

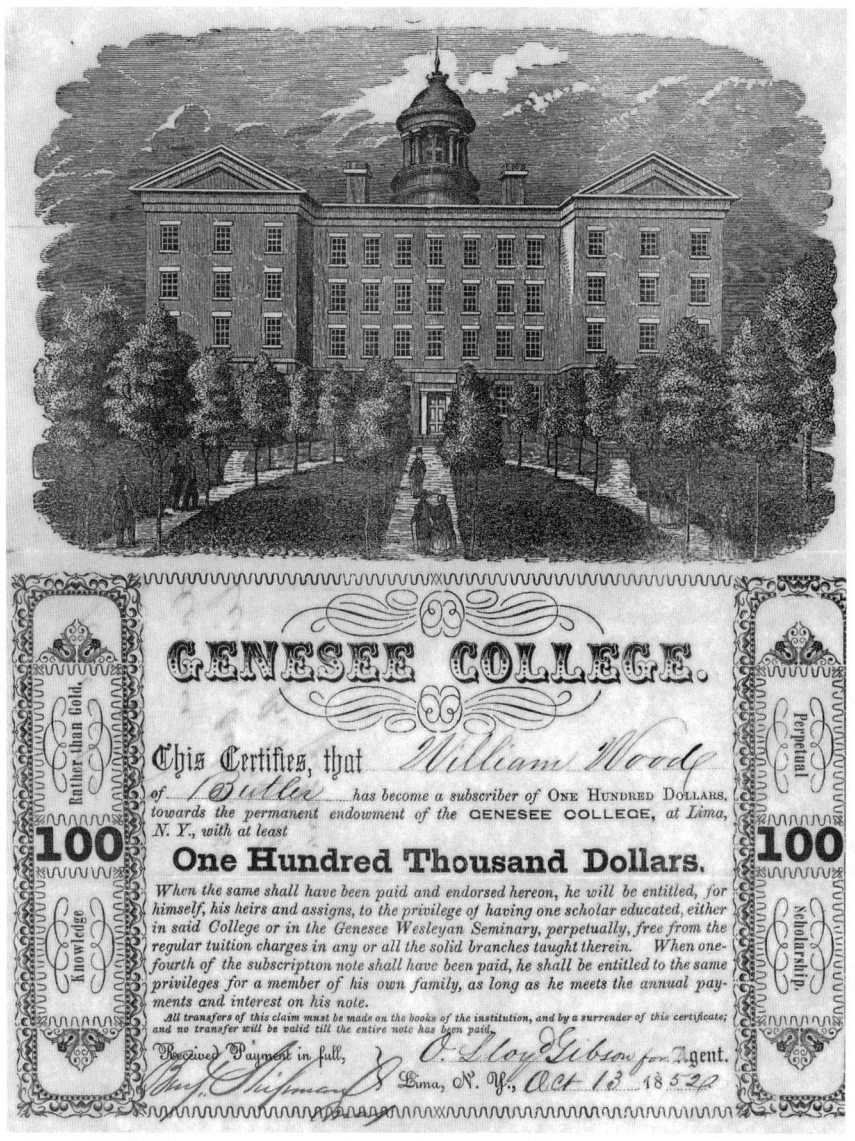

FIGURE 6. Genesee Wesleyan Seminary, Lima, New York, circa 1848. By 1840, Genesee Wesleyan Seminary was the largest and one of the most heavily capitalized educational institutions in New York State, a position it retained off and on through ensuing decades. Capitalizing on this success, leaders of the institution and of the sponsoring Methodist Conference launched a campaign in 1848 to found an affiliated college, which opened in a new building under a separate charter in 1850. To establish the new institution, agents drew on the same practice of fundraising through the sale of subscription scholarships that they had used twenty years earlier. An etching of the seminary building appeared on the new scholarship certificate, along with the slogan "Knowledge Rather than Gold." Courtesy of Syracuse University Archives.

13

Education as an Object of Capital Investment

> Whereas, the village of Lima has favoured us with several inviting considerations not easily to be enumerated in this place, the committee ... recommend to the conference Lima as the most eligible point for the location of our contemplated Seminary.
>
> Report of the Seminary Committee, July 1830[1]

As objects of capital investment during a period of increased capital accumulation and mobility, educational institutions like the academy at Lima played significant roles in mediating economic change. They did so in a number of ways. Strongly rooted in local social networks and economies, schools became one way of storing the value of surplus labor and goods produced through the intensification of agriculture in the decades after the Revolution. As a result of this broad pattern of investment, ordinary rural households in the North achieved a significant expansion of schooling by 1820. At the same time, the integration of domestic commodity markets and the expansion of mortgage lending and banking made commercial capital increasingly available after 1820. Together, the increased availability of both rural and commercial capital made it possible for individual households and groups of households to contemplate new forms of investments. Among the objects of such investments were new educational institutions. For many ordinary households, education may actually have been a preferred form of investment, because schooling offered a means of realizing the value of even fairly small amounts of surplus goods or labor. It also offered the advantage of socializing costs and benefits. Through contributions from multiple households, families could secure a higher quality and quantity of services than they could obtain on their own. They could also attract outside funding. In the process, educational institutions helped to forge new economic relationships, promote and enforce new

---

[1] "Report of the Seminary Committee Adopted by the Genesee Annual Conference at its session in Rochester, A.D. 1830," in "Journal of the Genesee Wesleyan Seminary," 1830–1854, Account Book #178, GWSC.

norms of economic behavior and discipline, and stimulate economic development. In fact, in the period from 1820 to 1840, educational institutions proved to have far more real power for mobilizing and realizing the value of capital than many commercial enterprises.

This chapter places the founding of the academy at Lima in the process of economic change and development commonly referred to as the capitalist transition. At first glance, the notion of investigating an educational institution as a site of capitalist transformation may seem strange. An academy, after all, was not a profit-making institution. It thus was not "capitalist" in what later became the conventional sense. The academy at Lima was, however, a highly capitalized and financially successful institution. Eventually, the academy's initial capital base of $11,000 in local subscriptions was augmented by $10,000 in long-term commercial loans, $12,000 in short-term commercial credit from banks and individuals, $60,000 in additional subscription "stock" from thousands of subscribers in hundreds of towns throughout western New York, and $10,000 in state capital. This combination of multiple sources of funding contributed to a level of capitalization and long-term financial success that exceeded that of many capital enterprises at the time, including that of a local textile mill.

Education as an Object of Capital Investment

At its July 1830 meeting in Rochester, the Genesee Annual Conference entertained five bids for the site of its proposed conference seminary and took up the task of choosing among them. That task occasioned heated debate and considerable conflict. On the face of it, the town of Perry had the strongest bid. Located on the west side of the Genesee River and settled somewhat later than Lima, Perry had been the site of considerable Methodist activity since at least 1825, when it became a circuit, and since 1828 had grown in membership to a level that rivaled that of Lima's Bloomfield Circuit.[2] Having hosted the meeting that appointed the seminary committee in 1829, Perry also had a head start in raising a bid for the seminary site. It certainly had the broadest base of support – 380 subscribers for a town of 2,792 people, perhaps as much as 80 percent of its households. It also made the most generous land offer. Instead of charging from $50 to $100 an acre for a five- to ten-acre building site, as did the other competing towns, Perry offered twenty-five acres for free. Not only that, but it offered the largest supporting farm, and it did so at the lowest price. At $20 an acre the conference could have acquired 130 acres in Perry for $900 less than it would cost to acquire just 100 acres in either Lima or Brockport.[3] In the end, however, after several calls for order, some

---

[2] The numbers of people "in society" on the various circuits of the Genesee Conference for 1829 and 1830 are published in *Minutes of the Annual Conferences of the Methodist Episcopal Church for the Years 1829–1839* (New York: T. Mason and G. Lane for the Methodist Episcopal Church, 1840): 30–31 and 72–73.

[3] Bids from the five towns that competed for the seminary site are described in the "Report of the Seminary Committee." Calculations for the proportion of Perry households represented by its 380 subscribers are based on an estimated average of 6 persons per household, which was

final horse-trading, and a second vote, the conference accepted the recommendation of the seminary committee and chose Lima for the site. By way of explanation, the committee referred mysteriously to "several inviting considerations" offered by Lima but "not ... easily enumerated." Although never spelled out, these considerations appear to have included matters of social geography and access to commercial capital.

Geographically, the five towns that competed for the site of the academy all lay near the center of the conference territory from east to west, on either side of the Genesee River. Two of the towns, Lima and Henrietta, lay east of the river. Three of the towns – Perry, LeRoy, and Brockport – lay west of the river. Looking from north to south, however, the towns were much less centrally located, with four of the five clustered toward the northern end of the territory. Only the town of Perry could claim any proximity to the conference's southern regions. Three of the towns, by contrast – Brockport, Henrietta, and Lima – were linked to Rochester by direct transportation routes. This Rochester connection proved important to attracting extra financial and political support for Lima.

When it came to the contents of the bids, all five of the towns offered land and financial support in the form of subscriptions, but the terms of the offers varied. The land offers varied both in the amount of acreage offered and the cost to the institution. Though all five towns offered a building site, the size of the site varied from two to three acres (Henrietta) to twenty-five acres (Perry). Curiously, both Henrietta and Perry offered the building site for free. The three remaining towns (Lima, Brockport and LeRoy) offered the sites at costs ranging from $50 to $100 an acre. In addition, three of the five towns – Perry, Lima, and Brockport – offered supporting farms, but of different sizes and costs per acre. Lima and Brockport both offered 100-acre farms at a cost of $30 per acre, while Perry offered a 130-acre farm at just $20 per acre.

With regard to subscription support, the five bids differed both in the number of subscriptions they offered and in their total value. Brockport offered the largest total value at $16,820, though it also had the smallest number of subscribers (129). The next largest total was Lima's. Officially, it included $11,650 in subscriptions from 170 people. A close look at the actual list reveals, however, that Lima's subscribers numbered 166 rather than 170, including 8 subscriptions from Rochester and its vicinity that had clearly been added later, probably at the meeting. Even with these additions, the pledges actually totaled $11,173 rather than the $11,650 claimed – a difference of $477. By comparison, Perry offered a total of $10,463. Without the Rochester pledges, the Lima total would have exceeded Perry's by just $150, hardly enough to cover the huge difference in land costs between the two towns' bids, which amounted to $1,400.[4] Moreover, when subscriptions from surrounding towns

---

the actual average number of persons per household in Lima the same year. Total population figures for Perry taken from the federal census. *Enumeration of the Inhabitants of the United States. 1830.* (Washington, DC: Duff Green, 1832).

[4] The list of original Lima subscribers appears in Subscription Book, 1830–1837, Account Book #102, GWSC.

are subtracted, only 115 of Lima's pledges came from the town of Lima itself, a figure representing just 40 percent of households, as compared with the 80 percent of households represented by Perry's 380 subscribers.[5]

When land and subscription support are considered together as capital assets, Perry seems to have offered the highest level of capitalization with the broadest base of support and the least amount of risk. Apparently many attendees at the meeting shared this assessment, for the seminary committee's recommendation that Lima be chosen as the site was greeted with considerable opposition. After passing the committee's first resolution that they support the seminary "be its location wherever it may," members immediately broke into conflict, moving and seconding that "Lima be stricken from the second resolution wherever it occurs, and that Perry be inserted in its stead." Later it was proposed that the location be left undecided until various contenders had made presentations to the whole body, and then that the location be decided by ballot. The conference eventually returned to the latter half of this proposal, but in the meantime, committee member John Copeland further agitated the meeting with a speech in support of Lima. Whatever he said proved so contentious that the group had to pass a special resolution to enable Copeland to finish his speech. When he had done so, the meeting went into such an uproar that another resolution passed reminding members of the *"enlightened, correct,* and *dignified* manner" in which meetings should be conducted. In the voting that followed, the first ballot produced no majority. On a second ballot, Brockport was dropped as a candidate. Lima then won with twenty-six votes; Perry received fifteen votes and LeRoy and Henrietta each received four.[6]

The shift of support from Brockport to Lima suggests that proximity to Rochester played a role in constituency-building. In addition, it appears that leaders of the conference were influenced more by an appetite for risk than by an aversion to it. This disposition is suggested by a comparison of the terms of payment specified in the bids. All five towns offered a schedule of payment that extended over two to four years, with one-quarter to one-third of the total paid in six months or at the start of building and the remainder paid in equal annual installments. When it came to the method of payment, however, differences among the bids were significant. All of the towns but Lima specified that some portion of its financial support would take the form of labor and materials. Brockport offered free stone from a local quarry. LeRoy specified that

---

[5] The census lists 296 households for Lima in 1830. *Enumeration of the Inhabitants of the United States. 1830.* See footnote 3 for comparable statistics on Perry. It is possible that some number of the Perry subscriptions did not come from the town of Perry itself, but from surrounding towns. In that case, the proportion of Perry households represented by its subscription would decrease. Nonetheless, the high number of Perry subscriptions indicates that the proportion of local households represented by the Perry subscriptions was much higher than for Lima.

[6] Minutes of the Genesee Annual Conference of the Methodist Episcopal Church, July 29, 1830, Rochester, New York, "Journal of the Genesee Annual Conference," WNYCA.

Education as an Object of Capital Investment

$1,535, or 18 percent of its $8,500 in subscriptions, be payable in labor and materials. Similarly, Perry specified that $2,232 of its total, or 21 percent, be payable in-kind. The bid from Henrietta, meanwhile, consisted primarily of an existing academy building. Lima, by contrast, made no explicit statement that subscriptions would be wholly or partially paid in-kind. To the contrary, according to the seminary committee's report, Lima offered $11,650 *in cash*.[7]

This distinction among the five seminary bids places the founding of the academy in Lima at the heart of economic change in the early nineteenth century. The bids of Lima's four competitors reflected the norms of community building up to that time. As exemplified most recently in the building of the Methodist church in Lima, completed the previous year, subscribers to church and school building projects commonly paid some portion of their subscriptions in produce, goods, or labor that could be sold for cash on the market, bartered on local accounts, or employed directly in the construction process. Direct mobilization of surplus goods and labor from rural households in this way reflected the roots of such projects in local social economies. To promise to pay subscriptions wholly in cash, by contrast, implied market integration.

As it turned out, the claim that Lima's subscriptions would be paid wholly in cash contradicted the expectations of a number of subscribers and became a source of conflict as the project proceeded. Many subscribers would in fact pay their subscriptions in-kind or through direct exchange. What the promise of cash payment actually reflected, it seems, was a mixture of cunning and ambition on the part of both local and Methodist leaders who, each for their own reasons, were committed to making Lima the successful bidder. Members of the seminary committee clearly favored a site near Rochester, which in 1830 was a locus of evangelical activity and economic development in western New York. It is likely that the Reverend John Copeland, a member of the committee and also the presiding elder of the Rochester District at the time, helped to solicit the extra subscriptions from Rochester that edged Lima's subscription total over that of Perry, perhaps after the bids came in. It is also likely, given subsequent events, that at some time during the final days or moments of the bidding process, Asahel Warner mentioned the possibility of a major long-term commercial loan he could secure for the project. It was this prospect, more than any, perhaps, that induced the Genesee Conference to choose Lima.

The Role of the Local Credit Broker

When Asahel Warner became involved in founding the academy at Lima, he and his extended family had been at the center of economic, political, and cultural activity in their town for nearly forty years. As a young man of thirty, he and his father, William; his sister, Sarah; and his three brothers, Matthew, Daniel and William, migrated with their spouses from the Upper Hudson

---

[7] Report of the Seminary Committee.

Valley in eastern New York State to a newly platted township in the Genesee Valley of western New York. Other relatives followed. Having first visited the area in 1794, and settled there in 1795, the Warners were party to the political organization and naming of the town in 1796, to the founding of the first church society there in 1801, and to the construction of the "brick school house" in 1803. Since then they had served in virtually every town office, from fence viewer to assessor to supervisor to school commissioner. At the state level, Asahel had served six nonconsecutive terms as an assembly representative in the state legislature from 1807 to 1819, and Matthew had served one term beginning in 1820. In addition, Asahel held the title of local postmaster for years while Matthew heard civil cases as a judge in the county court of common pleas from 1808 to 1817, and as a local justice of the peace in the early 1820s. After playing leading roles in financing the construction of the academy, the Warners became involved in financing a local textile mill. As a later chronicler stated, "the history of the town of Lima is intimately connected with that of the Warners."[8]

Like virtually all new settlers of western territory, the Warners first held capital in the form of land. Everywhere, the Warners and their in-laws – the Bristols, the Burchards, the Annables, and others – acquired real estate. Gradually, some became involved in other pursuits. Brother-in-law James Spier, for example, built and operated a hotel at Lima's four corners in the 1820s.[9] Brothers Asahel and Matthew, meanwhile, became local financiers. As major landholders by local standards, the Warner brothers enjoyed greater access to cash and commercial credit than many of their neighbors. By using their land as security, they could obtain loans from banks or, more often, from private mortgage lenders. Asahel in particular enjoyed a long-term financial relationship with a major mortgage lender and financier in New York City,

---

[8] This quotation comes from a newspaper account of a Warner family reunion in 1894. That year was the 100th anniversary of the Warners' settlement in the town as well as the 50th wedding anniversary of Andrew Jackson Warner, one of Matthew Warner's sons, who remained a resident of Lima his whole life. (This Andrew Jackson Warner was not the same as the slightly younger Rochester architect of the same name and roughly the same generation.) The extremely lengthy newspaper account includes detailed geneological information from the seventeenth through the nineteenth centuries. Unfortunately, the surviving copy I have seen provides no publication information, LHS.

[9] Some account of founding families in Lima, including the Burchards (sometimes spelled Birchard), is provided in Neil Adams McNall, *An Agricultural History of the Genesee Valley, 1790–1860* (Philadelphia: University of Pennsylvania Press, 1952) and in Orasmus Turner, *History of the Pioneer Settlement of Phelps and Gorham's Purchase and Morris' Reserve* (Rochester, NY: William Alling, 1851). Also, a partial account of the interrelationships between families, particularly among the Bristols and the Warners, appears in the Last Will and Testament of Eliphalet Bristol, dated August 25, 1830, a copy of which is contained in the Warner Papers, LHS, Item #545. Additional details and points of comparison and confirmation can be found in local histories by Mabel Furner Jenks, *Lima, 1788–1964: The Crossroads of Western New York, Outline of the History of Lima Written for the 175th Anniversary Celebration*, (n.p., 1984 [1964]), LHS; and by Fran Gotcsik, "Lima Village History," pp. 1–38 and "A Short History of Lima, New York," pp. 1–65, unpublished papers, LHS. For early land

Isaac Bronson, and later with his sons and heirs, Arthur and Oliver Bronson. Beginning in the early 1820s, Asahel secured a series of mortgage loans from the Bronsons for himself and family members, while occasionally also arranging loans for other area residents and advising the Bronsons of the security of other local investments.[10] At the same time, he and his brother made smaller loans of their own to local townspeople. In this way, the Warners served as brokers between large-scale commercial credit networks and local economic relations.[11] Eventually, Asahel would play a similar role for the academy.

To succeed in the role of credit-broker, the Warners had to negotiate a delicate social balance. During much of the nineteenth century a fundamental tension existed between the norms of economy practiced at local levels, in small towns and rural areas, and the norms of economy that prevailed in the world of translocal trade and high finance, in major coastal cities and merchant houses. At the level of operation represented by the Bronsons' lending business in New York City, which involved hundreds of bonds and mortgages throughout the state and in other states as well, few deviations from the rule of prompt and regular cash payments of interest were tolerated. At the local level represented by the Warners' credit relations in Lima, by contrast, a different rule applied. Among neighbors most debts had no set term of obligation or schedule of payment. Nor could creditors expect to earn interest or be paid in cash. The challenge for the Warners and others who made their way by mediating between cultures was to avoid getting caught in a culture clash.

The Warners' experience managing this challenge was rooted in substantial land ownership. In the initial two decades after settlement, they concentrated first on establishing their household estates through land acquisition.[12] Through marriage, inheritance, and mortgage-borrowing, they accumulated substantial estates by local standards. In 1820, Asahel owned a total of 607 acres in Lima, the second largest estate in town. Only 190 (31%) of these acres were "improved," suggesting that he held the rest for possible re-sale. By contrast, the rest of the Warner family owned land primarily for their own working farms or to settle their children. In 1820, the parental Warner estate (William Sr. died shortly after his arrival in 1795, leaving his fourth wife, who died in 1819, and a number of children) comprised an additional 350 acres and was the seventh largest estate in town, while brothers Matthew, Daniel and William, Jr. owned 230, 150, and 93 acres, respectively. On each of these farms the Warners kept over half the acreage in some kind of cultivation or

---

sales and purchases in what became the Town of Lima, see the Record of Deeds for Ontario County, OCRAIMS.

[10] Evidence of Asahel Warner's dealings with the Bronsons of New York City can be found among miscellaneous items in the Warner Papers, LHS; in multiple account books, GWSC; and especially in Box 44, Folder 10, Asahel Warner, Lima, 1821–1844, BFP.

[11] Evidence of these loans to local townspeople appears in miscellaneous items in the Warner Papers, LHS.

[12] This account of property acquisition in Lima by the Warners is pieced together from miscellaneous items in the Warner Papers, LHS.

pasturage. Matthew made the most intensive use of his land by far, with 78 percent of his land assessed at the highest possible value.[13]

As substantial landowners, the Warners participated in the intensification of agricultural production that characterized the U.S. economy in the decades following the Revolution. To improve land and make it agriculturally productive, the Warners relied primarily on household labor and the labor of neighbors traded through local exchange. Asahel and Matthew, like their father, each had a number of children, as did their siblings. Daughters as well as sons contributed to production through dairy-making, orchard-tending, sheep-herding, and the production of field crops. Household labor included not only that of the Warners' own family members, but also of wards and apprentices housed through agreements with neighbors. Beginning as early as 1806, Matthew, in particular, became legal guardian to a series of young men and women, some of whose fathers had died. In formal contracts with their surviving parent, Matthew agreed to supply these youth with the customary benefits of apprenticeship. These included food, washing, lodging, apparel, and a good common education in reading, writing, and ciphering, as well as knowledge of a skill or trade (i.e., farming). In exchange, Warner enjoyed the benefit of the youths' labor until the age of majority, at which time he released them from further obligation with agreed upon payments of cash or goods. When Jonas Humprey reached the age of majority in 1820, for example, he received $197.50 in cash.[14]

Beyond these specific contractual arrangements with neighbors over their children, Matthew also engaged extra labor for capital improvements and agricultural production through local exchange relations. In 1819, for example, Matthew secured the benefit of a neighbor's labor in digging an irrigation ditch, in exchange for which the neighbor gained a lease for use of the ditch and the water forever.[15] For the Warners, the management and distribution of labor was as important to successful household economy as were the acquisition and disposition of land and the production and exchange of commodities. At times they even exchanged land for labor. In 1821, for example, Matthew made a mortgage agreement with Eli Kimball whereby the latter eventually acquired title to a few acres of Warner land. Kimball paid this mortgage in part with cash and produce, but he also cancelled at least a quarter of the debt with fourteen years of occasional labor such as hay-making, boot repair, and chimney building.[16]

---

[13] County Tax Records for the Town of Lima, 1820, OCRAIMS.
[14] Receipt from Jonas Humphrey to M. Warner for $197.50 paid to Humphrey at age of majority by Warner, his guardian, June 1820, Item #533, Warner Papers, LHS.
[15] Copy of agreement between M. Warner and James Sterling for digging ditch on M. Warner property to be leased to Sterling and his heirs, dated 1819, Item #300, Warner Papers, LHS.
[16] Bill and receipt for labor performed by Eli Kimball on his account with Matthew Warner for the period 1824–1835, dated March 22, 1835; also, lease-mortage of land from Eli Kimball to Matthew Warner, dated 1821, Item #221; and receipt for final sale of land from Matthew Warner to Eli Kimball, dated March 28, 1835, Item #349, Warner Papers, LHS.

Education as an Object of Capital Investment

As farmers the Warners produced a number of agricultural goods that had exchange value both on commercial markets and in local trade. These goods included apples, cider, butter, wool, and pork as well as field crops such as corn, oats, and wheat. The Warners probably traded some commodities almost as soon as they settled in Lima. As early as 1791, grains could be processed and traded at grist mills on Zebulon Norton's lands in the northeast corner of town, on Honeoye Creek. Once Norton accumulated sufficient grain in his stores, he would transport it for resale at markets in Montreal, Baltimore, or New York. Later, in 1806, a second local landowner, James K. Guernsey, formed a partnership with Norton to establish a two-way trade in Lima. By 1808 Guernsey owned a separate store that reportedly bought up saleable agricultural commodities such as potash, pork, corn, and wheat from a wide region. In exchange he either paid cash or traded imported goods from the East on account.[17]

Guernsey continued this business with a series of partners until 1823, the year the Erie Canal opened as far as the Genesee River. At that time he moved twenty-five miles northwest of Lima to the town of Pittsford, where the canal and the river joined just south of Rochester.[18] When the canal opened, local opportunities for commercial trade of agricultural goods widened considerably. Even though Lima was not on the canal, it experienced a notable quickening of commercial activity. A number of new merchant partnerships formed in the region and began competing to buy up area grain harvests. In 1825, for example, Matthew Warner supplied more than fifty-one bushels of corn on contract to a store in Mendon, the next town north.[19]

Eventually, the Warners did some of their own commodities trading directly on the market. On more than one occasion they pulled together a shipment of wheat from area farms. A receipt from 1835, for example, shows a schedule of the fares charged to Matthew Warner for shipping wheat flour from Lima to New York City via road, canal barge, and packet boat. Matthew traveled with the grain to New York on this occasion. Once there, he wrote back to his brother Asahel to report on the prices of both imported goods such as coffee, tea, and sugar, and domestic agricultural products such as pork, flour, and corn. Noting the sudden rise in prices that had occurred even since he left home, Matthew asked his brother to "tell my boys if they have not sold what corn and oats we had to spare to hold on and not to feed too much. Corn is

[17] Evidence of the Guernsey and Norton partnership appears in an advertisement dated October 1806 and published in a January 1807 issue of the Canandaigua *Western Repository*, OCHS. Guernesey's early trade is described in Turner, *Pioneer* Settlement, 503. On Norton, see also Diane Ham and Anne Bollock, "History of the Town of Mendon, 1813–2000 and Village of Honeoye Falls," booklet issued by the Honeoye Falls–Town of Mendon Historical Society (n.p., 2000).
[18] Orasmus Turner, *History of the Pioneer Settlement*, p. 375.
[19] Receipt from Atwell and Grout to Matthew Warner as per Able Parker, May 17, 1825, Warner Papers, LHS.

worth 75 cents and oats 50. Mr. Hutchinson wants the corn and will pay that or more."[20]

At the same time as the Warners traded commodities directly on the market, however, they also traded some of the same goods on long-term debt accounts with their neighbors. Over the period from 1834 to 1838, for example, Matthew enlisted the services of a local blacksmith, Ransom Smith, for a number of jobs, such as repairing wagons, pitchforks, a carriage, and a sleigh. Warner in return pastured two of Smith's cows in 1836, gave him five bushels of corn in 1837, and provided one and a half bushels of apples in 1838 before balancing his account with a cash payment of $6.61.[21] Meanwhile, Warner continued to trade household agricultural products with local merchants on account. With the merchants Grout and Sumner, for example, Matthew traded hogs and plough points for store items from 1829 to 1832.[22] Similarly, over a five-month period in 1836, Matthew's household acquired a number of items, including linen and silk cloth, from merchants Godfrey and Cargill. To balance the account for these imported goods, Matthew (or his wife) made payments in the form of butter as well as cash.[23]

Cash, as these examples indicate, could be useful in local exchange but was not absolutely necessary. Those who recorded debts and credits on slips of paper or in formal account books often stated the value of a good or service in monetary terms, but this was a matter of accounting. As with any other service or commodity, the value of cash depended on its usefulness to the parties involved. Although cash had its virtues, it was not, to borrow a phrase coined by another historian, "good to eat."[24] Moreover, cash was often scarce. Until 1811, when the charter of the first bank of the United States expired, only a few money banks existed at all in the State of New York, and these exclusively in the trade cities of New York and Albany. With that charter's expiration, New York chartered ten new banks. Still, the closest of these to Lima was the Bank of Utica, still 150 miles to the east and well beyond the reach of local exchange. An office of the Utica bank was authorized for Canandaigua in 1815, and the Bank of Rochester was chartered in 1824, but it was not until the liberalization of New York bank policies and the expansion of savings banks in the 1830s that bank notes appear to have become widely available.[25] The first savings banks in the area were Ontario Savings Bank

---

[20] Letter from Matthew Warner to Asahel Warner regarding joint affairs in New York City, May 6, 1835, Item #48, Warner Papers, LHS.
[21] Bill and receipt from Ransom Smith to Matthew Warner, 1834–1838, Item #236, Warner Papers, LHS.
[22] Bill and receipt from Grout and Sumner to Matthew Warner, 1829–1832, Item #269, Warner Papers, LHS.
[23] Bill and receipt from Godfrey and Cargill, for June–October, 1836, Item #255, Warner Papers, LHS.
[24] Michael Merrill, "Cash is Good to Eat: Self-Sufficiency and Exchange in the Rural Economy of the United States," *Radical Historical Review* 3 (Winter 1977): 42–71.
[25] The dates of various New York bank charters were compiled from Adolph Julius Rodenbeck, *The Statutory Record of the Unconsolidated Laws* (Albany, NY: J. B. Lyon Co., state printers, 1911).

Education as an Object of Capital Investment 225

of Canandaigua, chartered in 1830 and operational in 1832, and Rochester Savings Bank, founded in 1831.[26] In the meantime, credit-brokers like the Warners remained a crucial source of currency and credit for both individual and corporate community enterprises.

Education and Economic Development

Historians have provided somewhat competing accounts of the process of economic development that led to what some refer to as a "take-off" period for the U.S. economy – a point, often put at around 1840, when growth in per capita output and income accelerated and became a "normal condition" of society. Nonetheless, scholars agree on many of the central characteristics of this process. At its core, economic development involved a shift of resources from agricultural to nonagricultural activities. This meant that instead of investing increased wealth in the acquisition of additional land or livestock, or in the improvement of existing agricultural holdings, successful farmers and rural merchants after 1820 increasingly invested a portion of their "savings" – that is, surplus labor and goods beyond the level necessary to sustain their households – in nonagricultural enterprises.[27] Scholars typically focus on textile mills as objects of this development. However, textile mills were not the only enterprises to shift resources from agriculture to nonagricultural activities, to employ "surplus" labor and goods, or to promote the formation and investment of rural capital. In Lima, a coalition of small-scale land dealers, commercial farmers, local merchants and professionals, and ordinary craftsmen and tradesmen drew on existing networks of trust and association to generate a substantial base of corporate capital for founding an academy. To the extent that this initial capitalization represented a shift of resources from agricultural to nonagricultural activities, it was part of the broader process of economic development.

According to economic historians, several factors facilitated the shift of capital from agricultural to nonagricultural activities during the antebellum period. These included the formation of translocal commodities markets through which farmers and merchants could realize the value of surplus labor and goods beyond the amount absorbed by local exchange. Although historians have argued about the precise timing and the extent of such market formation and integration, most would now agree that the intensification of agriculture and the creation of domestic commodities markets occurred in the Northeast in the period from 1780 to 1820 – a chronology that fits the

---

[26] See Emerson Willard Keyes, *A History of Savings Banks in the United States from Their Inception in 1816 down to 1874*, 2 Vols. (New York Bradford Rhodes, 1876 and 1878), Vol. II.

[27] An excellent survey of the literature on antebellum economic development is provided in Howard Bodenhorn, *A History of Banking in Antebellum America: Financial Markets and Economic Development in an Era of Nation-Building* (Cambridge: Cambridge University Press, 2000): 1–27.

Lima case. By 1820, Lima clearly exhibited the characteristics of a commercial farming economy.[28]

Another factor associated with economic development was the increased availability of cash and other negotiable instruments that allowed farmers and merchants to "store" their savings in a nonperishable form and to employ that savings in multiple ways. This increase in the money supply began around 1820 and is typically associated by historians with the expansion of banking. In his study of antebellum banking, Howard Bodenhorn points out two important functions of banks in the capitalist transition. First, banks were important because they performed the valuable function of collecting the capital from one group of people who sought to "save" it and directing it to another group of people who "needed" it. This redirection of capital had important strategic as well as geographic dimensions. It involved the movement of capital from one sector of economic activity to another (i.e., agriculture to manufacturing) as well as from one place to another (i.e., town to city or city to town). Second, banks were important in the antebellum era as a source of currency and thus as a means of capital accumulation or "savings." According to Bodenhorn's estimates, 76 percent of all currency in circulation during the antebellum period was issued directly by banks. In the absence of alternative financial instruments, households seeking to "save" current surplus labor and goods for future use chose to store it in the form of money. Bank currency thus had an important influence on capital accumulation, because it provided a means of storing "savings."[29]

Bodenhorn's analysis of banking highlights the significance of increased currency and capital mobility in fostering economic development. A focus on banking also makes sense as a way of assessing capital savings and mobility from a state or regional perspective. When considered from a local or rural perspective, however, an emphasis on banks as the primary source of currency and credit may be misleading, especially for the early republican era. In 1830, the concept of the ordinary "savings" bank was still in the process of being invented, and was still very much an urban phenomenon. Rather than taking deposits from ordinary households, most early banks pooled the capital of major financiers and investors. They then lent that money to provide a return to their investor-shareholders in the form of interest. These were not long-term loans, however, nor did they go to ordinary households. Instead, early banks

---

[28] The leading authority on the emergence of commodities markets in this period is Winifred Barr Rothenberg, *From Market-places to a Market Economy: The Transformation of Rural Massachusetts, 1750–1850* (Chicago: University of Chicago, 1992). The claim here about the character and chronology of Lima's participation in the commercial farming economy is based on the model of antebellum economic development developed by Linda Pritchard in "Religious Change in a Developing Region: The Social Context of Evangelicalism in Western New York and the Upper Ohio Valley During the Mid-Nineteenth Century" (unpublished Ph.D. dissertation, University of Pittsburgh, 1980). See the previous chapter for a discussion of the model and the data used to place Lima in the model. Also see Appendix Table 4.

[29] Bodenhorn, *A History of Banking*, 5–22; esp. p. 17.

issued short-term loans of three to six months designed to help merchants to bridge the gap between the purchase of commodities and their subsequent resale. Larger, long-term loans were available mainly to major merchant capitalists who themselves often held shares in a bank.[30]

The main form of commercial credit available to ordinary households on a long-term basis was a mortgage loan. This form of capital was not generally available through commercial institutions, however, but through individuals. In Lima and western New York, the first and primary source of commercial credit in the 1820s was private mortgage lending. Increases in bank loans followed in the 1830s with the liberalization of state banking and the founding of the first savings banks outside major cities. By the 1840s and 1850s, according to Bodenhorn's data, banks in certain regions regularly issued short-term loans to farmers and small-scale manufacturers. In 1830, however, few households or enterprises could readily "save" or "borrow" money through a commercial lending institution. Instead, they had to rely on local capitalists and credit-brokers.

The Making of a Capitalist

Before the mid-1820s, the Warners' commercial activities consisted primarily of land sales and purchases and the trading of agricultural commodities, the latter first with merchants like Guernsey and Clark, and then directly on New York markets. Beginning in the 1820s, however, the Warners increased their commercial exposure through mortgage-borrowing, money-lending, and other forms of capital investment. For Asahel, and to some degree also for Matthew, the role of local financier probably first developed out of experience with land sales. As was common in the early decades of settlement in western New York and elsewhere, both men had engaged in the practice of selling land through mortgage agreements. Typically used in sales involving small amounts of land not yet cleared of timber, this sales arrangement involved no initial outlay of funds on the buyer's part. Instead, the landowner effectively advanced title to the land as a form of exchange credit on which the buyer then made payments of cash, produce, and labor. By this method major speculators like Oliver Phelps, Nathaniel Gorham, James Wadsworth, and John Ellicot sold many lots to householders of modest means. They also sold many of the same lots more than once, for failure to maintain payments resulted in reversion of the

---

[30] Ibid. On early savings banks, see Keyes, *A History of Savings Banks*. On the development of banking more generally in New York and in the context of trends nationally, see Bray Hammond, *Banks and Politics in America: From the Revolution to the Civil War* (Princeton, NJ: Princeton University Press, 1957); L. Ray Gunn, *The Decline of Authority: Public Economic Policy and Political Development in New York State, 1800–1860* (Ithaca, NY: Cornell University Press, 1988); and James Roger Sharp, *The Jacksonians versus the Banks: Politics in the States after the Panic of 1837* (New York: Columbia University Press, 1970).

title to the original owner.[31] Although Asahel and Matthew Warner were not nearly as involved in land trading as these speculators, they also sold some parcels of land on this basis. In 1815, for example, Olive and Matthew Teas made a mortgage agreement for a few acres of Warner land in the amount of $400. After fourteen years of settlement and labor on the site, however, Matthew Teas died and the land title reverted to Matthew Warner.[32]

In arrangements such as these, landowners like the Warners earned only small incomes, but they also took virtually no risks. It was the settler who invested years of labor in an all-or-nothing enterprise for which he earned no equity. Meanwhile, the value of the land increased as a result of the settler's efforts to clear and improve it. Should the mortgage end in default, the original landowner could not only regain title to the land but also resell it to a subsequent buyer at a higher price. Although this form of mortgage had the advantage of security, however, it only applied to property a landowner already owned and actually wished to sell. For Matthew especially, who owned much less land than Asahel and who already used most of that land for household production, such arrangements offered only limited opportunities for increasing either his household's assets or its cash income. Also, with the greater demand for western New York commodities fostered by the canal, land values in the Genesee Valley rose significantly. In this context, the Warners sought not to get rid of their holdings, but to realize more of the value of the land they already owned. To do this they used their land to gain access to cash, augment their holdings, and invest in local development. One of the forms of investment in which they engaged was local mortgage lending.

Mortgage lending differed from the mortgage sales agreements in which the Warners previously had been involved in several respects. First, instead of selling land they already owned on time, the Warners in these cases advanced cash to local landowners, using the owners' lands as security. Second, the Warners made such cash advances to locals who were substantial landowners in Lima already, rather than to the settlers of little means with whom they had previously made mortgage sales agreements. Third, if a mortgagor defaulted on the loan, the Warners gained title to the lands that had been offered on security. This meant that the Warners stood to gain title to land they did not already own in Lima. Finally, to avoid default, the mortgagor had to make regular payments of interest. In contrast with the Warners' previous mortgage sales agreements, which conformed to the norms of local social economy, mortgage loans involved considerable outlays of cash and were subject to the norms of market economy and commercial credit.

[31] This practice of mortgage land sales is described in McNall, *An Agricultural History*, 17–77. It is also apparent in the records for the 1790s and early 1800s of the Court of Common Pleas for Ontario County, OCRAIMS. See also D. W. Meinig, "Geography of Expansion, 1785–1855," in John H. Thompson, ed., *Geography of New York State* (Syracuse: Syracuse University Press, 1966): 140–171.
[32] Deed for land mortgaged by Olive and Matthew Teas, originally dated August, 1815, signed over to Matthew Warner in 1829, Item #27, Warner Papers, LHS.

Perhaps the most significant mortgage loan Matthew made in the 1820s was to Benjamin Hovey. In March 1826, Hovey mortgaged several town lots to Matthew for $800.³³ Hovey at this time operated a carding machine business in Lima under the name Benjamin Hovey and Company. At the company's store in the center of town, Benjamin and his father and brother, Ebenezer and Levi, sold carding machines for household wool production. The resulting wool in turn could then be sold to the Hoveys, exchanged with local households, or traded with other merchants for transport to market. At the same time as Hovey engaged in the wool business, he also was a substantial landowner. In 1820 he and his company owned a total of 350 acres valued at nearly $6,000.³⁴ This made his estate the eighth largest in Lima. Although existing records do not reveal the nature of the farming in which Hovey engaged, it is possible that he maintained a sheep herd. In any case, by the end of the 1820s, Matthew Warner had acquired all of Hovey's property and an interest in wool production.

Matthew effected this acquisition of property and investment interests through a combination of actions, of which the $800 mortgage loan of 1826 was only one. They included outright land purchases, but also the seizure of Hovey property to satisfy outstanding debts.³⁵ Indeed, Matthew's involvement with the Hoveys and with the role of local financier may have developed as much from his experience as a local constable, county judge, and justice of the peace as from his less extensive experience in land sales.³⁶ The first piece of property Matthew acquired from Hovey came to him through a court suit and judgment. In 1820, the State of Connecticut, which had served as a major mortgage lender to purchasers of western New York lands in the first decades of the century, seized Hovey property valued at $3,093.62, or half of Hovey's estate, for payment of debts. A number of years later, in March of 1826, Matthew acquired this same property from the State of Connecticut at a public auction for a fraction of its value, at $206.87.³⁷ Although this sale

---

33 Mortgage of land by Benjamin Hovey to Matthew Warner, dated March, 1826, Item #378, Warner Papers, LHS.
34 County Tax Records for the Town of Lima, 1820, OCRAIMS.
35 Notice regarding debt of Benjamin and Ebenezer Hovey to Isaac Spencer, Treasurer of the State of Connecticut, dated March 6, 1820, marked sold at public auction and deeded to Matthew Warner, 1828, Item #483; Receipt to Edward Watterous for several promissory notes against Benjamin Hovey from Matthew Warner, n.d., Item #574; and Deed from Benjamin Hovey to M. Warner for 130 acres valued at $2200, dated June 27, 1829, Item #475, Warner Papers, LHS.
36 Matthew Warner's early service as justice on the Ontario County Court or "General Sessions of the Peace" is recorded in Ontario County General Sessions Records, Box 1, 1794–1840, OCRAIMS. Warner appeared as justice for most years between 1808 and 1819 and may have also served before 1808 (records are missing for 1803–1808). In the 1820s, Matthew Warner also served for a few years as a justice of the peace after the office became a locally elected one. This service is recorded in the Lima Town Book, 1818–1840, LHS.
37 See footnote 31; also bill to Benjamin Hovey from Matthew Warner regarding outstanding notes and debts, dated 1829, Item #455; Warner Papers, LHS.

represented a substantial loss, such losses were not uncommon in sales at public auctions, especially in the pre-canal period. This acquisition may even have been arranged in advance by Hovey and Warner. The fact that Hovey mortgaged additional property to Warner in the same month suggests that he may have done so to acquire the money to buy back the original property. At the greatly discounted rate he paid for it, Warner could have sold the property back to Hovey at a very low price and still have made a profit. Such cooperation among neighbors was not unknown. In this case, however, Hovey never regained full title to the property. In 1828, Hovey again defaulted on a number of commercial debts, including not only the 1826 mortgage loan to Matthew, but other mortgages and promissory notes as well. To settle these debts, Hovey was eventually forced to sell his remaining land to Matthew for a total of $2,200 in 1829.[38]

For Matthew Warner, the series of transactions that led to the acquisition of Hovey land had several significant consequences. First, the acquisition more than doubled the amount of property Matthew owned during the 1820s. According to one local historian, Matthew's property now included virtually all of the town's central village district as well as substantial farm lands.[39] Second, acquisition of the Hovey property increased Matthew's capacity for agricultural production, not only of grain crops that he eventually traded directly on the market, but also of wool for the production of cloth. At the same time that Matthew increased his assets and production capacity, however, he also increased his liabilities. To make the final purchase of Hovey's land, Matthew took out a substantial mortgage loan of his own from his brother-in-law, James Spier, for $1,900.[40] A third consequence of the acquisition, then, is that it increased his financial risks. Finally, Matthew's involvement in the Hovey affair launched him in the role of local financier and developer. Perhaps emboldened by his success with the Hovey property, Matthew went on to offer other financial services. In the early 1830s, he would become a surety agent on a number of loans to neighbors from Ontario Bank.

Serving as a surety agent meant that Matthew guaranteed a loan made to someone else by promising to pay off the loan in case of default. In return for putting his own property and credit at risk in this way, the agent (Matthew) received some portion of the loan as a fee. Loans of this kind took the form of promissory notes, with surety agents signing along with the actual borrowers. Thus, after Erastus and Abel Morse signed a note promising to pay Ontario Bank $280 in 1833, Matthew added his own signature – "Matthew

---

[38] Ibid.
[39] Jenks, *Lima: 1788–1964*, 10. Unfortunately Jenks provided no references to sources for her information.
[40] Receipt from James Spier regarding payment of $1,900 on 1828 mortgage from Matthew Warner, paid by Matthew's relatives and heirs, August 29, 1840, Item #432; also, mortgage agreement, Item #438, Warner Papers, LHS.

Warner, surety."⁴¹ For banks in this period, the repayment period was almost always three months, though such loans were often renewed. Matthew's papers include a series of notes for $280 dated exactly three months apart. Matthew's initial involvement in the surety business was associated with the liberalization of lending policies at Ontario Bank in nearby Canandaigua. In 1832 alone Matthew served as surety agent on at least five different loans to individuals by Ontario Bank and received at least one loan from the bank himself. The period from 1832 through 1834 was a high point of activity for Matthew in this regard, and it facilitated his subsequent nonagricultural investments.⁴²

To a certain extent this expansion of property and financial activity was appropriate to Matthew's stage of life. In 1830 he was sixty-four years old and had three grown males at home and five children under the age of twenty. He was preparing to settle several sons and daughters in homes and estates of their own. At this point in life he was supposed to accumulate property. To say that Matthew had reached the peak of his wealth and influence is to say that he had successfully followed the course that most householders hoped to follow.⁴³ At the same time as the course of Matthew's economic activity represented the fulfillment of normal life cycle expectations, however, it also coincided with broader economic changes peculiar to the time and place in which he lived. The land purchases that Matthew and Asahel made in the 1790s, for instance, were part of a major expansion of national wealth through the appropriation and sale of new federal and state lands in the decades immediately following the Revolution. Similarly, the mortgage-lending that the brothers did in the 1820s was part of a broader expansion of mortgage-lending to ordinary farmer households (as opposed to major land speculators) in the interior that occurred during that decade. Isaac Bronson, the New York financier, is credited with leading this expansion in western New York State, and his $6000 mortgage loan to Asahel Warner in 1821 was among the first he made in the territory.⁴⁴ In the same way, the financial services Matthew provided as a surety agent for bank loans in the early 1830s was part of a broader expansion of credit and note circulation fostered by changes in federal and state banking policies in that decade.

---

[41] Promissory note from Erastus and Able Morse with M. Warner as surety, January 1833, Item #106; also renewals of those notes, April 1833, Item #203, and July 1833, Item #252, Warner Papers, LHS.

[42] Warner Papers, passim.

[43] There is a large literature providing a life cycle perspective on the norms of property accumulation, labor distribution, and employment for rural household economies. One of the most illuminating accounts is provided by Laural Thatcher Ulrich in *A Mid-wife's Tale; The Life of Martha Ballard, Based on Her Diary, 1785–1812* (New York: Random House, 1991), esp. 262–285 and 309–345. See also Daniel Vickers, "Competency and Competition: Economic Culture in Early America," *William and Mary Quarterly* 47:1 (January 1990): 3–29.

[44] Bronson's investments in land and mortgages in New York and the Midwest are described in detail in John Denis Haeger, *The Investment Frontier: New York Businessmen and the*

For leading local landowners and credit-brokers like the Warners, the limited increase in the availability of cash and commercial credit from mortgage-lenders and banks in the 1820s and 1830s had created certain opportunities. Using their own substantial landholdings as collateral and their personal and political connections with outside investors and commercial institutions, they became sources of cash and commercial credit for their neighbors, effectively assuming the role of local financiers. In 1830, they were poised to use the capital and credit they had accumulated to make substantial new investments. Both men chose to invest in nonagricultural enterprises. In 1830, Asahel took the lead in financing the academy. In 1834, Matthew began raising capital for a local textile mill in which Asahel also became involved. The very different histories and levels of success achieved by these two enterprises highlight the significance of social and cultural institutions like the academy in the transforming economy.

Economic Development of the Old Northwest (Albany: State University of New York Press, 1981) and in Grant Morrison, *Isaac Bronson and the Search for System in American Capitalism* (New York: Arno Press, 1978). According to these accounts, Bronson did not get into the land mortgage business in western New York until the 1820s. Asahel Warner's first mortgage with Bronson was dated 1821. "Mortgage Indenture, August 27, 1821," and "Memo: Asahel Warner property mortgaged to I. Bronson, August, 1821," Box 44, Folder 10, Asahel Warner, Lima, 1821–1844, BFP.

14

Varieties of Trust – Education and Economic Competition

> The committee announced they were ready to receive proposals for doing the work of the Seminary buildings. None presented.
> Minutes of the Seminary Building Committee, December 28, 1830[1]

> Fine specimens of drawings were presented both by Mr. Warner of Geneseo and Mr. Elbridge of Rochester. ...
> Minutes of the Seminary Building Committee, January 4, 1831[2]

The coalition that founded the academy in Lima brought together two different social capital networks, two different patterns and scales of political organization, and two different economies and norms of capitalization. Local credit-brokers like Asahel Warner and Augustus Bennett mediated relationships between and among these norms and networks. Almost immediately, however, the same norms and networks also came into conflict. The first conflict arose over the method by which the value of the institution's capital would be realized. In July of 1830, when the Genesee Annual Conference awarded the site of the academy to the town of Lima, all it had in hand was a list of I.O.U.s totaling approximately $11,000 and a plan for generating more. In this respect the academy resembled many other corporate enterprises at the time. Ordinary "investors" or subscribers to corporate projects generally did not hand over large amounts of capital that they had already "saved" in some form of money. Instead, they promised shares of capital that they expected to create *in the future*. The art of capitalization under these conditions lay in realizing the value of promised capital at a level and pace sufficient to meet capital costs. The question was how the value of that capital could best be realized. The norms and networks of rural social economy represented one answer to this question, while those of a translocal Methodist economy represented another.

---

[1] Minutes of the Seminary Building Committee, December 28, 1830, "Journal of the Genesee Wesleyan Seminary," Account Book #178, GWSC.
[2] Ibid., January 4, 1831.

This chapter considers the capitalization of the academy at Lima as a case study of conflict and change in norms of economic behavior during the capitalist transition. To trace capitalization of the academy at Lima is to reimagine the meaning of capitalism as it was being created. It is to rediscover "the market" and "the economy" as relative terms, to recognize "cash" as just one form of currency, to watch first-hand the creation of "negotiable instruments," to see the market as just one way of realizing the value of surplus goods and labor, and to understand how economic collapse and depression were integral to the consolidation of wealth and reconstruction of politics that made capitalist economic development possible. In this account, the "definition of capitalism" is a process of change rather than a settled idea.

Two Different Models of Capitalization

The Methodist model for capitalizing the seminary was essentially market-based. After accepting Lima's bid for the site, Methodist leaders established a joint stock association and created a negotiable instrument, or security, which they sold to investors in return for future education benefits. Subscribers for a full $100 share in the institution received a "certificate" entitling the subscriber, "his heirs or assigns" to four years of free tuition. As this terminology indicates, the certificate could be used by a member of the purchasing household or traded or sold to third parties. Thus, a subscription certificate constituted a kind of "negotiable instrument" – a debt-based security – that could be used for storing capital.[3] Among educational institutions, the practice of offering free tuition as a dividend or return on joint stock "shares" was not unusual, though the terms of such arrangements varied from case to case, and the practice became more common after 1830. Methodists in particular systematized the practice, eventually referring to it in explicitly commercial terms as the "sale of subscription scholarships."[4]

Initially, however, these "subscription scholarships" represented the *promise* of capital for the seminary, the value of which still had to be realized. According to the terms of the joint stock agreement laid out by the Genesee Conference leadership, subscription stock was "payable one fourth within

---

[3] The terms of these subscription scholarships and their trade and use by certificate holders are discussed throughout the Minutes of the Board of Trustees, Account Book #178, GWSC.

[4] The prevalence of this practice is readily apparent to anyone who explores the archives and manuscript collections for nineteenth-century institutions and voluntary associations. For summary accounts of the use of the practice for capitalizing educational institutions, specifically academies and colleges, see Edward Herring O'Neil, "Private Schools and Public Vision: A History of Academies in Upstate New York, 1800–1860" (Ph.D. dissertation, Syracuse University, 1984): 74–76; and Colin Burke, *American Collegiate Populations: A Test of the Traditional View* (New York: New York University Press, 1982): 40–47. For an account of a later campaign to sell subscription scholarships in the Genesee case, see Nancy Beadie, "From Academy to University in New York State: The Genesee Institutions and the Importance of Capital to the Success of an Idea, 1848–1971," *History of Higher Education Annual* 14 (1994): 3–28.

six months from the time of subscribing and the remainder in three equal annual payments thereafter." The assumption in this case was that payments would be made in cash and on commercial terms. Subscribers would first acquire cash through exchange of their household's goods and labor on the market. They would then use the cash to make payments on their subscriptions. Theoretically, at least, the full cash value of the subscriptions would be realized over a designated period on market terms.

The market was only one way to realize the value of capital, however. A second method was that represented by the norms of rural social economy, which local leaders in Lima had been using for school and community building projects for nearly thirty years. Under these norms, the value of capital could be realized through direct application of goods and services to the project of creating a specific capital asset, without recourse to the market. Although Methodist leaders had reported in July of 1830 that Lima's $11,000 in subscriptions would be paid in cash, it soon became clear that local subscribers had something else in mind. In keeping with the norms of community building, they assumed that some portion of the academy's local capital would be realized in the form of materials and labor employed directly in construction.

The conflict between these norms and assumptions was first revealed within the first few months of the project, as plans for erecting the seminary building got under way. The first meeting of the building committee occurred in Lima on August 15, 1830, just two weeks after the site of the seminary was chosen. At this point, the building process appeared to be under local control. According to the official minutes, the first meeting took place at the home of Frederic House, the Methodist layman and local subscriber who had recently served as builder of the new Methodist chapel in Lima. Asahel Warner served as chairman and Erastus Clark, a local merchant and major subscriber, as secretary. Also present was Augustus Bennett, the Methodist lawyer from the town of Avon who had played an important role in putting together the land deal and mediating the bid for the seminary, and who soon became the institution's first official treasurer.[5]

At the meeting participants decided that "stone" would be the principle building material, and that the committee should "make arrangements to quarry the necessary stone."[6] At the next meeting, on October 6, 1830, the committee "Resolved that Frederic House be authorized on behalf of the committee to contract with any person or persons at his discretion, to quarry and draw the stone necessary for the Seminary buildings."[7] At the third meeting, on December 8, 1830, House reported that he had "closed a contract with the owner of the stone quarry for the exclusive use of it for one year, at $1 per cord for the whole building ..." and that he had "contracted with one Darrow to

---

[5] Minutes of the Seminary Building Committee, August 15, 1830.
[6] Ibid., August 15, 1830.
[7] Ibid., October 6, 1830.

get out and quarry the stone fit for drawing, for one dollar per cord, one half of the stone to be ready by the first of February next."[8]

Having initiated the first stage of construction, the committee passed a series of three resolutions regarding the contracting of work and the payment of subscriptions. The first resolution concerned the unskilled labor and team work involved in drawing stone to the seminary site:

Resolved, That the name of Asahel Warner be added to F. House with the full power to make contracts for drawing the stone. And they are hereby instructed to contract with the subscribers (if they make any with them) *in such manner, that the stone they draw shall apply on their entire subscriptions, and not on any one installment.*[9]

This resolution assumed that subscribers would exchange labor and services directly against their subscriptions. It thus confirmed the norms of rural social economy. The second resolution concerned the contracting of skilled construction work:

Resolved, that the committee publish proposals to mechanics and other contractors, to make proposals and put in their offers to do any part of the work on the Seminary at the time of the next meeting; and in such publications, that due notice be given, that *payment for said work be made in subscription notes against subscribers....*[10]

Like the first resolution, this conformed to common norms of rural social economy. Presumably, mechanics and contractors who had subscribed to the project would receive their own subscriptions in payment for at least part of their work, thereby canceling their debt at the same time as they contributed labor or materials to the project. In addition, they might also receive as pay subscriptions from their neighbors, on which they would then collect as they would any other ordinary debt-based account. The third resolution passed on December 8 involved a third form of payment on subscriptions:

Resolved that a special agent be appointed to obtain notes on subscriptions in Lima, and that Frederic House be such an agent.[11]

This resolution implied that House would visit subscribers who had not otherwise contracted to do work and obtain from each of them an individual promissory note in the amount of their subscriptions, as a form of interim payment. (As a legal financial instrument, a promissory note could more readily be traded with third parties.)

Up through this point, plans for building construction developed within the norms of past practice for local community building projects. Subscribers, it seemed, would have the opportunity to trade goods and labor directly on their accounts. Otherwise they would be asked to convert their subscriptions into personal promissory notes. The process so far remained under the control

---

[8] Ibid., December 8, 1830 (emphasis added).
[9] Ibid.
[10] Ibid.
[11] Ibid.

Varieties of Trust

of local residents, and thus subject to face-to-face negotiations among neighbors. All that changed rather suddenly just a few weeks later, however, when control of the building process shifted to Methodist leadership. *firm local*

Competition and Conflict

In what appears to have been a surprise to local residents and subscribers, at the next round of building committee meetings, outside contractors from Rochester and Geneseo presented competitive bids for constructing the seminary buildings. That the prospect of competitive bidding came as a surprise to local residents and subscribers is indicated by the cumulative nature of the local response to the challenge the bids represented. According to the official minutes, the committee announced on December 28 that it was ready to receive proposals to do the work on the seminary buildings, but "none were presented."[12] The next day, however, attendance at the building committee meeting was so large that it had to be moved to the town house. At the meeting, a Mr. Eldridge from the city of Rochester presented "a front view of the Seminary." Following the Eldridge presentation, perhaps under pressure from the crowd, the committee voted to adjourn for a week, as "some proposals were not ready."[13] At the same time, the committee approved a two-part resolution overturning their earlier decision regarding the use of subscriptions:

Whereas, at a meeting of the committee on December 8th a resolution passed, specifying, with other things, the manner of payment to be made to contractors; Therefore, Resolved, *that so much of said resolution that pertains to manner of payment be reconsidered*;

Resolved: *That cash be raised by loans or otherwise, sufficient to pay one fourth of the expense of building*, and that three fourths of the expense be paid to contractors in subscriptions and notes: and that said one fourth be paid in two semi-annual installments from the time of making the contract; provided, if contractors do not furnish materials they shall receive but one eighth of the amount in cash.[14]

Implications of these decisions were several. First, the resolutions presented the possibility that building materials would be purchased with cash rather than traded on account. Second, the introduction of commercial "cash" loans would create an ongoing need for cash to pay the interest and eventually the principal of the loan. Most importantly, however, when combined with the possibility of an outside contractor, the new terms of payment suggested a possible shift in the norms of collection on individual subscriptions. Instead of negotiating arrangements with a neighbor like Asahel Warner, with whom many residents already had longstanding debt accounts, a subscriber would be negotiating payment with a stranger with whom he had no relationship, who might bring his own outside labor and employees to do the work, and

---

[12] Ibid., December 28, 1830.
[13] Ibid., December 29, 1830.
[14] Ibid., January 6, 1831 (emphasis added).

who might therefore insist on cash payments rather than trade or barter on account. The norms of the market, in other words, might supplant or compete with the norms of rural social economy.

This competition became reality at the next scheduled meeting of the building committee, at which the final contract decisions were made. At this meeting, two outside contractors proposed "to do the whole job" – the same Mr. Eldridge from Rochester, and a Mr. Warner from Geneseo (no relation to the Lima Warners). Both outside contractors, according to the minutes, presented drawings of the seminary that conformed to "the original design of Rev. L. Grant," the Methodist superintendent of the project on behalf of the conference. Also bidding for the role of general contractor now, however, was one local candidate. Though he presented no drawings – or other qualifications, for that matter – a man named George W. Little joined the competition, presenting a proposal for "doing the whole job and furnishing materials." In addition, the committee received several independent proposals for carpentry and mason work, including some from local craftsmen. It appears, however, that the balance of power had now shifted within the committee. The committee was no longer contemplating the possibility of negotiating the exchange of goods and labor on multiple independent accounts with local subscribers. Instead, it sought the consolidation of accounts in a single contract for the "whole job." The Little proposal represented a bid for the whole job on behalf of local subscribers.

That Little should have become the contractor of record for the seminary is surprising. Little appears to have been a man with no landed estate. The few surviving references to Little in existing documents indicate that he was a doctor. Little's identity as medical practitioner would not seem to make him a likely candidate for a building contractor. More important, perhaps, was his position as town clerk, an office he had held for five consecutive years, since the shift in local politics in 1826. This position may have lent him authority as a spokesperson for the town itself. It may also have lent him an air of independence. Little had subscribed to the academy project along with other local residents like House and Warner. Unlike House or Warner, however, Little did not subscribe for $500 or $600, but for $100.[15] Also unlike these and other major subscribers, Little had no direct stake in either the land deal or the supply of materials for the building, and no official position on the building committee or board of trustees. If "conflicts of interest" had become an issue within the building committee or the board of trustees, then Little's candidacy for the position of building contractor made some sense.

Of course, the very notion of a "conflict of interest" was itself market-based – an idea wholly contrary to the logic of rural social economy. In the tradition of rural social economy, it was precisely those with a direct stake in the future of the community who could be depended on to get the project done – and to take the financial risks that were often necessary to bring a

---

[15] List of original Lima subscribers, Subscription Book, Account Book #102, GWSC.

project to completion. From this perspective, the prospect of awarding the contract for a major building project to someone who had no interest in the locality or roots in local social relationships was not only contrary to local expectation, it was imprudent. Without the "interest" created through a history of participation in local credit networks, a builder would lack the social and economic leverage necessary to realize the value of surplus goods and labor – or capital – that local residents had pledged.

In the end, it was the capacity of the Little bid to bridge two worlds – the world of rural social economy and the world of the market – that explains not only the success of Little's bid but ultimately the success of the academy itself. Behind the decision to choose Little as the contractor lay a compromise that drew both on the norms of commerce and on local social networks to achieve maximum levels of capitalization. Considered in the context of broader patterns of economic change, this interaction between competing norms and networks was significant.

The Meaning of Economic Change

A number of scholars have explored the significance of different forms of economic activity in the early national era. One question is how far rural householders actively sought new opportunities on the market, and how far they sought to preserve older norms of household production and neighborly exchange. Early debate on this subject focused on the concept of "self-sufficiency" in the thought and behavior of early American farmers. While some saw the yeoman farmer as expressing entrepreneurial individualism, others emphasized the noncommercial character of early household production.[16] Scholars on both sides soon essentially agreed, however, that individual farmers seldom supplied all of their own needs. Rather, they met their needs through a combination of household production and exchange with neighbors. At some point they also combined this neighborly exchange with the sale of goods and labor on the market. The question then was when and to what extent participation in markets occurred, and how rural householders regarded this participation.

The historian James Henretta and others emphasized the importance of familial goals in shaping this economic decision making. When considered over the course of a life cycle, farmers seem to have been oriented neither singularly toward the market nor necessarily toward household production, but toward satisfying family obligations, particularly the demands of "settling" children in households of their own. Building on the work of Henretta, scholars identified the concept of "competency" as capturing this family-centered commitment.[17] "Competency" was a state of "comfortable independence,"

---

[16] For an excellent review of this literature on self-sufficiency, see Alan Kulikoff, "The Transition to Capitalism in Rural America," *William and Mary Quarterly*, 3rd Ser. 46 (1989): 120–144.

[17] Ibid. James Henretta, "Families and Farms: *Mentalité*," in Pre-Industrial America," *William and Mary Quarterly* 35 (January 1978): 3–32; Christopher Clark, "Household Economy,

in which a family possessed sufficient property to absorb the labors of its members and provide "something more than a mere subsistence." To achieve this purpose, household members might trade some surplus goods on the market or lend their labors to an outwork system, but not to the extent that the household became dependent on the market for basic goods or lost control of household labor or property.[18]

Community exchange networks were essential to maintaining this independence as they provided some security against the vagaries of the market. John Schlotterbeck, for example, argued that in some upper south communities, norms and networks of social economy intensified during disruptions of overseas markets and declines in market prices. Recognizing the threat that these fluctuations could pose to their security, farmers consciously combined commodities production with a more mixed production of goods for exchange with neighbors. In Schlotterbeck's account, the social economy of neighbors represented an ideal of communal independence that farmers in certain areas of the country defended right up through the Civil War.[19]

If these ideas of family and communal independence at one time dominated economic decision making, another question is when and how these notions changed. The historian Christopher Clark argued that in western Massachusetts, rural householders initially became involved in commodities markets and factory outwork as a means of achieving older ideas of family independence and community life. During the period from 1790 to 1820, participation in commodities markets and the emergence of capitalist production and labor relations were "restrained." Crucial innovations in the economy were generated from within the rural social structure itself. Increasingly, in the 1810s, 1820s, and 1830s, rural households experimented with combining household production with participation in new markets and forms of outwork production. Gradually, however, the balance of power between farmers and the merchants and manufacturers who mediated participation in the market changed. In order to meet the expanding demand for cash, rural householders became more dependent on selling their goods and labor on the market. Thus, although they entered the market in order to preserve their old way of life, they helped to bring about a capitalist transformation that undermined their independence. Clark identified this shift in power as beginning in western Massachusetts in the 1830s and 1840s.[20] In the process, many farmers lost

---

Market Exchange and the Rise of Capitalism in the Connecticut Valley, 1800–1860," *Journal of Social History* 13 (Winter 1979): 169–189; Daniel Vickers, "Competency and Competition: Economic Culture in Early America," *William and Mary Quarterly* 47:1 (January 1990): 3–29.

[18] This definition of "competency" comes from Vickers, "Competency and Competition."
[19] John T. Schlotterbeck, "The 'Social Economy' of an Upper South Community: Orange and Greene Counties, Virginia, 1815–1860," in Orville Vernon Burton and Robert C. McMath, Jr., eds. *Class Conflict and Consensus: Antebellum Southern Community Studies* (Westport, CT: Greenwood Press, 1982).
[20] Christopher Clark, "Household Economy."

their status as independent farmers or migrated to the West. By the 1850s and 1860s, the viable independent farmers that remained took on characteristics of capitalist employers and producers themselves.[21]

In Clark's account, farmers and other rural householders began as the initiators of economic change but later became the victims of capitalist markets and production as represented by merchants and manufacturers. Other scholars have questioned this division between the thinking and behavior of farmers, on the one hand, and of merchants and manufacturers on the other. They have sought ways of understanding "how the economic cultures of merchants and manufacturers, as well as of farmers, changed during the period of transformation."[22] Using a model developed by the economist Peter Temin, Naomi Lamoureaux analyzed this shift in consciousness as an interaction between individual personality and changing institutional contexts. The model posits three modes of human behavior, each associated with a different institutional structure: "customary" behavior, associated with community; rationalist "instrumental" behavior, associated with the market; and "command" behavior, associated with hierarchy. In this model, some individuals are more disposed toward one mode of behavior than another, while some tend to act more autonomously with respect to their institutional contexts than others. Under conditions of structural or institutional change, "autonomous" individuals behave more instrumentally with respect to their individual interests, while others fall back on custom. Applying this model to the issues of the capitalist transition, Lamoureaux hypothesized that in the late eighteenth and early nineteenth centuries, certain "autonomous" farmers took the lead in pursuing the instrumental behavior and opportunities associated with markets. As the expansion of markets developed, more and more farmers followed, "propelling a shift from communal to market-based institutions." Eventually, the nature of customary behavior itself changed, from that represented by communal exchange to that represented by the market.[23]

Lamouroeux's analysis poses the question of who took the lead in promoting expanded participation in markets and why. The case of the academy at Lima provides an opportunity for exploring this question. In Lima, a coalition of commercial farmers, local merchants, craftsmen, and professionals competed for the opportunity to establish an educational institution that might foster further commercial growth and economic development. At the same time, they acted to defend certain norms of social economy. As in the past, a local credit-broker took the lead in negotiating the tension between these norms and networks. This time, however, the stakes were higher and the conflicts more intense. A close look at the dynamics of capitalization in the

---

[21] For a full account of the dynamics, evidence, and chronology of this shift see Christopher Clark, *The Roots of Rural Capitalism: Western Massachusetts, 1780–1860* (Ithaca, NY: Cornell University Press, 1990).

[22] Naomi Lamoureaux, "Re-Thinking the Transition to Capitalism in the Early American Northeast," *The Journal of American History* 90:2 (September 2003): 437–461.

[23] Ibid.

academy case reveals how market integration and the transition to capitalism looked in the context of everyday life.

Bonding and Bridging

The building committee's decision to choose the Little bid for construction of the seminary buildings took full advantage of the norms of rural social economy, even as it also courted market competition. First there was the matter of who the Little bid represented. Although the minutes identify Dr. G. W. Little as the builder selected by the building committee on January 6, 1831, subsequent records refer to the building contractors sometimes as a three-way partnership among Little, House, and Warner, but more often as a two-person partnership of House and Warner. One retrospective account referred to the seminary building as having been "erected by F. House and A. Warner on contract of G. W. Little."[24] Clearly, the Little bid represented a cooperative response by Warner, House, and other local subscribers to the threat of outside competition.

Then there was the matter of how the contractors were paid. According to the official minutes, the committee resolved on January 6 that

the proposal offered by Dr. G. W. Little conformable to a resolution of the committee pertaining to payment be accepted, and that a contract be closed with him accordingly.[25]

From this statement it is not clear to *which* resolution pertaining to payment the Little bid conformed – whether the original resolution dated December 8, which implied payment would be entirely in subscription notes, or the later reversal of that resolution, which specified that a quarter of the payment would be made by cash loan. In the end, one could say that payment conformed to both resolutions. First, the committee decided to pay the contractor with subscriptions, directing:

that the business of drawing the contract and selecting and consigning subscriptions to the contractor be done by A. A. Bennett Esq. and John C. Copeland.[26]

In fact, by the time the committee announced its decision, on January 6, the consignment of subscriptions had already taken place. According to the subscription account books, the consignment by Bennett and Copeland had actually occurred January 5. By the time the committee heard the formal presentations of the various bidders, in other words, the contractors had not only been chosen, *they had already been paid.* Specifically, 173 different subscriptions had been signed over to the builders, with a face value totaling approximately

---

[24] Summary history of seminary financing dated 1840 in Account Book #102.
[25] Minutes of the Seminary Building Committee, January 6, 1831.
[26] Ibid.

$10,000. At the same time, another 14 subscriptions totaling $1,460 in face value were signed over to Bennett and Smith, the owners of the land for the building site. Included among these 187 total subscriptions with a total face value of $11,460 were the vast majority of subscriptions pledged by Lima's original subscribers.[27] In this way, subscription payments on the building and land contracts preserved the norms of rural social economy. Local subscribers would be able to pay their subscriptions through the direct exchange of goods, labor, and services of value to landowners and contractors.

This was not the whole story, however. The payment arrangements worked out by local and Methodist leaders involved not only an exchange of subscriptions but an influx of commercial capital. In a complex set of arrangements involving multiple plots of land and multiple mortgages, Asahel Warner agreed to secure a $5,000 cash loan to the seminary to help finance construction. Specifically, what Warner did over the next several months was mortgage his own farm to the New York financier Isaac Bronson for $5,000. He then advanced this same $5,000 to the seminary in the form of a mortgage loan on its property. The major portion of this money – $3,950 – went to the builders – that is, House and Warner himself – to provide cash for certain aspects of construction. The remaining $1,150 appeared in the treasurer's book as a cash payment to the seminary (i.e., to the treasurer, Augustus Bennett) signed over by Warner.[28]

A curious element of this arrangement was that in addition to the $5,000 mortgage loan on the main seminary site (sold by Bennett and Smith), Warner arranged a mortgage sale of thirty-nine acres of his own land for $1,170. These thirty-nine acres became a supporting farm and the site of an ostensible experiment with manual labor education. They also became the site of a curious experiment in capitalist entrepreneurship by Asahel Warner, who maintained a financial interest in the farm and associated manual labor experiment for several years. No payment for the land, either in cash or in subscriptions, was recorded at the time of the sale. Instead, Warner advanced the sale of the land to the seminary at 7 percent interest on its value. For four years, then, Warner received interest on both a $5,000 mortgage loan and a $1,170 mortgage sale, though he had advanced no money on the second mortgage and retained title to the land until the manual labor experiment came to an end and the seminary paid the principal in 1835.[29] What was the significance of these financial arrangements?

---

[27] Records of subscriptions signed over to builders compiled from Account Books #102 and #59, GWSC.
[28] Evidence of the loans, interest payments, and interest rates compiled from the Treasurer's Book, Account Book #56, GWSC; Account Book #102; and Box 44, Folder 10, BFP. The $5,000 loan from Bronson to Warner was dated July 10, 1831; Warner's $5,000 loan to the Seminary was dated August 16, 1831.
[29] Ibid.

The Social Dimensions of Risk

The significance of Warner's capitalist entrepreneurship looks quite different depending on the perspective from which it is viewed and on the ends with respect to which it is judged. From the perspective of Loring Grant, the Methodist preacher who served as superintendent of the seminary building project, the goal was maximum capitalization of the seminary. Through artful pressure and negotiation, he essentially achieved his goal. A seasoned political operator in his own right, Grant was not satisfied to leave the capitalization and building process to local parties. By bringing competitors into the picture, Grant managed first to secure his vision of the institution, and second to get local subscribers contracted to fulfill that vision for the amount of capital available. He also managed to get Warner to make use of his commercial connections, about which Grant had no doubt been aware from the start. To accomplish all this he skillfully invoked the culture of an expanding market economy, including the norms of competition.

It should be noted, however, that Grant had no personal financial stake in the academy project. His only risks were those of ambition. All he stood to gain or lose was power and standing within the Methodist hierarchy. By contrast, the move involved substantial risk for Warner. Should the subscribers fail to make good on their subscriptions or the seminary close before completing its interest payments, Warner stood to lose not only an ongoing source of income, but also his family farm to the commercial capitalist Isaac Bronson.

Interestingly, Bronson seems to have regarded the seminary deal with skepticism. Having supplied commercial credit to Warner for at least a decade and employed him occasionally as something of an agent in his own affairs, Bronson cannot have been entirely indifferent to Warner's fortunes. Indeed, to some extent Bronson must have valued and even encouraged the role of community builder that Warner assumed in Lima and the vicinity. It did, after all, potentially increase the value of Bronson's whole field of investment in western New York. At the same time, Bronson questioned some of the specifics in this case. Writing in July of 1831 with regard to the $5,000 mortgage he had just granted on Warner's farm, Bronson queried Augustus Bennett about the security of Warner's finances and the status of Warner's outstanding debts. Later, in October 1831, having learned of Warner's own mortgage to the seminary, Bronson again wrote Bennett, inquiring about the value of the seminary's assets and the security of its land title. As the linchpin of a vast western credit network, Bronson constantly solicited and received information about financial solvency, risks, and failures in his domain, so he may or may not have had a specific reason for concern. In any case, however, of all the parties involved in the project, Bronson took the most skeptical view of its prospects.

By comparison, Bennett's view of the academy project might be regarded as the most liberal and individually opportunistic. In responding to Bronson's queries, Bennett was evasive. Rather than responding immediately in July and

October, when he first received Bronson's letters, he waited until December 6, 1831, when building construction was largely complete. This allowed Bennett to state the value of the seminary property as exceeding the amount of Warner's loan to the institution, a claim he could not have made prior to that time. By Bennett's account, the land exclusive of buildings was worth just $2,000, though Warner's loan on the land's security had been for twice that amount. With the large stone edifice since added, Bennett placed the value of the property at $18,500, thereby retroactively justifying the amount of the mortgage loan.[30] Bennett, of course, had his own stake in these arrangements, and thus a reason for reassuring Bronson of the security of Warner's finances. In addition to selling the land to the seminary in the first place, he had also become treasurer of the institution. Although in the long term this position would in fact cause Bennett substantial trouble, in the short term he gained directly from his role. From this perspective, the least that Bennett could do was reinforce Warner's reputation with his chief creditor, Isaac Bronson.

Whether Bronson was in fact satisfied by Bennett's reassurances is another matter. In response to Bronson's query regarding the security of the seminary's title to the mortgaged land – which, after all, he himself had been party to selling to the seminary – Bennett seems less than convincing:

In regards to the lands mortgaged by the officers of the Seminary to Major Warner, I cannot be at the trouble of tracing the chain of title, I can merely say that I have well known the several alienations it has undergone and hands through which it has passed for twenty-five years past and so well knew the title to be good, that I paid out two or three thousand dollars for that and the remainder of the small farm, and together with a joint owner with me, gave a warranty deed to the Trustees of the Seminary.[31]

And, in response to Bronson's query regarding the status of Warner's other financial obligations, Bennett was similarly evasive.

But my Dear Sir – you need feel no inquietude about your security on Major Warner's property, true the old man is careless but there is nothing *now* that encumbers his estate but your demand –

You are to regard this as an answer to yours of July 15 written from Geneva. Be in no haste for my answer to the appalling list of judgments against my old friend the Major – I called his attention to them particularly the other day, and he assured me they were every one paid to the utmost farthing, but I agree with you they ought to be discharged of record....[32]

Given the larger history of Warner's political and financial dealings, his decisions regarding the discharge of debts were probably more knowing than careless. But it all depends on the norms and standards by which they are judged. As professionals with no significant financial investment in the academy

---

[30] Correspondence from A. A. Bennett to Isaac Bronson, dated E. Avon, December 6, 1831, Folder 10, Box 44, "Asahel Warner, Lima, 1821–1844," BFP.
[31] Ibid.
[32] Ibid.

project and thus nothing to lose, men like Grant and Bennett could afford to be enthusiastic about the opportunities offered by the market. Bronson, however, whose engagement in financial markets was one of the most extended of anyone's in the country at the time, was much less sanguine.

But, of course, Bronson's concerns were not the same as those of Asahel Warner. Although Bronson had a long established relationship with Warner that may have been grounded in some social or family tie, the nature of his relationship to the particular loans in question and to the whole seminary project was primarily commercial. The standards of judgment he brought to the affair were thus ones of financial security and viability. Warner, by contrast, had to consider not only his own financial stake in the academy as its largest individual subscriber and then its largest creditor, but also the interests and normative expectations of his neighbors and fellow subscribers, for which he bore some responsibility. No doubt he traded on such expectations in helping to solicit their subscriptions in the first place. He also carried those interests and expectations with him to the annual meeting of the Genesee Conference back in July 1830, when he and his collaborators said whatever they said to convince the seminary committee to choose Lima over the town of Perry. In a very real sense, then, Warner's standing with his neighbors was at stake in his capacity to influence the outcome of negotiations. While Bronson was in a position to gain financially from the arrangement no matter what happened to the seminary project, Warner's only security lay in success. From this perspective, Warner's role in the commercial capitalization of the seminary was no less pragmatic than Bronson's, but pragmatic with respect to different norms and ends. It was not autonomy from communal social relations that led Warner to increase his market exposure, in other words, but his long-term embeddedness in those relationships. Without the expectations imposed by his thirty-year history of leadership within the local social economy, it is unlikely that he would ever have taken the financial risk that he did.

And yet without that financial risk, the scale and significance of the enterprise at Lima would have been much diminished. Ultimately, the academy owed its long-term financial success to the combined advantages of rural social economy and commercial capitalization. First, the consignment of subscriptions in payment for the construction of the seminary building and title to the land on which it was sited effectively maximized the value of the institution's initial capital. Although the builders and landowners still had to do the hard work of collecting payments on those subscriptions in the form of goods, labor, services, or cash, the value of that capital had effectively already been realized by the institution itself in the form of real capital assets, that is, title to the land and to the large stone edifice the builders were now legally contracted to create. Altogether, the institution realized 91 percent of the face value of its initial subscriptions from Lima and neighboring residents through direct exchange on its land and building contracts. As subsequent events would show, this was a much higher rate of return than the institution would ever achieve through cash collection on other subscriptions. Moreover, the capital assets acquired through this direct exchange effectively secured additional capital in the form of mortgage loans, first from Asahel Warner, then from Isaac Bronson, and finally from the State of New York. In the end, then, these initial financial arrangements contributed substantially to the size and long-term financial success of the institution.

At the same time, however, the influx of commercial capital and the associated financial risk incurred both by the institution and by the town's leading credit-broker, Asahal Warner, demonstrably affected the balance of power between local residents and outsiders in subsequent battles over governance of the institution and over the kind of institution the seminary would be. At the local level, these battles played out as part of a conflict over manual labor education. At the state level, they played out as part of a legislative battle over incorporation and the increasing influence of evangelical culture and institutions in politics. In these ways, competition and conflict between the norms and networks of the local social economy, on the one hand, and those of the translocal Methodist economy, on the other, continued. Ultimately, the case of the academy at Lima illuminates both the place of education in the capitalist transition, and the conflict and loss that attended that transition and gave education its cultural meaning. Illuminating the political and cultural significance of education in this process of economic conflict and change is the project of the book's remaining chapters.

15

Controlling Capital – Education and the Politics of Economic Change

> ...nothing but the most strong and oft repeated assurances that the institution should be purely literary and scientific of the most liberal cast, so far as its conduct and management were concerned, could have induced your memorialists to make the liberal donations they did.
>
> "Memorial from sundry inhabitants of Lima, in the county of Livingston, remonstrating against the further incorporation of the Genesee and Wesleyan Seminary at Lima," January 7, 1834[1]

On the surface, the battle that developed in the 1830s between the residents of the town of Lima and the regional body of the Methodist Episcopal Church was a conflict between political liberalism and religious sectarianism. That, at any rate, is how the local residents portrayed it. In their 1834 petition to the legislature protesting against the "further incorporation" of the seminary, forty-seven "inhabitants of Lima" complained that "priests and coadjutors" at the institution used the most "ardent and exciting means" for "proselyting [sic] the students to methodism[sic]." By contrast, the petitioners described their own vision of education as "purely literary and scientific" and "of the most liberal cast."[2] They positioned themselves, in other words, as defenders of liberal ideas. It does not take much skepticism to realize, however, that this somewhat ritualized account of student experience in the twilight of the Second Great Awakening – true as it may have been – was a rhetorical strategy aimed at achieving a particular political end. Nor does it detract from the seriousness with which Methodist preachers took their mission to recognize that by the 1830s the Methodist Episcopal Church had transcended its once marginal status to become not only the largest church in the United States, but a highly effective political organization, particularly in New York. Against

---

[1] "Memorial from sundry inhabitants of Lima, in the county of Livingston, remonstrating against the further incorporation of the Genesee and Wesleyan seminary at Lima," dated January 7, 1834, recorded January 22, 1834, No. 51, *Documents of the Assembly of the State of New York* (Albany, NY: E. Croswell, printer to the state, 1834).
[2] Ibid.

such a force, Lima residents were well advised to marshal whatever rhetorical resources they could. To take their version of events at face value, however, is to miss much about the larger transformation of society, politics, and economy of which their drama was part.

This chapter considers the academy at Lima as a site of political organization and conflict in the Jacksonian era. Historians have long debated the factors that shaped the emergence of the Second American Party system. In particular, they have puzzled over the political connections between religion and economics in this period. To explore this question some scholars have analyzed ethnic and religious divisions in statewide electoral returns, while others have looked at the process of economic change in urban or industrial locations. The Lima case, by contrast, illuminates the interaction between economy and culture in a rural context. It shows how an economic issue like labor competition could be converted into a cultural issue, such as religious sectarianism, through the medium of state politics and the process of incorporation.

Economic Competition and the Idea of Manual Labor Education

The conflict between local residents and Methodist leaders over economic competition from outsiders did not end with the cash loan Asahel Warner brokered in 1831. A year later, in 1832, when construction of the academy building was largely complete and trustees began planning the recruitment and enrollment of students, a related conflict developed over the challenge to local labor represented by the idea of manual labor education. If anything, this idea aroused even more opposition than the earlier conflict, with seventy local citizens signing a petition against it. Although the parties eventually reached a compromise, a year later hostilities again developed over governance of the institution and, more specifically, over the terms of its corporate charter. This time, the conflict became the subject of a statewide petition campaign. It also played out as part of the emergence of the Second American Party System.

Trustees of Genesee Wesleyan Seminary began referring to their intention to establish a "manual labor department" in January 1832, as the academy prepared to enroll its first students. At the time, the concept of manual labor education was approaching a peak of popularity in New York and elsewhere in the country. Beginning in the late 1820s and continuing into the 1840s, a number of institutions adopted the idea.[3] One of the most successful of these was the Oneida Institute of Science and Industry in the town of Whitesboro, near Utica, New York. Founded in 1827 by an evangelical Presbyterian minister and chartered by the state in 1829, the institution was located on a farm

---

[3] For a review of the manual labor education movement see Jeffrey A. Mullins, "'In the Sweat of Thy Brow': Education, Manual Labor, and the Market Revolution," in Scott C. Martin, ed. *Cultural Change and the Market Revolution in America, 1789–1860* (New York: Rowman and Littlefield, 2005): 143–180.

that also came to include wagon, carpentry, and blacksmith shops. By its own account, the Oneida Institute aimed at "uniting manual labor with classical education," language common to other similar experiments at the time. The implication was that somehow the combination of learning and labor would lead to the mutual improvement of both.[4]

In practice, however, the central dynamic of the relationship between the liberal and mechanical arts in the manual labor experiments of the 1830s was neither intellectual nor technological but financial. Students exchanged labor for education – or, more precisely, for the room and board costs associated with residing at the institution. At the Oneida Institute students were initially required to work twenty-one hours a week to defray room and board costs and to receive the ostensible physical and character benefits of manual labor education.[5] In the Oneida case, in other words, the manual labor idea was a way of extending the norms and networks of local barter economies to the site of a translocal educational institution. It offered students a way of realizing the value of their labor in exchange for education and at the same time enabled the trustee-operators of the institution to meet basic supply and labor needs without recourse to cash.

Something like the Oneida model seems to have been what the trustees had in mind for the seminary at Lima. In the Lima case, however, the idea of manual labor education proved highly controversial. The first sign of controversy appeared at the beginning of the trustee meeting in April 1832, when the secretary, Augustus Bennett, "laid before the Board a memorial signed by about seventy citizens of Lima."[6] After turning the memorial over to a committee, the board resolved to invite the citizens of Lima to join the meeting the next day to discuss the committee's report. Apparently, members of the board believed that local residents could be led to accept the manual labor plan after some discussion. In fact, however, the discussion with local residents proceeded all the following morning with no sign of resolution. If anything, opposition to the plan became more ardent and assertive. In the afternoon, two local members of the board moved that "a committee be appointed to report on the circumstances and propriety of the appointment of a steward as made by the board of trustees."[7] This motion was first ruled out of order,

---

[4] On the Oneida Institute see Milton Sennett, *Abolition's Axe: Beriah Green, Oneida Institute and the Black Freedom Struggle* (Syracuse, NY: Syracuse University Press, 1986): 31–47. According to George Frederick Miller, *The Academy System of the State of New York* (Albany, NY: J. B. Lyon Company, 1922): 93, the institution was chartered as the "Oneida Institute of Science and Industry" in 1829. For comparison of the language used to describe the manual labor idea, see "An Act to incorporate the Genesee manual labor seminary," Passed March 27, 1834, *Laws of New York*, 57th Session, Chap. 53 (Albany: State of New York): 53–54 and "An Act to Incorporate the New-York State Agricultural School," Passed May 6, 1836, *Laws of New York*, 59th Session, Chap. 259 (Albany: State of New York): 341–345.

[5] By 1831, the institution reduced the work commitment to 18 hours a week. Sennett, *Abolition's Axe*, 35.

[6] Minutes of the Board of Trustees, April 10, 1832, Account Book #178, GWSC.

[7] Ibid., April 11, 1832.

and subsequently carried after the ruling itself was overruled. A committee was then duly constituted. Whatever the new committee's conclusions were, however, they did not quell the controversy. The committee was asked to read its report twice. At first the report was tabled. Then a motion for indefinitely postponing consideration of the report lost, followed by a motion to amend the report that also lost. The parties had apparently reached a standoff.[8]

From a local perspective, the issue was economic competition. Allowing students to labor in exchange for room and board meant bringing outside labor into competition with local households for the domestic, farm, and mechanical labor that they might otherwise perform. In the tradition of rural social economy, local households would have hoped or expected that their own youth or other household members could exchange goods or labor with the institution for credit on existing debts or for other services the institution had to offer, that is, tuition. By promising room and board in exchange for labor, the trustees seemed to reserve any benefits of labor exchange to students from out of town. The steward appointed to negotiate these exchanges, moreover, was a man that residents already knew to be inimical to local interests: Reverend Loring Grant, the Methodist minister who had already stirred up considerable local resentment as building superintendent. Finally, by allowing students to trade labor for room and board, the trustees threatened to undercut local households in their own bids to attract students as boarders. Competition between the institution's boarding facility and local boarding houses would in fact be a source of conflict for decades to come.[9]

For all these reasons, local opposition to the manual labor plan proved fierce. In the short run, the board resorted to bluster and subterfuge as a means of resolving the issue. With a majority of its members Methodist ministers, the board managed to pass a resolution reasserting the trustees' prerogative to decide whatever they wanted about the issue, without actually making or declaring any such decision:

Resolved that the institution be a manual labor institution so far, and so soon, as circumstances will admit. And that it be considered the constitutional duty of the trustees to carry the above resolution into effect, whenever they deem it practicable.[10]

With this official prevarication, the board effectively adjourned, to reconvene without notice two days later in Penn Yan, a town forty miles southeast of Lima. At the Penn Yan meeting the trustees got down to specifying the kind of manual labor arrangement that some of them had apparently had in mind all along:

Resolved that the steward be authorized to employ any student desiring to labor, and if he can furnish the work out of school hours, for the first term, and report to the board

---

[8] Ibid.
[9] Evidence of competition between the institution's boarding facility and local boarding establishments appears throughout the records of the board of trustees.
[10] Minutes of the Board of Trustees, April 11, 1832.

at their next meeting what each student has earned, that he may be allowed deduction from his board bill, at the rate of five shillings per day, for a man's day's work.[11]

In the near term, this decision paved the way for agents of the seminary to recruit student laborers to work on the building and adjoining farm over the summer in anticipation of enrolling the institution's first full class of students in the fall. To some extent, then, Methodists appear to have prevailed in the contest over manual labor education.

In other ways, however, local residents appear to have won a compromise. At their June 1832 meeting, the trustees resolved that "it is inexpedient to depend upon the students for perfecting and completing the outdoor arrangements around and connected with the Seminary, except in such matters as in the opinion of the steward, can be profitably and timely performed by the job."[12] Also, in the first official "advertisement" for the seminary in August 1832, the trustees made only oblique reference to manual labor education:

Advertisement

This Institution has recently been established in the town of Lima, Livingston County, N. Y. under the patronage of the Genesee annual conference of the Methodist Episcopal church. Its original design contemplates instruction in Letters and Science, combined with Agriculture and the Mechanic Arts....[13]

In this description, the nature of the relationship between instruction in letters and science and agriculture and mechanic arts is vague. Although some might read the manual labor idea into it, the phrasing implies that agriculture and mechanic arts might be subjects of study rather than fields of student labor. In other respects as well, the description of the institution seems to have gestured toward local preference: "It is hardly necessary to add," the advertisement concluded, "that the principles which are to govern, and characterise [sic] the school, are perfectly liberal, everything of a sectarian cast being entirely excluded in the course of instruction."[14]

As it turned out, however, the conflict was far from over. The economic issue embedded in the conflict over manual labor education was about to be transmuted into an issue of religious sectarianism through the medium of state politics and the process of incorporation. To understand how this occurred, it helps to remember the peculiar significance of incorporation in the early republican era. A grant of incorporation conferred on a corporate body the power to accumulate, hold, and defend property in common, under a designated name or title. This power pertained first of all to the acquisition of real estate, but also to the accumulation of "paper," that is, stock, bank notes, promissory notes, and other negotiable instruments, including subscriptions.

---

[11] Ibid., April 13, 1832.
[12] Ibid., June 19, 1832.
[13] "Advertisement," Bulletins of Genesee Wesleyan Seminary, 1832, Account Book #170a, GWSC.
[14] Ibid.

Most importantly, an act of incorporation conferred the status of a body corporate in court and thus the capacity "to sue or be sued" for collection of debts. The power to sue for collection of debts in turn implied the power to negotiate the terms on which such debts would be collected, whether in the form of cash, labor, goods, or materials. In short, acts of incorporation were about the control of capital.

Incorporation Acts

In September of 1832, the trustees voted to "make application to the legislature for an act of incorporation."[15] Four months later, at their January meeting, the trustees drafted, amended, and approved a petition to the New York State Legislature for their first corporate charter. Unfortunately, no copy of this original draft survives. It is clear, nonetheless, that the charter that actually passed in April 1833 differed from what most of the trustees intended and initially approved. The charter passed by the legislature was minimal in its provisions. It consisted of six articles, each tightly organized around an essential function. The first and longest of these was the effective article. It listed the thirteen men designated as the institution's first trustees and declared that they thereby constituted a body corporate "for the purpose of establishing, maintaining and conducting a Seminary of learning for the education of both sexes." The remaining articles specified the powers of the corporation and its trustees. Central to these were the accumulation and use of property, that is, the power "to purchase, take and hold real and personal estate," and to "lease, sell or otherwise dispose of the same."[16] These powers were further elaborated in certain sections of the revised statutes to which the corporation was declared subject, including the power to "sue and be sued in court."[17] In addition to these matters regarding the disposition of property, the charter specified that the trustees had the power to elect the faculty of the institution, form regulations and by-laws, prescribe the course of study, attend examinations, regulate the government and instruction of students, and "fill all vacancies that should occur in their board."[18] In other words, the power of the trustees extended to the control of both cultural and financial capital.

The question was who would be eligible to exercise that power. According to the charter that actually passed the legislature, the board would be self-perpetuating; that is, existing trustees would choose their own successors. Although it was true, as local residents later claimed, that the provision for a self-perpetuating board of trustees was "in conformity with established usage"

[15] Minutes of the Board of Trustees, September 26, 1832.
[16] "An Act to Incorporate the Genesee and Wesleyan Seminary," Passed April 30, 1833, *Laws of New York*, 56th Session, Chap. 304 (Albany: State of New York): 481.
[17] Part 1, Chapter XVIII (of Incorporations), Title III (of the General powers, Privileges and Liabilities of Corporations), *Revised Statutes of the State of New-York* (Albany, NY: Packard and Van Benthuysen, 1836), Volume I, pp. 602–603.
[18] "An Act to Incorporate the Genesee and Wesleyan Seminary," Passed April 30, 1833.

among Regents institutions, it was not in conformity with Methodist expectations. The charter of the Methodist seminary founded earlier at Cazenovia specified that all the trustees of the institutions would be appointed by the regional body of the Methodist Episcopal Church.[19] Although in 1833 the Cazenovia institution was the only Regents academy under such direct church control, it established a precedent that Methodist leaders like Loring Grant and John Copeland – who had been involved in organizing the earlier academy – had reason to believe could be repeated in the Lima case.[20] That this was in fact their expectation is further indicated by the terms of the joint stock arrangement in the "Report of the Seminary Committee," dated July of 1830. According to this document, the board of trustees and the board of visitors to the institution would each consist of nine persons, "five of whom in each board would be members of the Conference, and all of whom would be chosen by the conference," according to "the directions and provisions of the Bill of Incorporation when said bill shall be granted by the legislature of the state."[21]

With all this apparently established in advance of the charter application, it is somewhat surprising that the charter granted to the seminary in April 1833 made no specific mention of the Methodist Church and no provision for involvement in the institution's governance by the Genesee Conference. How did that occur? This is where politics came in. In 1832–1833, when the trustees first applied to the legislature for incorporation, state politics was still firmly under the control of the Albany "Regency," the Van Buren political machine that took shape in the 1820s and was closely affiliated with Andrew Jackson at the federal level. Known formally as the "Democratic Republicans," or more commonly as "Democrats" or "Jackson men," the Regency is typically regarded as the first modern political party, defined and advanced by rigorous party discipline and an elaborate spoils system.[22] This power remained essentially intact (though not unchallenged) at both the state and federal levels through most of the 1830s – until the Panic of 1837. Even as Van Buren and Jacksonian Democrats reached the peak of their power, however, in the early to mid-1830s, opposition coalesced, particularly in western New York. Rooted in the anti-Masonic movement that first became a factor in state politics in 1828, the Whig Party came together from various anti-Jackson forces in 1833–1834.[23] The initial passage and subsequent battle over

---

[19] "An Act to Incorporate the Seminary of the Genesee Conference," Passed April 6, 1825, *Laws of New York*, 48th Session, Chap. 86 (Albany: State of New York, 1825): 125–127.

[20] For an account of the context of incorporation of the Seminary at Cazenovia, see Chapter 10; also Miller, *The Academy System*, 92.

[21] "Report of the Seminary Committee," 1830.

[22] See, for example, Richard P. McCormick, *The Second American Party System: Party Formation in the Jacksonian Era* (Chapel Hill: University of North Carolina Press, 1966): 115–117.

[23] This is the standard account of the rise of the Whig Party and the Second American Party System in political history. See McCormick, *The Second American Party System*,

Controlling Capital

the seminary's corporate charter occurred as part of the emergence of this new two-party system.

Economy and Culture in the Emergence of the Second American Party System

Historians of Jacksonian-era politics have long debated the factors that shaped the emergence of the Second American Party System in the United States in the 1830s and 1840s.[24] In his 1961 study of the "concept" of Jacksonian politics in New York State, Lee Benson strongly disputed the then-prevailing view that voting behavior was shaped primarily by economic interests. More specifically, Benson rejected the notion that Jacksonian Democrats necessarily represented populist, nonmonied interests, while the emerging Whigs represented the interests of capital – that is, merchants and manufacturers. Citing countervailing evidence such as early antipathy between Jacksonians and the Workingmen's Party in New York City, and early anti-Mason support for populist measures such as the abolition of imprisonment for debt and an end of "licensed monopolies," Benson portrayed the early anti-Masonic core of the Whig Party as populist reformers and the Jacksonians as an established party with a genius for the effective populist "counterattack."[25] At this stage, in other words, the difference between Jacksonians and the anti-Mason core of the developing Whig Party was far from clear. In matters of economic policy, Benson argued, the two parties had as many commonalities as differences. To explain the emerging Second American Party System, he suggested, historians must thus look to other factors.

Writing a decade later, but building on Benson's earlier analysis of New York, the historian Ronald Formisano also firmly rejected the significance of economic issues, specifically "laissez-faire political economics" during the "birth of mass political parties" in the State of Michigan in the 1830s and 1840s. Although economic issues may have been important in national party platforms, Formisano argued, they did not distinguish the parties at the state level. At the national level, Democratic conceptions of "negative liberalism" were opposed to Whig conceptions of a "positive liberalism" in matters of both economic growth and morality. "In Michigan," however, "neither Democrats

---

104–124; Harry L. Watson, *Liberty and Power: The Politics of Jacksonian America* (New York: Noonday Press, 1990), esp. 172–197; Jabez D. Hammond, *History of Political Parties*, Vol. II, pp. 369–488; and Dixon Ryan Fox, *The Decline of Aristocracy in the Politics of New York* (New York: Columbia University, 1918): 352–405.

[24] For an incisive discussion of this issue of interpretation, see Richard P. McCormick, "Ethno-Cultural Interpretations of Nineteenth-Century American Voting Behavior," *Political Science Quarterly* 89:2 (June, 1974): 351–377; for more general surveys of the issue see Watson, *Liberty and Power*, pp. 172–197; and Charles Sellers, *The Market Revolution: Jacksonian America, 1815–1848* (New York: Oxford University Press, 1991): 202–236 and 364–395.

[25] Lee Benson, *The Concept of Jacksonian Democracy: New York as a Test Case* (Princeton, NJ: Princeton University Press, 1961), passim; especially pp. 165–207.

or Whigs could be regarded as laissez faire..." and "it is difficult to find differences between parties on state economic matters, in policy or practice."[26] In Formisano's analysis, Democrats' "laissez faire" ideology conflicted with Whig activism not so much in political economy but rather over issues of religion and morals.

In particular, Formisano argued that the emerging Whig Party of the early and mid-1830s was strongly associated with "the evangelical impulse to Christianize America."[27] This impulse was represented by what he called "the benevolent system" – an interlocking directorate of organizations such as temperance societies, Bible societies, and Sunday school unions. Grounded in the image of a party devoted to moral reform, the emerging Whig Party framed its opposition to the reigning Jacksonian Democrats as an attack on corruption. Democrats, meanwhile, responded by raising the specter of "a Union of Church and State," in which Whigs imposed a kind of "evangelical authoritarianism," with "arbitrary laws" regulating moral conduct.[28] Religion in this way became a defining feature of the Second American Party System, serving as a strong positive referent for those joining the developing Whig coalition and as a strong negative referent for Jacksonians opposed to evangelical social control.

In many ways the Lima case fits this scenario. Understood in this context, the fact that the 1833 seminary charter made no mention of the Methodist Church and no formal provision for Methodist influence over the institution is not surprising. It is a reflection of the continued domination of the state legislature by Jackson forces. In fact, according to Formisano, similar controversies over the chartering of denominationally sponsored educational institutions animated politics in Michigan at about the same time. Beginning in the late 1820s, Baptist, Methodist, and Presbyterian leaders all lobbied the then–Territory's Legislative Council for grants of incorporation to denominational colleges. Although a few charters were granted, the power to award degrees was withheld from such institutions in favor of concentrating all such power and resources in the establishment of a nondenominational state university. Abandoning his own effort to establish a Baptist denominational college in Michigan in 1836, one minister described the "prevalent antipathy among politicians against denominational movements" that, it was feared, aimed "to secure a sectarian control of the educational interests of the country."[29] If Jacksonians managed to frustrate such denominational ambitions in Michigan in 1836, it is not surprising that they did so in New York in 1833.

Still, the fact that Methodist leaders of the academy at Lima were surprised by the version of the seminary charter that passed in 1833 raises the question

---

[26] Ronald P. Formisano, *The Birth of Mass Political Parties: Michigan, 1827–1861* (Princeton, NJ: Princeton University Press, 1971): 109 and 102–128, passim.
[27] Ibid., p. 111 and pp. 102–127, passim.
[28] Ibid., p. 110.
[29] Ibid., p. 108.

Controlling Capital

of how exactly it happened. Presumably, the draft bill for incorporation that the board of trustees sent to the legislature in January 1833 *did* include provisions for Methodist control of the board or it would not have been approved by its majority-Methodist membership. Something apparently happened between the time the trustees applied for the charter and its approval. In this context, Asahel Warner's role is of interest. As a former state assemblyman, Warner presumably had something to offer in the way of experience and connections for pushing through an act of incorporation. The fact that another local trustee resigned to make way for him on the board immediately after the trustees voted to apply for incorporation suggests that the trustees sought his assistance for the purpose.[30] More important than his legislative experience, however, may have been his association with the Democratic majority in the legislature. Although the Methodist leadership had its own connections in the legislature, they tended to be with anti-Jackson forces.[31] Given their anti-Jackson associations, Methodist leaders may have decided they could use the help of a Jacksonite like Warner to negotiate the passage of a seminary charter.

What happened when the delegation got to Albany is another matter. Whether the nondenominational terms of the charter were dictated by the Jacksonian leadership or introduced by local lobbyists like Warner is unknown. One thing is clear, however. Anyone who hoped to check Methodist power through the nondenominational terms of the 1833 charter made a miscalculation. If anything, the decision triggered an increase in Methodist activism and political organization. The official minutes of the board of trustees make no mention whatsoever of the April 1833 charter. Nonetheless, work on a substitute charter began immediately. By January 1834, the legislature had received petitions from throughout western New York to change the charter to give Methodists control over the institution's board of trustees. Of thirty-seven petitions received by the legislature on the topic, only one opposed the change. That was from Lima residents.

The Argument against Denominational Control

As artifacts of political strategy, the petitions opposing and supporting the bill to re-charter the seminary in 1834 provide evidence of who regarded themselves as sharing common interests, how they conceived their claim on the state, and how they framed the issues of the case. Of the forty-seven local residents who petitioned against the new charter, forty-three can be precisely

---

[30] Minutes of the Board of Trustees, September 26, 1832.
[31] These Whig associations are indicated by the role of Reverend Glezen Fillmore, Millard Fillmore's cousin, on the seminary board and in the seminary's charter application. See Robert J. Rayback, *Millard Fillmore: Biography of a President* (Buffalo, NY: Published for the Buffalo Historical Society by Henry Steward, Incorporated, 1959); DeAlva Stanwood Alexander, *A Political History of the State of New York* (Port Washington, NY:Ira J. Friedman, Inc., 1909), Volumes I and II; and the Methodist periodical *The Ladies Repository: A Monthly Periodical Devoted to Literature, Arts and Religion*, Volume 21, Issue 5, June 1861, pp. 366–367.

matched with the names of original local subscribers. Altogether, the value of their subscriptions totals $4,215. Among signatories to the petition, dated January 7, 1834, were two of the town's leading merchants, who had each subscribed for $500; several shopowners, craftsmen, and professionals who had subscribed for more than $100; and a number of landowners and others who subscribed for $100 or less.[32]

The petitioners began by asserting the nature of their claim on the institution. Identifying themselves as "sundry inhabitants of the town of Lima" who "together with other inhabitants of the said town ... subscribed for the building of a literary institution in that town, about the sum of ten thousand dollars," they asserted (accurately) that these subscriptions "constituted about two-thirds the whole expense" for "erection of the buildings now known as Genesee Wesleyan Seminary." Of this sum, they went on to explain, "not over two thousand dollars were given by members of the Methodist sect" or "others who had any particular partialities for that sect."[33] The petitioners presented themselves, in other words, as subscriber-investors with a claim on the institution due to their founding influence and financial stake in its capital assets.

This claim was essential to the logic of the narrative and argument that followed. First, the petitioners referred to the existing 1833 charter for the institution, which, they noted, the legislature had passed "in conformity with established usage." Then they turned to the proposal currently before the legislature. Recently, they explained, they had learned that "a petition is in circulation praying an alteration" in the existing act of incorporation. The proposed alteration, they pointed out, would "invest the Genesee conference, a body composed exclusively of Methodist priests, a part of whom reside in this State and a part in Pennsylvania, with the sole power of appointing trustees to the institution, and filling all vacancies in that body."[34] In addition, the Lima petitioners "were not a little surprised to learn," they went on to explain, that according to supporters of the new charter "subscribers were induced to make donations to the institution" with the promise "that the trustees should be appointed by the conference." The petitioners begged to differ with this account:

Your memorialists will not pretend to judge of the motives of all who may have given to the institution, but they beg your honorable body distinctly to understand, that no such motives influenced them; on the contrary, the proposal to confer on the conference the power which is now sought, constituted a primary objection, with them, to making any bestowment for the institution; and nothing but the most strong and oft repeated assurances that the institution should be purely literary and scientific of the most liberal cast, so far as its conduct and management were concerned, could have induced your memorialists to make the liberal donations they did.[35]

[32] "Memorial from Sundry Inhabitants of Lima," 1834 and Account Book #102, GWSC.
[33] "Memorial from Sundry Inhabitants of Lima," 1834.
[34] Ibid.
[35] Ibid.

If the application for a new charter was to be based on promises made to subscribers, in other words, then the forty-seven Lima petitioners had also been given promises that should be taken into consideration. Specifically, they had been promised that the institution would be "purely literary and scientific of the most liberal cast."

It was at this point, then, after establishing their claim on the institution and stating what promises they had received, that the Lima petitioners began arguing that promises had been violated. Rather than establishing the school on liberal terms, the petitioners argued, the Methodist Conference had made it "wholly subservient to sectarian views and purposes." This was manifested in the selection of trustees and faculty for the institution. A majority of the trustees and all the instructors were Methodists, and half or more were not only members of the Methodist "sect" but also "priests." Instead of receiving a liberal education, students were subject to regular religious meetings, held by a resident or circuit preacher at the institution, who used "the most ardent and exciting means" for "proselyting" them to Methodism. Students were "pursued by priests and coadjutors, even to their rooms, to bring them to the adoption of their religious opinions."[36]

Considered as political strategy, this argument was astute. In making it, the Lima petitioners not only voiced a specific complaint against Methodist control of the institution but invoked an already politicized rhetoric about the threat posed by growing evangelical influence in politics and government. By complaining about Methodist "priests and coadjutors" actively "proselyting students to Methodism," local residents tapped into the rhetoric of resistance to "evangelical authoritarianism" that Benson and Formisano ascribed to Jacksonian Democrats in New York and Michigan. In doing so, they appealed to the still-prevailing power of Jacksonian forces in the state legislature to prevent passage of the bill rechartering the seminary under Methodist control.

It was not only with respect to religion that the petitioners tapped into prevailing political rhetoric, however. The forty-seven local residents who opposed the new corporate charter also connected the charge of religious sectarianism to an anti-corporate critique that would gain increasing currency among Democrats in the bank wars of the 1830s and 1840s. Directly following their account of Methodist proselytizing – indeed as part of the same extended sentence – the petitioners protested the unchecked power the act would confer on the Genesee Conference, itself a corporation:

> ... and as a means of perpetuating this domination of the priests, it is now sought to confer *on a self-constituted body, without the control of the Legislature, the irrevocable power, without limitation,* of appointing trustees to the institution.[37]

Much the same stance against unregulated corporate power would soon be assumed by a faction of the Jacksonian coalition in their campaign against

---

[36] Ibid.
[37] "Memorial from Sundry Inhabitants of Lima," 1834 (emphasis added).

banks. In the spring of 1834, just after the new seminary charter passed the legislature, leaders of the Workingmen's Party of New York City demanded that local Democratic candidates for state office pledge to oppose "the chartering of monopolies."[38] Although directed primarily against banks, this anti-corporate rhetoric was framed in broad terms, as applying to all corporations.[39] The petitioners from Lima appealed to similar anti-monopoly rhetoric and the constituencies of the developing anti-bank movement in arguing their case. As they did so, they effectively forged a link between economic and cultural issues in Jacksonian politics. In their formulation, granting Methodists monopoly power over a local educational institution was problematic in both economic and cultural terms. It was a matter of both economic and religious liberty.

Money and Influence in Local Politics

If not for certain complications, this strategy on the part of local residents might have worked. As it turned out, however, the forty-seven Lima residents who argued against a new charter for the seminary were not the only local residents who petitioned the legislature on the subject. In a separate petition dated three weeks later, three local leaders of the seminary project – Frederic House, Asahel Warner, and Ralph P. Smith – argued in support of the bill to recharter the seminary. Curiously, these three petitioners, who together had subscribed for a total of $1,600 and who had served as the primary landowners and builders involved in construction of the institution, made no direct mention of their financial roles in the project. Instead, they presented themselves simply as witnesses. According to their account, the intentions of the Genesee Conference with respect to control of the institution were clear from the very first meeting in Lima at which the possibility of competing for the site of the seminary was discussed. At that meeting, "it was understood that the contemplated institution was to stand related to the Conference as that at Cazenovia did." Accordingly, "their act of incorporation [i.e., Cazenovia's], passed in the year eighteen hundred and twenty-five, was read to the said meeting, as the model of the contemplated Seminary." The decision to solicit the site of the seminary was thus informed by an understanding that the resulting institution would be under Methodist control. "Such control," as these petitioners put it, "was anticipated by every intelligent subscriber."[40] In this way, three leading local entrepreneurs of the seminary project undercut the position and strategy of other Lima petitioners.

---

[38] Jabez Hammond, *Political History of New York*, 489–491 and 500–503.
[39] By the summer of 1835, the anti-monopolists, or loco-focos, would become a significant faction within the state Democratic Party. The following year they adopted a slate of principles as the "Equal Rights Party," including "hostility to any and all monopolies by legislation." Ibid.
[40] "Memorial of Frederic House, Asahel Warner, and R. P. Smith, relative to the incorporation of the Lima Seminary," dated January 27, 1834; recorded January 31, 1834, No. 96,

At first glance, the alliance with the Methodist leadership on the part of Asahel Warner is surprising – a surprise reinforced by the fact that Asahel's own brother, Matthew, signed the opposing local petition against Methodist control. A close look at the finances of the situation reveals the logic of Asahel's actions, however. All three signatories of the local counterpetition were creditors of the institution or of Methodist subscribers. Both House as builder and Smith as landholder had received Methodist subscriptions as well as local subscriptions in payment on their land and building contracts. Warner, meanwhile, held a $5,000 mortgage against the institution. As the seminary's chief commercial creditor, he could not afford to lose either the legal or practical leverage necessary for collection on this debt. Given the determination of the Methodist leadership to achieve denominational control, failure of the new charter could mean that the larger Methodist network might feel little responsibility for ensuring the institution honored the debt. In such an eventuality, Warner stood to lose not only his claim on the institution but his own family farm. From this perspective, Warner may have come to see that he had an economic interest in aiding passage of the recharter bill.

This economic interest complicates the politics of the Lima case. Since the work of Benson and Formisano, most scholars have accepted that religion was a significant factor in shaping the emergence of the Second American Party System.[41] At the same time, a number of scholars have reasserted the significance of economic issues in party formation and have explored the interaction between religion and economic issues at the local level. Typically, this analysis has been framed in terms of social class and social control. In his richly anthropological study of a Pennsylvania mill town, for example, Anthony F. C. Wallace demonstrated that certain early industrialists, and their wives and daughters, took the lead in organizing Sunday schools, promoting temperance, and establishing churches to evangelize workers. He then showed how these same industrial leaders interpreted workers' subsequent participation or nonparticipation in industrial strikes in evangelical terms – as signs of the relative success or failure, extent and sincerity, of evangelical conversions. Some of these leaders became active in politics, promoting policies that facilitated the concentration of capital, the integration of markets, and broad economic development. In this account, then, evangelical religion was a source of cultural authority and social control for an entrepreneurial class seeking to increase its command of labor and its own economic advancement.[42]

Similarly, in his study of society, religion, and politics in Rochester, New York, in the 1820s and 1830s, Paul Johnson argued that religious revivalism played an important role in restructuring the economic and political

---

Documents of the Assembly of the State of New York (Albany, NY: E. Croswell, printer to the state, 1834).

[41] See Watson, *Liberty and Power*, pp. 172–197.
[42] Anthony F. C. Wallace, *Rockdale: The Growth of an American Village in the Early Industrial Revolution* (New York: W. W. Norton & Co., 1972).

authority of the entrepreneurial class. In Johnson's analysis, this authority had been significantly disrupted by the anti-Mason agitation of the late 1820s. In Rochester, as in Rockdale, merchants and manufacturers took the lead in forming temperance societies, Sunday schools, and churches aimed at cultivating moral order among the growing city's relatively large population of workingmen. Before the revivals of 1830–1831, neither the Democrats nor the anti-Masonic leadership seemed inclined to enforce such order through political authority, given that they relied on votes from these groups for their power. During the revivals of 1830–1831, however, the city's social, political, and economic elite achieved a new level of class solidarity and cultural authority. According to Johnson's analysis, converts in the revival of 1830–1831 came disproportionately from businessmen, professionals, and master craftsmen in the city – the "influential people." Converts in later revivals, by contrast, from 1832–1837, were more often journeymen workers in the shops and businesses of these influential men. Quoting observations from contemporaries of the time, Johnson concluded that evidence of moral reform – that is, membership in temperance societies and evangelical churches – increasingly became a condition of employment. At the same time, leaders began to use their political authority to enforce moral provisions such as Sabbatarian laws and stricter qualifications for grocery (or liquor) licensing. This new moral order in turn provided the local political base for a developing Whig Party. As in Rockdale, evangelicalism became a new source of authority and of economic and social control for an ownership class.[43]

To some extent, Warner's actions in Lima fit the Rochester scenario. Like the political and economic leaders Johnson described, Warner's authority as a leader had been disrupted by the political changes of the 1820s. As a result of constitutional revisions, the restructuring of state politics and government, geographical redistricting, and the rise of anti-Masonry, Warner lost state office and local influence. The role he assumed in promoting the academy seems to have been aimed at recovering that influence and renewing local solidarity in the midst of new religious and political divisions. At the start of the project, in 1830, an alliance with an outside organization like the Genesee Annual Conference also seemed to offer to a landowner and petit capitalist like himself the prospect of economic opportunity. To the extent that Warner seized this opportunity it could be said that he, too, "used" the rise of evangelicalism to advance his "class" interests.

But Lima was not Rochester and Warner was neither a shopkeeper nor (yet) an industrialist. As a leading landowner in a town of mostly independent farmers, Warner would not seem to have had the same interest in the social control of a nascent proletariat as did the shopkeepers and mill owners of Wallace's and Johnson's accounts. The primary source of Warner's economic and political leverage in Lima was as a creditor rather than as an employer.

---

[43] Paul E. Johnson, *A Shopkeeper's Millenium: Society and Revivals in Rochester, New York, 1815–1837* (New York: Hill and Wang, 1978).

Although his local credit relations certainly involved the exchange of labor as well as goods, the suppliers of this labor were not entirely or even primarily dependent on him for their livelihoods. In most cases they had their own independent means of production. The Lima case in this respect does not seem to fit Wallace's or Johnsons' social control analysis of the relationship between religion and economic issues in Jacksonian society and politics. Nor does Warner seem to have been particularly invested in the promotion of evangelical culture. As a leading Freemason and a Jacksonian Democrat, Warner was more strongly associated with the opponents of the developing Whig coalition than with its proponents. By the standards of Benson and Formisano, then, Warner's alliance with the Methodists also appears anomalous.

This apparent anomaly disappears, however, when the impact of Methodism on Warner's role as credit-broker is considered. As a leading landholder and creditor in the town of Lima for nearly forty years, Warner had long brokered local interests in state politics and commercial credit relations. Because of his relationship with the New York financier Isaac Bronson, and with political networks such as the Jacksonian Democrats, Warner had access to cash, credit, and political influence that his neighbors often wanted. Indeed, his position of local leadership depended in large part on his access to this translocal financial and political capital. As long as his own creditors were primarily local, Warner's interests lay with whatever measures stimulated the local economy and promoted local influence in state politics. Thanks to the translocal organizational power of the Methodist church, however, Warner had become chief creditor of an institution whose capacity to honor that debt lay with thousands of households outside the town of Lima. The balance of his economic interests thus shifted from inside to outside the locality. When defense of those interests became a political matter through the process of incorporation, Warner shifted political alliances as well.

The Politics of Economic Change

The new seminary charter, dated May 1, 1834, constituted a Methodist victory in many ways. Although Warner's alliance with Methodist leaders certainly contributed to this victory, it was not the only factor contributing to their success. Just as important was the mobilization of political capital by Methodists. When the New York Legislature considered the Methodist application to recharter the seminary, it examined not only two petitions from local residents but thirty-five additional petitions from groups of Methodist subscribers in twelve different counties in western New York.[44] All thirty-five petitions argued in favor of a new corporate charter.

In this kind of political activism, Methodists enjoyed a clear advantage. The same organizational system that made for the effective mobilization of

---

[44] *Journal of the Assembly, State of New York* (Albany: State of New York, 1834): 39, 81, 87, 95, 101, 128, 183, 195, 238.

financial capital for the seminary also effectively mobilized political capital. Traveling preachers and seminary agents riding the circuits, stations, and districts of the Genesee Conference to raise subscriptions could at the same time solicit petition signatures. In addition to this organizational advantage, Methodists also enjoyed a geographical advantage in state politics. As a translocal organization roughly congruent with the whole of western New York, the Genesee Conference had constituencies in every senate and assembly district in the region. The twelve counties from which the Methodists raised petitions together represented one-fifth of all counties and one-quarter of all assembly districts in the state.[45]

For the assemblymen representing these western regional districts, Methodists were a particularly important constituency. Although the state as a whole remained firmly Democratic in 1834, the assemblymen representing these districts were all elected as anti-Jackson candidates.[46] In the end, all but one of the twenty-three assemblymen representing these districts voted in favor of changing the seminary charter.[47] In the face of this systematically organized and geographically extensive political base, the local and personal politics of a town like Lima could not successfully resist for long.

The success of this political effort on the part of Methodism was part of a larger political transformation in New York in 1834 – namely, the emergence of the Whigs as a cohesive and competitive opposition party at the state level. In April 1834, while the bill to recharter the seminary was still under consideration by the legislature, anti-Jackson forces in New York City first adopted the term "Whig" in municipal elections. By August 1834, city Whigs had forged a coalition with anti-Jackson forces in western New York to hold the first Whig convention and nominate its first candidate for governor.[48] In western New York in particular, evangelical networks such as those represented by the Genesee Conference of the Methodist Church were an important base of this developing opposition. To the extent that the controversy over the seminary charter helped politicize this Methodist base as an anti-Jackson force, it helped build the Whig coalition.

Still, the Methodist victory on the charter included some concessions to local concerns. As requested by Methodist petitioners, the new charter provided for Methodist control of the board, specifying that the trustees "shall be appointed by the Genesee annual Conference of the Methodist Episcopal

---

[45] Ibid. The petitions represented 12 of 55 total counties (22%) and 8 of 33 total districts (24%). The counties and districts from which Methodist petitions were submitted to the Legislature were Allegany (30th), Erie (32nd), Livingston (30th), Monroe (28th), Niagara (33rd), Ontario (26th), Seneca (25th), Orleans (33rd), Tioga (22nd), Genesee (29th), Wayne (25th), and Yates (27th).
[46] Jabez Hammond, *Political History of New York*, Vol. II; Fox, *Decline of Aristocracy*.
[47] The roll call vote was taken on April 28, 1834. Of 128 total members, 88 voted in favor and 10 against (30 did not vote). *Journal of the Assembly* (1834): 935–936.
[48] Hammond, *Political History of New York* and Fox, *Decline of Aristocracy*.

Church."[49] Beyond this new provision, however, the charter included some other changes that Methodists had not requested. Article 6 specified that "No part of the funds of the corporation hereby created, shall ever be applied for the support of theological or other studies than those of literature and fine arts."[50] On the face of it, this provision addressed the issue of religious sectarianism that Lima residents had raised in their January 1834 petition against the new charter. Implicitly, however, the focus on literature and fine arts also excluded applied arts, such as agriculture and mechanical arts, and thus the idea of manual labor education.

Evidence suggests that these latter provisions were added to the bill in response to political pressure and that the issue of manual labor education played a role in the outcome. When the committee on colleges, academies, and common schools first brought the bill to the floor of the Assembly on April 17, 1834, the discussion was apparently inconclusive. The bill was tabled and then referred to a "select committee" the following day. On April 19 the bill came back to the Assembly floor, with the select committee reporting that it had "gone through the said bill, made amendments thereto, and agreed to the same."[51] Although the contents of the amendments were not recorded in the minutes, they presumably represented some modification of the provisions drafted by the Methodist leadership in the original bill.

Events immediately surrounding passage of the 1834 charter further illuminate the issues. On April 30, 1834, the seminary's trustees held a special meeting and voted to "raise $1000 for the New York debt, and to pay Major Warner in part."[52] The next day, the board voted that "there be a committee of three to enquire into the experience of introducing the manual labor department at the School and to report at the next meeting of the Board."[53] Although the content and results of this report were never recorded in the minutes, the outcome is clear. By July of 1834, the operation of the boarding hall and supporting farm had been contracted out to a layman.[54] At the same time, any reference to "agriculture and mechanic arts" disappeared from descriptions of the institution.[55] By the end of the year, Warner had received final payment for the farm and signed the title for it over to the institution.[56] It appears, then, that ending the seminary's experiment with manual labor education – and thus the threat of student competition with local farmers, boarding houses,

---

[49] "An Act to Incorporate the Genesee Wesleyan Seminary," Passed May 1, 1834, recorded in Account Book #178, GWSC.
[50] Ibid.
[51] *Journal of the Assembly* (1834): 811, 821, and 823.
[52] "Minutes of the Board of Trustees," April 30, 1834, Account Book #178.
[53] "Minutes of the Board of Trustees," April 31, 1834, Account Book #178. Since there are only 30 days in April, the trustee vote seems to have been backdated to appear prior to that of the charter, May 1.
[54] Ibid., July 13, 1834.
[55] "Catalogue ... of Genesee Wesleyan Seminary," 1834, passim.
[56] This payment and transfer of title is recorded in Account Books #56 and #102, GWSC.

and tradesmen – was a condition of the charter's passage. In the battle for institutional control, in other words, locals made their mark by insisting that the seminary's corporate enterprise would be more cultural than economic. In the end, though, the education offered by the academy at Lima would still derive its meaning less from the content of its studies than from its place in a transforming economy.

16

Success – Education and the Culture of the Market

> The school has been in operation for more than two years; and its success has equaled, and in some respects exceeded, the most sanguine expectations of its friends.
>
> Catalogue of the Officers and Students of Genesee Wesleyan Seminary, Lima, New York, for the year ending July 1834[1]
>
> Arrangements are made to give instruction in any of the branches taught in Colleges, Academies, Select and Common Schools, according to the wants of the Students. ...
>
> Ibid.

In the wake of their political victory, Methodist Seminary officials anticipated the future of the institution with considerable optimism. "Having obtained a Charter in accordance with the wishes and original design of its friends," the July 1834 catalog stated, the institution was "now enabled to take a course which promises permanency and success."[2] Without specifying exactly what this "course" was, school officials predicted that the institution "will soon rise to a level of eminence unequalled by any other of its grade in the country." In this they proved correct. Among other things, Methodist agents succeeded in raising additional capital funds. By the end of 1834, the total in new subscriptions made the seminary one of the most highly capitalized academies in the state. Enrollments, meanwhile, approached 400 students, making the institution one of the largest in New York. These students enrolled in a wide range of subjects, including classical and higher English studies, a fact that made the seminary a candidate for Regents status and funding. All this was evidence of the seminary's success, particularly of its successful strategy of using Methodist networks to raise capital, recruit students, and mobilize political support.

---

[1] "Catalogue of the Officers and Students of Genesee Wesleyan Seminary, Lima, New York, for the year ending July, 1834," p. 16. Bulletins of Genesee Wesleyan Seminary, Box 14, GWSC.
[2] Ibid.

This chapter shows how the structure of the academy's success shaped the character, curriculum, and culture of the institution. At the same time as Genesee Wesleyan owed its successful capitalization and incorporation to its roots in local and translocal social networks, it also operated largely on market principles. Like virtually all academies and venture schools, it depended heavily on tuition for operating funds, and thus on attracting paying students. This dependence on market-based demand for instruction in turn shaped the content of the studies the seminary offered and the composition of its student population. To appeal to the largest potential student market, the seminary offered instruction in a wide range of studies on a pay-as-you-go basis or, as the catalog put it, "in any of the subjects taught in Colleges, Academies, select and common schools, according to the wants of the Students."[3] At the same time, to maximize its income from tuition and Regents funding, it encouraged both male and female students to pursue coherent curricula of higher study. Together, the combined effects of Methodist control, student choice, and Regents funding shaped an eclectic literary institution that facilitated traditional academic study at an individualized pace.

Permanency

The seminary's strategy of using Methodist organizational networks to raise funds, recruit students, and mobilize political capital proved highly effective and mutually reinforcing. In the months immediately following passage of the new charter, Methodist agents of the seminary stepped up their fundraising activities. In the process they contributed to long-term increases in the institution's enrollments as well as to the political leverage necessary to secure further benefits from the state, including access to Regents status and funding. This tripling of the value of capital raised by subscription may not have been fully foreseen at the time the Genesee Conference organized the seminary as a joint stock association in 1830, but it was fully exploited.

Ever since the Genesee Conference first established the joint stock arrangement for selling "shares" in the seminary, agents had actively solicited subscriptions through Methodist networks in western New York. The first big push occurred during the first ten months after the seminary's organization and yielded more than $8,000 in subscription pledges, of which about half went toward construction of the seminary building. A relatively high proportion of this first round of Methodist subscriptions – approximately 50% – was in amounts of $100, thereby conferring the benefit of free tuition to students.[4] That fact helps to explain the high student enrollments the seminary achieved in its very first year of operation. In the year extending from March of 1832,

---

[3] Ibid.
[4] The number and amount of subscriptions raised, and the number and proportion in $100 amounts, are compiled from the running record of subscriptions kept in Account Book #102, GWSC.

when the seminary enrolled its first students, to March of 1833, the seminary reported a total enrollment of 341 students, making it at once one of the largest academies in the state.[5]

This complementary relationship between subscription fundraising and student enrollment accelerated in years to come. During the initial two years of the seminary's organization, the work of raising subscriptions had been done by a single agent. Once the seminary began enrolling students in 1832, however, the trustees appointed a second agent to cover the huge territory represented by the conference. With each man raising between $5,000 and $7,000 a year in new subscriptions, the institution's financial capital quickly grew. By January 1834, when Methodists submitted their first petitions in favor of a new seminary charter, the total value of subscription pledges raised by Methodist agents exceeded $30,000, thereby bolstering Methodists' political claim to a controlling interest in the institution.[6] During the same period, enrollment increased by 9 percent, from 341 to 376 students. These 376 students came from 115 different towns in western New York and beyond, further establishing the institution's territorial and political reach.[7]

This already substantial success would receive an additional boost in the months that followed, as agents both solidified the Methodist victory in the legislature and anticipated the institution's next political move. Subscription records for the seminary show that in the fifteen-month period immediately following the date of the new seminary charter (May 1, 1834) and immediately preceding the institution's application for Regents status and funding in July 1835, Methodist agents dramatically increased the rate at which they raised new subscriptions. Together the two agents raised nearly $20,000 from 327 new subscribers. Close to half (46%) subscribed for $100, effectively ensuring a supply of future students.[8]

The value of subscriptions raised under Methodist auspices now exceeded $50,000, the goal that Methodist leaders had originally established five years earlier when they first organized the seminary as a joint stock association and "opened shares" for sale.[9] With this goal reached, seminary officials could convincingly argue that the institution had achieved the level of success and

[5] "Catalogue of the Officers and Students in the Genesee Wesleyan Seminary, Lima, Livingston Co., N.Y., for the year ending March 30, 1833," Bulletins of Genesee Wesleyan Seminary, Box 14, GWSC. Because Genesee Wesleyan Seminary was not admitted to the Regents until 1836, and because the Regents collected enrollment data only for subcategories of students in the 1830s, Genesee's total enrollment in 1833 cannot be directly compared with that of other institutions. Even by the standards of later years, however, an enrollment of 341 students would put the seminary in the top 5–10% of academies in the state.
[6] Data compiled from Account Book #102.
[7] Data on hometowns of students compiled from "Catalogue of Genesee Wesleyan Seminary," 1834, 5–14.
[8] Data compiled from Account Book #102.
[9] Ibid. Terms of the joint stock arrangement are recorded in "Report of the Seminary Committee Adopted by the Genesee Annual Conference at Its Session in Rochester, A.D. 1830," Account Book #178, GWSC.

permanency required of Regents institutions. A successful application for Regents status would in turn make the institution eligible for shares of state funds. Because these funds were distributed annually to Regents academies on a per pupil basis for students enrolled in "higher studies," officials actively promoted enrollment in those subjects even as they also accommodated a full range of market demand. In this way, the structure of the seminary's success shaped the culture of the institution.

Higher Study

As presented by the seminary catalog for 1834, the subjects of study offered by the institution were organized into five departments. The English Department represented subjects of a common education, including spelling, reading and writing, geography, English grammar, history and book-keeping. Headed by a male teacher who worked with a male assistant, the department allowed students to pick up their educations wherever they had left off. It also served as a training ground for students who wished "to prepare themselves for teaching others."[10] For decades, Genesee Wesleyan consistently enrolled about 40 percent of its students in common English studies, a relatively low figure compared with other New York academies.[11]

Beyond basic English education, the seminary modeled its curriculum on two prevailing traditions of higher study: the collegiate model and the model of female education. Traditionally, collegiate and female models of "higher" study were grounded in different core curricula. The collegiate model was grounded in ancient languages and classical literatures (including extensive study of Latin, some Greek, and less Hebrew), mathematics, and rhetoric, with a capstone course in moral philosophy and political economy.[12] At Genesee Wesleyan, this curricular model was represented by a total of three departments, each headed by a male "professor": the Department of Languages, the Department of Mathematics and Natural Philosophy, and the Department of Moral Science and Belles-letters. By contrast, the tradition of female education was represented at Genesee Wesleyan by a single "female department."[13] As developed since the late eighteenth century and especially since the 1810s by leading female educators like Sarah Pierce, Emma Willard, and Catharine Beecher, this tradition of higher study was grounded in the sciences and modern languages, English rhetoric and composition, and history, with an integrative course in natural theology and mental or intellectual philosophy. At

---

[10] "Catalogue ... of Genesee Wesleyan Seminary," 1834, p. 17.
[11] *Annual Report of the Regents of the University of the State of New York* (Albany: State of New York, passim).
[12] On the collegiate curricular tradition in the United States, see Douglas Sloan, *The Scottish Enlightenment and the American Collegiate Ideal* (New York: Teachers College Press, 1971); and Bruce Kimball, *Orators and Philosophers: A History of the Idea of Liberal Education* (New York: Teachers College Press, 1986).
[13] "Catalogue of Genesee Wesleyan Seminary," 1834, 18–20.

leading female institutions, the whole of this course might be taught by female faculty.[14] At the coeducational Genesee Wesleyan, female pupils received some of their instruction from "the male professors in those departments" and the rest from the female "preceptress" who headed the department, a female assistant, and a female "Teacher of Drawing and Music."[15]

Under each of the several departments, the seminary catalog listed specific subjects of study, often with specific texts. The description for the Department of Languages, for example, included long and detailed lists of texts in Latin and Greek, including grammars and literary texts, and somewhat shorter lists in Hebrew, French, and Spanish. The description for the Female Department, meanwhile, listed all the subjects of a basic English education (reading, writing, arithmetic, grammar, geography and history); together with mathematics (algebra and geometry); physical and natural sciences (natural philosophy, astronomy and botany); rhetoric, logic, the elements of criticism, intellectual philosophy, and natural theology; languages (Latin, French, and Italian); and ornamental studies (music, drawing and needlework).[16]

These departmental descriptions implied a level of curricular order and coherence that was rarely experienced by individual students, however. The tension between curricular ideals and the reality of market-based education is readily indicated by the section of the seminary's 1834 catalog entitled "General Remarks." The section began with the statement that "the system of instruction ... is designed to give a thorough education in all the branches usually taught in our College." Similarly, "In the FEMALE DEPARTMENT, provision is made to give instruction in all the branches, both solid and ornamental, usually taught in female Seminaries."[17] Just as quickly as it invoked the idea of thoroughness, however, the catalog acknowledged the difficulty of its pursuit in practice. "This system ... can be strictly adhered to only in the case of those who take a regular course," it noted. Otherwise, a more market-based principle applied: "Arrangements are made to give instruction in any of the branches taught in Colleges, Academies, Select and Common Schools, according to the wants of the Students. ..."[18]

This claim to compete with every possible institution and offer instruction in every possible subject appears exaggerated if judged by the standard of the

---

[14] On the female educational tradition in the United States, see Nancy Beadie, "Emma Willard's Idea Put to the Test: The Consequences of State Support of Female Education in New York, 1819–67" *History of Education Quarterly* 33:4 (Winter 1993): 543–562; Lynn Templeton Brickley, "Sarah Pierce's Litchfield Female Academy, 1792–1833" (Ed.D. dissertation, Harvard University, 1985); Kathryn Kish Sklar, *Catharine Beecher: A Study in American Domesticity* (New Haven, CT: Yale University Press, 1973); Kim Tolley, *The Science Education of American Girls: A Historical Perspective* (New York: Routledge-Falmer, 2003); and Margaret A. Nash, *Women's Education in the United States, 1780–1840* (New York: Teachers College Press, 2005).
[15] "Catalogue ... of Genesee Wesleyan Seminary," 1834, 19.
[16] Ibid.
[17] Ibid., 16.
[18] Ibid.

modern university, but not when considered in relation to the norms of the time. With a comparatively large faculty of eight, five males and three females, the seminary could offer a more elaborate set of curricula than most academies and colleges, which often had much smaller student bodies and employed just two or three faculty. When it came to school enrollment, moreover, students were likely to mix the subjects of a common education with higher study if they could. By offering a wide range of studies on a market basis, Genesee Wesleyan simply proposed to accommodate the norms of school attendance at the time.

Norms of School Attendance

When Clarissa Pengra began attending Genesee Wesleyan in 1834, she was eighteen years old, somewhat above the average age of academy students at most institutions but well within the wide range of ages common to academies at the time. Most academies enrolled youth as young as eight or ten and as old as twenty-five or thirty, with the average age at an institution falling somewhere between fourteen and nineteen and the majority of students between the ages of fourteen and twenty-two. Because of the discontinuous character of most students' school experience, young people anywhere in this age range could be found almost anywhere on the educational spectrum, from the elementary study of reading, writing, arithmetic, and geography, to "higher" and collegiate studies in sciences, philosophy, and modern and ancient languages. As the historian Joseph Kett explained in his study of adolescence, "the broad age span common to most academies was not the result of prolonged education, but of a combination of late starts and random attendance stretched out over a number of years, with sizable gaps between sessions attended, and with attendance in any given year rarely embracing more than a month or two."[19]

Academies thrived in the antebellum period precisely because they accommodated these late starts and gaps in education. Kett suggests that it was rare for more than one-third of the students attending an academy in one term to return the next.[20] Persistence from one year to the next was even more infrequent. The case of Frances Smith, who attended Ontario Female Seminary in the town of Canandaigua, seventeen miles east of Lima, was fairly typical. Frances attended the academy for just a month or two in early 1831, departing in April. She then studied at home for the rest of that year in the town of Caledonia, about fifteen miles west of Lima, returning to the academy for a month or two at the beginning of 1832. A third sojourn at the academy occurred eighteen months later, in October 1833. Altogether Frances probably spent a total of six months at the academy over a thirty-six-month period.[21]

[19] Joseph Kett, *Rites of Passage: Adolescence in America: 1790 to the Present* (New York: Basic Books, 1977).
[20] "Catalogue ... of Genesee Wesleyan Seminary," 1834, 19.
[21] "Diary of Frances Connors Smith [Wells]," 1831–1837, passim, Box 10, William H. Emerson Family Papers, 1758–1953, URSC.

Based on such evidence, scholars have often assumed that the experience of attending an academy lacked academic seriousness. Theodore Sizer, for example, suggested that the academy "fit the American ideal" in that it provided "a veneer of education."[22] Other scholars have reinforced this characterization by calling attention to the contradiction between the course rosters and attendance records of academies. On one hand were the elaborate multi-year courses of studies advertised in most catalogs. On the other were the highly erratic attendance patterns of most academy students. As Kett put the issue, "few students appear to have remained long enough in a given academy to have benefited from whatever advantages such sequences [of graded curriculum] offered."[23]

Complaints about the instructional challenge presented by sporadic student attendance were common among educators. Most famously, Emma Willard critiqued the market-based character of female education in 1818 for undermining the educational authority of teachers, precluding the benefits of systematic instruction, and making educators "victims of their [students'] caprice."[24] Nonetheless, academies accommodated parental and student demand with policies that allowed students to take only the subjects they wanted and to pay only for as long as they wanted to take them. The section on "Terms and Vacations" in the Genesee Wesleyan catalog for 1834 illustrates this point: "It is desirable that students always enter at the commencement of a quarter, if practicable, that they may take a regular course with the classes. But at whatever time they enter they are required to pay for only the balance of the quarter."[25]

Under such policies, instruction was shaped directly by student and parental choice. The papers of Frances Smith, a student at the nearby Ontario Female Seminary of Canandaigua, illuminate how such choices worked. First among the decisions that the Smith family made about Frances's education was where and when Frances would continue her studies. On two occasions, the family decided to employ a tutor to instruct Frances at home rather than send her to school. In one instance, the instructor taught all the children in the family. In the second instance, a tutor was hired on short-term basis specifically to prepare Frances to resume her studies at the academy. Explaining the first situation to a friend, Frances wrote that she would not be able to return to the academy as she would like. "The instructress which I have is competent to instruct me in any of the higher branches I should wish to pursue, and she will probably remain with us a year, so you see all hope is precluded."[26]

---

[22] Theodore R. Sizer, ed. *The Age of Academies* (New York: Teachers College, 1964): 15.
[23] Kett, *Rites of Passage*, p. 19.
[24] Emma Willard, *An Address to the Public: Particularly to the Members of the Legislature of New York, Proposing a Plan for Improving Female Education* (Middlebury, VT, 1918; org. 1819), 7. Willard's address was delivered in 1818 but published the following year. See Beadie, "Emma Willard's Idea."
[25] "Catalogue ... of Genesee Wesleyan Seminary," 1834, p. 16.
[26] "Diary of Frances Connors Smith [Wells]," June 5, 1831.

At the same time as Smith's correspondence shows how family decisions shaped the terms of study, it also shows how choices were made about the content of that study. When, as Frances explained to her friend, she had the option of being instructed at home "in any of the higher branches of education which I should wish to pursue," Frances chose to continue studying the branches of education she had been studying when she left the academy: intellectual philosophy, geometry, and music. A year and a half later, when she was no longer under formal tutelage, Frances noted in her diary that she had been "looking over Paley's theology," a standard component of the female educational tradition, and recorded her intention to "make it a study" that summer. Finally, with the help of a second special tutor, Frances prepared to return to the seminary by "reviewing" studies on which she expected to be examined. Upon successful examination she went on to study new subjects – algebra, astronomy, and rhetoric.[27]

These references to a self-directed pursuit of an academic course of study put a somewhat different slant on the academic seriousness of academies and their students. Viewed from the perspective of Frances Smith's diary, the elaborate courses of study published by academies – the contents of which were relatively consistent across institutions – appear to complement rather than contradict student attendance patterns. *Given* that most students only attended school for a couple of months at a time, and *given* that periods of academy attendance were often separated by a year or more, the existence of published curricula helped students to bridge the gaps in their school experience through independent study and to maximize academic progress during the period they did attend.

Effects of Student Choice on Academic Culture

The Smith case illuminates the effects of student and parental choice on the experience of individuals, but it reveals little about the combined effects of such choices on institutions. Data from Genesee Wesleyan provide some evidence on this point. The catalog for 1834 published an unusual breakdown of the numbers of pupils studying various higher level subjects. A close look at those numbers provides a rare opportunity to assess the cumulative effects of student choice on academic culture. The results show that gendered curricular ideals shaped the choices that students and parents made but did not strictly define the academic culture of the institution. They also highlight how the structure of tuition pricing and Regents funding gave academies like Genesee Wesleyan incentives to compete for female students and encourage their pursuit of higher study.

As formally presented in the 1834 catalog, academic culture at Genesee Wesleyan Seminary seems highly gendered. The section of the catalog listing the teaching staff, for example, was divided into two parts. The first part,

[27] Ibid. October 10, 1833; and February 7 and 8, 1834.

TABLE 4. *Number and Proportion of Male and Female Students Studying Various Higher Level Subjects at Genesee Wesleyan Seminary, 1834*

Subject	Number of Males	% of Males	Number of Females	% of Females
History	11	5%	56	38%
Latin	74	32%	3	2%
French	10	4%	23	16%
Algebra	103	44%	7	5%
Geometry	44	19%	15	10%
Trigonometry	21	9%	1	.7%
Chemistry	20	9%	33	23%
Logic	29	13%	13	9%
Rhetoric	48	21%	50	35%
Intellectual Phil.	7	3%	6	4%
Natural Philosophy			85	59%
Drawing			37	26%
Music			20	14%
Criticism			14	10%
Ancient Geography			13	9%
Botany			11	8%
Astronomy			7	5%
Natural Theology			3	2%
Italian			3	2%
Comstock's Phil.	57	25%		
Greek	31	13%		
Book-keeping	17	7%		
Olmsted's Phil.	7	3%		
Mensuration I	7	3%		
Mensuration II	4	2%		
Conic Sections	6	3%		
Navigation	5	2%		
Spherical Trig.	4	2%		
Hebrew	3	1%		

Data compiled from "Catalogue of the Officers and Students of Genesee Wesleyan Seminary, Lima, New York, for the year ending July, 1834," pp. 10 and 14 compared, Box 14, Bulletins, 1833–1861, GWSC.
Total # of female students = 144. Total # of male students = 236.

entitled "Faculty," included all the male professors, the male teacher, and his male assistant. The second part, entitled "Female Department," included the female preceptress, her female assistant, and the female teacher of music and drawing. This pattern continued into the next section of the catalog, which contained a roster of students. The 232 male students were listed first, followed by the 144 female students attending during the same period. Gender undoubtedly organized student life as well, including living arrangements in the boarding facility and most extracurricular activities, for which students at the seminary, as at most comparable institutions, organized into separate male and female societies.[28]

Evidence from the catalog suggests that the actual instructional experiences of students were also highly gendered, though perhaps not as completely as the formal titles of the faculty and curricular departments might lead one to expect. At the end of each of the rosters of male and female students, the catalog for 1834 provided two separate lists showing the numbers of male and female students pursuing various academic subjects. The two lists had a number of subjects in common, as well as a number that appeared only on the male or only on the female list. A close look at these figures provides rare insight into the normative significance of different subjects (see Table 4).

One thing of note is the wide variation in the numbers of student studying various subjects *within* each of the two gendered lists, with few subjects approaching a majority of either male or female students. For example, among the subjects studied by male students, the numbers ranged from a low of just 3 or 4 students each in Hebrew and certain forms of applied math, to a high of 103 students (44% of all males) in algebra. Similarly, among the subjects studied by female students, the numbers ranged from a low of just one student in trigonometry and 3 students each in Latin, Italian, and Paley's natural theology, to a high of 85 students (59% of all female students) in natural philosophy, the highest proportion of male or female students enrolled in any subject. All other subjects had enrollment rates of less than 50 percent, with most less than 30 percent and a number less than 10 percent. Right away this suggests that instructional experience at the academy was not that of a cohort moving together step by step through a common curriculum. To the extent that students followed a curriculum, they seem to have done so at an individual pace.

A second observation is that the variation across gendered lists was partly a matter of emphasis. Ten subject areas appeared on both the male and female lists. However, the proportion of male and female students studying each of those ten subjects differed dramatically by sex in most cases. The greatest convergence between male and female enrollments occurred in the subject of rhetoric, studied by forty-eight males and fifty females. Female enrollment in rhetoric represented a higher proportion of all female students (35%) than did male enrollment of males (21%). The numbers and proportions of students enrolled in other subjects were more skewed by sex, however. For

---

[28] Evidence of student societies at Genesee Wesleyan, including programs of the societies' various activities, is available in Box 13, GWSC. On student societies at another coeducational academy in New York at this time, see Kathryn Kerns, "Farmers' Daughters: The Education of Women at Alfred Academy and University before the Civil War," *History of Higher Education Annual* 6 (1986): 11–28.

example, 38 percent of female students studied history, but only 5 percent of males. Meanwhile, 44 percent of males studied algebra, but only 5 percent of females.[29]

A third observation is a greater emphasis on the sciences in female instructional experience than in that of males. This emphasis is exhibited in several ways. First, in the only scientific subject common to both the male and female subject lists, chemistry, the proportion of female students enrolled (23%) substantially exceeded the proportion of male students enrolled (9%). Second, the female subject list included sciences studied only by females and not by males. This included botany and astronomy, each with relatively small female enrollments at 8 and 5 percent, respectively, but with no male enrollments. More impressively, the female subject list was topped by natural philosophy (59%).[30] The subject of natural philosophy, or physics (consisting of mechanics, hydrostatics, pneumatics, acoustics, magnetism, electricity, heat, and optics) was not explicitly identified on the male subject list, though the items listed as "Comstock's Philosophy" and "Olmstead's Philosophy" were equivalent.[31] The numbers of male students pursuing these two subjects together still constituted a much lower proportion of male students (28%) than of female students pursuing natural philosophy (59%).[32]

This greater emphasis on sciences in the instructional experience of girls at Genesee Wesleyan matches what other scholars have found regarding the formal curricula of male and female institutions. As the historian Kim Tolley has put the point, the normative curricular ideal for educated youth in the nineteenth century was "Science for Ladies, Classics for Gentlemen."[33] At the same time, data from Genesee Wesleyan reveal several incongruities between the formal organization of the curricula and the instructional experiences of students. As portrayed in the catalog, the highly gendered departmental structure of the institution allowed little overlap in the instructional experiences of male and female students, at least at higher levels. A closer look, however, shows

---

[29] "Catalogue ... of Genesee Wesleyan Seminary," 1834, pp. 10 and 14 compared.
[30] Ibid.
[31] Comstock and Olmsted authored two textbooks in natural philosophy. A comparison shows that the presentations of the subject were nearly identical in the two books. There were hundreds of editions of each published, of which the following appear to be the earliest. Denison Olmsted, *An Introduction to Natural Philosophy: Designed as a Text Book for the Use of the Students in Yale College: Compiled from Various Authorities* (New Haven, CT: Hezekiah Howe, 1831–1832); and John Lee Comstock, *A System of Natural Philosophy in which the Principles of Mechanics, Hydrostatics, Hydraulics, Pneumatics, Acoustics, Optics, Astronomy, Electricity, and Magnetism, Are Familiarly Explained* (Hartford, CT: D. F. Robinson, 1830–1831).
[32] "Catalogue ... of Genesee Wesleyan Seminary," 1834, pp. 10 and 14 compared.
[33] Kim Tolley, *The Science Education of American Girls: A Historical Perspective* (New York: Routledge-Falmer, 2003); specifically Chapter 2, pp. 35–54; originally published as Kimberly Tolley, "Science for Ladies, Classics for Gentlemen: A Comparative Analysis of Scientific Subjects in the Curricula of Boys' and Girls' Secondary Schools in the United States, 1794–1850," *History of Education Quarterly* 36 (Summer 1996): 129–153.

that many of the students enrolled in the ostensibly "male" departments were women. The catalog clearly stated that "Pupils studying Languages or higher branches of mathematics, will receive instruction from the Professors of those Departments." Presumably, then, all the female students of French and the few of Latin and Italian received instruction from the professor of languages. Meanwhile, in the Mathematics Department, the numbers of female students at first appear to be relatively small. An additional note under that department, however, indicates that all the students of chemistry and natural philosophy – the vast majority of whom were female – also received instruction in that department. Finally, a close look at the Department of Moral Sciences and Belles-letters shows that slightly more than half of the students receiving instruction from that professor were female. Although the subjects listed under the department were all strongly associated with the male collegiate curricular ideal, the enrollment figures show that several of those subjects (metaphysics, moral philosophy, political economy) enrolled no students. Meanwhile, other subjects (elements of criticism and natural theology) enrolled only female students, and the remainder (rhetoric and logic) enrolled comparable numbers of male and female students. Altogether, despite the fact that the total enrollment at Genesee Wesleyan was 63 percent male, enrollment in the Department of Moral Science and Belles-letters was 51 percent female.[34]

Overall, seminary officials portrayed the academic culture at Genesee Wesleyan as more strictly defined by gender than it actually was. That portrayal was itself a strategic response to the market, however. Throughout the antebellum era, female academies numbered among the largest and most successful educational institutions in New York.[35] It was that popularity and success that Genesee Wesleyan strove to imitate and with which it had to compete. In the 1830s, the most well-established female academy in the Lima vicinity was Ontario Female Seminary in nearby Canandaigua, a Regents institution. Beyond the Regents system, many independent venture schools also competed for female students, and in the mid-1830s such a school existed in Lima. Conducted by two female teachers, Misses Baker and Merriman, the school advertised instruction in "those branches usually taught in well regulated Academies," with particular emphasis on "the female department," which offered instruction in music and in academic subjects for "junior" and "senior" level students.[36] Concerned about such competition, trustees of Genesee Wesleyan in October 1835 tried to negotiate a merger with the school, a proposal that, initially at least, local residents rejected.[37] Meanwhile,

---

[34] "Catalogue ... of Genesee Wesleyan Seminary," 1834, pp. 10 and 14 and 17–19, compared.

[35] This statement is based on an analysis of the *Annual Report of the Regents of the University of New York* for the period 1835–1850. For a full discussion of this analysis see Nancy Beadie, "Female Students and Denominational Affiliation: Sources of Success and Variation Among Nineteenth Century Academies. *American Journal of Education* 107:2 (1999): 75–115.

[36] "Advertisement," dated October 20, 1835, published in the *Livingston County Register*, Vol. II, No. 1, December 22, 1835, LCHO.

[37] Minutes of the Board of Trustees, October 6, 1835, Account Book #178, GWSC.

the seminary continued to compete for female students by promoting its own version of female education, embodied by a distinct female department.

The structure of tuition pricing reinforced the competition for female students and was one way in which institutions competed directly. In 1834, Genesee Wesleyan offered common English studies at $3 per quarter and "higher" studies for $5. These rates matched those charged by the Misses Baker and Merriman and were somewhat lower than those charged by many female academies in the state, including the institution at nearby Canandaigua.[38] Beyond these base rates, Genesee, like most institutions, charged extra fees for certain subjects. Female students often ended up paying more tuition than their male counterparts due to their enrollment in subjects for which institutions charged extra fees. These included the ornamental subjects of drawing and music, in which only female students typically enrolled, as well as special lectures in chemistry, for which female students dominated. In 1834, Genesee Wesleyan charged $5 extra for music, $1.50 for drawing, and $1 for chemistry, fees that were lower than those charged by the school operated by the Misses Baker and Merriman the following year.[39] Later, when the Baker and Merriman school disappeared, the price for music and drawing instruction at Genesee went up to $10 and $5 per quarter, respectively, while general charges for higher studies remained at $5.[40] With those prices, a female student might pay two to four times as much per quarter in tuition as her male counterpart. Add to that the prospect of additional per pupil funding from the Regents, and an academy like Genesee had multiple incentives to compete for female students and encourage their pursuit of higher study.

Success

In July of 1835, having achieved its initial capitalization goal of $50,000 and settled its $1,700 mortgage debt with Asahel Warner for its supporting farm, the seminary's trustees voted to petition the Regents of New York "to be

---

[38] "Catalogue ... of Genesee Wesleyan Seminary," 1834, p. 20. In 1826, Ontario Female Seminary advertised its tuition rates in the core academic subjects as $25 per year, or $8.25 per quarter for four quarters. Instruction in music or in French, Latin, or Greek was offered at extra charge. Advertisement in *The Ontario Repository*, April 19, 1826, reprinted in the *Daily Messenger*, 175th Anniversary edition, April 28, 1972, held as part of the Ontario Female Seminary Collection, OCHS. In 1836, Albany Female Academy advertised an elaborate set of tuition rates ranging from a low of $3 per quarter for the lowest, or sixth, department to a high of $8 per quarter for the highest, or first, department. An extra charge of $5 per quarter was levied for the study of French or Spanish. "Circular and Catalogue of the Albany Female Academy, 1836 (Albany, NY, 1836) reprinted in Sizer, ed. *The Age of Academies*, 168–174.

[39] Fees at the school taught by Baker and Merriman were advertised as $5 in the senior department, $3 in the junior department, and $10 for instruction in music. "Advertisement," December 22, 1835.

[40] "Catalogue of the Officers and Students of the Genesee Wesleyan Seminary, Lima, New York, for the Year Ending October 3, 1839," (Rochester, NY: William Alling, 1839), Box 14, GWSC.

taken under their supervision." Reflecting lessons learned during the charter controversy the previous year, the trustees specified as part of the resolution that agents circulate petitions "as far as practicable among the donors of the Seminary" in support of the measure.[41] Once again, Methodist leaders would owe victory to the successful mobilization of its political capital. As it turned out, the Regents proved resistant to the seminary's application, probably due to its church control. When the institution finally won designation as a Regents institution in March of 1836, it was by special legislative act rather than by a direct decision of the Regents. The legislature effectively circumvented the Regents by amending the seminary charter to confer the desired status: "The Genesee Wesleyan Seminary is hereby made and declared to be subject to the visitation of the regents of the university."[42]

Admission to the Regents proved the value of the seminary's Methodist networks financially as well as politically. To the value of capital raised by subscription could now be added not only the recruitment of students and the political leverage of subscribers but also a share of Regents funds. Because of the seminary's high enrollments, this value quickly proved substantial. By special provision in the 1836 act, the seminary received its first share of funds in 1836.[43] In this first year, for which the seminary seems to have received a partial share, the amount of the allocation was modest. At $242.30, the funds covered the equivalent of the female head teacher's salary.[44] The following year, however, the seminary received more than two and half times that amount, or $611.22, for enrolling 183 students (58% of its total enrollment) in higher studies. According to the Regents report, this level of enrollment in higher level study was exceeded by only two other institutions, both of which were female institutions. Albany Female Academy and Troy Female Seminary earned per pupil funding for a total of 312 and 300 students of higher level study, respectively.[45] Through a peculiarity of the state's funding formula, however, the money Genesee Wesleyan received from the Regents actually exceeded that received by those institutions. In accordance with early

---

[41] Minutes of the Board of Trustees, July 1835.

[42] "An Act to amend the act, entitled 'An act to incorporate the Genesee Wesleyan Seminary, passed May 1, 1834,' Passed March 9, 1836," *Laws of New York*, 59th Session, Chap. 44 (Albany: State of New York, 1836): 67.

[43] Ibid.: "... and the said regents are hereby authorised out of surplus funds, to pay to the trustees of said institution a sum equal to the distributive share of the literature fund for the present year, to which the said seminary would be entitled, if it were already subject to the visitation of the regents of the university."

[44] Receipt of this amount was recorded in the "Treasurer's Book," March 16, 1836, "From New York State per hand of A.A. Bennett, late Treas," Account Book #56, GWSC.

[45] "Schedule 1," *Report of the Regents of the University of the State of New York*, for the year 1837 (Albany: State of New York, 1838): 40–44. The Regents report for this year provides data on the number of students enrolled in classical and higher English subjects at Genesee Wesleyan for the year reported, which for this year was 183, and for the number of students enrolled on the date the report was filed, which for this year was 127. Figures for the total number of students enrolled in both lower and higher subjects for the year, which for this

legislative provisions, the total amount of funds that an institution received depended not only on the size of its enrollment in higher level subjects, but also on the senate district in which it was located. Literary funds were first divided among the districts and then among the institutions within a district. For this reason, Genesee Wesleyan Seminary actually received the second largest allotment of any institution in the state, even though it ranked third in the state in terms of enrollment.[46] Over the next few years, financial returns on Genesee Wesleyan's Regents status would increase further, due both to increased enrollment at the institution and increased funding from the state. By the late 1830s, seminary officials could legitimately say they had achieved their goal of rising "to a level of eminence unequalled by any other of its grade in the country."[47]

---

year was 314, compiled from the "Bulletins of Genessee Wesleyan Seminary," Account Book #170a, and for years when bulletins were not available, from "Report of the Trustees of Genesee Wesleyan Seminary to the Genesee Annual Conference, made September 14, 1844, Account Book #190, GWSC.

[46] *Report of the Regents of the University of the State of New York*, for the year 1837.

[47] "Catalogue of Genesee Wesleyan Seminary," 1834, p. 16.

17

Panic – Education and the Discipline of the Market

> ...the alarming crisis in which we have arrived in consequence of our pecuniary embarrassments requires immediate and vigorous action on the part of the Board....
>
> Special Trustee Meeting, Lima, December 26, 1837[1]

> I want you should write and let me know how my dear Father gets along with his Trouble.
>
> Letter from Frederick B. Warner to the Matthew Warner family, February 18, 1838[2]

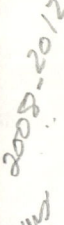

Even as the seminary achieved unrivaled success in raising subscriptions, recruiting students, and mobilizing political capital, it also confronted considerable financial challenges. These arose from the institution's high level of commercial indebtedness, on the one hand, combined with the difficulty of collecting the hundreds of smaller debts owed to the institution by students and subscribers, on the other. To manage the gap, the trustees regularly renewed a number of short-term bank notes. That method of managing the institution's finances worked as long as commercial lenders were willing to renew such loans. But all that changed in 1837. In March of that year, substantial failures in international credit markets precipitated a six-year depression known as the Panic of 1837.[3] Like many enterprises, Genesee Wesleyan found itself pressed by the demands of its commercial creditors, while unable to renew its short-term bank notes. Also like other enterprises, the seminary responded by pressing its debtors, tightening demands on subscribers and

---

[1] Special Trustee Meeting, Lima, December 26, 1837, Minutes of the Board of Trustees, Account Book #178, GWSC.

[2] Letter from Frederick B. Warner to the Matthew Warner family, February 18, 1838, Warner Papers, LHS.

[3] A blow-by-blow account of the Panic is provided by Bray Hammond, *Banks and Politics in America from the Revolution to the Civil War* (Princeton, NJ: Princeton University Press, 1957): 451–499.

parents who owed money on subscriptions or tuition bills, and initiating legal action against individuals who failed to pay. By December 1837, however, the trustees regarded the institution as in deep financial trouble. At a special meeting held December 26 to address "the alarming crisis in which we have arrived in consequence of our pecuniary embarrassments," they undertook "immediate and vigorous action."[4]

Meanwhile, other local enterprises also faced financial crisis. During 1835 and 1836, Matthew Warner had assumed the role of financier for a textile mill in the hamlet of West Bloomfield, on Lima's eastern border. Raising funds from a combination of local, regional, and metropolitan sources, he formed a partnership with two operators to establish a state-of-the art woolen manufactory. In May 1837, however, as a result of the Panic, the partners lost ownership of the mill and Matthew faced complete liquidation of his personal property.

To compare the fate of the local academy with that of the local textile mill is to learn much about the state of the economy at the end of the 1830s. Both cases illuminate the limits of the market revolution and capitalist transition at the time. Despite the rhetoric of market culture and efforts to enforce market discipline on the part of trustees, actual seminary accounts show that prompt payment of tuition and regular payments on subscriptions were the exception rather than the rule. Meanwhile, though banks and other commercial lenders contributed to economic development by investing capital in new forms of production such as textile mills, the brief history of the mill at West Bloomfield shows the inadequacy of the short-term credit they offered for the challenges such enterprises faced. While the two cases reveal the limits of the market, however, they also reveal the value of social networks and the significance of social institutions in the capitalist transition. In the case of the textile mill, local family and friendship networks went a long way toward saving the mill and its local investors from immediate financial ruin. In the case of the seminary, translocal social networks provided the institution with the means of redeeming politically what could not be redeemed on the market. Ultimately, however, the consequences of the Panic were quite different for the two enterprises. Although the trustees seriously contemplated the possibility of financial ruin at the end of 1837, the Panic eventually led to a consolidation of wealth and financial stability for the seminary. In contrast, local investors lost their stake in the local textile mill and bankruptcy eventually overtook the Warner family. Together, the two cases show how social institutions helped to mediate the transition to a capitalist market economy that otherwise did not yet fully exist.

"Pay as You Go" – The Rhetoric and Reality of Market Culture

At the end of 1836, the seminary had substantial commercial credit obligations. These included two relatively large, long-term loans used to cover capital costs,

---

[4] Special Trustee Meeting, Lima, December 26, 1837.

as well as a number of short-term loans from banks and individuals used to cover operating costs. Altogether, these debts required at least $1,400 a year in cash to pay interest. In addition, the institution had about $3,500 in annual salary costs and another $1,000 in miscellaneous other expenses, bringing the annual operating expenses to approximately $6,000 a year.[5] To meet these obligations, the institution had three main sources of income: tuition, subscription payments, and – after July, 1836 – Regents funding, which that year amounted to $241. From the first years of its operation, however, cash collections on tuition and subscription debts proved problematic. Throughout 1834, 1835, and 1836, seminary officials tried a number of measures aimed at improving collection rates, including special rhetorical pleading, new accounting procedures, collection agents, church discipline, and threats of legal action. A review of these efforts provides some insight into the state of market culture and discipline at the time.

In its catalog for 1834, the first to be published after Methodists gained full control of the institution, the trustees emphasized that the institution operated on a cash basis, and that payment of all fees was required quarterly and in advance of attendance. The timely payment of such fees, the bulletin suggested, was not simply institutional policy but constituted a moral imperative arising from a shared interest that true "friends" of the institution had in its success. Invoking a notion of "friendship" that apparently applied primarily to Methodists, the trustees admonished supporters to "continue their patronage, and inculcate among those who wish to enjoy the benefits of the institution, ... the importance of consulting its prosperity as well as their own interest, *by strictly adhering to the terms, in entering their children as students, and in making payment...*"[6]

In making this appeal, trustees of the institution drew on an already well-established rhetoric of market culture in the Methodist press. Beginning in the mid-1820s, Methodist periodicals regularly addressed issues of economy and credit within the church and in society at large. Admonishing youth to "pay as you go," *The Christian Advocate and Journal and Zion's Herald* warned in September 1829 that a habit of obtaining goods on credit would lead to

---

[5] "Treasurer's Book," #56, passim, and "Day Book," #102, pp. 260–303, GWSC. The figures reported here are compiled from a number of sources, including the running account of expenses in the "Treasurer's Book," a retrospective summary of various expenses that appears in the back pages of the "Day Book," and the texts of the annual reports the trustees were required to submit to the Regents after the institution acquired Regents status in 1836. The Regents did require that the institution report annual income and expenses in several categories, and these figures seem at least roughly congruent with the institution's own accounts, with the exception that with respect to indebtedness and interest payments the institution seems to have reported only on its formal, long-term commercial mortgage and charter house loans, not on any of its smaller loans from individuals or short-term loans from banks. As a result, these categories are significantly understated.

[6] "Catalogue of the Officers and Students of Genesee Wesleyan Seminary, Lima, New York, for the year ending July, 1834," p. 16. Bulletins of Genesee Wesleyan Seminary, Box 14, GWSC, *emphasis added*.

financial ruin. Rather than obtaining goods on credit, which was "sure to beget extravagance, and extravagance embarrassment and want," the wise youth would practice "paying for everything as it is purchased," a habit "sure to induce a rational economy in expenditures."[7]

Increasingly in the 1830s, one context for which the Methodist press promoted immediate cash payment was that of the church itself. Especially with respect to the collection of "quarterage," or the support of traveling preachers, the press advocated a more regular, cash-based model of payment than had been the norm. In a series of editorials beginning in 1829 and revived often thereafter, the *Advocate* promoted the practice of class leaders calling on class members on a weekly basis for cash payments on their church pledges instead of the quarterly payment of in-kind goods and services that often prevailed in rural areas. By the mid-1830s, some circuits in upstate New York, including Lima's local circuit, had ostensibly adopted such a system.[8] Similarly, Genesee Wesleyan Seminary tried to promote norms of commercial cash collection with its debtors. Yet, a close look at payment records shows that the practice of economic relations differed substantially from the rhetoric.[9]

In the case of Genesee Wesleyan, the trustees undertook a number of measures aimed at enforcing the principle of pay-as-you-go, including new accounting procedures. Although official policy had always been that tuition was due in advance of receiving instruction, in practice this had not occurred. After asking the principal, Samuel Luckey, to report on the collections of the "tuition department" in July 1834, the trustees determined that there were "tuition accounts unsettled in the amount of about $1200," a substantial sum when annual enrollment numbered just under 400 students and tuition for academic subjects was $3–5 per term.[10] To address the problem, the trustees established a committee to "fill out all the charges for tuition on Mr. Luckey's book into regular individual accounts and put them into the hands of the Treasurer."[11] Thereafter, the trustees resolved, the principal would be responsible for keeping both a day book, in which he recorded daily income and expenses, and separate debt account books for tuition in both the male and female departments.[12]

These efforts, too, were apparently ineffective, however. In December 1834, the trustees reiterated that "after the next vacation, no student [shall]

---

[7] *Christian Advocate and Journal and Zion's Herald,* September 18, 1829, Vol. 4, Issue 3, p. 12.
[8] "Bloomfield Circuit Book, Genesee Conference, 1828–1880," microfilm, CUDRMC.
[9] This statement about the practice of keeping class books is drawn from an examination of miscellaneous class books from several areas of upstate New York, including several from the city of Elmira, MMC.
[10] Minutes of the Board of Trustees, July 15, 1834; Bulletin of Genesee Wesleyan Seminary, 1834, pp. 14 and 20. Total enrollment in 1834 was 386 students. Tuition in common English studies was $3 per quarter and $5 for higher English or classical studies.
[11] Minutes of the Board of Trustees, July 15, 1834.
[12] Ibid.

be admitted to the institution without cash payment in advance or satisfactory security or endorsements on certificates in advance."[13] Again, the demand proved difficult to enforce. Perhaps in response to complaints from the principal regarding the burden of keeping accounts, the trustees resolved that a clerk be appointed to receive tuition money at the institution.[14] Seven months later, in July of 1835, the board announced yet another set of arrangements. In the future, the "steward" would collect tuition and teachers would be instructed "not to give lessons to any students until a certificate is furnished by them from the steward evidencing that their tuition bills are adjusted."[15]

As these repeated actions indicate, school officials had difficulty enforcing a principle of pay as you go. A factor that may have contributed was confusion surrounding subscription scholarships. According to the stated terms of the original joint stock arrangement, subscriptions were payable "one fourth within six months from the time of subscribing and the remainder in three equal installments thereafter."[16] For a $100 subscription, this meant that the subscriber should pay $25 six months after the date of subscription and another $25 annually each of three years thereafter. Left wholly unspecified was whether the use of tuition benefits depended on meeting these terms. Could a subscriber begin using benefits right away, whether or not he had paid anything on the subscription? In September of 1835 the trustees specified that subscribers could receive "six months gratuitous tuition when they shall have paid $12.50" or one-eighth the full cost of a subscription, and that they would receive additional tuition benefits "in the same proportion when larger sums are paid."[17] For every $12.50 paid, in other words, the subscriber received six months of free tuition.

Still, none of these clarifications of policy necessarily changed behavior. At their April 1836 meeting, the trustees considered methods of enforcing market discipline. In one case, they decided simply to turn the note over to an agent for further collection. In a second case, the trustees empowered the agent to "adjust" a note according to his discretion. In a third, the trustees determined to "adopt a disciplinary course" to collect a note, implying that the subscriber would be disciplined through the church. Similarly, in a fourth case, trustees decided to "furnish a complaint" against a debtor who happened to be a Methodist preacher, and to lodge that complaint with the minister's presiding elder. By contrast, in a fifth case, they decided to put the note "in a legal way for collection."[18]

As this set of decisions indicates, the church and the courts represented alternative methods of enforcement for payment of debts. In fact, according to official church policy, Methodists were *required* to turn to the church before

[13] Ibid., December 31, 1834.
[14] Ibid.
[15] Ibid., July 22, 1835.
[16] "Report of the Seminary Committee," 1830.
[17] Ibid., September 8, 1835.
[18] Ibid., April 5, 1836.

going to the courts to negotiate the payment of a debt by a Methodist church member. Moreover, if at anytime a member should "refuse to refer the matter to arbitration ... or shall enter into a law suit with another member before such measures are taken, he shall be expelled, unless the case be of such a nature as to require and justify a process at law."[19] Some scholars date the decline of church-enforced discipline in cases of debt to the late eighteenth century.[20] However, records from upstate New York show that churches did serve as alternatives to the courts in credit disputes well into the nineteenth century.[21] Nor were such practices unknown to Methodists in Lima. A surviving circuit book for Lima's own circuit shows that, in 1832, a committee heard a series of appeals in a credit dispute arising out of building the local Methodist chapel three years earlier.[22]

How effective the threat of such discipline was in forcing payment of debts depends on the standard of success. In the seminary case, agents clearly got more successful in their collection efforts in 1835 than they had been previously. In July of that year, agents began reporting collections of as much as $2,000 apiece in cash per quarter, as compared to just a few hundred dollars reported now and then in previous years. Altogether, the institution's agents collected about $4,000 a year on outstanding debts between April 1835 and October 1837 for a total of approximately $10,000 over two and a half years, a not insubstantial sum.[23] Measured in relation to previous collections, then, the effort to improve the institution's income on debt accounts was a success.

---

[19] *The Doctrines and Discipline of the Methodist Episcopal Church*, 22nd Edition (New York: N. Bangs and J. Emory, 1824): 40–42.

[20] Bruce Mann, *Republic of Debtors: Bankruptcy in the Age of American Independence* (Cambridge, MA: Harvard University Press, 2002): 260. In this book, Mann focuses on the development of early U.S. bankruptcy laws. For evidence of actual debt and collection practices he relies primarily on the papers of major creditors and financiers. Although such men no doubt were among the most influential in the development of bankruptcy law, there is "room to doubt," as Christopher Clark suggests, that the same "separation of economic calculation from moral considerations" prevailed at the popular level. Christopher Clark, "The Consequences of the Market Revolution in the Rural North," in Stokes and Conway, eds. *The Market Revolution in America: Social, Political, and Religious Expressions, 1800–1880* (Charlottesville: University of Virginia Press, 1996): 23–42. On debt, credit, and bankruptcy issues, see also Bruce Mann, *Neighbors and Strangers: Law and Community in Early Connecticut* (Chapel Hill: University of North Carolina Press, 1987); and Peter J. Coleman, *Debtors and Creditors in America: Insolvency, Imprisonment for Debt, and Bankruptcy, 1607–1900* (Madison: University of Wisconsin Press, 1974).

[21] Curtis D. Johnson, *Islands of Holiness: Rural Religion in Upstate New York, 1790–1860* (Ithaca, NY: Cornell University Press, 1989): 57 and 189–190. Johnson estimates that 7% of all church disciplinary cases in Cortland County, New York, pertained to commercial matters. It should be noted that the figure of 7% covers the whole period from 1801 to 1849; it is likely that cases of church discipline in commercial cases were more frequent before 1840 than after. Also, not all denominations were well represented among the surviving disciplinary records that Johnson examined. Methodist records were among those underrepresented.

[22] Bloomfield Circuit Book, April 1832.

[23] Figures compiled from the agents' reports recorded in Minutes of the Board of Trustees, 1835–1837.

It was not enough, however, to meet the challenges presented by the Panic of 1837, which threatened even highly capitalized enterprises like the seminary and the local textile mill with bankruptcy.

Capitalist Entrepreneurship and Commercial Credit Markets

In the years 1835 to 1837, Matthew Warner undertook a form of entrepreneurship that economic historians have regarded as pivotal to the capitalist transition. Drawing capital from multiple sources, he formed a partnership with two textile operators to establish a state-of-the-art woolen manufactory. At the time, the investment held the promise of bringing together all of Matthew's experiences and resources as a landholder, farmer, producer, trader, and financier. The factory would take the wool produced on his own and other farms and turn it into cloth on land the family owned at the old mill site on Honeoye Creek, known as West Bloomfield. The resulting cloth could then be sold locally or on New York markets, as some of Matthew's other commodities had been in the past. In economic terms, Matthew engineered a shift of rural capital from agricultural to nonagricultural production.

Matthew's partners in the enterprise, Amon Lamphere and Othaniel Gilbert, developed the textile mill in West Bloomfield from a local carding mill they already operated. Common in the United States since the early nineteenth century, power carding mills generally operated in communities where yarn and cloth production still took place at home. A family took its raw wool to a carding mill to be worked up into rolls and then took the rolls home to spin them into yarn and weave them into cloth.[24] The shift from a custom carding mill to a full-scale textile mill was a common form of business expansion in the 1820s and 1830s. A textile mill was a different order of business than a carding mill in a number of ways, however. For one thing, a textile factory required a larger inventory of equipment and higher capital investment than a carding mill. Instead of the $600 or $800 required to establish a small-scale carding operation, the average woolen manufacturer invested between $15,000 and $20,000.[25] Though still small by comparison with that of major cotton mills in Rhode Island and Massachusetts, this level of investment required an entrepreneur to go beyond local networks of merchants and landowners for financing.

---

[24] A good description of early carding operations and how they fit into local rural economies in both eastern and midwestern regions of the United States is provided by Norman L. Crockett, *The Woolen Industry of the Midwest* (Lexington: University Press of Kentucky, 1970): 3–17, 25–26, and 29. Other studies of the early wool industry include James Burnley, *The History of Wool and Woolcombing* (London: Sampson Low, Marston, Searle and Rivington, Ltd., 1889); Peter M. Molloy, *Homespun to Factory Made: Woolen Textiles in America, 1776–1876* (North Andover, MA: Merrimack Valley Textile Museum, 1977); *Wool Technology and the Industrial Revolution: an Exhibition* (North Andover, MA: Merrimack Valley Textile Museum, 1965).

[25] Crockett, *Woolen Industry*, pp. 25 and 31.

A textile mill also differed from a carding mill in its relationship to wool producers. Instead of engaging the carding mill as a service for their own production, farmers sold or traded their wool to the mill outright, relinquishing further interest in production. Because of the greater production capacity of a power loom operation, moreover, local households competed with farms from a broader area to sell or trade their wool. The average woolen factory consumed more than 20,000 pounds of wool a year and drew its supplies from an area extending fifty miles in any direction. Larger mills often used buying agents to obtain fleeces from a wider territory. Finally, in order to sustain production at a level sufficient to pay back investors, a full-scale textile factory had to go beyond the sporadic exchange of labor and services or the employment of live-in wards and apprentices that characterized production within a local exchange economy. The average woolen mill employed ten full-time laborers for nine to ten months a year. Larger mills employed twenty-five or more workers. To recruit and retain workers some mills developed household settlements specifically dedicated to millwork.[26]

The woolen textile mill at West Bloomfield was fairly large as compared with other nineteenth-century woolen mills. According to one historian of the industry, the average midwestern mill of 1870 owned five looms and two sets of carding machines.[27] By comparison, an 1836 inventory shows that Lamphere and Gilbert owned eight carding machines and twenty looms, a set of equipment that gave them as much as four times the production capacity of the average midwestern mill of a later era.[28] Although no employment records for the West Bloomfield mill survive, it is reasonable to conclude that the factory would require a labor force of at least forty people to operate its equipment at full capacity.[29] In addition, other workers would be required to clean and pick the raw wool, dye the yarn, and full the finished cloth. According to a local history, the factory employed sixty people at the height of its operation.[30] As indicated by its substantial inventory of equipment, Lamphere and Gilbert's factory was close to the cutting edge of both technological and business

---

[26] Ibid., pp. 54–72. The average size of manufacturing operations in the midwest is stated on p. 79; examples of operations are provided throughout. Crockett describes a few operations with 100 to 200 employees, but these cases all date from the very last decade of the nineteenth century (see p. 62, for example). For the period before the Civil War, the woolen factories specifically described by Crockett all seem to have employed fewer than 50 people.

[27] Ibid., p. 79.

[28] Inventory of equipment mortgaged to Elisha Eggleston of West Bloomfield, October 15, 1836. Item #196, Warner Papers, LHS.

[29] This estimate is based on a comparison of operations described by Crockett, *The Woolen Industry*; see especially p. 79.

[30] Mabel Furner Jenks, *Lima, 1788–1964: The Crossroads of Western New York, Outline of the History of Lima Written for the 175th Anniversary Celebration* (n.p., 1984 [1964]; available through the Lima Historical Society): 39. Unfortunately, Jenks cites no sources for her information. The relative precision of her statements suggests that she had sources of some kind, though no corresponding sources seem to survive in the collections of the Lima Historical Society.

development at the time. According to textile historian Peter Molloy, the early power looms that first appeared in the United States in 1815 were used only for cotton weaving because they were too harsh to be used with woolen yarn. It was the 1830s before power looms were adapted for use in woolen mills.[31]

To finance this expanded operation, Matthew Warner helped Lamphere and Gilbert raise capital from both private and institutional lenders in New York, Rochester, and elsewhere in the western country. It is difficult to know for sure who initiated the effort to expand. Although Lamphere and Gilbert assumed ownership of the factory and borrowed capital in their names, evidence suggests that Matthew was involved in the factory's financing from the beginning. A letter from Matthew to his brother Asahel written from New York City in May 1835 makes clear that the two brothers were trying to raise capital for something that Matthew obliquely referred to as "the business in which we are engaged." These efforts included the sale of certain "notes" and attempts to sell "the Norton land" located on or near the mill site.[32]

In soliciting capital directly on New York markets, Matthew ventured outside his ordinary circles of trade and influence. He and his brother had experience with land sales and mortgages, including Asahel's fifteen-year relationship with New York's leading mortgage lender, Isaac Bronson. But mortgage lending was an old and traditional business as compared with the entrepreneurial capitalism represented by textile manufacturing. The latter was not a business in which Bronson, a fiscal conservative, invested.[33] Moreover, the mortgage business with which the Warners were familiar occurred almost entirely by letter. It did not require the kind of personal visit to merchants and financiers that Matthew undertook in the spring of 1835. A sense of the unease Matthew felt in New York financial circles is suggested in his letter when he explained his inability to bring his business to a definitive conclusion. "Everybody is busy and cannot spare much time," he wrote. "It is hard doing anything with any of them." New York City lenders also proved less interested in discounting the promissory notes he offered than western New Yorkers had. "The notes are many of them sold to men in our country," Matthew explained to his brother. "I think, however, that we shall succeed in selling the Norton Land."[34]

In fact, Matthew does not appear to have succeeded in selling the land at this time. Despite these difficulties, however, the factory project achieved

---

[31] Molloy, p. 82.

[32] Letter from Matthew Warner in New York City to Asahel Warner of Lima, May 6, 1835, Item #48, Warner Papers, LHS.

[33] An analysis of the Bronson family's financial activities, investment philosophies, and policy perspectives is provided in John Denis Haeger, *The Investment Frontier: New York Businessmen and the Economic Development of the Old Northwest* (Albany: State University of New York Press, 1981). See also Grant Morrison, *Isaac Bronson and the Search for System in American Capitalism* (New York: Arno Press, 1978); and idem, "A New York City Creditor and His Upstate Debtors: Isaac Bronson's Moneylending, 1819–1836," *New York History* 61:3 (July 1980): 255–276.

[34] Letter from Matthew Warner in New York City, May 6, 1835.

a substantial level of capitalization as compared with other woolen mills. Eventually, Matthew helped Lamphere and Gilbert raise $30,000 in capital from at least seventeen different private lenders and several different banks. The resulting list of investors matches fairly well the description Matthew provided of the buyers of "notes" in his New York letter. Private lenders included one or two that the Warners explicitly identified in their papers as New York lenders, that is, "The New York Debt" and/or "B.V. Baker, New York." Others were merchants and money-lenders in the western country, with some of whom Matthew had had dealings in the past, such as William Parker, a merchant with whom Matthew had previously traded goods; Samuel Sibley, a merchant with whom Matthew had conducted legal business; and William Pitkin, a financial agent with whom Matthew had had dealings at Rochester Bank. Also among the pool of investors were several local householders with whom Matthew had ongoing relationships as neighbors, exchange partners, and fellow townsmen, including the merchant Erastus Clark, the lawyer Melancton Brown, property owner Anthony Yorks, and Elisha Eggleston, a landowner whose family had long operated a tavern in Lima.[35]

In the end, then, Warner, Lamphere, and Gilbert financed their venture with capital drawn from a combination of local, regional, and metropolitan sources. About one-third of their investment capital came from commercial banking institutions and private lenders in New York and other cities with little or no stake in the locality. Another third came from private lenders in western New York with connections to business in Lima. Finally, a last third came from local merchants and townsmen who presumably had some commitment to local development.

Potentially this mixture of funding sources had the virtue of infusing urban capital into a local development project while including enough local money to retain significant local influence and control. Unfortunately, however, the factory project linked households like Matthew Warner's not only to the greater availability of cash and credit in the early to mid-1830s, but also to the severe contraction of that availability in the Panic of 1837. The first signs of trouble appeared in October of 1836, when Lamphere and Gilbert mortgaged their equipment in a temporary agreement with a local townsman, Elisha Eggleston, for $10,750. Although Eggleston was a private money-lender and local resident, the terms of the mortgage loan were the same as those that might be offered for a short-term bank loan. Lamphere and Gilbert agreed to pay the full value of the loan, with interest, in three months' time. In case of default, the material in the inventory would be "liquidated."[36]

This loan occurred with the first tremors of the 1837 Panic. In New York and other major commercial cities, business failures began occurring in the last months of 1836. Textile operations, especially cotton manufacturers, were

[35] "Statement of Liability of Lamphere and Gilbert and Matthew B. Warner," West Bloomfield, May 19, 1838, Item #436, Warner Papers, LHS.
[36] Inventory of Equipment, October 15, 1836.

among the first to be affected as British banks cut off credit for buying cotton and the prices for finished cloth reportedly declined to rates below the cost of production. Domestic merchants and money-lenders who had invested in such establishments in turn responded by recalling their loans and credit.[37] The factory at West Bloomfield appears to have experienced a similar recall, perhaps from their New York lenders. To deal with this demand, the proprietors of the factory turned to local merchants and property owners like Elisha Eggleston and Erastus Clark, and then to short-term loans from local banks. If the downturn in the market had proved to be short term as well, this strategy might have worked. As time went on, however, credit continued to tighten and suits for loan repayment increased. Matthew had signed his name as surety agent to more than twenty different loans and promissory notes. At the end of May 1837, the month commonly identified as the height of the Panic, Lamphere and Gilbert were forced to surrender ownership of the factory, and Matthew Warner faced liquidation of virtually all the rural capital he had accumulated over forty years.[38]

Crisis Turned Political Opportunity

Like the textile mill, the seminary experienced a tightening of commercial credit in 1837. At a special meeting held December 26, 1837, to address the crisis, the trustees undertook a number of actions. They instructed the steward to "adhere strictly to the resolutions regarding collections of tuition," with pupils who neglected to comply to be dismissed. To assist in this matter, the trustees voted to "take legal measure for collecting in all such cases as [the agent] deemed expedient." They also authorized their agent to get the best he could get and to receive "uncurrant money when he cannot get that which is currant at his discretion [sic.]." Second, they voted to appeal to the state for relief – to consider "the expediency of petitioning the Legislature for an appropriation in favor of the Seminary." Third, they appealed to their Methodist constituency, voting to "publish notice of the present state and future prospects of the institution" in two Methodist periodicals, *The Auburn Banner* and the *Christian Advocate and Journal*.[39]

This appeal through Methodist periodicals at the end of 1837 indicates that the trustees glimpsed a political solution to Genesee Wesleyan's financial problems. A convergence of two developments in government and politics

---

[37] A blow-by-blow account of the Panic is provided in Bray Hammond, *Banks and Politics in America: From the Revolution to the Civil War* (Princeton, NJ: Princeton University Press, 1957): 451–499. See also James Roger Sharp, *The Jacksonians versus the Banks: Politics in the States after the Panic of 1837* (New York: Columbia University Press, 1970).

[38] Some of the terms of this arrangement are discussed in "Letter from Richard L. Clark to Matthew Warner with advice regarding his claims as surety agent," May 23, 1837, Item #57, and in a variety of other items in Warner Papers, LHS.

[39] Special Trustee Meeting, Lima, December 26, 1837, and Trustee Meeting, January 23, 1838, Minutes of the Board of Trustees, Account Book #178, GWSC.

offered a reason for hope. The first of these, initiated before the Panic, involved the distribution of income from federal funds. The second, a direct consequence of the Panic, involved shifting politics at both the state and federal levels. In response to the Panic, Jacksonian Democrats had been swept from many offices at the state level in the fall 1837 elections.[40] With the Whigs in power for the first time in the Assembly, Methodist constituencies and western regions of the state gained new leverage in state politics. At the same time, the state had come into a major influx of capital from the federal government, the income of which was likely to be used to support education.

In 1836, while Andrew Jackson was still in the White House, the federal government experienced a substantial budget surplus. In accordance with Jackson's commitment to limited government at the federal level, Congress voted in June 1836 to return the surplus to the states in the form of "deposits" in proportion to the states' respective proportions in the Senate and House of Representatives. These "deposits" of federal funds were to be transferred in four equal parts in the year 1837, beginning in January and continuing through October. Because of the earlier decision of the Jackson administration to veto renewal of the Second National Bank of the United States, many of these funds were already in state banks. Ostensibly, these federal funds were on "deposit" and thus liable to eventual recall by the federal government. In practice, however, such funds became a source of permanent capital for use by the states. Most states, like New York, devoted some or all of the income on such capital to support of education.[41]

In April 1838, the New York State Legislature passed "An Act to appropriate the income of the United States deposit fund to the purposes of education and the diffusion of knowledge."[42] The act specified three different types of allocation, two for common schools and one for "higher" schooling. With respect to common schools, the act allocated an annual sum of $110,000 in interest income to school districts for teacher salaries and another $55,000 for district libraries.[43] Meanwhile, for "higher" schooling, the law made two kinds of provisions, one for colleges and another for academies. For academies, the legislature allocated a total of $28,000 in interest income to be distributed on an annual per pupil basis, through the same Regents system that

---

[40] Dixon Ryan Fox, *The Decline of Aristocracy in the Politics of New York* (New York: Columbia University Press, 1918): 402 and 381–439, passim.

[41] In some states, such as Massachusetts, the provision of federal deposit funds became the occasion for establishing a new system of state funding for schools and academies that had theretofore operated entirely on local taxes and tuition or rate bills. In New York, by contrast, the law had the effect of strengthening existing systems of school funding. See Chapter 8 and Fletcher Harper Swift, *A History of Permanent Common School Funds in the United States, 1795–1905* (New York: Henry Holt and Co., 1911).

[42] "An Act to appropriate the income of the United States deposit fund to the purposes of education and the diffusion of knowledge, Passed April 17, 1838" *Laws of New York*, 61st Session, Chap. 237 (Albany: State of New York, 1839): 220–223.

[43] Ibid.

distributed shares of the existing Literature Fund. In addition, the Regents made substantial allocations to individual colleges. Altogether, the legislature allocated a total of $165,000 annually for common schools, $28,000 for academies, and $15,000 a year for several years to individual colleges.[44]

The seminary was in an outstanding position to take advantage of this development. In particular, as a result of its high student enrollment, the seminary stood to enjoy a substantial increase in per pupil funding for academies. In 1837, the academy had enrolled a total of 314 students, 183 of whom were eligible for per pupil funding from the state, at a rate of $3.34 per student. For the year 1838, the academy enrolled a total of 421 students, 235 of whom were eligible for per pupil funding at a rate of $7.58 per student, more than double the rate of the pervious year.[45] Altogether Genesee Wesleyan received a total of $1,783 from the state, the largest total amount of Regents funding awarded to any institution that year, and enough to cover 54 percent of the seminary's total salary costs for ten teachers.[46] After 1838, the per pupil funding Genesee Wesleyan received per student began to decline as the total number of academies and eligible students increased for the state as a whole. Nonetheless, Genesee Wesleyan's share of total state funds continued to rank among the highest due to its large enrollment. In 1839, Genesee Wesleyan would enroll the largest number of Regents students of any academy in the state, a position it maintained off and on into the 1850s.[47]

Capitalizing on its position, the seminary board went one step further, and in January 1839 it made a special application for additional funds. Again the trustees may have been inspired by a re-assessment of their political situation. In the recent November elections the Whigs had again gained seats in the legislature. At the opening of the new Whig-controlled Assembly on January 1, 1839, the members chose as speaker none other than a representative from Lima's own Livingston County, George W. Patterson.[48] At a special meeting of Genesee Wesleyan's Board of Trustees just two days later, members of the seminary's board drafted a memorial to the legislature requesting a special appropriation and voted to ask Patterson to act as one of its three "agents" in the matter. Four months later, agents reported "that success had so far crowned the exertions of the committee as to procure the passage of an act authorizing a loan of ten thousand dollars for the term of ten years at six per cent."[49] Although it would take nearly a year for the trustees to actually receive the money, the seminary had effectively survived its financial crisis. Eventually, in 1843, the state converted its $10,000 loan into a series of grants,

---

[44] Ibid.
[45] *Report of the Regents of the University of the State of New York*, for the years 1837 and 1838.
[46] Ibid., for the year 1838.
[47] Ibid., for the years 1838–1860.
[48] Jabez D. Hammond, *The History of Political Parties in the State of New York*, Vol. II (Albany: C. Van Benthuysen, 1842): 504.
[49] Minutes of the Board of Trustees, May 5, 1839.

permanently freeing the institution from the commercial debt incurred during its initial capitalization.

One way to explain the substantial financial success of the seminary in the aftermath of the Panic of 1837 is to say that it was the right kind of institution in the right place at the right time. The seminary's success was not merely accidental, however. To acquire the Regents status that made the institution eligible for state funding and to win its appeal for a special appropriation, the seminary mobilized the political power of its networks to lobby the state legislature. To achieve high levels of student enrollment, the seminary not only recruited students through its powerful organizational structure, but continued to raise and redeem the subscription scholarships that awarded free tuition to subscribers. To meet its annual operating costs, especially the costs of faculty salaries and interest on commercial loans, the seminary simultaneously expanded its commercial capitalization and appealed to subscribers, parents, and students as Methodists to pay their debts to the institution. Finally, and perhaps most importantly, to frame the sense of common purpose and commitment that made it possible to mobilize students, funding, and political support for its endeavors, the seminary drew not only on the structure of Methodism but on the culture of Methodism – on the shared experience, norms, and identity shaped by the Methodist *Discipline* and promoted through a strong Methodist press. To achieve financial stability, in other words, the seminary drew on social, political, and cultural capital. By comparison, capitalist enterprises like the textile mill in West Bloomfield had much less to call on.

Bankruptcy

Although the terms of bankruptcy were somewhat unsettled in the 1830s, New York had established some procedures for debtor relief.[50] In May 1837, Lamphere and Gilbert worked out an agreement with their creditors that looked much like a bankruptcy settlement, with the important exception that it did not offer the protection of legal indemnity against future claims. What Lamphere and Gilbert did was surrender ownership of the factory to their creditors in lieu of immediate payment of their debts. The factory itself continued to operate with Lamphere and Gilbert as managers rather than proprietors. Proceeds of the sales were then returned to the factory's creditors in proportion to their shares of ownership in the company and deducted from the debts owed to them. In effect, then, the creditors became investors in the factory as a business corporation. At the same time, the locus of ownership in the factory shifted. Instead of consisting of a few local residents, owners became a mixture of locals and outsiders.[51]

---

[50] Coleman, *Debtors and Creditors*.
[51] This arrangement is described in the Letter from Richard Clark, May 23, 1837 and further illuminated by the later "Deed from Erastus Hanchett to Matthew Warner for land which Warner sold to Hanchett in May, 1837," dated May 1840, Item #78, Warner Papers, LHS.

A lawyer advised Matthew Warner against participating in this agreement. As surety agent, the lawyer explained, Matthew himself should have first claim to property held by Lamphere and Gilbert. He should not agree to share that right with anyone else.[52] Whether Matthew chose to ignore this advice, found himself out-maneuvered, or believed that a share in the enterprise would eventually be more profitable is unclear. Treated as one of a number of Lamphere and Gilbert's creditors, Matthew acquired a one-twelfth share in "the land, building and appurtenances formerly owned by Lamphere and Gilbert" and in the factory's "apparatus, machinery and stock."[53] Meanwhile, however, Matthew remained subject to claims from the factory's other creditors.

The consequences of this development for Matthew and his family were both immediate and protracted. Within a very short time, from May 1835 to May 1837, Matthew went from serving as a conduit for the infusion of outside capital and power into the local community to trying desperately to prevent outside banks and private lenders from sucking out of him and his family all that he and his household, with the help of neighbors, had labored to produce over the previous forty years. Recognizing the seriousness of the situation, Matthew took pre-emptive measures. In a May 27, 1837 agreement he transferred all his personal property to two local townsmen, Seth Johnson and Erastus Hanchett. This included "all goods, wares, merchandise, debts, furniture, waggons, oxen, swine, etc. of Matthew Warner." According to the agreement, the property was transferred "for sale to pay off all debts, including those which may be legally chargeable against him on account of having become surety for Lamphere and Gilbert or any other person."[54] In a separate agreement Matthew also transferred a large amount of land and his share in the factory company to Hanchett. The idea was to avoid the slow whittling away of his property that would occur if he were forced to settle one claim at a time. Without actually declaring bankruptcy, he put himself in the position of invoking bankruptcy and forcing a single blanket settlement should he need it. This gamble rested, among other things, on the trust that his neighbors would hold onto the property until otherwise directed, or until he could reclaim it himself. In fact, the property was not sold, and Matthew's land and share in the factory company were eventually returned to him.

Despite the partial success of this maneuver, however, Matthew and his family experienced a sense of crisis. This experience was conveyed by one of Matthew's sons, Frederick Warner. In a letter to his family written in February 1838, Frederick discussed his father's declared interest in emigrating from New York State to start over on the Michigan frontier. He also made

---

[52] Letter from Richard Clark, May 23, 1837.
[53] "Deed from Erastus Hanchett to Matthew Warner," May 1840.
[54] "Contract transferring to Seth Johnson and Erastus Hanchett all goods, wares, mechanary [sic], debts, furniture, waggons, oxen, swine, etc. of M. Warner for sale and to pay off all debts....," May 27, 1837, Item #56, Warner Papers, LHS; also see reference in "Deed from Erastus Hanchett to Matthew Warner," May 1840.

clear that he and his father had fully expected the family's personal property to have been sold by the time of the letter. Sent to Michigan to scout out prospects for possible relocation of his parents, as well as to make his own way on a new frontier, Frederick asked his siblings to "write and let me know how my dear Father gets along with his Trouble," and went on to say "I feel very sorry to hear that they have sold Father's personal property." What most affected Frederick about news of his father's losses, however, was that it made him "think of my situation." In describing the conditions he encountered in Michigan, Frederick captured something of the difficulties of the time. "I told you that I thought we should not see such hard times but the prospect is very much turned. The Canada wave has made a great overturning in this country. As respects provision, it is very hard to get because there is so much bad money here."[55] Conditions worsened over the course of 1838 so that in December Frederick described he and his family as "in a state of starvation." "I have been under the necessity of selling my team to feed my family," Frederick explained. "May the God of the universe bless you all" for "clothing the destitute."[56]

For Matthew as well, conditions continued to be dire. Throughout 1837 creditors of the factory continued to press their claims in court. By the end of the year, Matthew and the factory's proprietors had at least twelve major judgments against them. In May of 1838, one year after Lamphere and Gilbert had divided ownership of the mill among its creditors, a statement of the liabilities of the three men showed $29,056.00 in debts still outstanding.[57] At the same time as Matthew and his family lived under the threat of total bankruptcy, however, the factory itself went into full operation. Matthew himself seems to have served as a kind of buying agent, acquiring wool not only from local farms but from farmers elsewhere in central and western New York. Throughout this period, Matthew retained at least an indirect interest in its operations. In September of 1838, for example, a farmer from the town of Cayuga, New York, some 60 miles to the east of Lima, wrote to Matthew offering to supply him with 1,300 pounds of wool on time.[58] Later this same farmer became a major creditor of Matthew's.

Eventually, by maintaining production and sales, Lamphere and Gilbert managed to pay off more than $12,000 in debts over two years to individual investors, so that the total debt stood at just over $17,000 in 1840.[59] Of this

---

[55] Letter from Frederick B. Warner, February 18, 1838.
[56] Letter from Frederick B. Warner to Matthew and Huldah Warner, December 3, 1838, Item #206, Warner Papers, LHA. .
[57] "Statement of Liabilities," May 19, 1838, Item #436, Warner Papers, LHS.
[58] Letter from L. Willard of Cayuga, New York, to Matthew Warner, Esq., September, 25, 1838, Warner Papers, LHS.
[59] This analysis of the partners' debt payments is based on a comparison of Statement of Liabilities, May 1838, Item #436; Statement of Notes to be Settled, 1840, Item #174; and Notice of Paid Judgments, 1840, Item #433, Warner Papers, LHS.

remaining amount, about $9,000 was owed to banks and $8,000 to individuals. At this point the eventual retirement of the debts may have seemed within reach. In May of 1840, Matthew reclaimed the land and share in the factory company he had transferred to Erastus Hanchett and enlisted the aid of his brothers Asahel and William and his sons William and Orson in securing a mortgage to pay some of the judgments against him.[60] Drawing on his brother Asahel's long-term financial relationship with the Bronson family of New York City, Matthew and his sons and brothers mortgaged $8,000 worth of property to the Bronson sons, Oliver and Arthur, and applied the resulting funds to the payment of $6,000 in bank debt and $2,000 to individuals. To cancel the debts, the Warners' simply signed over the outstanding notes and had the Bronsons pay them directly in New York.[61] At this point, a reasonable person might have supposed the worst fallout of the Lamphere and Gilbert affair to have passed and the prospects for the Warners' financial recovery to have permanently improved. This prediction would have failed in anticipating a deciding event, however: the death of Matthew Warner in June of 1841.

The Economic Significance of Social Capital

A comparative analysis of the financing of the local textile mill and the academy reveals important differences. The first important difference was the largely noncommercial character of the seminary's initial capitalization. Unlike the entrepreneurs of the textile mill, who borrowed capital to acquire production equipment and facilities, the seminary covered three-quarters of the costs of its initial land purchase and building construction through local subscriptions. These subscriptions served as a kind of noncommercial capital. In the tradition of social economy and debt-accounting they were applied directly against land and building costs, without any associated interest.

The second important difference was the long-term nature of the seminary's first major commercial loans. In addition to Warner's $5,000 mortgage loan, dated August 1831, the institution received a $4,000 loan from the Methodist-affiliated Charter Fund in Philadelphia in 1832. The relatively long-term nature of these two loans meant that for the first few years, while the seminary completed construction, enrolled its first students, and acquired its first corporate charter, it did not have to face the prospect of either paying or renewing major loans. By contrast, the textile mill, which relied on short-term capital for its initial capitalization, was forced into delinquency before it ever had the chance to produce its first goods for market.

---

[60] Deed from Erastus Hanchett to Matthew Warner for land that Warner had sold to Hanchett three years earlier, May 1840, Item #78, Warner Papers, LHS.

[61] Bond for $8,000 for payment to Oliver and Arthur Bronson of New York City, August 6, 1840, Item #42; Mortgage for $4,000 to Oliver and Arthur Bronson, marked "Exhibit H," Item #79; Receipt for $4,000 from Matthew Warner, Item #296; and List of notes signed over to be paid by Oliver and Arthur Bronson, Item #433, Warner Papers, LHS.

If these had been the only differences between the two enterprises, however, their fates might have been much the same. The third major difference was the joint stock association, which provided the seminary with substantial additional capital, both financial and political. A retroactive analysis of the seminary's accounts shows that the financial value of the stock was limited. The process of collection on Methodist subscriptions occurred over a period of twelve years, from November 1831 through September 1843. Although subscribers occasionally made payments in amounts of $12.50 or $25.00 in accordance with the institution's official policy, these were rare exceptions. Payments came in many amounts: 50 cents, $1.50, $3, $8, and up. In some cases payments did not begin until three to six years after the time of subscription. In other cases payments extended over a six- to twelve-year period. In most cases (55%) the full value of the subscription was never realized, and in a quarter of cases (25%) no payment was ever received on the pledge. Together, over the twelve-year period, from 1831 to 1843, agents of the seminary collected a total of about $24,000 in cash on the joint stock subscriptions, or about 44 percent of the face value. If costs of collection are factored in – that is, agents' salaries and travel costs – the proportion of face value realized is substantially lower, just 30 percent.[62]

These slow and relatively low rates of collection confirm the limits of a cash-based economy at the time. Despite the pervasive rhetoric of "pay as you go" both within and beyond the culture of the church, despite the threat of church discipline and court action to enforce payment, and despite the dedicated efforts of two full-time agents, the seminary succeeded in collecting substantially less than half its subscription debt – and then only over an extended period. Clearly the development of market discipline and culture was still incomplete. If the financial value of Methodist subscription stock was limited, however, the political value was substantial. The same network of thousands of small debtors throughout western New York who failed to honor fully their subscription and tuition debts provided the institution with a strong political base from which to claim shares of state funds. By drawing on these networks the seminary redeemed politically what could not be redeemed on the market.

From the perspective of a fully integrated capitalist market economy, the fact that the seminary had to draw on political resources to redeem the value of its initial capital might be regarded as an institutional weakness. But to view the case this way is to misunderstand – or to miss altogether – the significance of social institutions in the capitalist transition. Many enterprises claimed thousands of dollars of capital that could never be realized. Agents of such enterprises often threatened to sue for payment, and the power to take such debts to court was an important factor driving the application for corporate

[62] Collection rates on the more than 1,200 joint stock subscriptions raised between September 1830 and September 1837 were determined by compiling the amount and proportion collected on each individual account recorded in Account Book #59, pp. 30–302, GWSC.

status by "body politics." But blood can't be squeezed from a stone. In the volatile conditions of the Jacksonian era – a product on the one hand of the furious undertaking of so many new enterprises and, on the other, of change in the norms of debt and credit relations – there were infinitely more legally enforceable claims for payment than there were means of satisfying them. To imply that enterprises would have been more successful *if commercial capital had been more available and market discipline had been more complete* is to beg the whole question of how that transition occurred. Institutions like Genesee Wesleyan contributed to the process of economic integration precisely by drawing on resources that mere commerce could not command. By using Methodist organizational power, invoking Methodist loyalty, enlisting Methodist periodicals, enforcing Methodist discipline, and most of all by converting social capital into political capital, institutions like Genesee Wesleyan helped to forge a capitalist market economy and culture that otherwise did not yet fully exist.

18

Friends – An Education in Trust

> We are under such straits as never before presented to us, being far from any friend.
>
> Letter from Frederick B. Warner to the Matthew Warner family, February 18, 1838[1]

> Who are willing to think themselves friendless in this changing life? Surely no one in their senses.
>
> Diary of Clarissa Pengra, April 1839[2]

In the six years following the Panic of 1837, the market taught many lessons. For some youth, including Matthew Warner's son, Frederick, the demise of personal and family fortunes occasioned by the Panic led to despair. For others, including another of Matthew's sons, A. J. Warner, the same events led to a new life rooted less in rural production and more in the trade of goods and services on the market. Education helped youth like A. J. negotiate that transition. It provided not only the instrumental knowledge necessary to the work of a teacher or clerk but also an initiation into the social norms and networks of a mobile middle class. At institutions like Genesee Wesleyan, men and women forged connections with youth from a wide geographic region, with some of whom they became "friends." "Friends" were valuable as a source of advice regarding important life choices. They also provided links to new opportunities and eased the transition to life in a new place. In these ways, friends could help bridge the experience of social and geographic dislocation common in a mobile society. As the Genesee Wesleyan student Clarissa Pengra put the point in 1839, "Who is willing to think themselves friendless in a changing life? Surely no one in their senses."[3]

---

[1] Letter from Frederick B. Warner to Matthew and Huldah Warner, February 18, 1838, Item #264, Warner Papers, LHS.
[2] Diary of Clarissa Pengra, identified as "Livingston and Onondaga County Woman's Diary, 1838–1842," April 1839, Microfilm #6230, CUDRMC. I have identified the woman as Clarissa Pengra.
[3] Ibid.

This chapter considers the meaning of education in a transforming economy. To establish oneself in society had always required the trust, patronage, and credit of friends and family. And yet, in the boom and bust economy of the 1830s and 1840s, when towns, businesses, and fortunes rose and fell with great rapidity, and when just a third of a town's population endured in the same place from one decade to the next, it could be difficult to know who one's friends were. Many watched as neighbors, relatives, and friends left for points further west. Others, like Frederick Warner, made the move themselves. In some cases migrants disappeared for good, successfully settled in a new territory or lost to illness, death, or a continual chain of migration. In other cases, migrants returned, but without the property, security, and hope they had lost to the hazards of speculation and the hardships of frontier life. The challenge for youth like Clarissa, Frederick, and A. J. was to acquire social and cultural capital that retained value through misfortune and transcended time and space.[4] Education offered the prospect of meeting that challenge.

The Hazards of a Changing Life

The Panic of 1837 taught the value of trust and friendship. It was a lesson learned through both positive and negative experiences. In the case of Matthew Warner, family and friends more than once cooperated to help him secure his property against the claims of outside creditors. When Matthew died in 1841, however, there was little they could do to prevent the loss of capital that he had accumulated with their help over the previous forty years. Ultimately, the Panic effected a shift of economic power from inside to outside the community. In other words, it taught both the value of friendship and its limits in a transforming economy.

When Matthew Warner died in 1841, the administrators of his estate undertook a final settlement of his accounts. This meant going through all of Matthew's papers and account books, totaling up debts and credits with each of his local and distant exchange partners, and making the final payment or collection necessary to balance each account. Since Matthew's debts clearly would not be satisfied with cash on hand, his personal property was put up for sale at public auction in November 1841.[5]

---

[4] For a good discussion of comparative rates of persistence and geographic mobility within local town populations, see Don Harrison Doyle, *The Social Order of a Frontier Community: Jacksonville, Illinois, 1825–70* (Urbana: University Illinois Press, 1979): 93–97 and 261–271. Doyle's analysis indicates that persistence rates (the proportion of a town's population in one census that appears again in the town's census the following decade) ranged widely from 20% to 50% depending on the size, location, and age of town. (Frontier communities had lower persistence rates.) Rates for the frontier community of Jacksonville were 27% for the period from 1850 to 1860 and 21% for the period from 1860 to 1870.

[5] Publication Notice, estate of Matthew B. Warner, August 11, 1841, Surrogate Court Records, Book 5, p. 380; Settlement Papers, estate of Matthew B. Warner, November 4, 1841, p. 465; and Schedules A, B, and C, Inventory, January 6, 1842, Surrogate Court, LCCO.

The story of Matthew's rise and demise as a financier and entrepreneur illuminates the dynamics of commercial expansion from a local perspective. For forty years Matthew and his brother Asahel had assumed leading roles in the political, economic, and cultural life of the town of Lima. They had begun by establishing a stronghold of local land ownership and had quickly gone on to take initiative in virtually every congregational effort, political action, educational endeavor, and construction project in town. The Warners had represented their neighbors in state and county offices and had negotiated relationships for the town with outside agencies. From this perspective, Matthew's investment in the woolen factory was another in a long line of efforts to develop local resources and institutions, to create a town life with a full range of production capacities as well as of educational opportunities and church affiliations. As an entrepreneur, Matthew expressed a geographic loyalty combined with personal opportunism characteristic of his time. He had courted New York lenders and solicited capital on New York markets, but he had done so to invest in a local factory that used the produce of local farms and employed the labor of local families. Potentially, at least, the woolen manufactory could have renewed and reinforced local social networks by injecting new sources of credit into exchange relationships and providing new possibilities for production and exchange. In fact what happened, however, was that it facilitated a shift in the locus of economic power from inside to outside the locality.

To consider the process of commercial development from this perspective is also to appreciate the significance of local friendship and exchange networks. For forty years Matthew produced and acquired goods through long-term social relationships as well as through the market. He traded apples and cider, butter and wool, wheat and pasturage for furniture, wagons, labor, and tools. At death, however, Matthew and his family lost these goods through a sudden reversal of this lifelong social process. Once his neighbors had helped him dig irrigation ditches and raise chimneys. Now they helped his family alienate his property and turn it into the cash to pay his debts to strangers.

Where would Mathew have been without this network of friends and family? His son Frederick helps us to imagine this possibility. Unlike his parents and his aunts and uncles, who had migrated to Lima more than forty years earlier with an extended network of relatives and a wealth of resources in land and access to capital, Frederick ventured west to Michigan with minimal resources and few connections except those with his own wife and children. In his letters Frederick remarked on the difficulties of this experience in the wake of the 1837 Panic, writing in February 1838 that things were hard, very hard, much harder than he had expected. Adding to the conditions of physical and financial hardship in Frederick's account, however, was a condition that he described as one of friendlessness. Chastising his siblings for failing to write and forgetting that they had "a brother in the wilderness," Frederick went on to express the despair he felt over his situation. "It seems to me that I am an outcast to all friends and relations in this world, but may that good Lord and Redeemer preserve me in all my affliction. We are under such straits as never before presented to us being far from any friend."[6]

The Instrumental Economic Value of Education

In this context, education had some instrumental value. While Frederick Warner struggled to make a home on the Michigan frontier, his younger brother, Andrew Jackson Warner, studied at the local academy. Tuition receipts and institutional records show that despite (or perhaps because of) his father's financial difficulties, A. J., as he was known, managed to continue his education at Genesee Wesleyan for at least a month or so in the winter of 1837–1838 and again in 1839. Like most students in this era, both male and female, A. J. attended school for only short periods, alternating school attendance with seasonal labor. Eventually, however, A. J.'s experience at the academy became a point of departure from farm life to town life and commercial occupation. Although he had labored on a farm for much of his youth, A. J. Warner became an independent music teacher rather than a farmer.[7]

Teaching was a common route to new ways of life. For one thing, it offered a means of combining paid labor with continued education. Males in particular could alternate winter teaching with periods of seasonal farm labor and higher school attendance. This point is amply illustrated by the experience of one male diarist of the late 1840s and 1850s, who stated straight out that "I attend school winters; my assistance being required summers on the farm." In fact this diarist, Eli Rogers, worked on a number of farms, hiring himself to a Mr. Adams in the fall of 1848 at the age of sixteen and to a Mr. Browning the ensuing summer, attending a district school in the winter in between, and attending Alfred Academy in the fall of 1849. He then taught district school in the winter of 1850, attended the academy in 1851, taught common school again in the winter of 1852, and then taught in several "writing schools" before returning again to the academy as a student in the fall of 1854 at the age of twenty-two.[8] In Eli's case academy attendance and school teaching were both occupations initially combined with farm work, with teaching eventually helping to pay for further education.

Although Eli's ultimate adult occupation is unknown, the similar early trajectory of Genesee Wesleyan's most famous student, Henry Raymond, is suggestive of some possibilities. As a youth Henry, like Eli, combined academy attendance with common school teaching and work on his family's farm, enrolling in Genesee Wesleyan over a period of three years, from 1832 to 1835.

---

[6] Letter from Frederick B. Warner, February 18, 1838.
[7] "Receipt of A.J. Warner," June 7, 1838 [Wrb 117], Warner Papers, LHS; "Bulletin of Genesee Wesleyan Seminary, 1839," GWSC; newspaper article, "The Warner Centennial Celebration," *Lima Recorder*, June 28, 1894.
[8] "Diary of Eli Rogers," Library, NYSHA.

After leaving the seminary as a student, Henry taught school in the town of Wheatland, twenty miles away, the hometown of a friend he had made at the seminary, Alexander Mann. Eventually, at the urging of the same friend, Henry determined to go to college. By mortgaging the family farm his father managed to send him to the University of Vermont. From there Henry went to New York City, worked for Horace Greeley at the *Herald Tribune,* and eventually became a founder and longtime editor of the *New York Times.*[9]

Young women also taught school and attended academies as ways of making lives for themselves. If anything, the combination of school teaching and academy attendance proved more valuable for women, who could by this means pursue something of a career, as they could not in any other field. Evidence suggests that in the field of teaching women were rewarded for years of education and experience. At Genesee Wesleyan, the education and experience of head female teachers sometimes exceeded that of male members of the faculty; and occasionally their salaries also approached those of male colleagues.[10] Though such success was not easy to achieve, women who began teaching in common schools or as assistants in large institutions had an incentive to acquire the education necessary to establish successful schools of their own or to work as senior teachers at academies.[11]

Clarissa Pengra was among the many young women who pursued education on this model. Clarissa attended Genesee Wesleyan over a period of three years, from 1834 to 1836. There she studied the principles of teaching, among other subjects, becoming an assistant teacher at the academy in 1837. After leaving the academy, Clarissa taught school for a year in the nearby town of Avon in 1839. She then went on in 1840 to teach in the more competitive school market of Syracuse, New York. As a woman in her twenties who already had teaching experience and two to three years of academy education, Clarissa at that time already exceeded the qualifications of the vast majority of common school teachers, especially in rural areas. For her, the move to a city school represented occupational mobility.[12]

Although much less evidence has been collected on connections between education and careers in fields other than teaching, it is likely that academy

---

[9] Augustus Maverick, *Henry J. Raymond and the New York Press* (Hartford, CT: A. S. Hale and Company, 1870): 13–27.

[10] Kim Tolley and Nancy Beadie, "Socio-Economic Incentives to Teach in New York and North Carolina: Toward a More Complex Model of Teacher Labor Markets, 1800–1850," *History of Education Quarterly* 46:1 (Feb. 2006): 36–72.

[11] This pattern was first explored by Anne Firor Scott in her study of the careers and life histories of alumnae of Emma Willard's school: Scott, "The Ever-Widening Circle: The Diffusion of Feminist Values from the Troy Female Seminary, 1822–1972," *History of Education Quarterly* 19 (Spring 1979): 3–24. It is reinforced by the data collected by Polly Welts Kaufman on women who had gone west to teach through Catharine Beecher's placement organization: Kaufman, *Women Teachers on the Frontier* (New Haven, CT: Yale University Press, 1984).

[12] Diary of Clarissa Pengra.

attendance helped students to improve their prospects in other occupations as well, especially as clerks in stores, merchant houses, banks, and land offices, and as navigators and surveyors. The experience of another academy student, Sidney Roby, is suggestive. At the age of fourteen, Sidney began attending an academy in the town of Brockport, New York, northwest of Lima. While there he studied a typical array of "higher" subjects, including Latin and English grammar and math and sciences, continuing at the school for most of three years. Sidney eventually left the academy in 1846 and took a position as a clerk in a saddlery store in New York City. Although this position probably came to Sidney through a family connection, his relatively steady attendance at the academy for three years distinguished him from most academy students, not to mention most youth of his age. In effect, his attendance at the academy helped to qualify him for the New York apprenticeship that provided his real education in business. In 1853 Sidney concluded his training in New York City and returned to upstate New York to establish his own store.[13]

As Sidney's experience suggests, a combination of academy study and work may have been more important than academy education itself for occupational advancement. In this respect, the flexibility with which academies accommodated students' discontinuous attendance patterns facilitated mobility. In a letter to A. J. Warner, a former academy student named William Graves made the value of this flexibility explicit. "Why in hell don't you go into a store or office or something of the kind?" Graves wrote in May 1838. "Don't always be going to school." Speaking from his own position as a bank clerk, Graves explained that school attendance was most useful when interspersed with work. "After you have been in a store for a year or two" he advised, "you can then go to school and learn more than you have before."[14]

Education and Social Networking

The instrumental economic value of academy attendance as a means of occupational mobility was only one dimension of its significance. Another important dimension was social. The diaries and correspondence of academy students like Clarissa Pengra and A. J. Warner reveal that academy attendance expanded students' social networks and conferred social credentials that could help them make "friends" across localities. In 1834, the second year of Genesee Wesleyan's operation and the first year Clarissa attended the institution, the seminary enrolled a total of 376 students. Of these, only 63, or 17 percent, claimed Lima as their hometown. Five years later, in 1839, when A. J. Warner attended the academy, enrollment totaled 475 and the proportion of local students had increased slightly but remained less than a quarter of the total. Other students came from neighboring towns, but together less than a

---

[13] James K. Somerville, "Homesick in Upstate New York: The Saga of Sidney Roby, 1843–47," *New York History* 72:2 (April 1991): 179–196.
[14] William Graves to A. J. Warner, May 1838, Warner Papers, LHS.

Friends

third of the students came from Lima or any of the five towns that bordered it.¹⁵ Altogether, Genesee Wesleyan students came from a total of 119 different towns in 1834 and 141 different towns in 1839.¹⁶

With its geographic breadth, a large academy like Genesee Wesleyan provided students like Clarissa Pengra and A. J. Warner with opportunities to forge relationships and peer networks that extended well beyond their hometowns. For Clarissa, Genesee Wesleyan remained an important locus of friendship and affiliation after she completed her education there and left town. In 1839, two years after leaving as an assistant teacher, Clarissa made at least two return visits to Genesee Wesleyan, commenting on the friendship she enjoyed there both times. "Just returned from Lima. Found my friends well. Had a pleasant visit." On one of these occasions Clarissa elaborated her statement about visiting the seminary to remark more generally: "I hope I shall always think I have friends. It is so satisfactory."¹⁷

Given norms of geographic mobility and sporadic school attendance, however, young people sometimes had difficulty keeping track of their school acquaintances, let alone sustaining long-term relationships. To overcome these difficulties they corresponded with each other. In May 1838, for example, A. J. Warner's academy friend William Graves wrote him from Auburn, New York, seventy-five miles east of Lima. Graves had attended the seminary with a friend from Auburn, Martin Grant. While at the seminary, the two Auburn youth had forged a friendship with A. J. Warner and his friend, Charlie Ingersoll. Since Graves could not return to the seminary in 1838, he tried to sustain the personal connections he had made with A. J. and Charlie through correspondence. In his letter he invoked nostalgia for the times the foursome had enjoyed at school and tried to goad the Lima boys into paying a visit to Auburn by claiming that the girls were "better and more beautiful" there than anywhere else.¹⁸

In his avid sociability, William Graves struck a note common to other surviving student correspondence. Recognizing the social dimension of academy experience, most academies published lists of students and their hometowns as part of their annual bulletins. These lists provided reference points for students as they tried to sustain communication with each other. At times, the students' letters also read as catalogs of names. "And you are once more at Phipps Union?" a former female academy student named Hattie wrote to a woman named Mary at Phipps Union Seminary, fifty miles west of Lima. "I wish I was placed in the same position, but no, I don't think I shall ever

---

¹⁵ "Bulletins of Genesee Wesleyan Seminary," 1834 and 1839; "Minutes of the Board of Trustees of Genesee Wesleyan Seminary, Account Book #178, GWSC.
¹⁶ "Bulletins of Genesee Wesleyan Seminary," 1834 and 1839, as compared with records of the Genesee Annual Conference of the Methodist Church, including the Journal of the Genesee Conference, WNYCA, and the published minutes of the Genesee Annual Conference, MMC.
¹⁷ Diary of Clarissa Pengra, Thursday, April 14, and Monday, July 29, 1839.
¹⁸ William Graves to A. J. Warner, May 1838.

come back to school. ... Has Minnie Mitchell returned to school? ... She intended to have returned this year. ..." and "Do you know where Georgia is this year?"[19]

Sporadic attendance patterns are important to understanding the tenor of such communications. The reason Hattie's letter to Mary survives in the records of Phipps Union Seminary is probably because it proved undeliverable, its intended recipient having disappeared from the academy's roster of students just as Hattie had herself. Socializing among academy students was not limited to periods of actual attendance at academies, however. Once they had made each others' acquaintance at school, many students pursued their friendships through visits in private families. In between periods of attendance at Ontario Female Seminary in Canandaigua, Frances Smith entertained a number of academy friends in her home and met more at their homes or the homes of mutual friends. Attempting to arrange one such visit in June 1831, Frances explained: "Our Friend and comrade Hosmer returned to the Seminary this week. I wish I could accompany her but our family arrangements are such that I cannot even entertain a thought of returning in the fall." In light of this absence, Frances went on to explore how she and her academy friend could continue their relationship outside of school. "Elsie, as we are deprived of the pleasure of attending school together more, I trust we may notwithstanding have it in our power to see one another frequently."[20]

Eventually, Frances did meet up with Elsie and two other friends at the sulphur springs in the town of Avon, next door to Lima, for a lively round of social visiting, sulphur baths, card-playing, singing, and games of ninepins. Frances used phrases such as "fine sport" and "high glee" to describe the time the girls spent together, expressing a great degree of pleasure and exhilaration. "Play'd whist until 9 o'clock. Retired to my sleeping apartment accompanied by Elsa, Mary L. and Millicent. We all slept in the same bed and a jolly one it was." When the foursome split up to go home, Frances felt a sense of loss. "We arose quite early and prepared for our departure – they to the delightful village of Canandaigua and I to the lone village of Caledonia 7 miles west."[21]

"Friendship": An Education in Trust

Beyond widening their circle of acquaintances and increasing their opportunities to socialize, young people sought long-term relationships of trust and respect characteristic of "true" and enduring friendship. "True" friends were intellectually and morally improving. They were also important sources of advice and influence regarding major life choices, such as those about further

---

[19] Letter from "Hattie" in Waverly to "Mary" at Albion, New York, dated October 6, 1863. Phipps Union Seminary Collection, Swan Library, Albion, New York.
[20] "Diary of Frances Connors Smith [Wells]," Letter to Elsie, Box 10, William H. Emerson Family Papers, 1758–1953, URSC, June 1831.
[21] Ibid., July 30, 1831.

education, future occupation, marriage, and settlement. As youth often learned, however, not all those who appeared to be friends could be trusted. "Friendship" was above all an education in trust.

Like Frances Smith, Clarissa Pengra expressed a sense of exhilaration over time spent with friends. "Nothing gives me more pleasure than to see my friends," she declared after a visit from her "old dear friend Miss Smith." At the same time, however, Clarissa clearly distinguished between those social encounters she found "improving" and those she did not. The visiting Miss Smith, Clarissa found, was "a noble, sweet-spirited girl. ... I wish I could imitate her."[22] With persons of character, in other words, friendship could be educational. On other occasions, however, Clarissa critiqued her social encounters as frivolous or even corrupting. Again, Clarissa expressed these criticisms in educational terms. After a stay at the home of her friend Mary Nowlin, Clarissa ruminated on what she had learned through the negative example of Mary's father. "Since Monday evening I have been at Capt. Nowlins. I have made no advancement in any kind of knowledge unless it is a truth of human nature. Man naturally loves power and when he once possesses it without restoring influences he becomes a tyrant and even the sacredness of the Parental Office is sometimes polluted by tyranny."[23]

By implication, Clarissa regarded good character as essential to true friendship. In addition to inspiring character improvement, however, true friendship stimulated the mind. Without such stimulation, social interaction was frivolous. After one social occasion, Clarissa commented on the poverty of a social life devoid of edification. "Saturday evening I attended a party at W. Mcguire's. Very pleasant pleasure but I do not think parties are beneficial. Why must common sense be turned to nonsense at a party more than at other places? Why should reason flee her empire and leave the mind a vacuum to be filled with winds? But so it is. One might as well entreat a moth not to fly into a candle as to try to force a thought into the mind at a party."[24]

As contrasted with the deadening effects of such frivolity, a more satisfying and beneficial social life allowed consideration of more serious matters. Indeed, the capacity for such conversation could be the basis for a lasting relationship. Recounting an early courtship experience with someone in whom she maintained a long-term interest, Clarissa clearly regarded the depth of conversation as an important indicator of the prospects for the relationship. "Mr. Butler called," she wrote in June 1839. "Road (sic.) out in company with him and several others. In the first part of our ride we talked about matters and things as they arose. Rather trifling. But in the latter part we were more serious and improving." Clarissa left the content of this conversation unspecified in her comment, but the context suggests a religious interpretation. "I find that every day brings me deeper in debt to my maker," Clarissa wrote in the

---

[22] "Livingston ... Diary," August 13, 1839.
[23] Ibid., February 14, 1839.
[24] Ibid., April 12, 1839.

very next sentence. A "serious and improving" conversation, in other words, brought one closer to God.[25]

In making this connection between her experience of friendship and her quest for religious justification, Clarissa may in part have been trying to bestow a kind of divine blessing on her developing relationship with Mr. Butler. She also pursued a more educational purpose common to evangelical thinking, however. The familiar religious phrases that Clarissa frequently recorded in her diary reflected an orientation toward life that she was trying to cultivate in herself. In many respects the diary was a way of developing such a world view. For evangelicals generally, and Methodists specifically, the practice of Christianity meant the practice of a discipline or *method* of self-examination through which one improved oneself, or increased one's piety and understanding. The local Methodist class or church meeting was one context in which this discipline was exercised; friendship and the private diary were others. Through an interactive process of experience and reflection, Clarissa practiced interpreting the episodes of her life in terms of her religious training. This interpretive experience in turn shaped experience itself by informing the content of her social interaction with friends. Potentially, such conversations with "true" friends could themselves approach religious experiences, as Clarissa suggested in a subsequent diary entry. "Our friends left this morning. What a blessing it is to hold communion a few hours with our friends on earth and how much greater will be the happiness in another world if we are permitted to hold communion that will never end."[26]

If friendship was potentially educational, however, the lessons it taught could be negative as well as positive. Geographic separation could test the presumption of trust among friends. In the spring and summer of 1831, Frances Smith strove to maintain connections with academy friends, but also to protect her reputation from gossip that circulated in her absence. Specifically, a rumor circulated that Frances had entertained a visit from a young man named Henry, a man in whom her academy friend Elsa also apparently had an interest. Having received a query regarding this visit from a third person named Fanny, Frances was defensive: "Now my Dear Fan," she wrote, "I cannot conceive by what authority ECB told you that H came to see me. I should be pleased to know where she got her information for I can assure you I knew

---

[25] Ibid., June 26, 1839.
[26] Ibid. Comments regarding the discipline of Methodism are based on an extensive reading of a wide variety of Methodist sources including personal papers, published memoirs and periodical accounts, and records of disciplinary guidelines and proceedings at the local, regional, and conference levels. In particular, I have made use of the Methodist Manuscript Collection at Syracuse University and of the National Archives of the Methodist Episcopal Church at Drew University in Madison, New Jersey. An insightful account of the social psychology and historical significance of Methodist discipline in the antebellum period is provided by Donald Mathews, *Religion in the Old South* (Chicago: University of Chicago Press, 1977), especially pp. 39–80.

it not until informed by you. ... I am perhaps feeling a little jealous that she took that method to find out."[27]

Issues of trust often became particularly acute when it came to courtship. As the diaries and letters of many nineteenth-century young women show, the norms of courtship required that women refrain from public displays of interest in a suitor. Indeed, the demand for discretion increased in direct relation to actual interest. For Clarissa this meant that the more involved she and Mr. Butler became, the more guarded she was about mentioning him by name. Although at the beginning she stated in her diary that "Mr. Butler called," she soon began referring to him as "Mr. ____" and to herself as engaged in thinking about "subjects which I will not name."[28]

Exceptions to the norms of discretion could be made in the case of certain friends in whom one might confide a particular romantic interest. Indeed, a few intimate friends were regarded as essential for providing advice about the character, prospects, and intentions of a suitor. Such friends might also help advance a courtship of which they approved. At one point, for example, Clarissa admitted in her diary to having made "a confidential friend" of a relative of Mr. Butler. "I hope I have not done it indiscreetly," she commented.[29] As Frances Smith discovered, however, such trust could be misplaced. When Fanny wrote Frances to inquire about Henry's visit she put Frances in a difficult position. Henry had not yet called on Frances, but may have declared an intent to do so. By probing Frances about this intended visit, Fanny provoked a conflict between the norms of discretion and the presumption of trust among friends.

In responding, Frances chose denial. Beyond refuting the specific matter of Henry's rumored visit, however, Frances went on to deny any interest in courtship whatsoever. "She [Elsa] need not fear me as a rival for I hope this idea of making a conquest will not enter my heart for some years. For I do not, and perhaps never shall, consider myself a fit candidate for matrimony. ... I feel no inclination to resign my freedom at present. I advise all girls to beware of 'artful man.' He's a deceiver."[30]

---

[27] "Diary of Frances ... Smith," letter to Fanny, April 5, 1831.
[28] Diary of Clarissa Pengra, April 25, 1841. For a fascinating and insightful discussion of courtship norms in this era, see Lynne Templeton Brickley, "Sarah Pierce's Litchfield Female Academy, 1792–1833," (Ed.D. dissertation, Harvard University, 1985): 446–540; also, Thomas A. Chambers, "Seduction and Sensibiltiy: The Refined Society of Ballston, New York, 1800," *New York History* 78:3 (July 1997): 245–272. Some insights from a somewhat later period can be gleaned from the large body of letters between female friends analyzed in Clare Putala, "'Reading and Writing Ourselves into Being – Then What?': The Literacy of Certain Nineteenth-Century Young Women'" (Ph.D. dissertation, Syracuse University, 1997). See also a direct study of romantic relationships between men and women by Karen Lystra, *Searching the Heart: Women, Men and Romantic Love in Nineteenth Century America* (New York: Oxford University Press, 1989).
[29] Diary of Clarissa Pengra, August 24, 1840.
[30] "Diary of Frances ... Smith," April 5, 1831.

This declaration of disinterest in marriage may have been genuine. Diaries and letters of other young women show that some were keenly aware of the loss of independence and identity that followed marriage. It does not appear to have been true, however, that no courtship interest existed between Frances and Henry. Two months after Frances replied to Fanny, Henry did come to visit Frances. In accordance with the norms of discretion, Frances said very little about the visit. She simply recorded that on the second of August 1831, at 9 o'clock, she "received a call from Mr. H. H. Martin on his way to the West." That he made the call in the morning, possibly spending much of the day, suggests that the call was serious. That Frances did not discourage his interest is suggested by the fact that he called again the following day.[31]

In denying an interest in being courted by Henry, however, Frances had taken a risk that her denial would get back to him. Interwoven in the norms of discretion and confidential friends were the hazards of betrayal. That Frances ultimately felt betrayed is revealed by a solemn statement she made several months later:

Jan. 1st 1832
Another New Year has come. ... I have learned more of the disposition of my fellow being than I learned in ten years prior to the last. It has been learned by bitter experience and never may it depart from me. *I have learned that all who have pretended friendship are not to be depended upon.* ... I never could believe half that was told me in regard to human nature, consequently I never was on my guard. I considered all were my friends who treated me with friendship, but alas to my sorrow I soon learned that they were interested friends of a moment. I then regretted that I had ever sought to extend my acquaintance beyond my father's family. ...[32]

For Frances, then, the benefits of expanded social networks were ambiguous. On the one hand, they enabled her to meet new people, to enter new social milieus, and to assert her identity in settings somewhat independent of her family and outside the shelter of home. On the other hand, what she learned from this experience was that many people cannot be trusted. The experience of friendship fostered by academy attendance was educational, in other words, but not necessarily positive.

Education and Mobility

An education in trust was valuable in a mobile society. Migration without friends could be financially and emotionally hazardous. "Friends" could provide links to work opportunities in a new place. They also could confer credibility. In this way friends bridged relations of trust in a new community and offered sources of social and financial security. To the extent that educational

---

[31] Ibid., August 2–3, 1831. On declarations of disinterest in marriage, see Anya Jabour, "'It Will Never Do For Me to Be Married': The Life of Laura Wirt Randall, 1803–33," *Journal of the Early Republic* 17 (Summer 1997): 193–236.

[32] "Diary of Frances ... Smith," January 1, 1832 (emphasis added).

institutions like Genesee Wesleyan helped students to forge translocal friendships and acquire social and cultural credentials, they eased the experience of dislocation common to migrant youth.

The special significance of friendship in the context of migration is apparent in the experience of Clarissa Pengra. In October of 1840, Clarissa took a job teaching in the young city of Syracuse, about eighty miles east of Lima. Recording the onset of her journey on November 2, 1840, Clarissa reported arriving in Rochester the evening before she was to catch a canal boat east. "I have left home and friend," she wrote with some ceremony, "and for the moment must depend upon myself." Later, having arrived in Syracuse and completed her first week of teaching, Clarissa again returned to the theme of home and the challenge of making friends in a new place. "One week of school has gone and I have spent one Lord's day in Syracuse. Been to church twice. Heard very good sermons but did not feel at home. I hope I am not a stranger among the Lord's people anywhere but there is a peculiar felling of attachment to one's own people and place that cannot be for any other."[33]

Although Clarissa described herself as friendless, she was not entirely without social connection in her new location. Clarissa had an aunt who resided in the town of Onondaga, just south of Syracuse. Onondaga also seems to have been a point of connection with Mr. Butler.[34] Often on weekends Clarissa journeyed south of Syracuse to Onondaga to stay with her aunt's family and continue her courtship by Mr. Butler. School teaching also clearly consumed much of her energy. Weeks often passed with Clarissa recording nothing in her diary. Notwithstanding these connections, however, Clarissa did experience a significant sense of dislocation in making her move to Syracuse. In an entry occasioned by receiving letters from home, however, Clarissa conveyed a sense of ambiguity about her move. "Nothing gives me so much pleasure as news from home," she wrote. And the next day, "I have this day been writing home. It brings many pleasant things as well as some anxieties. Reading a letter from my father, I find that my absence is felt by him. My Mother too is lonely without me. Is it then my duty to remain away?"[35]

The migration experience was something Clarissa had in common with many youth of the time. Some, like Frances Smith's suitor, Henry Martin, migrated "to the West." Others, like Clarissa, migrated to the growing cities of the North. Where exactly the young man Henry Martin went when he left for "the West" and what he expected to do when he got there are unknown, but in the 1830s many migrants from upstate New York headed for the newly opened Michigan territory, which they could reach efficiently by crossing into Canada at Buffalo or Lockport and travelling due west toward Detroit. Other parts of the old Northwest, including Ohio, Indiana and Illinois, were also common destinations for New Yorkers in this period, as were the in-state

---

[33] Diary of Clarissa Pengra, November 2 and November 9, 1840.
[34] Ibid., passim.
[35] Ibid., December 26, 1841.

cities of New York, Utica, Syracuse, Rochester, and Buffalo, all of which grew exponentially. Both men and women participated in migration. While single women migrated most often as teachers, single men migrated as farmers, like Frederick Warner, but also as ministers and missionaries, or as clerks in the banks, land offices, merchant houses, and legal offices that promoted both frontier and urban development in the 1820s, 1830s, 1840s, and 1850s.[36]

These migration paths and opportunities were familiar to young people like Clarissa Pengra, A. J. Warner, and Frances Smith. Over a three-year period, from 1831 to 1833, Frances Smith's diary refers to no less than four men migrating "to the West." In one instance the connection between Frances and the migrant does not appear to have been close: "Nat tells me that ABB has gone to Michigan," she reported in a letter dated June 1831. "He passed through this place and did not call upon me. Did you ever hear of such neglect? I did not shed many tears when I heard about it though." In the other instances the young men were close acquaintances, like Henry. Other young people were affected by the migrations of close family members. Just six months before her own departure for Syracuse, Clarissa's brother migrated to Michigan. A. J. Warner's brother Frederick made the same journey just a few years before.[37]

For some youth, the migration of a family member shaped their whole childhood. The academy student Sidney Roby, for example, effectively lost his father to westward migration when he departed for Michigan soon after Sidney's mother died, in 1832. Sidney grew up with his maternal grandparents and began attending Brockport Collegiate Institute, forty miles northwest of Lima, in 1843. Meanwhile, his father engaged in land speculation in Michigan, tried farming in Illinois, and made periodic sojourns to St. Louis and New Orleans. Throughout this period, Sidney's father communicated only rarely with his son. When Sidney finally met up with him again, after commencing work in New York City as a clerk, he had not seen him in fourteen years.[38]

Migration experiences such as these posed challenges to young people trying to make their way in life. Among these were physical risks. Frances discussed some of these risks with respect to the migration of John Hosmer, the brother of a good friend. Writing in May of 1833, Frances reported that "After dinner John Hosmer came to spend a few hours. Dressed myself and went down and spent what time I could with him. ... John left immediately after tea. He is on his way to Illinois. Poor fellow, he is quite out of health. I

---

[36] On Michigan migration, see Susan Gray, *Yankee West: Community Life on the Michigan Frontier* (Chapel Hill: University of North Carolina Press, 1996) and John Denis Haeger, *The Investment Frontier: New York Businessmen and the Economic Development of the Old Northwest* (Albany: State University of New York Press, 1981). On teacher migration see Polly Welts Kaufman, *Women Teachers on the Frontier* (New Haven, CT: Yale University Press, 1984).
[37] "Diary of Frances ... Smith," June 5, 1831; Letters from Frederick B. Warner in Romeo, Michigan, to the Warner family in Lima, New York, February 13, 1838 and December 3, 1838, Warner Papers, LHS.
[38] Somerville, "Homesick."

fear he will never return. There are so many perils to encounter on a trip of that kind that I think it presumptuous for a young person to travel alone as he intends. ..."[39]

Clarissa expressed similar concerns about her own brother's prospects for survival. This concern began well before his departure for Michigan. In October of 1839, for example, Clarissa wrote, "My brother has been home today. His health is poor, although he seems better than formerly. How little he knows a sister's anxiety for him." When this visit ended, Clarissa noted "Have just parted with my dear brother who has gone to PA to visit. May ... [he] return to us in health." These concerns intensified when Clarissa's brother went west. At the time, in May of 1840, Clarissa recorded a strong sense of foreboding. "Yesterday morning my Brother started for Michigan. We parted with him the evening before. It was a severe trial. I do not believe in presentiments, ... [nor] have I any communion with spirits, but I do feel as if he would never return."[40]

The risks of migration were not only physical, but mental. Separation from friends and family combined with pressures to succeed could lead to mental breakdown. In April 1833, Frances reported on such an eventuality in the case of a close family friend. "At 12 o'clock my father informed me of the death of Mr. T. Blakeslee by suicide, committed, it is supposed, in a fit of derangement (on the 30th) – How dreadful. ... A dependant wife and family of children are deprived of an affectionate husband and fond Father. In the prime of life, too. How melancholy. He left his place last fall for Ohio. Probably he became discouraged with the prospect before him. Allowed his feelings to become excited to such a degree as to produce insanity. And in such a state to put an end to his life."[41] That the experience of frontier life could result in depression and derangement was appreciated by people at the time. After thirteen years of largely unsuccessful attempts to make a new life in the West, Sidney's father Joseph was understood to have arrived at this condition. Reporting news he had received via a cousin, Sidney informed his grandfather that "the folks here think father is quite sick" and "I have heard them hint that they thought his mind was a little deranged."[42]

Young people pursued their own efforts to establish themselves against the knowledge of such failure, disappointment, and loss. In Sidney Roby's case the connection between the hazards of life his father encountered and his own education were made explicit. Admonishing his son to take his studies seriously, Joseph Roby warned Sidney that he needed to prepare himself "to battle with the world – its snares, its vices, its troubles, its evils – all of which you will have to experience." Given the great instability of society, Joseph explained, Sidney would have to be better prepared than he had been to deal

---

[39] "Diary of Frances ... Smith," May 8, 1833.
[40] Diary of Clarissa Pengra, October 9–10, 1839 and May 11, 1840.
[41] "Diary of Frances ... Smith," May 3, 1833.
[42] Somerville, "Homesick," 191.

with a world "where those who today are wealthy, respected and happy – are tomorrow destitute and left alone to grapple with poverty and distress."[43]

This idea of an unstable and potentially hostile society appeared in Clarissa's writing as well, albeit in softened form. "Who are willing to think themselves friendless in a changing life?" Clarissa asked at one point after recording a visit to her friends at the Seminary in Lima. "Surely no one in their senses." What Clarissa had in mind when she referred to "this changing life" is not clear, but her question followed a curious comment about friendship. "Saw many of my friends," she reported with regard to her visit. "Or those who appeared to be so."[44] Those who appeared to be friends might prove false, in other words. Life could change. Or, as Frances Smith had put the same point, "all who have pretended friendship are not to be depended upon."[45]

Clarissa may not have known the same kind of betrayal experienced by Frances Smith or the mental distress experienced by A. J. Warner's brother Frederick, Frances Smith's family friend Mr. Blakeslee, or Sidney Roby's father Joseph, but her adventure in Syracuse did not end well. Her Onondaga aunt died while she was there and her relationship with Mr. Butler disintegrated. Clarissa left Syracuse at the end of her second term of teaching, in the fall of 1841, and took up residence again in her family's home. The few entries that follow her return reveal only that she was struggling to reconcile herself to some disappointment. "Bitter and sad thoughts oppress me," she wrote on January 23, 1842. "My mind is not at rest."[46] Then, with only two brief intervening entries, Clarissa's diary abruptly ended. In her last diary entry Clarissa struggled to reconcile herself to her greatest sorrow, the death of the brother whose departure to Michigan she had regarded with foreboding two years earlier.

August 14, 1842
One week today since I followed my much beloved brother to the grave and it has been such a week of sadness as I never before realized. Yet I must thankfully acknowledge that I do not mourn without hope. Oh, no. I have reason to believe his spirit is in heaven.[47]

As she had been educated to do, Clarissa immediately reinterpreted her loss in terms of a life transcendent. "O Spirit of my departed brother," she prayed in the last line of her diary, "come dwell with me and be around me, constantly guarding my thoughts and actions."[48] Spiritually, as well as socially and instrumentally, education provided a means of negotiating the hazards of a changing life.

[43] Ibid., 190.
[44] Diary of Clarissa Pengra, April 14, 1839.
[45] "Diary of Frances ... Smith," January 1, 1832.
[46] Diary of Clarissa Pengra, January 23, 1842.
[47] Ibid., August 14, 1842.
[48] Ibid.

Conclusion – Education and the Creation of Capital

> Social capital ... refers to the features of social organization such as trust, norms and networks, that improve the efficiency of society by facilitating coordinated actions.
>
> Robert Putnam, *Making Democracy Work*, 1993, p. 167[1]

> Networks of national, state and local units allow associations to mediate between local people and political parties and legislators.
>
> Theda Skocpol, "The Tocqueville Problem," 1997, p. 470[2]

In retrospect, it is clear that few people in Lima had any idea what they were getting into when they forged a coalition in 1830 to win the site of a Methodist-sponsored academy for their town. Later, when they complained to the legislature, a number of townspeople would say that they had been betrayed, and in some ways, perhaps, they had. If so, however, the betrayal was more by history than it was by men. Looking around at what people in Lima would have seen on the eve of their successful bid for the academy in 1830, it is easy to understand how they might have been misled. A survey of local churches would certainly not have led them to believe they had anything to fear or much to expect from Methodists. The simple brick box that local Methodists just finished building outside the village the previous year was no match for the impressive steeple structure the Presbyterians had erected a few years earlier on a hill overlooking the town green. An examination of local church membership would reinforce the contrast. Although the number of Methodist church members had steadily increased in the Lima vicinity over the previous decade, this increased activity had occurred primarily in the hamlets that bordered the town. At the town center, the Presbyterian Church would continue to claim the largest number of church members for

---

[1] Robert Putnam, *Making Democracy Work: Civic Traditions in Modern Italy* (Princeton, NJ: Princeton University Press, 1993): 163.

[2] Theda Skocpol, "The Tocqueville Problem: Civic Engagement in American Democracy," *Social Science History* 21:4 (Winter 1997): 455–479; quotation from p. 470.

decades to come. Similarly, although the Methodist Smiths, with their cluster of mills, were significant local property-owners and employers, they certainly did not rival the Presbyterian Warners in social, financial, or political influence, whether at the local, county, or state level. In this way, a survey of local evidence alone might lead residents to underestimate the considerable social, financial, and political capital that Methodists would soon command not only in their town but in the state at large.

Of course, people in Lima also benefited from the substantial social, financial, and political capital commanded by the Methodist economy. The exceptional size and success of Genesee Wesleyan Seminary in attracting both students and state funds provided a stable if limited demand for labor, goods, and services, including housing for faculty, boarding establishments for students, farm labor, domestic service, shops, and merchants. Despite the financial losses of local investors in the textile mill at West Bloomfield, the failure of any significant manufacturing to develop within the town's borders, and a shift of political and economic leverage from inside to outside town, Lima did experience modest growth in the decades following the founding of its Methodist academy. Between 1830 and 1850, population density and per capita land values in Lima increased to those of a mixed commercial farming economy.[3]

Meanwhile, hundreds of local students enjoyed the benefits of ready access to higher schooling at one of the largest and best-staffed educational institutions in the state.[4] Although the proportion of the seminary's 660 total students in 1850 who were from the town of Lima remained relatively small at 17 percent, the proportion of local children who attended the institution at some point during their youth was high. Similar to the high rates of high school attendance Maris Vinovskis found for small towns in Massachusetts, an estimated 49.6 percent of all youth aged ten to nineteen in 1850 attended the seminary in Lima at some time in their youth.[5] In doing so, they gained access

[3] The town of Lima remained rural and primarily agricultural through at least 1860. According to the 1850 industrial census, Lima had two grist mills, one saw mill, an ashery, a stonecutter, a tanner, a shoemaker, a harness-maker, an iron furnace, and a tin-maker, but the largest establishment was a chair maker employing six persons. Manuscript schedule for the sixth census of the United States, 1850, LCCO. For data showing how per capita land values and population density of Lima compared with Linda Pritchard's model of economic development see Appendix Table 4. Linda Pritchard, "Religious Change in a Developing Region: The Social Context of Evangelicalism in Western New York and the Upper Ohio Valley During the Mid-Nineteenth Century" (unpublished Ph.D. dissertation, University of Pittsburgh, 1980).

[4] For a full account of the size, staffing, and relative success of Genesee Wesleyan Seminary as compared with other institutions in the state, see Nancy Beadie, "Female Students and Denominational Affiliation: Sources of Success and Variation among Nineteenth-Century Academies," *American Journal of Education* 107 (February 1999): 75–115.

[5] Maris Vinovskis, "Have We Underestimated the Extent of Antebellum High School Attendance?" *History of Education Quarterly* 28:4 (Winter 1988): 551–567. As Vinovskis has emphasized, annual enrollment figures are not an accurate reflection of the total share of a given age cohort who ever received high school or academy instruction, because attendance patterns were so discontinuous. A student who did not appear on a roster one year may well

not only to cultural capital but to the social capital represented by multiple social networks extending well beyond the locality. The 660 total students who attended the seminary in 1850 came from 234 different towns in New York State and 6 other states.[6]

Capitalizing on this considerable success attracting students and the state Regents funds associated with them, leaders of the seminary and of the sponsoring Methodist conference founded an affiliated college in 1850, known as Genesee College. Drawing on the same practice of fundraising through the sale of subscription scholarships used twenty years earlier, agents of the conference raised more than $100,000 in capital beginning in 1848. In 1850, a new college building opened on the seminary grounds under a separate corporate charter granted by the legislature in 1849. Although the total number of students enrolled at the college would never be more than 150, the combined enrollments of the two institutions soon exceeded 1,000, continuing the seminary's standing as one of the largest and most successful educational institutions in the state throughout the antebellum era. Over the years, with the help again of Methodist lobbying efforts, the college also won two grants of $6,000 each from the state legislature.[7]

In all these ways, the founding of the academy at Lima in 1830 contributed to long-term local growth and fostered the integration of local social and financial networks into a transforming political economy. More broadly, the larger educational expansion of which this and many other schools and educational institutions were a part stimulated the creation, accumulation, and mobility of social, financial, and political capital.

Current ideas about the relationship between education and economy for the most part rest on the concept of human capital. This is the idea that the education or schooling of a people increases their economic productivity and thereby contributes to economic growth. Given this premise, both states and individual citizens have an interest in common or mass schooling as a means of increasing production of and access to wealth. A related but somewhat distinct idea is that of intellectual capital. This is the idea that education produces

---

have appeared the year earlier or the year after. Here I have used Vinovskis' method for estimating attendance of a given age cohort. For a full discussion of this method and its application in the Lima case, see Nancy Beadie, "Academy Students in the Mid-19th Century: Social Geography, Demography, and the Culture of Academy Attendance," *History of Education Quarterly* 41:2 (Summer 2001): 252–263.

[6] Data on students compiled from "Catalog {"ue" in original} of the Officers and Students of the Genesee Wesleyan Seminary, Lima, New York for the Year Ending July Twenty-fifth, 1850 (Rochester, NY: Lee, Mann & Co, 1850), Box 13, GWSC.

[7] The grants from the state were made in 1854 and 1856. For a full account of the founding of the college, its operations, and subsequent events, see Nancy Beadie, "From Academy to University in New York State: The Genesee Institutions and the Importance of Capital to the Success of an Idea, 1848–1871," *History of Higher Education Annual* 14 (1994): 3–28. Eventually, in 1871, the college was removed to the city of Syracuse and re-founded as Syracuse University, with a substantial additional investment of capital from the city and citizens of Syracuse.

knowledge and that knowledge itself is an economic resource. Knowledge leads to technological innovation that in turn can be used to increase productivity and wealth. In this formulation the interest of the state lies less in mass education than in the production of more advanced forms of knowledge, that is, higher education.[8]

Both these formulations consider the relationship between education and economy from the perspective of the present, however. They assume a world in which the transition to capitalism and the process of modern state formation is complete. In these formulations labor is already a commodity, markets are already integrated, and the economy is already industrialized. Also in these formulations, the "state" has already amassed the financial and political capital necessary to direct substantial centralized resources into education. In fact, however, this was not the condition of the economy or the state in the early republican era. In 1820, labor, capital, and commodities markets were not fully integrated and agriculture was still the primary form of production. Moreover, in 1820, the social value of education commanded substantial resources that the state could not. From this perspective, the place of education in political economy looks quite different. The question is not when and why the state made schools an object of social spending, but how the considerable social, financial, and political capital already commanded by schools as voluntary associations came to be appropriated by the state.[9] The argument here is that the economic significance of schooling in the rural North during the early republican era lay not in the production of human or intellectual capital but in the creation and mobilization of social capital and its conversion into political capital for the modern liberal state.

Over the last twenty years, scholars from a wide range of fields have defined, used, and developed the idea of social capital. One way of distinguishing among different uses of the term is to consider the unit of analysis. At the macro level, scholars have used the concept of social capital to refer to the social factors that facilitate human capital formation and economic development.[10] In this formulation, ends are assumed and are ultimately economic, with the unit of analysis often the state or nation. Claudia Goldin and Lawrence Katz, for example, identified the substantial increases in high school enrollments in the period from 1910 to 1940 as an explanation for the significant economic growth that the United States experienced at mid-

---

[8] The idea of education as a means of "human capital" formation is usually attributed to Theodore Schultz, "Capital Formation by Education," *Journal of Political Economy* 68:6 (December 1960): 571–583; idem., "Investment in Human Capital," *The American Economic Review* 51:1 (1961): 1–17.

[9] For a comprehensive comparative historical analysis of education as an object of social spending see Peter Lindert, *Growing Public: Social Spending and Economic Growth Since the Eighteenth Century* (New York: Cambridge University Press, 2004).

[10] For a very helpful though now somewhat dated survey of this literature see Michael Woolcock, "Social Capital and Economic Development: Toward a Theoretical Synthesis and Policy Framework," *Theory and Society* 27:2 (April 1998): 151–208.

century. Drawing on national data sets, Goldin and Katz used the concept of social capital to explain variations in educational attainment and economic productivity across time and space.[11]

At a micro level, by contrast, scholars have used the concepts of social and cultural capital to describe the social and cultural resources within a particular community. In this formulation, social capital is a collective resource that a community uses to achieve its own ends. Economic development and opportunity might be among those ends, but so might education itself. The reference point for such development, moreover, is the community and its members, not the nation-state. Much of the literature that invokes this idea of social capital with respect to education is rooted in African American history. Historians of education have used the concepts of social and cultural capital to describe how African American communities in the antebellum North, the Reconstruction South, and twentieth-century cities have drawn on their own social and cultural resources to create institutions and opportunities in contexts where they were excluded from those controlled by whites.[12] Even when they have not used the term, leading African American historians like James Anderson, Vanessa Siddle Walker, Heather Andrea Williams, and Chris Span have all done much to illuminate how the process of social capitalization worked in the Reconstruction and post-Reconstruction South.[13]

---

[11] Claudia Goldin and Lawrence Katz, "Human Capital and Social Capital: The Rise of Secondary Schooling in America, 1910–1940," *The Journal of Interdisciplinary History* 29:4 (Spring 1999): 683–723; Goldin, "America's Graduation from High School: The Evolution and Spread of Secondary Schooling in the Twentieth Century," *The Journal of Economic History* 58:2 (June 1998): 345–374; John L. Rury, "Social Capital and Secondary Schooling: Interurban Differences in American Teenage Enrollment Rates in 1950," *American Journal of Education* 110 (August 2004): 1–22.

[12] V. P. Franklin edited a special issue of *The Journal of African American History* on "Cultural Capital and African American Education," in which the work referred to here appeared. See Franklin, "Introduction"; Adah Ward Randolph, "Building upon Cultural Capital: Thomas Jefferson Ferguson and the Albany Enterprise Academy in Southeast Ohio, 1863–1886"; and Chris Span, "I Must Learn Now or Not at All": Social and Cultural Capital in the Educational Initiatives of Formerly Enslaved African Americans in Mississippi, 1862–1869;" *The Journal of African American History* 87:1 (Spring 2002): 175–181, 182–195, and 196–205, respectively. In the same issue see also Carter Julian Savage, "Cultural Capital and African American Agency: The Economic Struggle for Effective Education for African Americans in Franklin, Tennessee, 1890–1967"; Richard M. Breaux, "'Maintaining a Home for Girls': The Iowa Federation of Colored Women's Clubs at the University of Iowa, 1919–1950"; Peggy B. Gill, "Community, Commitment, and African American Education: The Jackson School of Smith County, Texas, 1925–1954"; and Monica A. White, "Paradise Lost? Teachers' Perspectives on the Use of Cultural Capital in the Segregated Schools of New Orleans, Louisiana"; ibid., 206–235, 236–255, 256–268, and 269–281.

[13] James Anderson, *The Education of Blacks in the South, 1860–1935* (Chapel Hill: University of North Carolina Press, 1988). I am thinking in particular of the sections of Anderson's book where he describes the substantial funds raised by black communities for basic common schools above and beyond any support received from either public or philanthropic sources, as well as the financial and political capital mobilized from black communities for high schools and from black church denominations for colleges. Intensive studies of particular aspects

The juxtaposition of these two ways of thinking about social capital poses the question of how to theorize relationships between them. Substantial bodies of literature are devoted to this theoretical task. One way of formulating these relationships is to focus on the individual as the unit of analysis. In this formulation, social and cultural capital are socially constructed resources that can be appropriated or invoked by individuals to solidify or improve their status, to move from one social network to another, or to otherwise "capitalize" on their social standing in some way. Schooling is one place where this process of individual appropriation can occur. Through attendance at certain kinds of schools, an individual gains access to group membership and to the social capital resources of that group. This membership then serves as a kind of social credential that can be transferred to a new context. A number of historians have used this concept of social capital as articulated by Pierre Bourdieu to show how a wide range of higher level schools, from southern military academies to state normal schools, initiated students from largely rural backgrounds into forms of cultural knowledge, norms of social life, and networks of like-minded individuals that constituted a commercial middle class.[14] As the Lima case illustrates, much the same process occurred at academies in the North during the early republican period.[15]

Another way to analyze relationships between micro and macro ideas of social capital is to make translocal voluntary associations the primary unit of analysis. In this formulation, the "autonomous" or "bridging" capacities of social capital are highlighted. Analysis then focuses on identifying the structures and strategies used by such organizations to reproduce and extend their networks into new locations and to exercise influence at various levels of political association. As the Lima case illuminates, two of the most powerful such

of the larger picture described by Anderson are provided by Heather Andrea Williams, *Self-Taught: African-American Education in Slavery and Freedom* (Chapel Hill: University of North Carolina Press, 2005); Chris Span, *From Cotton Field to Schoolhouse: African American Education in Mississippi, 1862–1875* (Chapel Hill: University of North Carolina Press, 2009); and Vanessa Siddle Walker, *Their Highest Potential: An African American School Community in the Segregated South* (Chapel Hill: University of North Carolina Press, 1996).

[14] I'm thinking here in particular of Christine A. Ogren, *The American State Normal School: An Instrument of Great Good* (New York: Palgrave/MacMillan, 2005). With a finer grain of detail Benjamin Burks documented the same pattern among both black and white normal school students in postbellum Virginia. Benjamin Burks, "What Was Normal about Virginia's State Normal Schools: A History of Virginia's State Normal Schools, 1882–1930" (unpublished Ph.D. dissertation, University of Virginia, 2002). See also Jennifer R. Green, *Military Education and the Emerging Middle Class in the Old South* (New York: Cambridge University Press, 2008).

[15] See also Margaret Nash, *Women's Education in the United States, 1780–1840* (New York: Palgrave/MacMillan, 2005); Kathryn Kerns, "Ante-bellum Higher Education for Women in Western New York State" (unpublished Ph.D. dissertation, University of Pennsylvania, 1993); Doris Jeanne Malkmus, "Capable Women and Refined Ladies: Two Visions of American Women's Higher Education, 1760–1861" (unpublished Ph.D. dissertation, University of Iowa, 2001).

organizations in the early republican era were Freemasonry and Methodism. Both played significant though distinctive roles in mobilizing early support for education. They were also significant educational organizations in their own right. Each had its own elaborate curriculum, pedagogy, and system of certification for initiating new members and mediating relationships among different organizational units.

The analysis summarized here draws on all these ways of thinking about social capital. At the same time, it seeks to theorize relationships among them by treating schools as sites of interactions between different social networks. In the Lima case, the intensification of agriculture that occurred in the period from 1780 to 1820 was associated with the cultivation of social capital as a cultural community resource. The high levels of this local social capital that developed first through family connections and church societies helps to explain the high levels of school organization, attendance, and investment in schooling that townspeople had already achieved at the very beginning of the period of state intervention in common schools. This local school and community building created real wealth that local leaders and credit-brokers used to invest in new developments. At the same time, local leaders used their access to autonomous social networks to attract outside resources and foster local economic development. A local network of credit-brokers, commercial farmers, and ordinary craftsmen forged a coalition with a regional evangelical association to found a corporate educational institution. This autonomous organization in turn mobilized its own substantial sources of social capital to win outside support and ultimate control of the institution. At a micro-economic level, this process created a highly successful educational institution that stimulated the local economy and facilitated the forging of translocal friendship networks and the acquisition of social and professional credentials by students like Clarissa Pengra. At a macro-economic level, it helped to forge a constituency for policies that promoted state investment in education and development.

The significance of schools as historical agencies of politicization is a subject that merits further investigation. In the literature on social capital, the presence or absence of voluntary organizations is considered an indicator of the capacity for civic engagement. As explained by Theda Skocpol, "networks of national, state and local units allow associations to mediate between local people and political parties and legislators."[16] In many studies, however, the nature of this politicization process is more assumed than described. In one project, for example, Gerald Gamm and Robert Putnam collected time-slice data on the numbers and types of voluntary associations listed in city directories in 25 different towns and cities over a 100-year period from 1840 to 1940. They then charted variations in the level of associational activity in those places as a way of estimating their relative civic capacities. In this study, the presence or absence of voluntary organizations was itself an indicator of civic

---

[16] Skocpol, "The Toqueville Problem," 470.

capacity. The question of how, whether, or when these organizations actually engaged political issues, however, was not directly addressed.[17]

Schools are sites where that politicization process can be directly observed. In New York in the early republican era, rural schools were simultaneously voluntary associations and objects of policy and legislation. They also operated at more than one political level at a time. In Lima in the 1800s and 1810s, church-based schools expressed the religious pluralism of the local community and at the same time embodied the republican principles of religious liberty encoded in New York's first general incorporation law. In the 1820s, a local school became the site of a mini-rebellion by parents who challenged the district's tradition of allocating public funds only to male teachers. At the same time, those parents acted out the contest over terms of suffrage and the structure of political authority then being debated in the state legislature. In 1830, the founding of the academy became a way for local leaders to try to bridge local political divisions that had developed with the rise of evangelicalism and the anti-Masonic movement. At the same time, it also became the site of considerable political conflict over issues such as competition from outside labor, defense of religious liberty, and the "monopolistic" aspects of corporate power.[18]

This last set of issues was eventually fought out in the state legislature in a battle over the academy's charter that politicized both local networks and the translocal Methodist organization. Methodists essentially won this battle, and they did so by soliciting petitions from supporters. Methodists were of course particularly effective in this effort precisely because of their translocal organizational structure, which enabled them to mobilize political capital from virtually every senate and assembly district in the western half of the state. Eventually, these same Methodist networks became important as a constituency of the Whig Party.[19]

---

[17] Gerald Gamm and Robert D. Putnam, "The Growth of Voluntary Association in America, 1840–1940," *Journal of Interdisciplinary History* xxix:4 (Spring 1999): 511–557.

[18] Evidence of these various school-based political coalitions and conflicts lies in a large body of local church and school records for the town of Lima, in the trustee minutes and other account books for Genesee Wesleyan Seminary, and in state legislative records. These records include "Records of the First Congregational Society at Charleston," LPC; "Records of School District #4," and "Lima School Commissioners' Reports," LHS; Account Books #178 and #102, GWSC; "Memorial from sundry inhabitants of Lima, in the county of Livingston, remonstrating against the further incorporation of the Genesee and Wesleyan seminary at Lima, dated January 7, 1834; recorded January 22, 1834, No. 51, *Documents of the Assembly of the State of New York* (Albany, NY: E. Croswell, printer to the state, 1834); and *Journal of the Assembly, State of New York* (Albany: State of New York, 1834): 39, 81, 87, 95, 101, 128, 183, 195, 238.

[19] This politicization process had a good deal to do with the rise of political anti-Masonry, a movement that had strong evangelical roots, at least in western New York. See William Henry Brackney, "Religious Antimasonry: The Genesis of a Political Party" (unpublished Ph.D. dissertation, Temple University, 1976); and Kathleen Smith Kutolowski, "The Social Composition of Political Leadership: Genesee County, New York, 1821–1860" (unpublished Ph.D. dissertaton, University of Rochester, 1973).

Conclusion

Beyond providing examples of how the politicization of social networks worked, schools provide a window onto the structure of the state itself. To trace sources of funding for schools is to rediscover the meaning of the "modern liberal state" as it was being created. It is to recognize the significance of schools as corporations and the significance of corporations as politically sanctioned agencies of capital accumulation. It is to watch how freedom of religious association and freedom of economic association came to be embodied in the same principles of corporate law, how the politics of free banking and the politics of school funding came to be joined through the practice of political economy, and thus how the considerable social capital already commanded by schools as voluntary associations came to be a source of political capital for state investment in economic development.

Consider the source of early state funds for education. Where did they come from? In New York, as in virtually all other states, such funds were initially capitalized from the sale of "public" lands appropriated from Native Americans.[20] Proceeds from such sales were then invested in various enterprises, including banks. Interest on such investments then provided states with income that they distributed to schools.[21] As one rare scholar of the history of school funding concluded in a 1945 study, the use of bank enterprises to finance public education became "rather general before the Civil War," and in some instances "the money distributed to school districts by the State was derived entirely, or almost entirely from bank stock investment or taxation of banks."[22] In other words, the provision of the first state-level public funds for schools was directly tied to state investment in capitalist economic development.

This model of political economy received a significant boost as a result of the Jacksonian return of "surplus" federal deposit funds to states in 1836–1837.[23]

---

[20] New York established its common school fund in 1805 and its literature fund for support of academies and higher schooling in 1813, though in both cases it took several years for the funds to mature and begin yielding substantial income. By 1815, a total of seven states north and south had established such funds, including Delaware in 1796, Tennessee in 1806, Virginia in 1810, South Carolina in 1811, and Maryland in 1813. Thirteen additional states followed before 1830. They included original colonies like Georgia and New Jersey in 1817 and North Carolina in 1825. Also included were new states like Indiana in 1816, Illinois in 1818, and Kentucky and Mississippi in 1821. Fletcher Harper Swift, *A History of Public Permanent Common School Funds in the United States, 1795–1905* (New York: Henry Holt and Company, 1911).

[21] Ibid. In addition to appropriating proceeds from the sale of public lands, some states (Rhode Island, Delaware, and Virginia) capitalized their school funds from sources such as license and excise fees, fines, forfeitures, lotteries, and auctions.

[22] John Anthony Muscalus, *The Use of Banking Enterprises in the Financing of Public Education, 1796–1866* (Philadelphia: University of Pennsylvania, 1945): 7.

[23] The law directing the distribution of the surplus passed Congress in June 1836. The distribution of funds to the states began in January 1837. The law directing the allocation of funds within the state did not occur in New York until 1838. For an account of the events surrounding the return of surplus federal deposit funds to the states, see Hammond, *Banks and Politics in America*, especially pp. 453–457; and Edward G. Bourne, *The History of the Surplus Revenue of 1837* (New York: G. P. Putnam's Sons, 1885).

Most states, like New York, officially devoted some or all of the income on such capital to support education by adding it to the income realized on existing permanent school funds.[24] In some states, this money was sooner or later diverted to other purposes. Many states, however, kept the school fund in name if not in practice.[25] From a political perspective, this made sense. School funds provided a politically acceptable rationale for state investments in banks and other forms of economic development during a period when corporate power generally, and banking specifically, were extremely controversial.

Or, to put a similar point in a somewhat different way, the interests of capital were in this way tied to those of ordinary taxpayers and parents of school-age children. In the language of Governor DeWitt Clinton of New York, legislators succeeded in forging a "community of interest" and a "reciprocation of benefits" among the state's various constituencies.[26] This is where the substantial social capital already commanded by local schools, especially rural schools, became politically and economically significant at the macro-economic level. The practice of political economy was the art of knitting together various constituencies through the raising and expenditure of public funds. Schooling was an important site of such coalition building at both the local and state levels and continues to be one of the most important to this day.[27]

---

[24] The distribution of these funds in New York was directed by an 1838 law: "An Act to appropriate the income of the United States deposit fund to the purposes of the education and the diffusion of knowledge, Passed April 17, 1838" *Laws of New York,* 61st Session, Chap. 237 (Albany: State of New York, 1839): 220–223. In some states, such as Massachusetts, the provision of federal deposit funds became the occasion for establishing a new system of state funding for schools and academies that had theretofore operated entirely on local taxes and tuition or rate bills. In New York, by contrast, the law had the effect of strengthening existing systems of school funding. See Swift, *A History of Permanent Common School Funds.*

[25] Swift, *A History of Permanent Common School Funds.*

[26] In his oft-quoted "Memorial" to the legislature of the State of New York promoting the Erie Canal Project, DeWitt Clinton talked about the importance of binding a country's inhabitants together in a "community of interests" and "reciprocation of benefits." Though he was talking about "internal navigation" at the time, the logic of his argument applied to other internal improvement projects, including schooling. These phrases from Clinton's "Memorial" belong to the most widely cited passage of his writings, which is reproduced, among other places, in Nathan Miller, *The Enterprise of a Free People: Aspects of Economic Development in New York State during the Canal Period, 1792–1838* (Ithaca, NY: Cornell University Press, 1962): 42–43; and Evan Cornog, *The Birth of Empire: DeWitt Clinton and the American Experience, 1769–1828* (New York: Oxford University, 1998): 115.

[27] In some ways this policy became more significant after the Civil War, when federal power became a major factor in the economic development of the West. Examples include not only the Morrill Act, funded by the sale of federal lands that went to railroads, but huge grants of mineral rights in a state like Wyoming and of timber rights in states like Oregon and Washington. These rights were sold to private corporations with the justification that proceeds of the sale would fund education. On land grants see Earl D. Ross, *Democracy's College: The Land Grant Movement in the Formative Stage* (Ames: The Iowa State College Press, 1942); Carl L. Becker, *Cornell University: Founders and Founding* (Ithaca, NY: Cornell University Press, 1944); and Samuel D. Halliday, *History of the Federal Land Grant of July 2, 1862 ... as Relating to Cornell University* (Ithaca, NY: Ithaca Democrat Press, 1905). On mining and

Conclusion

In 1840, when Clarissa boarded the canal boat east to the city of Syracuse she embarked on a personal journey with historical resonance. It is tempting to see her as crossing a historical and sociological divide, from a rural world of reciprocity and trust among neighbors to a commercial world of competition among strangers. From this perspective, Clarissa's education, particularly her schooling at the Lima academy, provided a ticket from one world to the other. In reality, however, things were not that simple. For one thing, the rural world from which Clarissa came was not separated from the growing city of Syracuse, but connected to it in many ways. Although Clarissa described herself as leaving home and friend to depend on herself, she was not nearly as friendless as she made out. Family, church, and friendship networks were all connections that "bridged" the divide between rural and urban society and helped to ease Clarissa's transition to the city.

A second complication in the analogy between Clarissa's personal journey and larger shifts in economy and society is the reality of reversal. The concept of "capitalist transition" implies a directionality at the macro-economic level from which there is no return. For any particular person or place, however, the journey was not necessarily in one direction. The year 1840, when Clarissa made her journey to Syracuse, was also the midpoint of the Panic of 1837. In Lima, the Panic led to the bankruptcy of the local textile mill and that of several of its leading local investors. The academy was also threatened, though ultimately rescued by the claim that its considerable political capital gave it on the state. Meanwhile, after living and working for a time in Syracuse, Clarissa returned to her hometown with few of her original hopes and many of her anxieties fulfilled. Although she may well have recovered and gone on to a new career and new friendships in some other place, her diary ends on a note of keen despair.[28]

As historians, we often focus on formal institutions and thus on what through corporate power and political capital manages to last. One thing I have learned by simultaneously analyzing the significance of education in a transforming political economy and telling the story of schooling in a particular place is that corporate institutions may try to survive forever, but people can survive only for awhile. Though schooling occurs in institutions, learning occurs in a necessarily transitory life.

timber rights as sources of funding for schools, see Swift, *A History of Permanent Schools Funds*.

[28] Livingston and Onondaga County woman's diary [diary of Clarissa Pengra], 1838–1842, Microfilm, Collection #6230, CUDRMC. Holder of original material, Chris Densmore, University of Buffalo Archives. I have identified the woman as Clarissa Pengra.

Appendix

TABLE 1. *Per Capita Land Values and Improved Acreage, 1820, Lima and Neighboring Towns*

Town	Population	Total Acres	% Improved	Total Real Value	Per Capita Value
Lima	1963	21,094	56	$408.990.00	$208.35
Mendon	2016	20,601	32	$222,314.00	$110.27
Bloomfield	3631	34,946	na[a]	$522,532.00	$143.91

[a] The Bloomfield tax records did not include clear distinctions between improved and unimproved lands, so the proportion of improved land is not available for that town. The per capita land valuation indicates that the proportion of improved land was somewhere between that of Mendon and Lima.

Population figures taken from the federal census for 1820: *Census for 1820* (Washington, DC: Gales and Seaton, 1821). Total acreage, improved acreage, and real estate values calculated from 1820 county tax records for the towns of Lima, Mendon, and Bloomfield, OCRAIMS. I would like to thank Mary Jo Lanphear at the Ontario County Archives and Records Center and Taylor Kokjohn for assistance that made possible these calculations.

TABLE 2. *Percentage of Land Improved, Lima, 1820, as Compared with Clark's 4 Massachusetts Towns and Median % for Pritchard's 152 Counties*

Place	% Land Improved[a]
Lima, 1820	56
Clark's Four Towns, 1831	
Amherst	28.9
Hadley	34.9
Hatfield	37.9
Northampton	26.8

(continued)

TABLE 2 (continued)

Place	% Land Improved[a]
Clark's Four Towns, 1860	
Amherst	38.6
Hadley	42.0
Hatfield	49.5
Northampton	35.3
Average for Pritchard's 152 Counties, 1850	53.9
Average for Pritchard's 152 Counties, 1860	60.7

[a] Figure for proportion of land improved in Lima based on 1820 county tax assessment, OCRAIMS. See Appendix Table 1. Figures for Clark's four Massachusetts towns represent "Percentage of land under cultivation," based on aggregate valuations in Massachusetts General Court Records, Christopher Clark, The Roots of Rural Capitalism: Western Massachusetts, 1780–1860 (Ithaca, NY: Cornell University Press, 1990): 286. Figures for Pritchard's 152 counties represent median improved farm acreage in 1850 and 1860, 30–40 years after the 1820 Lima figures, with improved acreage figured as a % of total land. See note 9, Chapter 12, and Linda Pritchard, "Religious Change in a Developing Region: The Social Context of Evangelicalism in Western New York and the Upper Ohio Valley During the Mid-Nineteenth Century." Unpublished Ph.D. dissertation, University of Pittsburgh, 1980, p. 67.

TABLE 3. *Population Density, 1830, Lima and Surrounding Towns*

Town	Population	Square Miles[a]	People per Square Mile
Lima	1764	28.50	61.9
Avon	3362	44.25	75.9
Bloomfield	3861	57.75	66.9
Livonia	2265	39.00	58.1
Mendon	3057	39.80	76.8

[a] Figures given for the geographic areas of the respective towns are approximate, based on an analysis of town boundaries; they do not represent official figures.

Population figures taken from the federal census for 1830: *Enumeration of the Inhabitants of the United States. 1830* (Washington, DC: Duff Green, 1832).

Appendix

TABLE 4. *Population Density and Per Capita Land Values for Lima, 1820/1830/1850, as Compared with Pritchard's Categories of Economic Development, 1850–1860*

	Population Density	Town Size[a]	Per Capita Real Value[b]/ Farm Value	Price Index[c]	Adjusted Per Capita Value
Lima, 1820		1963	$208.35[b]	141	$295.73
Lima, 1830	62	1764			
Lima, 1850	85	2427	448.74[b]	94	421.74
Lima, 1850	85	2427	365.48	94	343.55
Pritchard's categories of economic development, 1850–1860					
Undeveloped	22	611	$167	97[d]	$159.08
Und-CF	40	1,151	$262		$254.14
Und-Mix	46	2,115	$269		$260.93
Und-Ind	43	2,080	$157		$152.29
Extractive	21	1,171	$177		$171.69
Commercial farming	41	1,118	$336		$325.92
CF-Mix	56	2,494	$361		$350.17
Mix	64	5,138	$370		$358.90
Industrial	163	16,988	$140		$135.80
Ind-Mix	55	4,428	$263		$255.11
Total average	49	1,739	$266		$258.02

[a] Figures for "town size" under Pritchard's model are averages of the largest towns in all counties in that category: Linda Pritchard, "Religious Change in a Developing Region: The Social Context of Evangelicalism in Western New York and the Upper Ohio Valley During the Mid-Nineteenth Century." Unpublished Ph.D. dissertation, University of Pittsburgh, 1980, pp. 108–109. See footnote 9, Chapter 12.

[b] Per capita real estate value for the town of Lima for 1820 is based on county tax assessment; see Appendix Table 2. Per capita real estate value for Lima for 1850 is based on the 1850 federal census. Corresponding figures for Pritchard's model are per capita *farm* values calculated from the federal census, so a second set of figures for Lima using farm values for 1850 is provided here.

[c] In order to compare data for Lima in 1820 to Pritchard's data, I converted per capita land values to constant dollars using the Composite Consumer Price Index developed by John J. McCusker, *How Much Is That in Real Money?: A Historical Price Index for Use as a Deflator of Money Values in the Economy of the United States* (Worcester: American Antiquarian Society, 1992).

[d] Because Pritchard's per capita figures represent an average for 1850 and 1860, I have used an average of the price indexes for 1850 (94) and 1860 (100).

Index

Abell, Asa, 203, 204
academies, academy education, 9
   and common schools, 123
   characteristics, 112
   coeducational, 127
   distinct from grammar schools, 108
   emergence of, 108, 116
   female, 278, 279
   genteel vs. productionist traditions, 127
   in New York State, 115, 116, 125, 270
   military, southern, 322
   per pupil funding, 280, 294
   Regents chartered, 119, 137
   single-sex, 127
academy
   definition, 112
   first use of term, 118
   idea of, 108, 114
      per Benjamin Franklin, 112
Academy of Philadelphia, 112, 113
accounting
   accounts, 286
      barter, 219
      informal, 103
      school district tax collection, 145
      settlement of, 39
      subscription account books, 242
      subscriptions, 99

      tuition account books, 285
   long-term debt, 20, 33, 224, 236, 237, 298
   account books, 224, 302
African Americans, 5, 11, 95, 109, 173, 321
Albany Female Academy, 280
Albany, New York, 131, 224, 257
Alfred Academy, 304
Allmendinger, David, 11
American Academy of Fine Arts, 161
American Home Missionary Society, 177, 197
Anderson, James, 11, 321
Andrews, Dee, 83, 92, 95
Anglican Church or Anglicanism, 109, 116–118, 134
anti-bank, anti-monopolism movement, 259, 260
anti-Jacksonians, 254, 257, 264
anti-Masonry, 140, 160, 180, 189–192, 195, 254, 255, 262, 324
   among Methodists, 190
   in New York State, 191
antislavery, 20, 172
apprentices and apprenticeship, 32, 43, 91, 110, 144, 152, 222, 289, 306
   farm labor, 222
Archer, Margaret, 120
artisans, 100, 162
Asbury, Francis, 99

attendance, school
    alternated with agricultural
        labor, 150
    high school, 318
    norms of, 272
    patterns, 9, 272, 273, 274, 307
    rates, 147
    universal, 16, 153
Auburn, New York, 307
Avon Methodist chapel, 188
Avon, New York, Town of, 50, 52, 85,
    180, 185, 188, 191, 206,
    208, 209, 235, 305, 308

Badger, Rev. Joseph, 36, 37, 49–53,
    56–61, 64, 66, 67, 68, 70,
    71, 87, 88
Baltimore, Maryland, 77, 92, 223
banks and banking, 8, 215, 226, 227,
    231
    Bank of Rochester, 224
    Bank of Utica, 224
    bank policies, liberalization of in
        New York, 224
    bankruptcy and foreclosure, 15,
        283, 291, 292, 295–297,
        327
    banks
        as business corporations, 24
        British, 292
    bonds, 34
    commercial, 291
    First Bank of the United States,
        224
    free banking
        politics of, 325
    lending policies, liberalization of,
        231
    lending practices, 8
    loans, 34
        commercial, 298
        interest, 133
        short-term, 252, 282
    money banks, 224
    Ontario Bank, Canandaigua, 230
    Ontario Savings Bank, 224
    Rochester Bank, 291
    Rochester Savings Bank, 225
    savings, 225, 226

    savings banks, 224, 226, 227
    Second National Bank of the United
        States, 293
    state investments in, 326
    state-chartered, 293
    stock, 133, 172, 173, 252
Baptists, 52, 80, 190, 196, 256
    academies, 200
Barnard, Rev. John, 55, 61, 62, 64,
    177, 184
barter, 14, 15, 33, 39, 145, 219,
    238, 250
Batavia, New York, 126, 200
Bath, New York, 126
Beecher, Catharine, 270
benefits, reciprocation of, 326
Bennett family, 188
Bennett, Augustus, 15, 176, 184–188,
    189, 191, 192, 204, 207,
    210, 235, 242–246, 250
Bennett, William, 188
Benson, Lee, 255, 259, 261, 263
Bloomfield, New York, 96, 98, 178,
    180, 184, 190, 208, 210
Bloomfield Circuit, 184, 187, 210
boarding facilities, 3, 186, 251, 265,
    276, 318
Bodenhorn, Howard, 8, 226,
    227
boosterism, 177, 179, 185, 192,
    196, 197
Boston, Massachusetts, 110,
    115, 116
Bourdieu, Pierre, 322
Bowles, Samuel, 9
Bristol, New York, 50
Britain, 108, 120, 162
British North America, 108, 122
Brockport, New York, 216–218,
    306
Brockport Collegiate Institute, 314
Bronson, Arthur and Oliver,
    221, 298
Bronson, Isaac, 15, 221, 231, 243–247,
    263, 290, 298
Bronson family, 298
Brown, Melancton, 49, 182, 291
Bruckney, William, 190
Buffalo, New York, 190, 193, 313

Index

Bullock, Steven C., 163, 165, 189
Burke, Colin, 198
Burpee, Samuel, 182
Butler, Mr., 309–313, 316

Caledonia, New York, 180, 272, 308
Canada, 50, 77, 297, 313
    Lower Canada, 77
    Upper Canada, 77
canals, 3, 20, 125, 140, 160, 161, 223,
    228, 313, 327
Canandaigua Academy, 124, 125,
    127–130, 135–137
    capitalization, initial, 131
    charter, 126, 129
    incorporation, 125, 126
Canandaigua, New York, 124–128,
    166, 168, 203, 223, 224,
    231, 272, 273, 278,
    279, 308
Canandaigua Lake, 125
capital
    accumulation of, 7, 13, 325
    as surplus labor and goods, 32
    commercial, 215, 217, 243, 247,
        300
    concentration of, 8, 188, 261
    corporate, 73, 75, 102, 177,
        225
    cultural, 17, 126, 178, 295, 302, 319,
        321, 322
    financial, 16, 17, 87, 264, 269, 318,
        319, 320
    human, 319
        formation, 10, 11, 320
    intellectual, 319
    mobility, 8, 226, 319
    mobilization of, 124
    noncommercial, 298
    political, 16, 17, 159, 161, 174, 195,
        211, 263, 264, 268, 280,
        282, 295, 300, 318–320,
        324, 325
    rural, 7, 225, 288, 292
    social, 16–19, 32, 34, 41, 56, 70,
        73, 87, 89, 159, 192,
        195, 210, 295, 298, 300,
        302, 317– 323, 325
        bonding and bridging, 87
    definition, 32–34
    idea of, 32
    theory, 87
    state, 216
    surplus, 73
    translocal, 263
    valuation, 233
capitalist market economy, 17, 299
capitalist production, 14, 100, 240
capitalist transition, 4, 7, 12, 13, 15,
    16, 102, 216, 226, 234,
    241, 247, 283, 288,
    299, 327
capitalization, 14, 16, 94–96, 122, 136,
    137, 183, 198, 216,
    218, 225, 234, 239, 241,
    268, 291, 295, 298
    commercial, 246
    corporate, 128
    local, 131
    norms of, 233
    social, 321
Carnegie, Andrew, 188
cash, 86, 96, 219, 220, 222–224, 227,
    228, 234, 235, 237
    value of pledges, 98
Caulkins, Thomas, 15, 142, 146, 148
Cayuga, Town of, New York, 297
Cayuga Lake, 193
Cazenovia Seminary, 203, 254, 260
    Regents status, 201
Cazenovia, New York, 74, 81, 172, 201,
    254
Chapman, Rev. Ezekiel, 36–44, 49
Charleston [Lima] Congregational
    Society, 18, 19
Chesapeake Bay, 77
Chesapeake region, 95
Christian Advocate and Journal,
    284, 292
Christian Herald, 56
church and churches
    alternative to courts, 287
    church members, 61, 63, 90, 91, 92,
        93, 207
    church membership, 61, 70
    church societies, 103
    disestablishment, 122
    established, 19, 120, 134

church and churches (*cont.*)
   examinations, 57, 70
      religious, 65
   excommunication, 60, 62, 63
   membership, 48, 89, 92
      by gender, 57
   trials, 55, 61, 62, 68
Church of England, 108
civic engagement, 139, 323
Clark, Christopher, 7, 8, 240, 241
Clark, Erastus, 176, 180, 182, 227, 235, 291, 292
class (social)
   class interest, 179, 185
   class solidarity, 262
   class spectrum, 153
   middle class, 12, 112, 172, 301, 322
   ownership class, 262
   working class, English, 100
classical studies, 110
Clinton, DeWitt, 158–160, 163, 166, 168, 169, 203, 326
   Masonic leader
      Grand Master of the State of New York, 160
Clinton, George, 118, 128
Clinton Academy, 115, 119
   Regents charter, 119
coalition building, education and, 191–192, 326
Colby College, 196
Coleman, James, 33
colleges, 123, 171, 195, 198, 268, 271, 272
   denominational, 256
   state support for, 293
Columbia College, 118
commerce, 126, 158, 178, 184, 239, 300
Common School Fund, New York State, 133, 170, 171
common schools, 9–11, 16, 107, 123, 133–135, 144, 146–148, 151, 153, 157, 265, 268, 271, 304, 305, 319
   attendance, universal, 147
      capitalization, 173
   commissioners, 164
   corporate status, 37

district schools, 44, 49, 109
expansion of, 171
funding, 133–135, 139, 170
   per pupil, 133
   state, 41
incorporation law, 45
investment in, 147
laws, 41, 42, 146, 153
rural, 14, 141
school commissioners, 37, 41, 43, 44, 139, 154
school districts, 34, 42–45, 47, 144, 155, 293, 324, 325
   boundaries, 42
   incorporation, 31
   libraries, 293
   Lima, New York, attendance rates, 147
   meetings, 156
school inspectors, 37, 42, 43, 47, 154, 180
school laws, 14, 45, 47, 144
school masters, 142
schoolhouses, 14, 15, 19, 29, 36, 44, 45, 121, 164, 180, 220
state intervention in, 323
state support for, 293
subscribers, 45
summer and winter schools, 141
support for, 128, 130
teachers, 305
common wealth, 161
communal social relations, 241
community building, 14, 19, 22, 28, 29, 30, 31, 32, 34, 35, 48, 104, 180, 181, 219, 235, 236, 323
community of interests, 158, 159, 161, 173, 174, 326
competition, 16, 122, 238, 242, 247, 249, 327
Congregationalism, 21, 38, 80, 109, 116, 189, 197
   congregational societies, 26, 28
Connecticut, 68, 116, 134, 142, 153, 229
Cooper, William, 126, 127
Cooper family, 97
Cooperstown, New York, 126

Index

Copeland, John, 218, 219, 242, 254
corporations, 25, 103, 118, 122, 131, 260, 265, 295
  religious, 65
  school corporations, 45
correspondence, 114, 274, 306, 307, 313
Cortland County, New York, 66
Cortland, New York, 92
Cott, Nancy, 11
courts, 220, 229, 297
  litigation, 299
courtship, 309, 311–313
craftsmen, 108, 111, 120, 172, 182, 184, 185, 225, 238, 241, 262, 323
Craig, Alexander, 145
credentials, social and cultural, 17, 70, 73, 76, 306, 313, 323
credit
  commercial, 34, 173, 179, 216, 220, 226–228, 244, 283, 284, 288–292, 300, 303
  noncommercial, 33, 70, 84, 227
credit-brokers, 14, 15, 90, 219–225, 227, 232, 233, 241, 247, 263, 323
crisis, financial, 166, 282, 283, 292, 294, 296
Cross, Whitney, 48, 206
currency, 70, 226, 234
  bank notes, 224
  financial instruments, 226
    cash, 224, 240, 285, 287, 291, 299, 303
    to pay interest, 284
    promissory notes, 136, 137, 230, 236, 252, 290, 292
    securities, 82, 234, 243
curricula, 112
  basic English education, 156
  classical studies, 109, 113, 114, 172
  gendered, 274–279
  grammar education, 156
  higher subjects, 142, 268, 270–272, 279
  liberal arts, 250
  mechanical arts, 250
  nonclassical studies, 114
  theological studies, 265

debt
  accounting, 20, 33, 224, 236, 237, 298
  collection, 25, 247, 253, 261, 283–288, 299–300, 302
  enforcement of payment, 286
  relief, 295
Delaware County, New York, 97
denominations (religious) and denominationalism, 29, 30, 35, 37, 62, 71, 75, 80, 86, 94, 100, 118, 119, 177, 185, 195–200, 203, 207
  affiliations, 49
  growth, 77
  Masonic membership denounced, 190
  nonevangelical, 65, 207
Detroit, Michigan, 77, 313
diffusion of intelligence, 15, 162
discipline, 55
  church, 60–65, 66, 70, 284, 286
  church as market discipline, 287
  moral, 65, 66, 69
  moral and educational, 56, 58–60
  religious, 62, 310
  social, 56, 88
Dixson, John, 43
Doyle, Don Harrison, 192
Dutchess County, New York, 97

East Avon, New York, 188, 207
East Hampton, Long Island, New York, 115, 119, 121
economic change and development, 6–8, 87, 89, 100–104, 173, 179, 207–208, 211, 225–227, 234, 239–242, 261, 320, 321, 323, 325–326
economic depression, 234, 282
economic transformation, 15, 17, 232, 266, 302
economy, 320
  political, 6, 16, 85, 108, 123, 131, 140, 141, 157, 161, 174, 256, 319, 320, 325, 326
  transforming, 15, 327
  social, 228, 240, 246, 298
    norms of, 241
    rural, 32, 34, 233, 235, 236, 238, 239, 242, 243, 246, 251

education
  agricultural, 158, 252, 265
  basic, 154
  collegiate, 270
  common, 166, 222, 270, 272
  effect of disestablishment of religion, 117
  female, 31, 270, 273, 274, 279
  liberal arts, 252
  manual labor education, 243, 247, 249–252, 265
  market-based, 271
  mechanical arts, 252, 265
  of both sexes, 253
  of girls, 11
  of teachers, 266, 271
  of women, 185, 305
  single sex, 111
  spiritual, 316
  support for, 123, 128, 293, 323
education funds, endowed by states, 135
Eggleston, Elisha, 291, 292
elections, 157, 159, 169, 249
Ellicot, John, 227
Ellicott, Joseph, 127
Elmira, New York, 193
endowments, 14, 19, 123, 126, 129, 131, 132, 134, 136
  land-based, 124, 129, 130, 135
  state-level, 135
Enlightenment, 162
entrepreneurship, 7, 8, 13, 127, 239, 243, 244, 261, 262, 288, 303
Episcopal Church, 79, 119
Erasmus Hall Academy, 115, 119, 121
Erie Canal, 160, 161, 223
evangelicalism, 12, 13, 37, 54, 55, 56, 66, 70, 87, 89, 92, 100, 102–104, 207, 211, 249, 262, 324
  and capital formation, 89
  and economic development, 100, 101
  and Freemasonry, 176
  anti-Masonic sentiment, 190
  as an educational movement, 58
  educational movement, 16
  evangelical societies, 57
  growing influence in politics and government, 259
  preaching, 196
  regional association, 323
examinations, 66, 69, 274
  religious, 58, 64, 70
exchange rates, New York, 142
expansion of the money supply, 173
extracurricular activities, 276

factories, 13, 289, 292
  textile, 288
  woolen, 283, 288, 289, 303
faculty
  female, 271, 272
  male, 272
  preceptress, female, 275
faculty housing, 318
Farmer's Hall, 121
farms and farming
  farmers, 7, 33, 34, 97, 153, 172, 182, 225, 239, 240, 241
    commercial, 323
    demand for education, 108
    initiators of economic change, 241
    landholding, 180
  farming, 51
    commercial, 13, 207, 208, 226
    families, 180, 182, 185
    neighborly exchange, 239
    production, 239
      mixed commodities and neighborly exchange, 240
    subsistence, 207
    towns, 207
  farms, 122, 186, 188
    inherited, 151
    mortgaged, 243
female institutions, 271, 277
Fillmore, Glezen, 204
financiers, 159, 226, 231, 243, 263, 290
  local, 220, 227, 229, 230, 232, 283, 288, 303
financing, 137, 187, 290, 298
  nondenominational, 198
Finney, Charles Grandison, 3, 48
First Methodist Church of Mendon, 90, 91
  members, 93

Index 339

First Universalist Church of Lima, 177
First Universalist Church, Cortland, New York, 66
First Universalist Society of Lima, 65, 66
   constitution, 65
   founding, 31
   membership, 65
   subscriptions, 31
Flatbush, Long Island, New York, 115, 119, 121
Flushing, Long Island, New York, 119
Formisano, Ronald, 255, 256, 259, 261, 263
France, 18, 120
Franklin and Marshall College, 197
Franklin, Benjamin, 20, 31, 38, 107, 110, 112–115
Free School Society of New York City, 161
freedom
   economic association, 325
   of conscience, 64, 153
   religious association, 325
Freemasonry, 159, 161, 162, 166, 167, 189, 191, 192, 193, 263
   condemned by Methodists, 177
   Grand Master for the State of New York, 162
   history, 162
   ideals of virtue and public service, 164
   lecturers, 163
   library sponsorship, 163
   Lima Masonic Lodge, 165
      charter, 162
   lodges, 165, 191
      as seminaries of learning, 163
   Masonic charter, Avon lodge, 191
   Masonic culture, 163
   Masonic enlightenment ideas, 164
   Masonic rituals, 163
   Masons
      public agenda of, 163
      social standing of, 162
   membership
      among political office holders, 165
      broadening of, 162
      levels of, 163

   political significance, in New York State, 165
   relationship to religion, 189
   Union Lodge no. 45 of Lima, 191
French-Canadians, 5
friendship, 3, 4, 15, 17, 52, 70, 97, 267, 283, 284, 301–303, 305–312, 315, 316
   translocal, 312, 323
   trust, 310, 311
frontier life, 315
funding, 28, 29, 159, 170, 197, 215, 216
   denominational, 198
   equity, 47
   per pupil, 146, 270
   public, 151, 153, 154, 295
   state, 42, 318
   voluntary, 123, 131
fundraising, 269, 319
   Methodist, 102
   subscriptions, 20, 236
funds
   federal deposit, 293, 325
   public, 139, 140, 146, 324–326
      bonds, 172
      loans, 172

Gamm, Gerald, 323
gender, 66, 69, 154
Genesee Annual Conference, 79, 83, 211, 219, 234, 246, 260, 268
   circuits, 264
   districts, 264
   stations, 264
Genesee College, 319
Genesee County, New York, 126, 127, 165, 166
Genesee River, 50, 81, 85, 125, 127, 216, 217, 223
Genesee Road, 19, 50, 125, 126
Genesee Wesleyan Seminary, 6, 16, 104, 164, 187, 200, 202, 203, 221, 236, 238, 244, 261, 264, 268–271, 277, 279, 282, 285, 287, 292, 295, 298, 299, 301, 304, 305, 307, 313, 316, 318, 319, 327

Genesee Wesleyan Seminary *(cont.)*
  academic culture, 274, 278
  agents, 252, 264, 269, 299
  Bill of Incorporation, 254
  Board of Trustees, 249, 250, 251, 253, 254, 256, 257, 265, 282, 283, 284
    memorials to state legislature, 294
  Board of Visitors, 254
  Building Committee, 233
  capitalization, 244, 279, 295, 298
  catalog, 267, 268, 270, 271, 273, 274, 275, 276, 277, 284
  charter, 16, 35, 253, 254, 256, 257, 258, 259, 260, 261, 263–265, 267, 268, 269, 280, 298, 324
    1833, 256
    terms of, 249
  Departments
    English, 270
    Female, 270, 271, 275
      preceptress, female, 271
    Languages, 270, 271
    Mathematics and Natural Philosophy, 270, 278
    Moral Sciences and Belles-Lettres, 270, 278
  designation as Regents institution won, 280
  enrollment, 268, 270, 272, 278, 280, 294, 306
    coeducational, 185
    gender differences, 276
  faculty, 272
    female, 305
    gendered, 274
    male, 305
  farm, supporting, 216, 217, 265
  finances, 283
  lobbying the legislature, 294
  manual labor education proposed, 249, 250
  Principal, 285
  Regents funding, 268
  Regents status, 281, 295
  site, 186
    competion, 217
  student labor, 252

  student population, 268
  students, 307
    ages of, 272
    attracting, 318
    geographic origins, 306
    subscription records, 269
    Treasurer, 243, 245, 285
    tuition, free for subscribers, 268
Geneseo, New York, 22, 172, 191, 233, 237, 238
Geneva, New York, 165, 245
Georgia, 116
  state constitution, 117
gerrymanders, 168
Gilbert, Othaniel, 15, 288, 289, 290–292, 295–297
Gintis, Herbert, 9
Glorious Revolution of 1689, 26
Goldin, Claudia, 320
good government, history and theory of, 152
goods, 103, 222, 298
  cultural, 86
  exchange of, 238, 243, 251, 263
  product of labor, 32
  spiritual, 86
  surplus, 32, 90, 215, 239
Gorham, Nathaniel, 128
Gorton, Thomas, 44, 45, 52
Goshen, New York, 121
gospel and school lots, 128, 129
Gospel of Wealth, 188
government, federal, 293
Grant, Martin, 307
Grant, Rev. Loring, 204, 238, 244, 246, 251, 254
Graves, William, 306, 307
Gray, William, 15, 139, 140, 151, 153, 156, 157
Greeley, Horace, 305
Grout, Henry, 176, 180, 182, 224
Guernsey, James K., 223, 227

Hamilton, Ontario, 9
Hanchett, Erastus, 296, 298
Hartwick Seminary, 197
Henretta, James, 239
Henrietta, New York, 180, 217–219

Index

history
  African American, 321
  women's, 11
Holland Land Company, 126, 127
Holland, E. A., 51, 68
Homer, New York, 65
Honeoye Creek, 23, 102, 223, 288
Honeoye Falls, New York, 189, 206
Honeoye Falls Methodist Church, 189
Hosmer, John, 314
House, Frederic, 176, 180, 182, 184, 235, 236, 238, 242, 243, 260, 261
Hovey, Benjamin, 229, 230
Hudson River, 77
Hume, David, 33

Illinois, 136, 177, 178, 197, 198, 313, 314
Illinois College, 177, 197
imported goods, 223, 224
incorporation, 20, 21, 22, 24, 25, 29, 35, 90, 94, 95, 113, 136, 137, 249, 252–254, 260, 263, 268
  corporate property ownership, 21
  of educational institution, 16
indemnity, legal, 295
Indiana, 135, 178, 199, 313
industrialists, 14, 188, 261, 262
industrialization, 9, 10, 188
influence, political, 35, 158, 174, 180
Ingersoll, Charles, 182, 307
inheritance, 66, 70, 221
institution building, 81, 95, 177, 195, 205
  Methodist, 195, 203
insurance companies, 24, 140
intensification of agriculture, 215
interest, 86, 99, 123, 221, 226, 237, 244, 284, 291, 295, 297, 298
  income from, 293
  on investments, 325
  rates, 8
internal navigation, 161
investment, 7, 16, 29, 90, 178, 180, 187, 215, 225, 228, 229, 244, 245, 303

investors, 226, 232–234, 289, 291, 295, 297, 327
Iroquois Trail, 125
Ithaca, New York, 190

Jackson, Andrew, 254, 293
Jacksonianism, 160
Jacksonians, 12, 249, 254–257, 259, 260, 263, 293, 325
Jacksonville, Illinois, 177, 178, 192, 197
Jamaica, Long Island, New York, 115, 119, 121
Jensen, Joan, 103
Johnson, Curtis D., 61, 62, 66, 92
Johnson, Paul E., 101, 261, 262
Johnson, Seth, 296
Johnson, Sir William, 114
joint stock
  arrangements, 254, 286
  associations, 234, 268, 269, 299

Kaestle, Carl, 9–11, 111
Katz, Lawrence, 320
Katz, Michael, 8, 9
Kentucky, 77
Kett, Joseph, 272, 273
Kimball, Eli, 222
Kings' College. *See* Columbia College
Kingston Academy, 112, 118
Kingston, New York, 121
Kulikoff, Alan, 8
Kutolowski, Kathleen, 165, 166

labor, 303
  competition from students, 251
  exchange of, 15, 32, 70, 99, 222, 247
  surplus, 7, 8, 32, 90, 97, 103
  transition from family labor to wage labor, 100
  wage labor, 10, 14
laissez faire ideology, 256
Lake Erie, 77
Lake Ontario, 50
Lamoureaux, Naomi, 241
Lamphere, Amos, 288–292, 295–297

Lancaster, Pennsylvania, 197
land, 178–180, 186, 217, 218, 228, 238, 243
　title, Native American, 128
landowners, 22, 96, 97, 130, 227, 228
laws
　common schools, 37, 41
　corporate, 325
　incorporation, 25
　Sabbatarian laws, 262
legal action, 29, 198, 261, 292
legislative codes, revision of, 157
lenders, 290, 291, 303
　commercial, 282, 283
　private, 291
lending, 221, 227
　mortgages, 97, 98, 133, 172, 173, 221, 222, 227–232, 243, 245, 247, 261, 279, 290, 291, 298, 305
　　mortgage sales agreements, 228
　short-term, 291
LeRoy, New York, 190, 217, 218
Leslie, Bruce, 197, 198
Lewiston, New York, 50, 190
Lexington, Kentucky, 165
liberal state, 16, 159, 169, 174, 320
　formation of, 158
　modern, 15, 325
liberalism, 248, 255
　political, 169
liberty, religious, 24, 25, 27, 44, 45, 116, 117, 324
libraries, 20
Lima, New York, 13, 14, 19, 20, 29–31, 68, 96, 128, 146, 156, 158, 159, 168, 176–179, 181, 182, 184, 190, 193, 211, 215, 217–219, 226, 246, 248, 252, 261, 264, 267, 282, 317
　academy, 108, 161, 247
　　bid, 88, 180
　　founding, 34
　population, 13, 178
　tax lists, 91

Lima Baptist Church, 47
Lima Congregational Society, 15, 19–23, 25, 27, 28, 30, 37–39, 44, 45, 47–49, 52, 56, 61, 65, 99, 147, 180
　builder of schoolhouse, 29, 30
　constitution, 19, 25, 27, 31, 46, 64
　incorporation, 19, 21
Lima Methodist Church, 187, 207, 209, 219
Lima Presbyterian Church, 63, 70, 183
Lima School District no. 4, 36, 44, 47, 52, 139–149
Lima School District no. 9, 147
Literary and Philosophical Society, 161
Literature Fund, New York State, 133, 135, 137, 171, 173, 294
Little, Dr. George W., 180, 238, 239, 242
Livingston County, New York, 3, 65, 168, 171, 188, 191, 248, 252, 294
Livingston family, 97, 136
Livingston High School, Geneseo, 172
Livonia, New York, 146, 180, 182, 190, 191, 207–210
lobbying, 257
　Methodist, 319
Locke, John, 26, 27
Lockport, New York, 313
lotteries, 129, 133
Lutheranism, 197

Maine, 163
Malkmus, Doris, 127, 199
Mann, Alexander, 305
manufacturers, 101, 173, 184, 227
Margo, Robert A., 142
markets
　competition, 122, 242
　　between student labor and local residents, 265
　　for students, 278
　norms of, 244

Index — Market Revolution —

market culture, 16, 17, 283, 284
market discipline, 216, 282–284, 286, 299, 300
market integration, 4, 5, 8, 219, 242, 261, 320
market principles, 131
market revolution, 4–6, 12, 15, 17, 283
market-based demand for schooling, 107, 108, 122, 146–150, 156, 159, 268, 270, 273
marriage, 27, 93, 221, 312
Marshall College, 197
Marvin, Jasper, 182
Maryland, 116
Massachusetts, 5, 7–9, 109, 116, 128, 129, 134, 135, 153–155, 240, 288, 318
Mendon, New York, 56, 85, 89–93, 95, 96, 98, 101–103, 178, 184, 191, 208, 209, 223
Mercersburg, Pennsylvania, 197
merchant houses, 221
merchants, 8, 13, 159, 173, 180, 184, 185, 224–226, 241, 291
Methodist Episcopal Church, 6, 35, 92, 122, 200, 256, 310
  academies, 176
    affiliated, 6, 14
    Regents status, 172
    sponsorship, 317
  academies, academy education, sponsorship of, 137
  agents, 267–269, 280, 319
  anti-Masonry in, 195
  areas of expansion, 77
  as a corporation, 259
  Charter Fund, 82, 298
  circuits, 72–75, 78, 83, 208
    circuit work, 205
  conferences, 78, 87, 208
    Genesee Annual Conference, 75–77, 81, 84, 176, 191, 193, 201, 202, 210, 216, 233, 248, 252, 254, 258, 259, 262, 264, 269

    circuits, 81
      Avon-Lima Circuit, 50
      Bloomfield Circuit, 81, 95, 98, 188, 190, 205–208, 210, 216
        membership growth, 81
      Lima Circuit, 287
      Sweetland Circuit, 74, 81
    committees, Seminary Committee, 176, 202, 204, 207, 215, 217–219, 254
    districts
      Bloomfield District, 205
      Buffalo District, 202
      Genesee District, 202, 204
      Ontario District, 202
      Steuben District, 202
    establishment and growth, 81
    seminary proposed, 216
  Niagara Conference, 83
  Oneida Conference, 193, 201
  quarterly conferences, 82
  districts, 79, 208
    boundaries, 79
  Doctrines and Discipline of the Methodist Episcopal Church, 58–60, 72, 74, 79, 82–84, 85, 89, 99, 295
  expansion in North America, 76
  fundraising, 268
  growth of, 77
  heirarchy, 244
  institution-building, 96
  largest church in the United States, 248
  leaders, 75, 80, 243, 265, 280
  membership, 93
  Methodist Book Concern, 82
  Methodist classes, 310
  Methodist culture, 295, 299
  Methodist discipline, 300, 310
  Methodist Economy, 71–73, 85, 86, 87, 247, 318
  Methodist system, 84, 87
  ministers and preachers, 75, 258
    candidates, 74, 75

Methodist Episcopal Church (*cont.*)
  celibacy preferred, 76
  located vs. traveling, 53
  probationary, 76
  professional hierarchy, 73
  salaries, 82
  superannuated, 53
  system of professional advancement, 74
 networks, 280
 organization
  Annual conference, 75
  translocal, 324
 organizational networks, 268
 organizational structure, 72
 periodicals, 82, 284, 292, 300
 political activism, 263
 population ranking, 77
 press, 284, 285, 295
 proselytizing, 259
 publishing, 86
 quarterage, 94, 98, 285
 rhetoric of market culture, 284
 stations, 208
 subscription stock, political value of, 299
 territorial units, 73
 translocal organizational power, 263
 writers, 86
Methodist Society of Norton's Mills, 65
Michigan, 178, 255, 256, 259, 296, 303, 304, 313–316
Middlebury Academy, 124–128, 135–137
Middlebury, New York, 126, 128
migration, 68, 302, 313, 314
 risks of, 315
Miller, George Frederick, 116
mill owners, 15, 97, 98, 100, 102, 187, 262
mill-sites, 42, 94, 96, 102, 207, 288, 290
mills, 96–99, 101, 102, 318
 carding, 288, 289
 carding and fulling, 102
 cotton, 288
 grist, 223
 Midwestern, 289
 production equipment and facilities, 298
 textile, 14, 216, 220, 225, 232, 283, 288, 289, 292, 295, 298, 318, 327
 water-powered, 96
 woolen, 289, 291
ministers and preachers, 29, 65, 81, 87, 88
 as lay leaders, 75
 as teachers, 109
 assignments, 83
 associates of Reverend Badger, 57
 careers, 39, 43, 84
 circuit, 15, 83, 98, 210
 combined preaching and teaching, 29, 43
 congregational support for, 103
 credentials, 74
 evangelical, 48, 52, 53
 independent, 52
 interim, 49
 itinerant, 4, 15, 37, 49–51, 53, 67, 70, 72, 83, 84
  itinerancy as entrepreneurship, 51
  logic and logistics of itinerancy, 53
  mobility, 53
 livelihoods of, 38
 Masonic membership of, 189
 ordained, 43, 58
 parsonages, 30
 permanent, 49
 professional, 102, 118, 201, 202, 205, 208
 quarterage, 89
 relationship to congregation, 51
 responsibilities, local and translocal, 83
 salaries, 75, 94
  augmented by teaching, 109
  how paid, 37
 salary disputes, 38
 settled, 37, 41, 43, 44, 50, 51, 53, 61
 settlement, 37–41, 53
 superannuated, 84
 surplus, 197
 traveling, 75, 80, 86, 264, 285
 visitors, 208
missionaries, 18

Index 345

Mitchell, Minnie, 308
mobility, 8, 306
   geographic, 56, 180, 181
   occupational, 305, 306
   social, 9, 301
Models of Academy Organization, 124
Molloy, Peter, 290
money, 21, 39, 99, 187, 226, 227, 233, 243, 291, 297
money-lenders, 291, 292
monopolies, 255, 260, 324
Montreal, Quebec, 223
Moon, Roxey, 55, 56, 60, 66–70
Morgan affair, 160, 191
Mormonism, 48
Morse, Erastus and Abel, 230

Native Americans, 5, 109, 125, 325
Naylor, Nathalie, 115, 119
negotiable instruments, 226, 234, 252
neighborly cooperation, 230
neighborly exchange, 239, 240, 291
neighbors, 40, 224, 230, 232, 236, 237, 246
New Bern Academy, 112, 115, 117
   charter, 117
New Bern, North Carolina, 117, 121
New England, 19, 21, 36, 38, 50, 68, 116, 124, 134, 135, 141, 197
New Hampshire, 50, 116, 117
New Orleans, Louisiana, 314
New York
   Colony of, 116, 118
      regions
         Hudson Valley, 121
         Long Island, 121
New York City, 9, 15, 77, 82, 92, 111, 115, 124, 131, 160, 164, 171, 220–224, 231, 243, 255, 260, 263, 264, 288, 290, 291, 298, 303, 305, 306, 314
   lenders, 291
   markets, 227
New York Gazette-Weekly Post Boy, 111
New York Herald Tribune, 305
New York High School, 171
New York State, 6, 9, 24, 37, 38, 95, 104, 108, 112, 122, 123, 128, 129, 131–135, 140, 142, 157, 173, 191, 203, 248, 255, 259, 267, 293, 295, 319
   academy founding, 124
   banks, 224
   canal fund
      bonds, 173
      mortgages, 172
   capital, income on, 326
   common school fund, 173
   constitution
      1777, 166
      1784, 25
      1821, 166–168
      1821 constitutional convention, 160, 168
   education, first state support of, 170
   laws
      1827 education act, 173
      incorporation, 120
   legislature, 16, 21, 24, 25, 31, 35, 118, 119, 128, 129, 133, 168, 177, 183, 220, 248, 253, 254, 256, 257–260, 263–265, 269, 280, 292, 293, 295, 317, 319, 324
      anti-Masonry in, 195
      Jacksonian leadership, 257
      Whig control, 294
   Masonic lodges, 164
   political transformation, 264
   politics, 166, 167, 255
   regions
      Catskills, 77, 128
      central, 48, 77, 297
      Cherry Valley, 128
      eastern, 97, 220
      Finger Lakes, 48, 77, 193
      Genesee country, 193
      Genesee region, 50, 68, 77, 80
      Genesee Valley, 13, 14, 48, 126, 220, 228
      Hudson Valley, 97, 136
      Long Island, 115, 119
      Mohawk Valley, 97

346   Index

New York State (cont.)
   Niagara, 77
   southern tier, 193
   Upper Hudson Valley, 220
   upstate, 13, 35, 48, 61, 77, 205,
      206, 285, 287, 306, 313
   western, 3, 13, 14, 16, 22, 32, 48,
      50, 51, 97, 125, 127, 128,
      140, 160, 167, 176, 185,
      189, 190–192, 207, 216,
      219, 220, 227–229, 231,
      244, 254, 257, 263, 264,
      268, 269, 291, 297, 299
   school laws, 37, 41, 49, 109, 142,
      146, 153, 156, 172, 173,
      174
   western region, 125
New York Times, 305
Newell, Silas, 127, 135, 136
Newton, Isaac, 162
Newton, Long Island, New York, 119
New-York Historical Society, 161
Niagara County, New York, 50
Nickerson, Michael, 79, 80
North America, 120, 134
   colonial, 120
North Bloomfield School, 32
North Bloomfield, New York, 47, 65,
   98, 102
North Carolina, 112, 115–117, 121,
   134
   legislature, 117
Northampton, Massachusetts, 110,
   153–156
Norton family, 95, 103, 178
Norton, Lyman, 102
Norton, Zebulon, 23, 94, 102, 223
Norton's Mills, New York, 23, 32, 42,
   47–51, 57, 65, 88, 102,
   206
Noyes, Alfred, 48

O'Neil, Edward Herring, 124
occupations, 185
   clerks, 4, 111, 172, 301, 306
   craftsmen, 258
   factory operatives, 4
   laborers, 4, 91, 100, 101, 152, 289
   manufacturers, 240, 241, 255, 262

   merchants, 7, 32, 108, 113, 120,
      172, 176, 182, 225, 227,
      229, 240, 241, 255, 258,
      262, 290
   mill owners, 32, 101
   mill workers, 101
   navigators, 113, 306
   of GWS subscribers, 184
   peddlar of factory clothes, 209
   professionals, 182, 225, 258,
      262
   proprietors, 32
   servants, 111
   shopkeepers, 101, 108, 120, 162,
      172, 262
   shopowners, 258
   surveyors, 113, 306
   teaching, 305
   tradesmen, 225, 266
   workingmen, 262
Ohio, 68–70, 77, 135, 177, 178,
   198, 313, 315
Olean, New York, 193
Oneida Community, 48
Oneida Institute of Science and
   Industry, 172, 249
Oneonta, New York, 197
Onondaga County, New York, 3
Onondaga, Town of, 313, 316
Ontario County, New York,
   124–126, 168
Ontario Female Seminary, 272–274,
   278, 308
Ontario, Province of, 9
Opal, J. M., 124
Ostrander family, 93
Otsego County, New York, 97
Otsego Patent, 128

Pain, Sally, 61
Paley's Theology, 276
Panic of 1837, 254, 282, 283, 288,
   291, 293, 295, 301–303,
   327
Parker, Rev. John, 206, 209
Parker, William, 291
Parmelee, Smith, 180
parties, political, 13, 195, 255,
   317, 323

Index

Democratic Party and Democrats, 159, 254–257, 259, 260, 262, 264
Jacksonian Democrats, 254–256, 259, 263, 293
Jacksonians, 254
People's Party, 160, 168
republicans, Bucktail, 166
Whig Party, 254–256, 262–264, 293, 294, 324
Workingmen's Party, 255, 260
partnerships, 93, 223
Partridge, Harriet, 15, 142, 146, 148, 157
patriarchal norms, 140, 152–155
Patterson, George W., 294
pedagogy, 323
Pengra, Clarissa, 3–6, 15, 17, 272, 301, 302, 305–307, 309–311, 313–316, 323, 327
Penn Yan, New York, 251
Pennsylvania, 68, 77, 95, 111, 127, 135, 197, 258, 261
per pupil funding, 134, 137, 293
Perlmann, Joel, 142
Perry, New York, 216–219, 246
petitions, 20, 190, 248, 249, 253, 260, 261, 263–265, 269, 324
 to the legislature, 257, 258
Phelps and Gorham, 125, 127, 129, 136
Phelps and Gorham Purchase, 124, 129
Phelps, Oliver, 128
Phelps, Oliver and Gorham, Nathaniel, 126, 136, 227
Philadelphia Academy, 20, 31
Philadelphia Gazette, 110
Philadelphia, Pennsylvania, 77, 82, 92, 112, 115, 121, 298
philanthropy, 187
Phillips, John, 45, 139
Phipps Union Seminary, 307, 308
Pierce, Sarah, 270
Pitkin, William, 291
Pittsford, New York, 50, 52, 53, 68, 223

pledges, 113, 136, 188, 217
 church, 285
 in kind, 98
 subscription, 269
 voluntary, 38
pluralism, 47, 48, 52, 56
 religious, 47
 social, 57
politics, 159
 denominational, 189
 local, 260
 of schooling, 139, 140, 154
 state level, 157, 158, 160, 249, 252, 254, 262–264, 293
populism, 157, 158, 161, 169, 255
Potts, David, 195, 198
Poultney territory, 126
Presbyterian Church, 119, 177, 256
 Missouri Presbytery, 197
 Ontario Presbytery, 61
 Pittsford, New York, 52
Presbyterians, 53, 119, 183, 190, 191, 197, 249, 317
 ministers, 177
Pritchard, Linda, 207, 208
production
 agricultural, 288
 household, 11, 86, 93, 103, 228, 239, 240
 means of, 101, 263
 outwork, 7, 13, 240
professionals, 184, 185, 241, 245
professors, male, 270, 275
property, 22, 25, 27
 as collateral, 230
 corporate, 112, 113
 held in common, 252
 ownership, 23, 28
 required for civic participation, 19
property owners, 90, 94, 318
 communal responsibilities, 152
 governance by, 109
proprietors, 22, 97, 126, 136, 297
public funds, 146, 151, 156
Putnam, Robert, 18, 33, 34, 317, 323

quarterage, 86
quit-rents, 97, 133

Raleigh, North Carolina, 117, 165
rate bills, 156
Raymond, Henry, 304
Reading, New York, 187
real estate, 113, 121, 137, 178, 179, 183, 220, 252, 253
reciprocation of benefits, 158, 159, 161, 173, 174
reciprocity, 34, 327
reformation, 208, 209, 210
Reformed Church
  Dutch, 119
  German, 197
    Pennsylvania Synod, 197
Regents of the University of the State of New York, 118, 128, 134, 170, 172, 279
  Board of Regents, 119, 120, 133, 137, 280
    Regents status, 133
  legislation enabling, 119, 120
  Regents academies, 6
  Regents charter, 131
  Regents charters
    female institutions, 172
  Regents funding, 133, 267–269, 274, 284, 294
    per pupil, 279
  Regents institutions, 270, 278
  Regents status, 172, 203, 267, 268–270
  Regents system, 135, 293
religion
  disestablishment of, 36, 38, 108, 116–120, 195
    in Pennsylvania, 135
  established, 25, 116
  evangelicalism, 35
  excommunication, 61, 87, 177
  organized, structure of, 37
  religious enthusiasm, 48
  religious fervor, 48
  religious obedience, 152
  religious societies, 20–23, 26, 31
  revivalism, 15, 30, 47, 48, 53, 56, 57, 88, 92, 95, 208, 261
    camp meetings, 82, 205, 207, 208, 211
  sectarianism, 30, 177

Revolution, American, 19, 24, 77, 97, 103, 112, 116, 117, 120, 123, 125, 128, 134, 135, 162, 167, 195, 215, 222, 231
Rhode Island, 288
Roby, Joseph, 315, 316
Roby, Sidney, 306, 314–316
Rochester District, 219
Rochester, New York, 3, 50, 101, 180, 193, 210, 211, 216–219, 223, 233, 237, 238, 261, 262, 290, 313, 314
Rockdale, Pennsylvania, 101, 261, 262
Rogers, Eli, 304
Rothenberg, Winifred, 7, 8
Ryan, Mary, 66, 92, 95

Sabean, David Warren, 63
Schenectady, New York, 114
Schlotterbeck, John, 240
Schoharie County, New York, 97
scholarships, 286, 295, 319
Schooling in Capitalist America, 9
schools and schooling
  academies, 107
  attendance, universal, 14
  charity schools, 29, 133–135, 152
  church schools, 109
  common schools, 15, 112, 154
  dame schools, 141
  district schools, 304
  English grammar schools, 114, 115
  enrollment
    coeducational, 111
    data, 112
    grammar schools, 116
    high school, 320
    rates, 9, 150, 276
  entrepreneurial, 108
  female, 154
  for girls, 153
  grammar schools, 29, 109, 114–116, 134
    English, 113
  high schools, 172
  higher schooling, 318
  investment in, 323

Index   349

Latin grammar schools, 108–110,
    113–115, 153
Latin schools, 115
law, common school law, 31
laws, 21, 173
    1827 education act, 172
    common school law, 144
    monitorial school, 171
    neighborhood schools, 31, 49
    normal schools, state, 322
    public support of, 14
    rate bills, 134
    reporting, 148
    school keeping, 141, 145
    school masters, 140
    school support, 124, 128, 133,
        135
        capital-based system, 135
        forms of, 129
        land-based model of, 128
        roots of, 15
    schools as corporations, 325
    select schools, 15, 265, 267,
        268, 271
    sponsorship categories, 109
    subscription schools, 107
    summer and winter schools, 150,
        155, 157
    summer schools, 139–144, 146,
        147, 148, 150–157
    Sunday schools, 261, 262
    supplementary rate bills, 109
    town schools, 109
    town support, two-tiered system,
        141, 142
    venture schools, 9, 107–112,
        114–116, 120, 121, 130,
        132, 134, 196, 268, 278
        English, 108
        market supply and demand,
            110
        urban, 113
    winter schools, 139–143, 145, 146,
        148–157, 304
    women's schools, 154
    writing schools, 304
sciences, enrollment in, by gender,
    277
sciences, physical, 121

scientific and literary societies, 171
Scramlin, John, 94
Second American Party System, 16,
    249, 255, 256, 261
Second Great Awakening, 16, 30, 37,
    47, 56, 57, 61, 66, 72,
    86, 100, 206, 211,
    248
Second Treatise on Government, 26
sectarianism, 195, 198, 248, 249,
    252, 259, 265
Sellers, Charles, 5
Seminary of the Genesee Conference
    (Cazenovia Seminary),
    Board of Trustees, 201
services, 97, 215, 224
    exchange of, 243, 251, 289
    financial, 230, 231
    shared, 20
shares, 94, 96, 103, 137, 233, 295
Sibley, Samuel, 291
Sines family, 94
Sizer, Theodore, 273
Sklar, Kathryn Kish, 153–155
Skocpol, Theda, 317, 323
Smith family, 94, 96, 98, 100,
    102, 189, 273,
    274, 318
Smith, Adam, 123, 131, 132, 173
Smith, Eldrick, 187
Smith, Frances, 15, 187, 207,
    272–274, 308–316
Smith, Justin, 162, 164, 189
Smith, Ralph, 176, 180, 184, 186,
    187, 204, 206, 243,
    260
Smith, Ransom, 224
Smith's Mills, New York, 32, 48
Soltow, Lee, 10
South Carolina, 116, 134
South Lima Church of God, 55,
    56–58, 60, 67–70
    membership, 57
South Lima, New York, 47–49,
    56, 57, 64, 207
Span, Chris, 321
speculation, 103, 178, 179
    hazards of, 302
    land, 97, 125, 314

speculators, 97, 126, 128, 129, 178, 227, 231
  land, 22, 125, 173, 187
Spier, James, 220, 230
St. Louis, Missouri, 314
state formation, 15, 16, 118
  modern, 320
Stephens, Francis, 44
Sterling, James, 55, 56, 62–66, 70, 153, 177
Steuben County, New York, 187
Stevens, Edward, 10
steward of accounts, 188, 292
stock, joint, agreements, 234
student fees, 112
students, 15, 111, 113, 198, 269, 271, 272, 298, 323
  academy students, 306
  boarders, 251
  competition for, 16
  demand, 111
  experiences, 276
  female, 12, 111, 115, 268, 271, 276–278
    competition for, 274, 279
  geographic origin, 319
  geographical distribution of students, 269
  male, 109, 111, 115, 142, 268, 275–277
  nonclassical, 115
  recruitment of, 268, 280, 282, 295
  rural backgrounds, 322
subjects of study, 271
  accounting, 114
  agriculture, 265
  algebra, 115, 271, 274, 276, 277
  applied studies, 111
  arithmetic, 109–111, 113–115, 132, 271, 272
  astronomy, 111, 113, 115, 271, 274, 277
  bookkeeping, 113–115, 270
  botany, 271, 277
  chemistry, 277–279
  chronology, 111
  ciphering, 222
  classical literature, 270
  classical studies, 108, 109, 150, 267
  classics, 115
  common school subjects, 115
  composition, 115
  criticism, elements of, 271, 278
  dialling, 110
  drawing, 113, 271, 275, 279
  English, 108–110, 114, 115
    basic, 271
    common, 109, 270, 279
    composition, 114
    grammar, 111, 113
  English composition, 113, 270
  English grammar, 270, 306
  English rhetoric, 270
  English studies, higher, 267
  fine arts, 265
  geography, 111, 113–115, 270–272
  geometry, 113, 271, 274
  grammar, 115, 271
  higher studies, 279
    sciences, 272
  higher subjects, 115, 306
  history, 113–115, 270, 271, 277
  languages, 114, 115, 278
    ancient, 132, 270
    classical, 113, 114
    French, 115, 271, 278
    Greek, 109, 114, 115, 270, 271
    Hebrew, 270, 271, 276
    Italian, 271, 276, 278
    Latin, 271
    modern, 113, 114, 270
    modern and ancient, 272
    Spanish, 271
  Latin, 109, 114, 115, 270, 271, 276, 278, 306
  Latin grammar, 109, 142
  Latin tongue, 110
  literacy, 152
    basic skills, 142, 150
  literature, 265
  logic, 271, 278
  mathematics, 109, 115, 270, 271, 276, 278, 306
  mechanical arts, 265
  mensuration, 110
  merchants' accounting, 111, 114

Index

metaphysics, 278
music, 271, 274, 275, 278, 279
navigation, 110, 115
needlework, 271
ornamental subjects, 271, 279
Paley's theology, 274
pedagogy, 305
penmanship, 113, 115
philosophy, 272
   higher branches of, 132
   intellectual, 270, 271, 274
   mental, 270
   moral, 270, 278
   natural, 271, 276–278
   natural (physics), 277
      acoustics, 277
      Comstock's philosophy, 277
      electricity, 277
      heat, 277
      hydrostatics, 277
      magnetism, 277
      mechanics, 277
      Olmstead's philosophy, 277
      optics, 277
      pneumatics, 277
political economy, 270, 278
reading, 109, 114, 115, 132, 141, 222, 270–272
rhetoric, 113, 115, 270, 271, 274, 276, 278
sciences, 111, 115, 132, 270, 306
   greater emphasis in female education, 277
   natural, 271
   physical, 271
spelling, 270
surveying, 110, 115
theology, natural, 270, 271, 276, 278
trigonometry, 115, 276
use of the globes, 111
writing, 109, 110, 113–115, 132, 222, 270–272
subscribers, 19, 21, 23, 28, 98, 180–185, 188, 210, 216–219, 233, 235–238, 242–244, 246, 259, 261, 263, 269, 282, 286, 295, 299

subscriptions, 19, 21, 23, 28, 29, 35, 38, 98, 99, 102, 113, 117, 119, 122, 130, 131, 135, 137, 179, 180, 183, 186, 188, 207, 216–219, 234–237, 242, 243, 246, 252, 261, 264, 267–269, 282, 284, 295, 298, 299, 319
suffrage, 16, 28, 157, 159, 166–171, 324
   eligibility, 156
   expansion of, 180, 192
   reform, 158
   universal, advocated, 160
   universal white male, 107, 157
   voting behavior, 255
Sumner, Ebenezer, 182, 224
Susquehanna River (basin), 77
Sutton, Massachusetts, 153, 156
Syracuse, New York, 3, 4, 6, 305, 313, 314, 316, 327

taxes, 22, 41, 156
   assessments, 43, 178
      highway tax, 23
   paid to churches, 116
   school taxes, 31, 43, 151
      relief for the poor, 145
   town-level, 140
taxpayers, 167, 326
teachers and teaching, 3, 15, 313
   common school, 154, 155, 304
   entrepreneurial, 107
   examinations, of teachers, 42
   qualifications, 170
   salaries and wages, 44, 121, 133, 143, 145, 293, 295, 305
      gender gap, 142
      ratio, male-to-female, 143
      room and board, 142, 143
      sources, 122, 147
         public funds, 144
         student fees, 110
   teacher training, 171, 270
teachers
   assistant, 6
   certification, 154, 155
      exclusively male, 155
      extended to women, 155
      gender, 155

teachers and teaching (*cont.*)
    female, 111, 122, 137, 142, 150, 154, 275, 278, 305
    male, 122, 137, 143, 149, 150, 270, 324
    principal teachers, 121
Teas, Olive and Matthew, 228
Temin, Peter, 241
temperance, 20, 261
    temperance societies, 73, 256, 262
Tennessee, 77
Thayer, Reuben, 22, 23
The Auburn Banner, 292
The Christian Advocate and Journal and Zion's Herald, 284
The Irony of School Reform, 8
title, 121, 136, 186, 222, 227, 228, 243–246, 265
Tocqueville, Alexis de, 18, 20, 317
Tolley, Kim, 109–112, 277
Toronto, Ontario, 9
Troy Female Seminary, 280
trust, 18, 33, 37, 40, 41, 70, 302, 327
    as social capital, 33
    relationships of, 34, 53, 308
trustees, 25, 121
tuition, 16, 110, 112, 121, 122, 132, 198, 234, 251, 268, 284, 285, 286, 295
    pricing, 279
    room and board, 250
turnpikes, 125, 140
Tuthill, Anson, 15
tutors, home, 273, 274

Ulrich, Laurel Thatcher, 103
Union Hall Academy, 115, 119, 121
    schoolmaster, 121
United States
    Congress, 293
    economy, 7, 222, 225
    federal government, 135
    regions
        Chesapeake region, 92
        Delmarva Peninsula, 77
        mid-Atlantic region, 142
        mid-Atlantic states, 177
        Midwest, 127
        North, 7, 8, 11, 13, 127, 215, 313, 321, 322
        rural, 159, 320
        Northeast, 36, 48, 87, 127, 142, 150, 225
        Northwest Territories, 135
        Northwest, Old, 313
        Ohio Valley, 207
        South, 11, 134, 135, 321
        upper, 240
        southern states, 177
        West, 77, 197, 241, 315
United States Deposit Fund, 293
Universalism, 65, 66, 153
    gender of members, 66
Utica, New York, 92, 190, 249, 314

Van Buren political machine, 254
van Cortlandt family, 97
Van Rensselaer family, 136
Vermont, 5
Vermont, University of, 305
Vinovskis, Maris, 9, 10, 11, 318
Virginia, 116, 134

Wadsworth family, 168
Wadsworth, James, 227
Wadsworth, William, 22
Walker, Vanessa Siddle, 321
Wallace, Anthony F. C., 95, 101, 261, 262
War of 1812, 103
wards, 152, 222, 289
Warner family, 168, 178, 219–225, 227, 228, 232, 238, 282, 283, 290, 291, 298, 301, 303, 318
Warner, A. J., 15, 301, 302, 304, 306, 307, 314, 316
Warner, Asahel, 15, 19, 23, 138, 158, 159, 162, 164, 166, 168, 174, 176, 180, 189, 192, 204, 219, 220–223, 227, 228, 231–233, 235–238, 242–247, 249, 257, 260–263, 265, 279, 290, 298, 303
Warner, Daniel, 219, 221

Index

Warner, Frederick, 282, 296, 301–304, 314, 316
Warner, Matthew, 19, 99, 168, 219–224, 227–232, 282, 283, 288, 290–292, 296–298, 301–303
Warner, William (brother of Asahel and Matthew), 219, 221, 298
Warner, William (father of Asahel and Matthew), 219, 221
Warner, William and Orson (sons of Matthew Warner), 298
Warsaw, New York, 127
Waterville, Maine, 196
wealth, 22, 93, 100, 120, 127, 179, 181, 185
   common, 173, 174
   (community assets), 34
   consolidation of, 234, 283
   created through labor, 27
   distribution of, 12, 93
   landed, 136
   of Lima residents, 183
   production of and access to, 319
   surplus, 32

Wealth of Nations, The, 123, 131, 173
Weeks, Smith, 42, 47, 102, 103, 189
West Bloomfield, New York, 48, 50, 283, 288, 289, 292, 295, 318
West Mendon Methodist Church, 96, 98, 99, 206
West Mendon, New York, 47, 49, 68, 83, 84, 88, 90, 93, 94, 98, 99, 102, 206, 207, 209
Wheatland, New York, 305
Whitesboro, New York, 172, 249
Wigger, John, 83
Wiley, Aldridge, 182
Wilkes Barre, Pennsylvania, 78
Willard, Emma, 31, 270, 273
Williams, Benajah, 15, 67, 72–77, 79, 80, 81, 83, 84, 87, 88, 95, 187, 193, 204–206, 208–210
Williams, Heather Andrea, 321
women, 66, 69, 90, 103
   church membership, 92
   in evangelical societies, 56
   in Methodist church societies, 95

Yorks, Anthony, 291